ABSOLUTE POVERTY AND GLOBAL JUSTICE

Law, Ethics and Economics

Series Editors:
Christoph Luetge, University of Munich, Germany
Itaru Shimazu, Chiba University, Japan

Law, Ethics and Economics brings together interdisciplinary books which deal with at least two of the three constituents. Among other subjects, this series covers issues in ethics and economics, law and economics, as well as constitutional issues in law, economics, philosophy and social theory. The focus is on theoretical analysis that goes beyond purely normative considerations, thus aiming at a synthesis of the desirable and the feasible.

Also in the Series:

Corporate Citizenship, Contractarianism and Ethical Theory
On Philosophical Foundations of Business Ethics
Edited by Jesús Conill, Christoph Luetge and Tatjana Schönwälder-Kuntze
ISBN 978 0 7546 7383 5

Public Reason and Applied Ethics
The Ways of Practical Reason in a Pluralist Society
Edited by Adela Cortina, Domingo García-Marzá and Jesús Conill
ISBN 978 0 7546 7287 6

Globalisation and Business Ethics
Edited by Karl Homann, Peter Koslowski and Christoph Luetge
ISBN 978 0 7546 4817 8

Deliberation and Decision
Economics, Constitutional Theory and Deliberative Democracy
Edited by Anne van Aaken, Christian List and Christoph Luetge
ISBN 978 0 7546 2358 8

Absolute Poverty and Global Justice

Empirical Data – Moral Theories – Initiatives

Edited by

ELKE MACK
University of Erfurt, Germany

MICHAEL SCHRAMM
University of Hohenheim, Germany

STEPHAN KLASEN
University of Göttingen, Germany

THOMAS POGGE
Yale University, USA

Routledge
Taylor & Francis Group
LONDON AND NEW YORK

First published 2009 by Ashgate Publishing

2 Park Square, Milton Park, Abingdon, Oxon OX14 4RN
711 Third Avenue, New York, NY 10017, USA

Routledge is an imprint of the Taylor & Francis Group, an informa business

First issued in paperback 2016

British Library Cataloguing in Publication Data
Absolute poverty and global justice : empirical data, moral
theories, initiatives. -- (Law, ethics and economics)
1. Poverty. 2. Poverty--International cooperation.
3. Economic assistance, Domestic. 4. Distributive justice.
I. Series II. Mack, Elke.
362.5-dc22

Library of Congress Cataloging-in-Publication Data
Absolute poverty and global justice : empirical data-moral theories-initiatives
/ by Elke Mack ... [et al.].
p. cm. -- (Law, ethics and economics)
Includes bibliographical references and index.
ISBN 978-0-7546-7849-6 (hardback) -- ISBN 978-0-7546-9673-5
(ebook) 1. Poverty. 2. Poor. 3. Poverty--Moral and ethical
aspects. I. Mack, Elke.
HC79.P6.A27 2009
362.5--dc22

2009020351

ISBN 13: 978-0-7546-7849-6 (hbk)
ISBN 13: 978-1-138-25505-0 (pbk)

Contents

PART 3 GLOBAL THEORIES OF JUSTICE AND RESPONSIBILITY

PART 4 POLICIES AND ACTIONS

List of Figures

List of Tables

Dedicated to Michael Ward (1939–2008), an active participant of the Erfurt workshop and a contributor to this volume.

Notes on Contributors

Norbert Anwander is Research Assistant at the Department of Philosophy, Humboldt University, Berlin, Germany.

Elizabeth Ashford is a Lecturer in Philosophy at the University of St Andrews, Scotland.

Barbara Bleisch is Head of the Post-Graduate Programme 'Advanced Studies in Applied Ethics' and Research Fellow at the Centre for Ethics, University of Zurich.

Eike Bohlken is the Director's Assistant at the Research Institute for Philosophy, Hannover, Germany.

Stefan Gosepath is Professor at the Institute for Intercultural and International Studies, University of Bremen.

Stefan Hielscher is Research Assistant at the Department of Economic Sciences, University of Halle-Wittenberg, Germany.

Stephan Klasen is Professor at the Department of Economics, University of Göttingen, Germany.

Peter Koller is Professor at the Department of Philosophy of Law, Karl-Franzens-University Graz, Austria.

Gerhard Kruip is Head of the Research Institute for Philosophy, Hannover, Germany, and Professor at the Department of Christian Social Ethics, University of Mainz, Germany.

Elke Mack is Professor at the Department of Christian Social Sciences and Social Ethics, University of Erfurt, Germany.

Lukas Meyer is Professor at the Department of Philosophy, Bern University, Switzerland.

Darrel Moellendorf is Professor of Philosophy, Director of the Institute for Ethics and Public Affairs, San Diego State University, USA, and Member of School of Social Sciences, Institute for Advanced Study.

Johannes Müller is Professor at the Jesuit University of Philosophy, Munich, Germany.

Else Øyen is Professor Emeritus, University of Bergen, Norway, and former Scientific Director of CROP.

Ingo Pies is Professor for Business Ethics, University of Halle-Wittenberg, Germany.

Thomas Pogge is Leitner Professor of Philosophy and International Affairs at Yale University, USA, Professorial Fellow at the Centre for Applied Philosophy and Public Ethics (Australian National University), and Research Director at the Centre for the Study of Mind in Nature (Oslo University), Norway.

Michael Reder is a lecturer at the Department of Philosophy of Social Sciences and Religion, Jesuit University of Philosophy, Munich, Germany.

Michael Schramm is Professor at the Department of Catholic Theology and Business Ethics, University of Stuttgart-Hohenheim, Germany.

Clemens Sedmak is Professor at the Centre for Ethics and Poverty Research, Salzburg, Austria, and Professor of Moral and Social Theology at King's College, London, England.

Judit Seid is Research Assistant at the Department of Catholic Theology and Business Ethics, University of Stuttgart-Hohenheim, Germany.

Johannes Wallacher is Professor at the Department of Social Sciences and Business Ethics at the Jesuit University of Philosophy, Munich, Germany.

Michael Ward († 2008) has been Principal Economist in the International Economics Department of the World Bank, Washington, USA.

The Erfurt Manifesto: Common Stance of all Contributors

An international group of economists, legal scholars, moral philosophers, development practitioners, political scientists and theologians met in Erfurt for a workshop of the German Research Foundation (DFG) on 'Absolute Poverty and Global Justice' and published the following manifesto at the end of July 2008. The discussions focused on absolute poverty and global inequality: their levels, trends, and determinants; their moral assessment; and their eradication through specific policies and structural reforms. While there were differences among the participants, they agreed on the following key findings and practical recommendations.

Facts

Absolute poverty in the world is unacceptably large, affecting at least one billion human beings. Despite great progress in poverty reduction in some countries, poverty has not been meaningfully reduced in most developing countries. Much faster progress against absolute poverty is possible through reductions of national and global inequalities which constrain economic growth in poor countries and households.

Moral Responsibility

Among the causes of poverty in developing countries are historical factors, such as colonialism and slavery, inadequate endowments, defective social institutions, ill-conceived national policies, and flaws in the international order which sustain absolute poverty and undermine efforts to reduce it. In particular, the international order offers too few opportunities for economic integration of the world's poorest populations and also encourages support – through trade, debt, and investment relations – of corrupt and authoritarian governments that foster or neglect poverty in their own countries. Rich countries contribute to absolute poverty by placing additional burdens of climate change on poor countries and their poor citizens. Diverse moral views imply that international agencies as well as the citizens, corporations, and governments of affluent countries bear a moral responsibility to reduce absolute poverty. These views variously invoke requirements:

- to avoid violating the human right to a decent standard of living;
- to help protect and fulfil the human rights of the poor;
- to respect and promote human dignity which is undermined by absolute poverty;
- to strengthen the legitimacy of international institutions by working toward absolute poverty eradication;
- to accord substantial weight, in the shaping of policies and social institutions, to the under-represented interests of future generations and the poor worldwide.

Actions

Because it is of the greatest moral importance and requires only modest efforts and resources, the goal of overcoming absolute poverty must be given much higher political priority by international agencies and by the citizens, corporations and governments of the affluent countries, including Germany. These agents and agencies ought to facilitate and promote the following initiatives:

- The global trading system must be reformed so that it better accommodates the needs and interests of poor countries and poor producers. Such reforms ought greatly improve access to rich country markets (including agriculture) for the goods and services poor countries can offer. Preferential trade access for poor producers may also be called for, at least temporarily.
- Affluent countries, such as Germany, must do more to support the existence of, and access to, global public goods such as vital medicines. Poor people must not be excluded by high monopoly prices from the medicines they need. And the current patent regime enshrined in the TRIPS Agreement should be complemented by additional mechanisms – such as advance purchase/market commitments and a Health Impact Fund – that encourage the development and affordable distribution of new medicines targeting diseases that are concentrated among the poor.
- Affluent countries, including Germany, should curtail economic interactions with regimes that violate basic human rights and fail to promote economic development and poverty reduction. Affluent countries might, in particular, refuse to buy natural resources from, and refuse to sell arms and grant loans to, such regimes and might treat natural resources bought from such a regime as stolen from their rightful owners: the country's population.
- Having produced the lion's share of greenhouse gas emissions, rich countries bear a weighty responsibility to ensure that emissions and climate change are slowed down and that poor countries can adjust to climate change without aggravating absolute poverty.

- The affluent countries must live up to their long-standing promise to increase their development assistance to the UN target (0.7 per cent of each country's social product) and to the intermediate targets agreed within the European Union. While the German aid budget has increased recently, it still falls far short of this goal. Moreover, far too much development assistance is spent on supporting domestic export firms and 'friendly' regimes abroad. A much higher share must be devoted to the poorest countries and to reducing absolute poverty.

Commentary on the Erfurt Manifesto

Michael Ward

Last month, a small inter-disciplinary group of philosophers, theologians, social ethicists and economic analysts meeting in Erfurt, Germany, re-positioned the debate on global poverty closer towards a matter of international injustice. The group convened in the Cathedral's Coelicum, aware of the deep humanistic and cultural tradition brought to the city by Martin Luther, Goethe and Schiller and the compositions of J.S. Bach. The meeting agreed that traditional approaches to global poverty alleviation have not worked. It recognised that efforts founded on a well-meaning charitable concern and individual donations in cash and kind, together with a general but neutral public notion of social responsibility that is reflected in official aid allocations, are not sufficient. The failure of these approaches implies the existence of more powerful overriding forces that combine to maintain the unequal societal status quo in the world. The group believes the persistence of global poverty to be a violation of basic human rights and that there is an imperative to take urgent and internationally agreed – if not at present legally enforceable – corrective action to restore the human dignity of both donors and recipients. While no individual can be held personally accountable, there should be some form of international legal obligation on richer members of the world to contribute to policies designed to ensure a progressive reduction in absolute poverty and preserve the notion and universality of a common justice.

This is more than a shared social responsibility of those with the capacity to provide assistance to those in dire need. It is the important formal recognition of the fundamental unacceptability of the persistent basic human condition of global poverty and an acknowledgement of an international legal obligation to rectify the situation. The need to eradicate extreme poverty and associated evils of appalling living conditions and poor sanitation that bring with them a continued exposure to endemic disease and a concomitant vulnerability to chronically high infant mortality and early death, should be deemed a criminal injustice and a priority for concerted international action. As a strategy, support for the poor should rank equally alongside current domestic policy objectives such as the provision of massive and seemingly unlimited financial support to failed banks and private business and continued engagement in socially and morally unacceptable military expenditures as well as excessive consumption. A new international institutional initiative, legitimised by a reconsideration of the common law of peoples, irrespective of their race and provenance, has to be developed. This should take full cognisance of a systematic theory of human justice that commands international authority and acceptance.

What empirical evidence did the group call upon to reach such a controversial conclusion? The necessity to observe some sort of corrective justice for past 'wrongs' was considered but not pursued because of poor documentation and the historical indeterminacy of individual attribution for such wrongful acts. Even if responsibility can be determined, there is also an almost insuperable practical and litigious problem concerning the appropriate level of compensation to be decided. Although past exploitation may possibly have been a contributory issue, the restitution and retribution approach does not address the more pressing contemporary concern to correct what is a continuing systemic and institutionalised injustice and the core need to alleviate, reduce and eventually eradicate present poverty.

Instead, the group noted the more than 300 million deaths, many of children, which have occurred as a result of disease in the last 18 years since the end of the Cold War. This figure is far more than has ever been slaughtered in wars, tribal genocide or ethnic cleansing during the entire twentieth century. These deaths constitute, clearly, a devastating indictment of civilised society and represent a massive violation of basic human rights. Unfortunately, there is no forum comparable to the International Court of Justice in The Hague presently in existence to expose this inhumanity and pursue the matter. There is a moral urgency to identify those concerned and to require the national and international community to account for the failure to provide the essential resources such as drugs and clean water to reduce the large numbers who are dying around the world.

There is a parallel responsibility to lift other burdens externally imposed on the poor that curtail their prospects, such as barriers to trade and market entry, legal and institutional obstacles to securing finance; and rich country agricultural subsidies to domestic over-producers and local farmers who grow food crops for bio-fuel purposes. The suppression of trade in generic medicines, the promotion of fungible loans and arms sales to oppressive regimes whose rulers also sell their people's natural resources and then embezzle the proceeds by sequestering the money into their own private foreign bank accounts have to be halted.

The associated path, therefore, is to focus on the best means to improve distributive justice. An empirical examination of the pattern of global income indicates that inequality has shifted only marginally at its extremes since the 1960s (and thus the immediate post-colonial period) to the present reveals that ill-defined and mostly unidentifiable power relationships continue to exert a strong unchanged pressure on the gross imbalances between the rich and the poor. The resulting coercive forces manifest themselves in the distortion of contractual justice and, consequently, unequal exchange relationships.

A projection of the global distribution of income to 2015 based on current trends and observed distributional characteristics indicates there is little prospect of any improvement in the overall pattern of inequality that has been consistently observed over the past 40–50 years. The same poor countries in Africa and South

Asia remain poor and the poor households living in those countries continue to subsist in absolute poverty. The mal-distribution of wealth and productive assets is even more substantial. The unwillingness to recognise this widespread abuse of economic power and the absence of basic human rights as a global injustice frustrates appropriate and proper action. The problem can be resolved only by global agreement on a new comprehensive and concerted strategy of national and international cooperation.

Among several solutions proposed, there were calls to provide better economic incentives and opportunities for the poor, for improved access to medicines, to regard purchases of natural resources from oppressive regimes that do not grant basic human rights to their citizens as trade in stolen property and for efforts to support new initiatives to help poor people adjust to the demands of environmental change.

The introduction of new financing sources that could include the establishment of a development fund based on a universal compulsory savings scheme made possible by the postponement of consumption by the richer members of society was regarded as a potential means to raise quickly and securely the money required to implement some of these desired actions and future development. Another idea called for the establishment of a Health Impact Fund that would reward new medicines, if priced at cost, on the basis of their global health impact.

At the close of the meeting, the Group issued the 'Erfurt Manifesto' as a joint declaration of intent outlining the suggested protocols and actions that should be followed up at the international level.

Michael Ward, Cambridge

Introduction
Justice for the Poor – A Global Paradigm in Progress and Dispute

Elke Mack[1]

Global Justice in Relation to the Absolute Poor

Every minute a human being dies due to poverty-related reasons. Among the absolute poor in Africa, south of the Sahara, and South East Asia, whose number exceeds one billion people, children in particular are the innocent victims of this enduring moral dilemma (cf. the contributions, including recent figures, by Stephan Klasen, Michael Ward and Thomas Pogge in this book). Not long ago, most of us, the members of the Western world could excuse ourselves from the moral responsibility of global poverty because there were insufficient resources available to alleviate the miserable conditions of the absolute poor. For the first time, following a long and successful period of globalisation and economic growth, the beginning of the twenty-first century presents a real opportunity to relieve those living in absolute poverty from their life-threatening situation,[2] and to change the structures which cause absolute poverty.[3] In fact, nobody would have to starve, suffer from avoidable illnesses, be poisoned by dirty water, live an extremely shortened life due to insufficiencies, and suffer from other poverty related constraints, if it just was a case of sufficient economic provision.

It therefore seems obvious that ethics scholars must research the avoidable reasons for the deepening gap between the well-off and the worst-off, as well as asking the core ethical question of who might be held responsible for the abolition of absolute poverty, and on what moral grounds.

---

1 References to authors without further detail (e.g. year and publisher) refer to contributions in this book.

2 Thomas Pogge claims that $300 billion US dollars would change the situation of the poor dramatically for the better (Pogge 2002, 7). Contrast his $300 billion dollar estimation to the hundreds of billions which western governments made available to combat the effects of the credit crisis in autumn 2008 – this proves the ongoing relevance of this estimate. ‘Billion’ being used in the US sense to signify 1,000 million in Europe.

3 Cf. Jeffrey Sachs, who is a strong advocate of geographic factors driving reasons of poverty and underdevelopment (Sachs 2005, 226). His thesis, however, does not reflect this and underestimates the much wider impact of institutional reasons for poverty, which ‘trump’ all other relevant factors (Risse 2005, 87).

In classical ethics, the principle of moral philosophy: '*ultra posse nemo tenetur*' applied only to an achievable extent or in general only to those who were able to help or change a moral dilemma. However, in a world with heavy interdependencies on cultural, economical and political configurations there seems to be no reason for this kind of reserve any more, but instead there is a need for broadening moral demands and duties up to the global level (Pogge 1992, 49; Gosepath 2002; Pogge 2002). In this context, the most difficult problem of moral philosophy seems to be that not all scholars, people or states agree there should be a universal obligation to erase life-threatening poverty through varying instruments in due time, be they political countermeasures, including distributional systems of whatever kind, or other means of international cooperation and intervention.

If you want to take the absolute poor seriously as autonomous human beings, it must be respected that they are supposed to live their lives within other nations, other continents or other cultural realms with respect to their own responsibility, individuality and cultural provenience. Consequently, any means to erase poverty may not touch the individuality, cultural identity and freedom of the poor as subjects. Although the world increasingly interconnects itself in economic and political terms (Höffe 1999, 14–20), its past and present forms of solidarity and cooperation have been insufficient[4] and sometimes paternalistic in character. Therefore it is not surprising that poverty could only be reduced in relative proportion to the world's population, but it has increased in absolute numbers during recent years (Worldbank 2008, 2).

Those who recognise a duty to change the situation – especially persons who are well-off and can spare, donate or invest something without harm – are unclear about the extent of their responsibilities. The role of citizens, social institutions, states or global society as a whole, is unclear in terms of their particular responsibility (cf. the contributions of Gosepath, Anwander, Bleisch and Bohlken; see also Pauer-Studer (2006); Bleisch and Schaber (2007)). Their contribution, influence, input to change or tolerance of the current world order is especially unclear, which is not really preventive as regards poverty. Even if a strict moral responsibility towards the extremely poor were accepted universally and consensually by states or people, it would still be an immense task to work out how the complex reduction of poverty could be implemented in the face of so many differing political, economic, cultural, geographic, climatic or social situations. The problem is so complex because most of the time poverty is *not* an outcome of specific economic problems alone, but a political, social, cultural, geographic or climatic one, caused, for example, by suppression within states, new forms of slavery or a lack of rights for certain minorities, social classes, groups or individuals, leading to increased inequalities and intensifications of poverty (Sen 1997; Rawls 2002, 132–137; Winters, McCulloch et al. 2004; Grimm, Klasen et al. 2007). This is one reason why a mere development program for growth

4 There are, however, numerous counter examples, e.g. the Tsunami disaster in 2004, which triggered off charity and institutional aid worldwide.

and prosperity of the least industrialised states does not go far enough. It needs to be supplemented by a variety of development processes, like environmental adjustments, reasonably planned policies, processes of democratisation and the establishment of the rule of law in terms of human rights, investment in public goods such as health care and education, and in extreme cases even by concerted political action of justified intervention and peace building measures (Moellendorf 2002, 102sqq.).

The argument, that poverty cannot be erased because it is too complex as an *object* to deal with, is not really an argument that discouraged the scholars dealing with the problem of poverty in this book. It rather stimulated them to make the poor *subjects* of 'A Global Theory of Justice'. This theory is developed in four main steps which give this book its specific structure:

In a *first chapter*, the empirical problem of absolute poverty is scrutinised through the means of economic analyses, and the most recent results in poverty research are presented and scientifically evaluated.

Due to a modern theory of justice, ethics is open to many reasonable, comprehensive doctrines as prior understandings of universal normativity – for example to secular humanism, to philosophical postulates or to religious values. In this publication, Christian theology is seen as a prominent and comprehensive doctrine in favour of global justice and is therefore presented by Christian Social Ethicists in the *second chapter*. In addition to these philosophical arguments, an 'Option for the Poor' is theologically justified (cf. Sedmak and Kruip) and religion, based on reason, is proved to be an outstanding integrative concept *pro homo* within the global domain (cf. Müller).

With regard to the empirical data and a reasonable understanding of the normative demands of poverty the *third chapter* is an attempt to argue for global norms and responsibility to eradicate absolute poverty as well as for normative claims of the poor, as members of a global society. The aim is to find principles and standards for a systematic 'Global Theory of Justice'. Therefore several approaches and normative claims for global justice are developed and true injustices and inequalities are revealed which should be removed in order to give the poor a chance for a dignified life.

In the *forth chapter* the normative theory is endorsed by implementation methods which consider initiatives by responsible agents, business and politics.

The Conceptual Debate

The motivating factor for this ethical debate lies in the scandal of so many preventable deaths and the misery of the world's poorest, rather than in some purely academic pursuit. The discussions arose with publications in moral and political philosophy in the 1970s (Singer 1972, 229–243; Beitz 1975). At the same time extensive discussions appeared in the religious and theological sphere with contributions from the Latin American Theology of Liberation[5] (cf. the history of the concept of a 'preferential option for the poor') which carried on during the 1980s producing a revised and amplified comprehension of the dimensions of poverty (Sen 1985; Sen 1997), and has enfolded during the prime time of globalisation since the 1990s in the social sciences, again mainly in moral philosophy (Pogge 1992; Pogge 1994; Rawls 1999). Since the 1990s the debate on '*Global Justice*' has become the new ethical paradigm for a world where absolute poverty represents one of the prior multidimensional problems for years to come, as the Millennium Development Goals show.[6]

The *concept of global justice* and an *ethics of human rights* are the endorsed ethical frameworks for the problem of severe poverty (cf. Koller's proposal to understand 'global justice as the "*totality of demands of justice that can be reasonably applied to international relations and the global order*"'). Within this framework we will discuss whether global justice must incorporate worldwide systems of distribution (Pogge 1994; Beitz 1999; Caney 2005); the guarantee of a life in dignity; the Aristotelian teleological development of anthropologically well-founded 'functionings' and 'capabilities' for the poor (Sen 1985; Nussbaum 1992; Nussbaum 2001; Nussbaum 2006); a universally sufficient supply of vital means to survive (cf. Meyer's contribution on intergenerational sufficiency, also Meyer 2008); only weak duties of charity for the poor within a communitarian concept (Krebs 2000; Krebs 2004), or, finally, ethically sufficient incentives for business to invest in least developed nations in a way that leads the poor economies to endogenous growth (cf. the contributions of Hielscher and Pies, and Schramm and Seid). The manifold suggestions show however, that the extent and concrete pattern of *advisable interaction* between those who live in abundance and those who cannot escape their poverty are not easily answered.

With regard to market forces in general, nobody really questions whether in order to fight poverty effectively, a modification of global organisations and institutions is overdue, especially in times of a likely revision of the world's financial order.[7] The ethical debate is trying to encourage a more competitive and social globalisation – which has the potential to make the world more prosperous – under a roof of human solidarity and justice. This can only be achieved by a set of transparent ramifications for markets and transactions which sanction one-sided market powers, heavy inequalities, ecological misuse and social as well as economic exclusion of the extremely poor. Although it is not advisable to underestimate the capabilities of well-governed domestic institutions, improving the lives of the poor relies strongly on just international organisations and institutions. Their task is to

---

5 The Theology of Liberation is deeply characterised by, but not limited to, its Latin-American origin (Medellin 1968; Gutiérrez and Inda 1973; Segundo 1976; Boff et al. 1987). Compare Gerhard Kruip's contribution in this book.

6 Millennium Development Goals (MDGs) are available at <http://www.un.org/millennium/declaration/ares552e.htm>.

7 See Hockett (2005); Moellendorf (2005) for justified proposals.

guide the forces of globalisation in terms of capital markets as well as in terms of the exchange of goods and services in a more transparent, balanced, rights-based and structured mode – constituted in a way that the participation of the poor is guaranteed and adequately honoured.

In the political realm, the majority of authors engaged in the ethical debate (apart from some political scientists) dropped the standpoint of a strict Westphalian 'statism' having recognised that states cannot be the sole nor sufficient actors of global moral responsibility. Statism is being fundamentally questioned, because a world of cooperation against poverty can only succeed if states are the legitimate representatives of their peoples and not sacrosanct just because they exist.[8] In current political ethics it is largely recognised that only the sovereigns themselves, namely the people and 'peoples' (Rawls 2002, 26–32), can be the source of collective legitimacy. Therefore ideas concerning the exclusion of illegitimate and failed states are strongly debated (Moellendorf 2002; Rawls 2002, 113–30). In 2005, the United Nations also committed themselves to a principle, named the 'Responsibility to Protect' (R2P). This international norm urges states to protect their populations from genocide, war crimes, crimes against humanity and ethnic cleansing. If a state is unable to guarantee this protection or itself commits one of the aforementioned crimes, the international community is automatically legitimised to take over the responsibility for this burdened society. The international community therefore is liable in the second degree.[9] One other suggestion brought forward consists of sanctioning undemocratic and totalitarian states by excluding them from the world's markets through international law, so they cannot earn capital for their unjust regimes by trading their resources on a global market (Wenar 2008). It seems ethically necessary to develop and establish many more peaceful political instruments against totalitarian states at the global level, forcing them to respect their own people, especially the poor, and to acknowledge the equal rights of all of their citizens, allowing them to 'affect the social-economic-political system in which they live' (Caney 2005, 156).

In this context a major question is whether today's global system itself should be named unjust (Pogge 2002), or whether it can only be criticised for not being just enough toward the absolutely poor (Risse 2005; Mack 2007b). Nevertheless both notions would seem to imply the need to improve several institutions as soon as possible (Sautter 2004). In this context the *quantitative* measurements of poverty and especially absolute poverty are criticised for the assumptions used and the methods applied by leading economists who are engaged in the debate; it is quite revealing to see that even after the reform of the World Bank's poverty

8 Cf. also the debate between David Miller and Kok-Chor Tan concerning this issue (Miller 1988; Tan 2001; Miller 2004; Miller 2005; Tan 2005), and Young (1998, 431–457) as well as O'Neill (1990; 2000).

9 Concerning 'R2P' see: International Commission on Intervention and State Sovereignty and International Development Research Centre (2001); Cooper and Voïnov Kohler (2009).

measurements there continues to be a need for improvements (cf. Ward, Klasen and Pogge in this book, also Ravallion 2003; Reddy and Pogge 2005). In contrast to these quantitative approaches there are also prominent suggestions of a better *qualitative* concept of poverty analysis, as stated above, from Aristotelian traditions as well as from Christian ethics which are traditionally human-good oriented (cf. the contribution of Kruip in this book).

On a formal and procedural level, cosmopolitan and most rights-based approaches accept the modern paradigm to work on the basis of *ethical consensus*. This means that norms and rights are best argued for when being built on a consensus of all the people concerned, and either justified on a hypothetical or on a factual basis.[10] Human rights, rights of interaction and fundamental principles of justice, focusing on the weakest and poorest within a world's society, have to be justified perpetually in front of those they are supposed to protect. It is a futile attempt to argue exclusively for an application of ontological principles in a world of controversial interests, pluralistic comprehensive doctrines and hermeneutical understandings as well as political powers, like traditional natural law approaches tried to do. It is similarly one-sided to argue for the stance that the possible consequences of actions and institutional arrangements alone will give us enough criteria for global justice because this can only lead us to situational ethics of trial and error. There are modern ethics which lie in between traditional natural law and positivism or pure consequentialism. Although consequences always matter in ethics, the mentioned *consensus principle* leads to the need for prior collective reflexion on relevant normativity; namely fundamental principles and their justification before all (Forst 2007, 294sqq.). One version of this reflection is also the *ex negativo* claim, that just global institutions may not reasonably be rejected by the persons concerned (Scanlon 1998). In this context we can assume on a practical level that human rights mirror a common moral understanding of humankind, in which the world found a factual consensus in 1948, regardless of which way one argues for them. In global ethics one should not retreat from this consensus of humankind, whether the granted rights are understood purely as claims on institutions or extensively as claims on all interactions among humans in general.

The deeper background leading to the necessity of finding a general consensus is the dignity of human beings. This is still the major normative core pursued by most ethical approaches based on a Kantian or Christian tradition, even if they do not explicitly mention it (cf. Moellendorf's argument in this book). Today the notion of dignity, having been criticised as being too vague or too thick in terms of a remaining metaphysical content, is supposed to be at least constituted by

---

10 This spectrum of argument is endorsed mainly by philosophers following a Kantian, contractarian or discourse tradition. Although neither Rawls' 'Theory of Justice' nor the Habermas 'Theorie des kommunikativen Handelns' [Theory of Communicative Action] converge as a whole, they both imply proper methodological foundations for a normative consensus. See Rawls 1979; Habermas 1981.

the two moral powers of (a) being able to pursue a conception of the good; and (b) by having a claim for justice (Rawls 1979). This means more, but in a way also less than a traditional account of dignity based on freedom and reason (Kant 1903, 60sqq.) or the theological theses of a creation by a personal God whose very image human beings are believed to be. But there are instrumental and pragmatic ethical approaches of Anglo-Saxon or economic origin that at least hold true to the principles of individuality and autonomy[11] although they do not refer to this as dignity. However, these normative arguments also protect a major element of the dignity of human beings in the form of fundamental human rights for the individual. Another way to reconstruct these rights is the argument for respecting the legitimate preferences of people.

If we contextualise the dignity of the poor in the debate on global justice, we can assume that the people concerned will claim a global order which at least guarantees *rights of inclusion and participation in society and working life*, *rights for subsidiarity instead of subsistence* (not only through bailouts or systems of social security, but through work by themselves), as well as the *right to veto further proceedings in the global order* (Mack 2007b, 319) if their interests are not sufficiently respected. Without these, the poor will not be able to achieve their own concept of the good or realise a claim for justice for themselves. This is also true for the economic discussion on establishing specific instruments, institutions and organisations to let the poorest participate in the world's growth. This can be achieved by regular trade and production without postponements and exclusions through certain market powers or mechanisms (export subsidies, strong import restrictions or patents secured by TRIPS preventing low priced medical supply for instance (cf. Pogges contribution, 'Medicines for the world') and without exploiting the working poor (no wages below the poverty level and labour rights for the poor), but also by establishing some instruments of distribution within states (like welfare-states) and also in a limited way among states.

Besides initialising and achieving further growth in the least developed states (Grimm, Klasen et al. 2007, 2sqq.), the second key claim for poverty reduction is *the reduction of extreme inequality* (Pogge 2002; Worldbank 2008, 40) by a certain degree of distribution (Beitz 1999, 150sqq.) in order to erase extreme poverty (cf. Erfurt Manifesto in this book). Although the world's overall Gini-coefficient reduced slightly (Worldbank 2008, 41), the researchers of this book agree on the demand to reduce the inequalities worldwide for three reasons: First, it takes too long to wait for endogenous growth in the least developed states to overcome absolute poverty. Second, it has been proved at a national level that if inequality increases to a certain degree, it has severe negative consequences for national economic development (Worldbank 2008, 51sqq.). It seems safe to assume that this negative correlation is most likely valid at the global level as well. Third, the

---

11 See for example the Charter of the European Union, as well as the 'Treaty establishing a Constitution for Europe' (in the latter especially the preamble and article I-2): The European Parliament (2000, 2004).

relative disadvantages for the rich in contributing some of their income or assets to the poor are to be weighed as ethically less severe than life-threatening severe poverty.

Three Normative Key Arguments in Support of Global Justice

Having analysed many arguments for and against the possibility of global justice, no one can really claim to have solved this complex problem of justice for the poor as well as the pragmatic problem of how to eradicate absolute poverty completely. However, considering three, admittedly simplified, patterns of the most prominent moral approaches for global justice, one comes to the conclusion that they all have some validity, but also have weaknesses and certain aspects that may be criticised. Since nobody in this book makes a stance for pure instrumental, positivistic or traditional natural law approaches, we leave them aside as positions at the margins of an even broader debate.

First, Rawlsian contractarian approaches are plausible with respect to the argument that we need to find principles for establishing and guiding 'a basic structure for a Society of Peoples'. However, Rawls' insistence on *peoples* as the sole negotiators in a global original position[12] has caused contradiction among cosmopolitans. Some global ethicists rather prefer the individual person as the normative starting point.[13] A contractarian view, however, is right about the ongoing need of an *overlapping consensus* on controversial global themes of justice among all peoples, representing every region, race, culture, gender, religion and comprehensive doctrine. It is also convincing in a Rawlsian tradition, and in tune with institutional theories of sociology and economics that it is important to establish better cooperative organisations at the global level in order to help enable the poor to improve their living standards (Rawls 1999; Sautter 2004). Those organisations have to adequately assist burdened states to establish just liberal or decent basic institutions, in order to be able to organise themselves, to establish endogenous growth within their economies and to reach at least the first step of development for their poor (Sachs 2005).[14]

But what is highly disputable in the Rawlsian approach towards global justice is the premise in the background of his proposal; namely that we still live in a non-permeable Westphalian world of states and that grave economic inequalities are not unjust *per se* (Rawls 1999, 114; Beitz 2000; Buchanan 2000).[15] To exclude redistribution as moral means on a broader than national realm and to connect global justice only to a duty of institutional assistance is also disputable, because it

12 Cf. Rawls (1999, 115).

13 Cf. Pogge (1992).

14 Cf. the 'Responsibility to Protect (R2P)'.

15 'It does not matter how great the gap between rich and poor may be. What matters are the consequences' (Rawls 1999, 114).

would not provide people with the possibility of making their living autonomously until far in the future, if ever. In this regard, it will not be possible to argue for more than subsistence and a minimum supply for the poor until institutions have a noticeable effect, which might be too late for many of today's absolute poor subsisting in life-threatening conditions. Therefore global distributive justice cannot be justified sufficiently by a traditionalistic Rawlsian approach because the institutions of the states and their narrow focus on a national understanding of social justice do not fulfil the normative demands of global solidarity among all people which would claim restricted but strict duties on the normative bases of reciprocity among all human beings.

Second, neo-aristotelian approaches justify some restricted claims of a global bailout with a clear limit or target, but intentionally also do not argue for a *general* international redistribution of income, goods or resources (Krebs 2000; Krebs 2004).[16] These accounts of justice do not aim for specific consequences in the light of egalitarian equality, but rely on a decisive equal normative starting point, namely the preservation of dignity for every human being. This dignity accords to all humans the justified claim to a fundamental provision of goods, given that everyone has a legitimate right to survival, a right to a 'good life' or to certain human capabilities (Nussbaum 2006). These ends are differing within an account of certain human claims for the person and its good life. However, there is the interesting unresolved question of how these human claim-rights can be realised without a thorough reshaping of worldwide distribution. It remains unclear how the provision for the rather extensive assets of a good life of the poor, as suggested by Nussbaum, can be made practically available. This would only be realistic if we were to transfer goods on a large scale, offer services and institutional assistance to the poor or assist burdened societies in economic terms to lift the poor to the first level of development. Taking different cultures and religions and their greatly varying ideas of '*the Good*' into account, we can also question whether the specific material contents of a good life can be agreed as precisely as Nussbaum considers it (Nussbaum 1992, 205).

Third, there are strong cosmopolitan or egalitarian approaches (cf. the already mentioned books by Pogge, Beitz and Caney). These make heavy claims for distributive justice which imply a reorganisation of the initial supply of assets for the poor with the help of global institutions, a reduction of global inequality and the building of a new just world order from scratch. Their primary intention is to equalise the standards of living, preventing inequalities in the division of income becoming too big and eradicating absolute poverty. The normative core arguments in support of these changes are the negative duties of responsibility (cf. Ashford and Pogge 2002) of the world's well-off towards the poor because the

16 Although in her most recent writings, Nussbaum seems to endorse an account of global justice which adopts large parts of the cosmopolitan ethical framework. She is, however, quite vague about how to combine these kinds of universalistic ethics with her own Aristotelian tradition. See Nussbaum (2006, 314sqq.).

existing order is harming their fundamental rights to an existence (cf. Bleisch). This last empirical premise is rejected by certain authors (cf. Risse 2005) who do not blame the global order for the existing injustice, but instead mostly accuse domestic factors, for example, bad governance within the countries concerned. A partial rejection is also put forward by scholars who see multidimensional empirical factors for underdevelopment and poverty in poor countries including particular climatic, geographic (Sachs 2005), or even religious and cultural reasons (Schramm 2008).

Even if one leaves aside the question of causation, the cosmopolitan approaches have a true validity in connecting the world to *one common society of people* with a necessary degree of reciprocity among all, or to *one family of humankind* (cf. Kruip) in which a special moral responsibility for the most disadvantaged exists. This notion arises from the thesis that it would be a 'fallacy of restricted universalism', if we made a difference between our fellow countrymen and all others (Black 1991, 357). Global equal rights on issues of fundamental justice are in the process of becoming a valid and strong moral principle at the beginning of the twenty-first century. Nonetheless, there remain severe conflicts between national and international material interests of nations and people as a result of political difficulties in deciding which one takes precedence when balancing competing moral goods.

Rather than going over the old causes of injustices, it seems more important to discuss the instruments available to relieve the suffering and put an end to the preventable deaths among the absolute poor as soon as possible. This is much more realistic, if it is clear that everybody who belongs to the cosmopolitan world is responsible in a bearable degree (cf. Bohlken; Anwander). The more the concept of a Westphalian world of untouchable national states becomes diluted, the more it becomes realistic to argue in favour of a world's 'society of responsibility', either among all states in the form of a responsibility to protect ('R2P', see above) or in favour of a multitude of legitimate collectively responsible actors, including business and transnational corporations as well (cf. Schramm and Seid in this book; Hielscher, Pies et al. 2007).

Human Solidarity Based on Consent and Interaction

Since all approaches mentioned present unresolved questions, an alternative argument could be put forward for an '*ethical paradigm of human solidarity, based on consent and interaction*' specifically on a global level, not so much an ethical paradigm which is based exclusively on the human person, as 'an individual member of the peoples on earth and his or her claim-rights'.

First, traditional ethical arguing consisted of only having to take the role of a patron who knew thoroughly what the deeper need of the persons concerned was. This thorough knowledge was even more necessary if one had to deal with foreigners, who were suffering but had a completely different cultural and mental background. But if one only pursues a static 'Rechtsethik' [ethics of rights], these poor are not invited into a global discourse as human subjects. Nor are they invited to articulate their moral needs and rights for themselves. It is presumed that we as ethical experts have prior universal knowledge of their existential needs and rights. To prevent any form of paternalism in modern global ethics there is no alternative to a process of an always renewed agreement on *every* fundamental question of global justice. This refers to the priority of rights as well as to the question of which particular human right one wants to realise first.

Second, human rights already represent a normative consensus for most of the world's population.[17] Still they are not sufficient to serve as ethical criteria in solving the fundamental problems of the absolute poor because the means of justice to take care of the most disadvantaged are not derivable or applicable from human rights alone. In a situation of malnutrition or social exclusion a right to freedom for the rich might contradict a right to equality for the poor, or even a right to free movement might contradict a right to nutrition for the same group of persons. It is also still not clear whether human rights ethics can lead to a duty of distribution worldwide or only within the same country and how far this duty would extend to subsistence, to specific economic and political participation or to an egalitarian portion of goods? Human rights can either be exclusively understood as claims towards local institutions or in the sense of duties to everyone who is entitled or able to fulfil them. This leaves the question of responsibility open to many interpretations.

What is missing in a plain ethics of human rights is a socially based view of permanent interaction within a globalised world which neither posits a zero sum game nor depicts a pure receiver–donator relationship between people. As mentioned before it can be proved on an empirical level that extreme inequality is worse than a society in which all participants have at least some assets to exchange (Worldbank 2008, 51sqq.). So some form of solidarity is already empirically perceptible and not only normatively demanded.

There are three principal categories for enhancing the interaction of a globalised world in favour of the poor: First, development *aid*, second, reshaped domestic and global *institutions* (including law and an international order) and third, *regulated market* transactions which benefit all (Mack 2005). Injustices of the global order notwithstanding, one still has to recognise that most of the world's welfare surplus develops through mutual exchange, interdependent production and international division of labour. Therefore, the first step to eradicate poverty has to be – also for ethics – *an inclusion of the poor*, not only in terms of their participation in a common moral framework, but also in terms of their possible contribution to the world's interactive work share and division of labour. Of course, mutual gains can only be earned under fair conditions and under the requirement that even the weaker part has something to exchange and contribute. This leads to the conclusion that the poor necessarily have to be on the first step of development, or

17 See Benhabib (2004).

in other words: The prerequisites for inclusion are certain capabilities of nutrition, health, education, shelter, freedom and civil rights, including the important liberty to engage in economic exchange or in the labour market in a meaningful way. Free economic development to mutual advantage can also only succeed, if the local institutions of developing countries are guided by law, are not corrupt or dominated by interest groups, so that economic entrepreneurship cannot exploit the poor, as is currently the case in many parts of the world. One important prerequisite is a global order preventing one-sided market powers (like protectionism, export subsidies or heavy internal subsidies within western economies).

Within an ethics of human solidarity based on consent it is not only necessary to search for a consensus in theory but to find a consensus in political and economic practice. Moral progress can only succeed if the normative claims of the persons concerned, in particular the poorest, are engaged in a local and global discourse and also if they, as human beings, have a chance to contribute to social, political, and economical interaction within a cosmopolitan world.[18] These demands for inclusion are, however, not sufficiently fulfilled by some foreign direct investments which are not aware of or do not care for specific unjust domestic situations. If the people concerned are excluded from democratic procedures, foreign direct investments that support corrupt or unstable regimes, for example, in Africa, cannot be prevented. As a result, they are then able to suppress their poor even more severely. The 'resource curse'[19] of many Sub-Saharan states is a major sign of the need for strong ethical guidelines in market exchanges, the rule of law and democratic inclusion of everybody. Therefore, economic interests are in tune with an ethics of human solidarity only if they are reciprocal on an equal basis[20] and in the interest of the poor themselves. Pro-poor economic gains are only possible within rights-based regimes which have a tax system that provides at least some social and financial distribution so that foreign investments are for the profit of all. Nevertheless one should not forget that gains in poverty reduction cannot be analysed exclusively in economic terms. Poverty has a deep anthropological complexity within its roots that can only be partially helped by increased income or economic growth alone.

Conclusions

All the contributors to this book agree that there is no alternative to the first element of global justice: Globally and domestically the institutional emphasis

18 One striking example is Nobel-prize winner Muhammad Yunus' Grameen Bank, which gives microcredits to the poor. For further information see Yunus (2008).

19 See Wenar (2008).

20 Most interestingly, the acceptability of an equal basis is one of the strongest requirements of the WTO for new members. The reality, however, shows another story. Cf. Hockett (2005); Moellendorf (2005).

on just governance comes first (Rawls 1979, 1). Rawls is generally right about an obligation of liberal and democratic states to assist burdened societies in developing just institutions until they can be self-sufficient and autarkical. For a global society this might also include the possibility of intervening in those sovereign states which suppress their poor in an intolerable manner (Moellendorf 2002, 118sqq.).

Viewing the world as one society of equal human beings and not primarily as a cooperation of states, many of the contributors to this book do not really see an alternative to at least a modest moral cosmopolitanism. Otherwise global ethics would provoke differences in claims of fundamental justice within and between states, in favour of fellow countrymen and against foreigners. The Communitarian or Aristotelian argument for distribution only within a national community simply reveals a pre-globalisation view of political ethics which is not up to the ethical paradigm of a global society. Even if one accepts the closer social solidarity within a common culture and nation, this must not lead to a pre-eminence of social justice in the domestic realm over fundamental claims of justice worldwide – namely the right to a decent life. Otherwise one would have to deny the possibility of a coherent and non-contradictory universally normative ethics on a formal level. On a material level, one would have to neglect the fundamental difference in moral gravity between global justice for the absolute poor and the social justice of solidarity within Western welfare states. It should be clear what has chief importance here: The absolute minimum for existence and the possibility for everyone to live a life in dignity.

A duty of assistance in a cosmopolitan interpretation cannot only include institutional reforms but also implies at least some politically initiated distribution or economically managed exchange of goods and resources either with the consequences of subsistence of the poor, or with a fair share of resources (Pogge 2005; Wenar 2008), or in the form of a global difference principle (see again Beitz 1999, 143sqq. and Mack 2007b) which would require a new or fundamentally improved global economic order. All three possible forms of distribution would include at least some reorganisation of the initial supply of assets among people, in order to provide all with basic capabilities and fundamental rights to provide for themselves. Here, opinions differ, whether or not self-sustaining growth in many African countries can be overcome either by foreign direct investment alone and a mere modification of domestic institutions or whether it needs political support to build incentives of foreign investment and the deliverance of capital, which would otherwise not flow (Klasen 2004; Klasen 2005).

Accepting Thomas Pogge's argument that it is a question of negative duty to prevent injustices in the world order towards the poor, it can be argued that a global *principle of distribution* can be justified to prevent the negative consequences of global inequalities against the poor. Inequalities are unjust if they are so grave that the poorest are unable to compete or to engage in a global process of mutual advantage. This might even be an argument that could convince Rawls because his objection to distribution was mainly based on rejecting disadvantage for the industrious states (Rawls 1999, 117–119), who would lose much of their earnings through egalitarian mechanisms of distribution. The problem is that Rawls does not take into account that inequalities do not only have a positive function by promoting exchange (through comparative advantage) but also have strong negative side effects in the sense of making the poorest so unattractive as market participants, even in their labour power, that nobody wants to deal with them out of economic interests alone. Bringing the world to mutually advantaged interaction without poverty, not only needs sound institutions, as Rawls demands. Initial solidarity has to overcome the disadvantage of poverty at least to the degree of subsidiarity (Mack 2007c, 312) which will always imply long term investments guided by institutions based on law and a democratic order.

The claim for global justice has to be formally universal in the sense of reaching and including every single person living in extreme poverty (cf. again Kruip, Sedmak) but may also be materially restricted in extension with regard to the principles of autonomy and subsidiarity on both sides of interaction[21] (Bischofskonferenz 2003, 18–21). Every human being, given his or her potential to live a decent life, has to master life on their own. This also applies to every state and nation, but only insofar as it is initially able to do so. Otherwise our claim for global justice would be paternalistic and would not seriously appreciate others as independent and free people who have a right to lead their life according to their particular cultural, social and economic manner. Even the Christian command of love cannot be reduced to one-sided benevolence but emphasises the interaction with the other, who always has a capacity to respond or react. If this is not the case, this capacity has to be fostered with respect to a human dignity which inherits demands of reciprocity among all humans. Nevertheless we would make our way of living absolute if we tried to egalitise the world – regardless of an equal dignity of all persons.

Concluding, there seems to be a period of transition within the development of the notion of justice. Initiated by globalisation, a process started in which the people on earth have begun to build up a global society and a conscience for solidarity among all the world's inhabitants not only in theory, but in practice. The claim for global justice is no more led by natural law or anthropological arguments of one human kind, but factually supported by processes of agreement and consensus building in theory and practice (international organisations relying on equal participants). Long after Kant initially reflected on this question, the concept of justice finally reaches out to be cosmopolitan and universal in the sense of equal interaction between all humankind providing multifold inclusion for every human subject. If the world's poorest and most disadvantaged do not have the right to veto and claim their stake in global society, ethics could not call itself global and comprehensive.

Nevertheless material global justice can be restricted in extent, for example by a modest form of equality and subsidiarity, in order to show tolerance and

21 Cf. Forst (2002, 230–232).

be respectful towards the culture, freedom, effort and individuality of different people. In this combination of universality and restrictiveness global justice becomes a realistic concept for a modest cosmopolitanism which can serve as a principle foundation for a future world order which includes the absolute poor as equal subjects.

Acknowledgements

In the name of all of the editors of this book, I would like to thank the German Research Foundation for financial support for this research program as well as the Erfurt Conference upon which this book is based. We also would like to thank Michael Hartlieb for excellent support in organising the conference and in putting together this book. One of the active participants of the conference and contributor to this volume was Michael Ward who sadly passed away unexpectedly in the Autumn of 2008. We would like to dedicate this volume to his memory.

References

Barry, C. et al. (eds) (2005), *Global Institutions and Responsibilities* (Blackwell Publishing Ltd).

Beitz, C. (1975), 'Justice and International Relations', *Philosophy and Public Affairs* 4:4, 360–389.

Beitz, C. (1999), *Political Theory and International Relations* (Princeton, NJ: Princeton University Press).

Beitz, C. (2000), 'Rawls' Law of Peoples', *Ethics* 110:4, 669–696.

Benhabib, S. (2004), *The Rights of Others. Aliens, Residents, and Citizens* (Cambridge: Cambridge University Press).

Black, S. (1991), 'Individualism at an Impasse', *Canadian Journal of Philosophy* 21:3, 347–377.

Bleisch, B. et al. (eds) (2007), *Weltarmut und Ethik* (Paderborn: Mentis).

Boff, L., Boff, C. et al. (1987), *Introducing Liberation Theology* (Tunbridge Wells: Burns & Oates).

Brock, G. et al. (eds) (2005), *The Political Philosophy of Cosmopolitanism* (Cambridge: Cambridge University Press).

Buchanan, A. (2000), 'Rawls's Law of Peoples: Rules for a Vanished Westphalian World', *Ethics* 110:4, 697–721.

Caney, S. (2005), *Justice Beyond Borders: A Global Political Theory* (Oxford: Oxford University Press).

Cooper, R. and Voïnov Kohler, J. (2009), *Responsibility to Protect* (Palgrave Macmillan).

European Parliament (2000), *Charter of Fundamental Rights of the European Union*. Available at <http://www.europarl.europa.eu/charter/pdf/text_en.pdf>.

European Parliament (2004), *Treaty Establishing a Constitution for Europe*. Available at <http://eur-lex.europa.eu/JOHtml.do?uri=OJ%3AC%3A2004%3A310%3ASOM%3AEN%3AHTML>.
Forst, R. (2002), 'Zu einer kritischen Theorie transnationaler Gerechtigkeit', in Schmücker, R. et al. (eds), 215–232.
Forst, R. (2007), *Das Recht auf Rechtfertigung: Elemente einer konstruktivistischen Theorie der Gerechtigkeit* (Frankfurt/Main: Suhrkamp).
Gosepath, S. (2002), 'Die Globale Ausdehnung der Gerechtigkeit', in Schmücker, R. et al. (eds), 197–214.
Grimm, M., Klasen, S. et al. (2007), *Determinants of Pro-Poor Growth: Analytical Issues and Findings from Country Cases* (Basingstoke: Palgrave Macmillan).
Gutiérrez, G. and Inda, C. (1973), *A Theology of Liberation: History, Politics and Salvation* (Maryknoll, NY: Orbis).
Habermas, J. (1981), *Theorie des Kommunikativen Handelns* (Frankfurt/Main: Suhrkamp).
Hielscher, S., Pies, I. et al. (2007), 'Wie können Corporate Citizens voneinander lernen? Anregungen für den Global Compact der Vereinten Nationen', *Discussion Paper* 2007:13 (Halle: Lehrstuhl für Wirtschaftsethik, Martin-Luther-Universität).
Hockett, R. (2005), 'Three (Potential) Pillars of Transnational Economic Justice: The Bretton Woods Institutions as Guarantors of Global Equal Treatment and Market Completion', in Barry, C. et al. (eds), 90–123.
Höffe, O. (1999), *Demokratie im Zeitalter der Globalisierung* (München: Verlag C.H. Beck).
Homann, K. et al. (eds) (2005), *Wirtschaftsethik der Globalisierung* (Tübingen).
Homann, K. et al. (eds) (2007), *Globalisation and Business Ethics* (Aldershot: Ashgate).
International Commission on Intervention and State Sovereignty and International Development Research Centre (2001), *The Responsibility to Protect: Report of the International Commission on Intervention and State Sovereignty* (Ottawa: International Development Research Centre).
Jigang, S. et al. (eds) (2007), *Politics and Ethics* (Peking: Ren min chu ban she).
Kant, I. (1903), *Grundlegung zur Metaphysik der Sitten* (Berlin: Preußische Akademie der Wissenschaften).
Klasen, S. (2004), 'In Search of the Holy Grail: How to Achieve Pro Poor Growth?', in Tungodden, B. et al. (eds).
Klasen, S. (2005), 'Armutsreduzierung im Zeitalter der Globalisierung', *Ibero American Institute for Economical Research Discussion Papers* 146. Available at <http://ideas.repec.org/p/got/iaidps/146.html>.
Koller, P. (ed.) (2006), *Die Globale Frage: Empirische Befunde und Ethische Herausforderungen* (Wien: Passagen-Verlag).
Krebs, A. (2000), *Gleichheit oder Gerechtigkeit: Texte der Neuen Egalitarismuskritik* (Frankfurt/Main: Suhrkamp).
Krebs, A. (2004), 'Gleichheit ohne Grenzen? Die Kosmopolitische Überforderung', *Information Philosophie* 5, 7–13.

Mack, E. (2002), *Gerechtigkeit und gutes Leben. Christliche Ethik im Politischen Diskurs* (Paderborn/München: Schöningh).
Mack, E. (2005), 'Globale Gerechtigkeitskriterien zur Beurteilung der Entwicklungsrelevanz von Globalisierungsprozessen', in Homann, K. et al. (eds), 305–318.
Mack, E. (2007a), 'Criteria for Justice in a Globalised World', in Homann, K. et al. (eds), 306–318.
Mack, E. (2007b), 'Globale Solidarität mit den Armen', *Jahrbuch für Christliche Sozialwissenschaften* 48, 297–336.
Mack, E. (2007c), 'Who is Responsible for Global Justice', in Jigang, S. et al. (eds), 349–362.
Meyer, L. (2008), 'Intergenerational Sufficiency Justice', in Meyer, L. et al. (eds), *Theories of Intergenerational Justice* (Oxford: Oxford University Press).
Miller, D. (1988), 'The Ethical Significance of Nationality', *Ethics* 98:4, 647–662.
Miller, D. (2004), 'Holding Nations Responsible', *Ethics* 114:2, 240–268.
Miller, D. (2005), 'Against Global Egalitarianism', *The Journal of Ethics* 9:1–2, 55–79.
Moellendorf, D. (2002), *Cosmopolitan Justice* (Boulder, CO/Oxford: Westview).
Moellendorf, D. (2005), 'The World Trade Organization and Egalitarian Justice', in Barry, C. et al. (eds), 141–158.
Nussbaum, M. (1992), 'Human Functioning and Social Justice: In Defense of Aristotelian Essentialism', *Political Theory* 20:2, 202–246.
Nussbaum, M. (2001), *Women and Human Development: The Capabilities Approach* (Cambridge: Cambridge University Press).
Nussbaum, M. (2006), *Frontiers of Justice: Disability, Nationality, Species Membership* (Cambridge, MA: The Belknap Press of Harvard University Press).
O'Neill, O. (1990), 'Justice, Gender and International Boundaries', *British Journal of Political Science* 20:4, 439–459.
O'Neill, O. (2000), *Bounds of Justice* (Cambridge: Cambridge University Press).
Pauer-Studer, H. (2006), 'Globale Gerechtigkeit und Moralische Verpflichtung', in Koller, P. (ed.).
Pogge, T. (1992), 'Cosmopolitanism and Sovereignty', *Ethics* 103:1, 48–75.
Pogge, T. (1994), 'An Egalitarian Law of Peoples', *Philosophy and Public Affairs* 23:3, 195–224.
Pogge, T. (2002), *World Poverty and Human Rights: Cosmopolitan Responsibilities and Reforms* (Cambridge: Polity).
Pogge, T. (2005), 'A Cosmopolitan Perspective on the Global Economic Order', in Brock, G. (eds), 92–109.
Ravallion, M. (2003), 'How Not to Count the Poor? A Reply to Reddy and Pogge'. Available at <http://www.socialanalysis.org>.
Rawls, J. (1979) *Eine Theorie der Gerechtigkeit* (Frankfurt/Main: Suhrkamp).
Rawls, J. (1999) *The Law of Peoples: with, The Idea of Public Reason Revisited* (Cambridge, MA: Harvard University Press).
Rawls, J. (2002), *Das Recht der Völker: enthält: 'Nochmals: Die Idee der öffentlichen Vernunft'* (Berlin: Walter de Gruyter).

Reddy, S. and Pogge, T. (2005), 'How Not to Count the Poor'. Available at <http://www.socialanalysis.org>.

Risse, M. (2005), 'How does the Global Order Harm the Poor?', *Philosophy and Public Affairs* 33:4, 349–376.

Risse, M. (2005), 'What We Owe to the Global Poor', *The Journal of Ethics* 9:1–2, 81–117.

Sachs, J. (2005), *The End of Poverty. Economic Possibilities for Our Time* (London: Penguin).

Sautter, H. (2004), *Weltwirtschaftsordnung. Die Institutionen der Globale Ökonomie* (München: Vahlen).

Scanlon, T. (1998), *What We Owe to Each Other* (Cambridge, MA: Belknap Press of Harvard University Press).

Schmücker, R. et al. (eds) (2002), *Gerechtigkeit und Politik: Philosophische Perspektiven* (Berlin: Akadmie Verlag).

Schramm, M. (2008), *Ökonomische Moralkulturen. Die Ethik differenter Interessen und der plurale Kapitalismus* (Marburg: Metropolis).

Segundo, J. (1976), *Liberation of Theology* (Maryknoll, NY: Orbis Books).

Sekretariat der deutschen Bischofskonferenz (2003), *Das Soziale neu denken. Für eine langfristig angelegte Reformpolitik* (Bonn).

Sen, A. (1985), 'Well-Being, Agency and Freedom: The Dewey Lectures 1984', *The Journal of Philosophy* 82:4, 169–221.

Sen, A. (1997), *Poverty and Famines: An Essay on Entitlement and Deprivation* (Oxford: Clarendon Press).

Singer, P. (1972), 'Famine, Affluence, and Morality', *Philosophy and Public Affairs* 1:3, 229–243.

Tan, K. (2001), 'Reasonable Disagreement and Distributive Justice', *The Journal of Value Inquiry* 35, 493–507.

Tan, K. (2005), 'Boundary Making and Equal Concern', in C. Barry et al. (eds), *Global Institutions and Responsibilities* (Oxford: Blackwell) 48–64.

Tungodden, B. et al. (eds) (2004), *Toward Pro Poor Policies – Aid, Institutions, and Globalization* (New York: Oxford University Press).

Wenar, L. (2008), 'Property Rights and the Resource Curse', *Philosophy and Public Affairs* 36:1, 2–32.

Winters, L., McCulloch, N. et al. (2004), 'Trade Liberalization and Poverty: The Evidence so Far', *Journal of Economic Literature* 42:1, 72–115.

Worldbank (2008), *Global Monitoring Report 2008. MDGs and the Environment. Agenda for Inclusive and Sustainable Development.* Available at <http://siteresources.worldbank.org/INTGLOMONREP2008/Resources/4737994-1207342962709/8944_Web_PDF.pdf>.

Young, I. (1998), 'Selbstbestimmung und Globale Demokratie. Zur Kritik des Liberalen Nationalismus', *Deutsche Zeitschrift für Philosophie* 46:3, 431–457.

Yunus, M. (2008), *Creating a World without Poverty: Social Business and the Future of Capitalism* (New York: Perseus Books Group).

PART 1
Poverty Data Under Scrutiny

Chapter 1

Levels and Trends in Absolute Poverty in the World: What We Know and What We Don't

Stephan Klasen[1]

Introduction

At the Millennium Summit in 2000, the world community agreed on eight Millennium Development Goals (MDGs) to ensure poverty reduction and sustainable development for all. Poverty was seen in a wider context, encompassing income poverty, hunger, lack of educational opportunities, gender bias, morbidity, and premature mortality which are taken up in the first six of the eight MDGs. The first Millennium Development Goal, agreed to by the world community at the Millennium Summit in 2000, calls for the eradication of extreme poverty and hunger. The targets agreed are somewhat more modest and refer to halving, between 1990 and 2015, the share of the population living on less than $1 a day, and halving the proportion of the population who suffer from hunger. For these two targets, three indicators were chosen. For the first target, the World Bank has been charged to regularly produce the relevant indicator, i.e. the share of the population that is living on less than a $1 a day. For the second target, there are two indicators. The first is to be monitored by UNICEF and WHO and refers to halving the share of children under five years of age who are underweight, and the second is to be monitored by the FAO and refers to halving the share of the population who are below minimum recommended levels of dietary intake.

While all of these targets appear quite clear and the indicators chosen to measure them appropriate, there is in fact a great deal of uncertainty about both levels and trends in absolute poverty and hunger in the developing world. In particular, the two indicators for hunger show a very different distribution of underweight children and populations with calorie deficiencies. Neither indicator, in turn, correlate particularly well with mortality indicators and there appear to be significant regional anomalies, although one would presume a close correlation at the regional level. For example, caloric deficiency appears to be worst in the Caribbean, the share of underweight children appears worst in South Asia, and infant and child mortality would seem to be worst in Sub-Saharan Africa.

1 The author would like to thank Francois Bourguignon, Francisco Ferreira, Elke Mack, Thomas Pogge, Martin Ravallion, Sanjay Reddy, Michael Schramm, and Michael Ward for helpful comments and discussion.

Standard models to explain these phenomena cannot account for these anomalies. As discussed in detail in Klasen (2008), these problems therefore appear to be due to significant conceptual and empirical problems with both hunger indicators, their underlying data, and the assumptions made to arrive at these aggregate measures. As a result, there remains significant uncertainty about where 'hunger' is indeed worst and how the share of hungry people is changing over time. As these issues are dealt with exhaustively in Klasen (2008), this chapter will not dwell further on them here. Instead the focus here will be on the first target and indicator: The share of the population living below $1 a day. The focus on this issue is particularly pertinent, as the World Bank has recently published extensive revisions to this indicator (Chen and Ravallion 2008). In fact, the revision of these numbers has been based on the derivation of a new international poverty line against which to measure levels and trends in poverty, as well as a recalculation of poverty levels and trends for all countries going back to 1981. Thus both the baseline for the first MDG target in 1990 has changed as well as the levels in each subsequent year, thereby also affecting the rate of progress towards this MDG. This chapter will critically review the way the World Bank measures this extreme poverty indicator, present key facts and figures on trends in extreme poverty using data from before and after the revision, and then focus on a critical appraisal of the recent revisions. While there is little reason to believe that these revisions seriously distort *trends* in extreme poverty in the developing world, it will be argued that the uncertainty about levels in *absolute* extreme poverty is very high and that the recent revisions have done little to reduce this uncertainty and might have indeed increased it. In fact, given the difficulties to measure poverty using an international poverty line, it will be suggested instead that it might be preferable to abandon the efforts to construct such an international poverty line and focus instead on creating consistent and comparable national poverty lines using a common set of methods that could in turn be used to estimate levels and trends in absolute extreme poverty in the world. The chapter is organised as follows: The next section will discuss the $1 a day poverty indicator, its conceptual underpinning and its empirical derivation. The following section will then critically review the revisions that were introduced in 2005 and present key facts and figures that have been affected by this revision. In the following section the implications of these criticisms and the advantages and disadvantages of an alternative procedure will be discussed with conclusions in the final section.

The World Bank's International Poverty Measure

Measuring poverty is clearly a challenging task. Among the questions to be asked are the domain in which poverty is to be measured, whether a poverty line separating the poor from the non-poor is invariant across space and time, whether one should consider just the incidence or also the depth of poverty, and whether poverty should be measured at the individual or household level.[2] These are all complex questions that merit detailed discussions as well as high-quality comparable household survey data. For a poverty indicator that attempts to measure levels and trends in poverty in a comparable manner across all developing countries, data availability and comparability issues will necessarily involve simplifications and short-cuts. In fact, until 1990 it was not possible to generate such poverty figures as the coverage of household surveys in developing countries was simply too sparse. In the 1990 World Development Report (World Bank 1990) the World Bank made a first attempt to measure poverty in a comparable way using an international poverty line and measuring poverty for the year 1985. This was based on an international poverty line of the purchasing power equivalent of $1 per capita in 1985 prices. There have been two major updates of this poverty line, once in the World Development Report 2000/01, where the poverty line was shifted to $1.08 in 1993 prices and recently again in Ravallion, Chen, and Sangraula (2008), when it was shifted again to $1.25 in 2005 prices. The one proposed in 2000 became the basis for the first target of MDG1 at the Millennium Summit. The methods for establishing the poverty lines have largely remained the same in these three versions which will be described below.

Before turning to this point, it is useful to point out a number of implicit choices and simplifications that are inherent in this approach to the measurement of poverty. First, the focus is entirely on the income dimension of poverty. Whether such income poverty is correlated with other forms of deprivation or a multidimensional view of poverty consistent with, for example, Sen's capability approach is not considered here (e.g. Sen 1985; Klasen 2000). While this is clearly a narrow view, it is defensible in the context of the MDGs where other forms of deprivation are captured in the other MDGs as well as the hunger target of MDG1.

Second, the international poverty line is invariant in space and time[3] and thus constitutes an *absolute* poverty line that tries to capture the share of people who are in extreme poverty where basic physical survival and health is at risk. *Relative* poverty concepts that are based on claims that poverty depends on socially acceptable standards of living in a given society are also not considered here. Clearly, this is a debatable choice, but may be also defensible if the focus is on developing countries where absolute, life-threatening poverty is still a very serious problem. It would clearly be inappropriate to use such an approach to measure poverty in industrialised countries; indeed one may wonder whether it is appropriate for poverty measurement in upper middle-income countries such as Brazil, Thailand, Mexico, or South Africa where absolute life-threatening poverty

2 For a discussion, see, for example, Sen (1984), Ravallion (1994), and Klasen (2000).

3 The poverty line is adjusted only for differences in prices across space and time.

is only affecting a relatively small share of the population while many more suffer from relative deprivation.[4]

Third, poverty depth is not considered in the target for MDG1, but all poor are treated the same and simply added up, regardless of whether their incomes are just below or very far below the poverty line. Considering the depth of poverty would indeed be preferable, but somewhat harder to communicate and also makes greater demands on the precision of the data.[5]

Fourth, the figures are per capita figures and do not account for differences in household size and composition which is likely to affect the needs of households as well as their ability to economise on resources. This will have the consequence that poverty in regions with large households and many children (such as many countries in Sub-Saharan Africa) is overstated relative to regions where household sizes and the number of children are small (such as China or South-East Asia).[6]

Lastly, inequality in intra-household resource allocation is not considered in these measures. If the per capita income of a household falls below the poverty line, everyone in the household is considered poor, even though some members might have better resource access than others. As a result, this approach is ill suited to examine the differential in poverty by gender or age group and it might indeed affect accurate poverty measurement (see Haddad and Kanbur 1990; Klasen 2007).[7]

While these are all shortcomings of this approach to measuring poverty, some of which that could be addressed with available data, some of these choices appear defensible in the context of the MDGs where there was a need for a straightforward comparable poverty indicator that would particularly capture levels and trends in extreme income poverty.

Bearing these methodological choices in mind, the big remaining questions are how this international poverty line is actually derived and how it is then used to measure poverty in each developing country so that poverty levels and trends can then be aggregated and compared. This is described in detail in Ravallion, Chen, and Sangraula (2008) and will be summarised here. Let us first turn to the construction

4 For a discussion, see, for example, Sen (1984). See Ravallion, Chen, and Sangraula (2008) for a defence of such an absolute approach to measuring poverty.

5 Most of the background papers by the World Bank team working on these numbers usually also prepare figures that consider the depth and severity of poverty. See, for example, Chen and Ravallion (2008).

6 In principle, this is also a solvable problem. The Luxembourg Income Survey which compiles comparable statistics mostly from OECD countries uses a common equivalence scale to deal with this problem. Possibly it would be harder to define such common equivalence scales for the very heterogeneous developing world.

7 There are also more detailed measurement questions such as the consistency of household surveys between countries and over time, as well as the consistency of income or consumption information in household surveys with the same information in national accounts which appear to suggest lower rates of extreme poverty and faster poverty reduction. See Chen and Ravallion (2008) and Bhalla (2004) for a discussion.

of the international poverty line. In all three versions presented by the World Bank (1990, 2000, and 2008), the starting point was always the national poverty lines of a large sample of developing countries, expressed in their national currencies. In order to render them comparable, the results of the so-called International Price Comparison Project (ICP) were used to turn these national poverty lines into international prices (expressed in international $). The ICP rounds, which take place every 3–10 years, compare prices of a large basket of goods and services in many different countries to generate exchange rates that appropriately reflect purchasing power differences between countries (see below and the contribution by Ward in this volume). These so-called purchasing power parity (PPP) exchange rates are used for the translation of national poverty lines into international $ in the hope that this approach will adequately reflect purchasing power differences and thus make these poverty lines comparable. For the 1990 exercise the 1985 ICP was used; for the 2000 revision, the 1993 ICP was used, and the latest poverty estimates are based on the 2005 ICP.

In a second step the poverty lines are plotted against per capita incomes and it is regularly found that among low income countries, the poverty lines, turned into international $, are very similar. The average of these poverty lines then is used as the international poverty line, which turned out to be $1.02 in 1985 prices in the 1990 World Development Report, $1.08 in 1993 prices in the 2000/01 World Development Report, and $1.25 in 2005 prices in the recent revision.

To measure poverty using these poverty lines, the following three steps are then undertaken. First, the international poverty line is turned into a poverty line in national currencies at the benchmark year using the PPP exchange rates from the particular ICP round (1985, 1993, and 2005, respectively). Second, this poverty line is adjusted using national inflation rates to generate poverty lines in national currencies backwards and forwards in time for all years since 1990 (or even since 1981). Third, the share of the population living below this poverty line is then determined using national household income or expenditure surveys.

It is important to emphasise that in each three rounds of calculation (1990, 2000, and 2008), poverty rates were recalculated not only for the most recent years, but for all years since the beginning of measurement of poverty at the global level (where the first data point is 1981). Thus we have three sets of poverty estimates for 1985, one based on the 1985 ICP round published in 1990, one for the 1993 ICP round published in 2000, and another one based on the 2005 ICP round published in 2008. The resulting numbers for the same year are, in some cases dramatically different and it is not obvious to say which estimate is the most accurate one, an issue that will be discussed in more detail below.

Poverty Levels and Trends Using the 2005 ICP Round

In late 2007, the World Bank made available the new PPP exchange rates from the 2005 ICP survey (World Bank 2007). Not only do they represent a more up-to-date set of price comparisons, but this round of the ICP was more comprehensive than all previous rounds, and particularly included China for the first time. In August of 2008, it then published new poverty estimates for developing countries going back to 1981 based on these figures. Table 1.1 compares the share of the population below $1.08 a day in 1993 prices by region and from 1990 to 2005 with the new figures which are based on the $1.25 poverty line in 2005 prices. As can be readily seen from the table, there are dramatic differences in levels of poverty in many regions of the developing world using these two methodologies. Changes are particularly extreme in East Asia and the Pacific, but also quite large in Sub-Saharan Africa, the Middle East, and South Asia. In China, using the 2005 ICP suggests that 60 per cent of the population lived in extreme poverty based on the ICP published in 1990, compared to 'only' 33 per cent using the previous ICP. This largely drives the results for all of East Asia. In India and in Sub-Saharan Africa, extreme poverty is now believed to have been much higher in 1990 than was previously thought. This, of course, has direct implications for the first target of MDG1 where the halving of poverty uses 1990 as a baseline. When the goal was agreed in 2000, based on the 1993 ICP, it implied that the share of the extremely poor should fall from about 29 per cent of the population in developing countries in 1990 to half that, i.e. 14.5 per cent in 2015. Using the 2005 ICP for this goal implies that now extreme poverty, expressed in 2005 international prices, needs to fall from nearly 42 per cent in 1990 to 21 per cent in 2015. Thus halving poverty is now based on a much larger share of poor people.

But also the most recent observations show large discrepancies. Poverty in 2005 is believed to be about ten percentage points higher in South Asia and Sub-Saharan Africa using the 2005 ICP rather than the 1993 ICP suggested. In all of the developing world, the 2005 ICP suggests that some 26 per cent of the population suffer from extreme poverty in 2005, compared to only 19 per cent when the 1993 ICP was used.

This not only affects poverty rates, but correspondingly the absolute number of people who live in extreme poverty. While the 1993 ICP round suggested that 1.5 billion people lived in extreme poverty in 1990 and this figure dropped to 930 million in 2005; the 2005 ICP implies that the number of extremely poor was 1.9 billion in 1990 and about 1.4 billion in 2005 (Chen and Ravallion 2008). These are large differences, suggesting that we have about 50 per cent more extremely poor people in the world.

While the differences in poverty levels introduced by the new revision based on the 2005 ICP are very large, the differences in poverty trends since 1990 are remarkably small, a point also emphasised by the World Bank (Chen and Ravallion 2008). The recent revision does not change the direction of poverty trends in any region or for the developing world as a whole. Also the size of poverty reduction in the different regions, and the developing world as a whole, changes remarkably little. Poverty reduction in China, and East Asia as a whole, remains very rapid, poverty reduction in South Asia also remains sizable, and continues to be the case that poverty reduction in Latin America, Eastern Europe and Central Asia, and

Sub-Saharan Africa was very small, and mostly concentrated in the period after 2000. As a whole, the figures thus suggest relatively little change to the assessment of overall progress in the first target of MDG1. Regardless of whether we use the old or the revised figures, the developing world as a whole seems to be on track to halving extreme poverty. Using 1993 prices, the poverty rate fell from 29 per cent in 1990 to about 18 per cent in 2005; using 2005 prices, the decline is from 42 per cent to 26 per cent; in both cases reaching the goal by 2015 is clearly within reach. At the same time, both sets of estimates suggest that this overall positive development is largely driven by over-achievement in poverty reduction in East Asia and quite good progress in South Asia. In contrast, Sub-Saharan Africa is highly unlikely to reach the goal, and it is also highly uncertain that Latin America or the Middle East will reach it.

Table 1.1 Share of population suffering from extreme poverty, 1993 and 2005 ICP rounds

Region	**1990**		**1996**		**2002**		**2005**	
Poverty line	1.25 (2005)	1.08 (1993)	1.25 (2005)	1.08 (1993)	1.25 (2005)	1.08 (1993)	1.25 (2005)	1.08 (1993)
East Asia and Pacific:	56.0	29.8	37.1	16.1	29.6	12.3	17.9	9.1
Of which China	60.2	33.0	36.4	17.4	28.4	13.8	15.9	9.9
Eastern Europe and Central Asia	1.5	0.5	4.5	4.4	5.6	1.3	5.0	0.9
Latin America and Caribbean	10.7	10.2	11.5	8.9	10.1	9.1	8.2	8.6
Middle East and North Africa	5.4	2.3	5.3	1.7	4.7	1.7	4.6	1.5
South Asia:	51.1	43.0	46.9	36.1	43.8	33.6	40.3	30.8
Of which India	51.3	44.3	46.6	39.9	43.9	36.0	41.6	34.3
Sub-Saharan Africa	54.9	46.7	57.5	47.7	52.7	42.6	50.4	41.1
Total	**41.6**	**28.7**	**34.8**	**22.7**	**31.0**	**20.1**	**25.7**	**18.1**
Total excluding China	35.2	27.1	34.2	24.5	31.9	22.2	28.7	20.7

Note: The first column refers to the share of the population below the new poverty line of $1.25 a day, the second one to the old poverty line. The differences in the figures are, to a very small degree, also due to changes in survey data; also note that the $1.08 figures in the 2005 column refer to 2004. Sources: Chen and Ravallion (2008), Chen and Ravallion (2007).

Given the process of arriving at these numbers, it is not surprising that the revisions only have a large impact on poverty levels, but not on trends in poverty reduction. All that has changed for poverty trends at the national level is that the poverty line has been changed at the benchmark year and then the same national inflation rates have been used to adjust the poverty line for each year between 1990 and now. Thus there has been a consistent shift of the poverty line across all years (either upwards, as in the case of most developing countries, or downwards, as in the case of very few developing countries); since the household surveys have not changed that are used to determine poverty using these adjusted poverty lines, it is not surprising that the trends are hardly affected. Trends in poverty using a consistent poverty line are mostly driven by changes in average incomes and the income distribution in national currencies rather than the location of the poverty line, and in this respect nothing has changed.[8]

Thus the new findings suggest that poverty is much higher than we previously thought, particularly in China, but also in Africa and India. At the same time, the new numbers have little impact on what we knew about the pace of poverty reduction and the progress towards meeting MDG1. Here the finding remains that progress on the whole looks quite promising, but is highly heterogeneous, with many regions projected not to meet the goal of halving extreme poverty.

In this context, one should also point that below the surface of even these uneven regional trends lie more disconcerting facts that were highlighted in last year's Global Monitoring Report on the MDGs, produced by the World Bank (World Bank, 2008). In particular, two very disconcerting facts are hidden beneath the figures in Table 1.1. The first is that more than half of the 149 developing countries included in the assessment of MDG progress lack the necessary data to assess whether there has been any progress in poverty reduction. Two groups of countries predominate among those with no data. One group consists of very small countries such as the many small island states in the Pacific and the small African countries where regular household surveys are not undertaken. The other group consists of unstable countries where violence, civil wars, state collapse, or extremely weak governments prevent the collection of data. While the first group is unlikely to affect overall trends by much, the second group includes some larger countries such as Afghanistan, Iraq, Somalia, Myanmar, or Eritrea where one might suspect that poverty trends are not favourable and this could have a noticeable effect. But the data represented in Table 1.1 include information from countries that comprise 90 per cent of the population of developing countries (Chen and Ravallion 2008), so that the overall regional and global trends are not seriously affected by these missing observations. It remains the case, however,

8 They will have a modest impact, however, as now these trends are evaluated at a different national poverty lines which have consistently been shifted upwards or downwards for all years, and we know from the work of Bourguignon (2003), Klasen and Misselhorn (2007), among others, that the location of the poverty line will affect the pace of poverty reduction.

that it is a serious problem that one simply lacks the data on poverty levels and trends for the majority of developing countries; this is a great challenge for the countries concerned as well as the international community to remedy this very unsatisfactory state of affairs.

The second disconcerting fact is that of those countries where information is available to monitor poverty trends, over 60 per cent are, at current trends, actually off track to meet the poverty reduction goal (World Bank 2008). If we take a country perspective, the news on progress in reducing extreme poverty is therefore actually quite bad: The vast majority of countries in the world either are unlikely to meet the target or lack the data to monitor progress. Conversely, the overall positive trend is entirely dominated by the good poverty reduction performance of a number of populous developing countries, most notably China, India, Indonesia, Bangladesh, and Vietnam.

Nevertheless the big question remains what to make of these large revisions in poverty levels in many developing countries. Similarly, the general approach of periodically revising these international poverty lines to generate a whole new time series of poverty estimates should be scrutinised further. This is taken up in the next section.

Problems and Open Questions Associated with the Recent Poverty Revisions

There are two different sets of questions associated with this approach to measuring extreme poverty in the developing world. The first set asks whether conceptually the current approach to measuring and periodically revising poverty lines in the developing world using this procedure is a promising way to accurately reflect levels and trends in absolute poverty. This is a subject on which there has been some debate in the past (e.g. Reddy and Pogge (forthcoming); Ravallion 2007); the focus here will not be to repeat this debate but reflect on the conceptual issues in light of the recent drastic revisions. The second set of questions involves potential empirical problems with the two ICP rounds in 1993 and 2005 that differ so much in their conclusions on relative price levels, and thus on poverty levels. This is also a topic that is discussed in more detail by Michael Ward in his contribution to this book, but this chapter will also weigh in on some of these issues. Our discussion will deal with these two issues in turn.

On the conceptual side, this chapter needs to address two difficult issues. The first is whether the PPP exchange rates generated by the ICP process are appropriate for the comparisons of the purchasing power of the poor. This is an issue central to the critique of Reddy and Pogge (forthcoming) and, in principle, it would indeed be preferable to only consider those items in the construction of PPP exchange rates that are of relevance to the poor. This was seen by all participants in these debates as an important way forward and several attempts have been made to move in this direction.[9] The most recent was by Deaton and Dupriez (2008) who constructed consumption baskets close to the poverty line and use those baskets to compare prices. This is conceptually superior, but data-intensive and only possible for a small set of countries. According to results presented in Chen, Ravallion, and Sangraula (2008), the empirical differences between these two sets of results in terms of setting a poverty line are rather small. This will not necessarily mean that this issue has no importance, however, as there is a second related point one must bear in mind. The overall PPPs that are used for the translation of the international poverty line into national currencies can be significantly affected by goods and services not heavily consumed by the poor and this can in turn affect levels of poverty. For example, Heston (2008) argues that in the 2005 ICP the biggest reason for the drastic downward revision of PPP adjusted per capita income (and thus the large upward adjustment of poverty levels) was due to changes in the assumptions about the productivity of government services. While this is an important issue to consider when comparing GDP levels, it is less clear that it is a relevant factor to consider when assessing poverty as the poor are arguably less affected by this change (see Reddy 2008). Similarly, Ward argues in his contribution that the finding that China was much more expensive than previously thought is based on baskets of goods that are internationally comparable, but largely out of reach of the poor so that also here the question is whether this change should really impinge on poverty measurement. The choices made in the 2005 ICP round to deal with these two difficult conceptual issues suggest that income levels are underestimated and poverty is overestimated, an issue to which we return below.

The second, equally difficult question relates to the intertemporal use of a single cross-country price comparison. As explained above, the poverty estimates from 1981 to 2005 are now based on the 2005 PPP exchange rates which are now used, in combination with national inflation rates, to derive poverty lines for each year. As has been pointed out by many scholars working on these price comparisons, the ICP rounds only provide valid comparisons of purchasing power adjusted GDPs at one point in time, the benchmark year. Thus the use of the 2005 price comparisons to compare poverty levels in 2000, 1995, let alone 1981, is not really an appropriate use of these comparisons. The reason is that the 2005 comparison is based on the global production and demand of goods available in 2005 and global demand and availability of goods changes over time which would affect price comparisons. While it appears rather innocuous to use the 2005 ICP to assess poverty levels in 2003–2006, it seems quite problematic to use these prices for comparisons of poverty levels in 1990, let alone 1981 when the world economy, the structure of world demand, and the availability of goods was quite different. This problem will keep getting worse. The next ICP round is planned for

9 See, for example, Reddy, Visaria, and Asali (2008) for one such example where the approach is to define a common conception of poverty based on nutritional adequacy and then compare poverty levels in three countries using this metric.

2011 and it seems highly dubious to base comparisons of poverty levels in 1990 or earlier on the assessment of global prices in 2011.

The obvious alternative to this approach would be to use all of the benchmark comparisons years (i.e. 1985, 1993, 1996, and 2005) in an assessment of purchasing power parity exchange rates for different time periods. This is the approach that so far has been taken by the various versions of the Penn World Tables provided by Summers, Heston, and Aten which provide PPP-adjusted GDP per capita levels.[10] The problem with applying this approach to poverty measurement is that it will lead to strong deviations of trends in poverty from what we know from national statistics. The extreme case would be China again. If we believed the 1993 ICP and the 2005 ICP to be true reflections of Chinese prices relative to world prices, then poverty would have fallen in China between 1993 and 2005 by only 10 percentage points (from 28 per cent to 18 per cent) which is entirely inconsistent with growth and poverty reduction using national data which show much faster poverty reduction.[11] A second problem with such an approach would be that the earlier ICP rounds were much more incomplete, omitting large countries such as China in all previous rounds and India in several rounds, so that it is unclear what estimates to use for these countries. A third problem is that there are reasons to believe that the earlier rounds were of lower quality than previous ones so that one might reasonably want to distrust some of their results (see Heston 2008; Ravallion, Chen and Sangraula 2008).[12]

So one is faced with a rather unpalatable choice between two problematic approaches: Either we rely on a single cross-country price comparison and pretend it tells us a lot about how relative prices were 15 or even 25 years ago across the world, which is the current approach, or we use the different comparisons and have to contend with the inconsistencies, the coverage, and the differential quality. Both choices appear to be quite problematic.

These conceptual problems appear to be really quite serious and they will get worse over time. Imagine that we are in 2015 where there has yet again been another ICP round and we will first have to generate a new international poverty line yet again, then produce an entirely new time series of poverty rates going back all the way to 1990 to determine what the new levels of poverty are and whether indeed we have met the goal.

Apart from these conceptual problems, there are also some measurement problems to deal with in this particular ICP round and the biases it might have produced. There are several reasons to believe that in general the quality of the

---

10 They do not only consider the benchmark years, but also national growth rates and try to render the two pieces of information consistent. For details see the documentation in Heston, Summers, and Aten (2006).

11 China did not participate in the 1993 ICP so its PPP exchange rates are based on estimates which may well be part of the problem for the drastic revision.

12 These arguments would also caution against just relying on earlier rounds of the ICP for global poverty measurement.

ICP is higher than in previous rounds. The country coverage was wider, there were more consistency checks, and it appears that the data gathering and analysis was more thorough (see, e.g. Heston 2008; Ravallion, Chen and Sangraula 2008). At the same time two particular empirical problems appear to arise. The first, also discussed by Ward in this volume and also confirmed by Heston (2008), relates to the choice of goods whose prices are being compared. There is the inherent tension between international comparability and national representativeness of goods. Ideally the goods whose prices are to be compared should be both highly comparable internationally (i.e. essentially the same good in all countries) but also representative of the purchasing habits of a population. In rich countries this is likely to be the case (e.g. one can compare the prices of identical shirts of the same popular brand that are both available and widely used). When we compare prices between a rich country and a poor country, the tension will arise. We will probably be able to find identical goods in both countries but in the poor country the good is likely to be consumed by a rich and import-oriented elite and thus not representative of the population (e.g. an international brand-name shirt will be bought only by a select group in China). One could alternatively replace the good in a poor country with a cheaper, domestically produced substitute which would be more representative of the population, but inherently less comparable to the good in the rich country. As with the conceptual problems, there is no easy way to resolve this tension and choose the 'correct' answer. The claim by Ward is that in the 2005 ICP one tended to emphasise international comparability over national representativeness, and this led to some of high reported prices in countries such as China, India, or parts of Sub-Saharan Africa, and thus the associated higher poverty levels, a claim also supported by Heston (2008), an adviser to the 2005 ICP round. This would essentially mean that poverty is overstated in these countries in the 2005 ICP round as the 'comparable' national goods are actually more affordable, leading to higher purchasing power and lower poverty.[13]

As a result, we are left with a great deal of uncertainty about the levels of extreme poverty and it appears to me that the conceptual and empirical problems are so severe that we can place relatively little confidence in the reported *levels* of poverty using these international poverty lines. To be sure the reported *trends* in global poverty are much less questionable where the changes implied by each revision have been always relatively modest due to the reasons described above.

13 A related issue refers to the already-mentioned assumption about the productivity of government services where Heston (2008) argues that the adjustments were possibly too large for China and India, thus making these countries look poorer as a whole, again leading to higher poverty levels there.

Is There an Alternative Approach to Measure Global Poverty?

Given these problems, the question arises whether there is an alternative approach to measuring extreme poverty at the global level. In principle there is and it is an approach that is already widely used, including by the World Bank, though not usually for measuring poverty at the global level. The approach, which has also been recommended by Reddy (2008) consists of creating *national* poverty lines using a procedure that is internationally consistent so that then poverty measured in this consistent way could be aggregated across countries. The most common way to generate consistent poverty lines is to anchor them in the costs of a basic needs bundle (Ravallion 1994). Such a basic needs bundle typically estimates the costs of purchasing a sufficient quantity of calories for poor households; additionally, it makes some allowance for non-food items as well.[14] With this poverty line, one would examine levels and trends in poverty, country by country, and then simply add up poverty across countries, without reference to an international poverty line. This would obviate the rather complex conceptual and empirical problems inherent in the current PPP-based international poverty lines.

While this is, in principle, rather straightforward and already is used in many countries to generate national poverty lines, there are also a range of conceptual and empirical issues one would have to deal with. The two most important conceptual issues are which basket to consider for the costs of basic calories, and the second is how to adjust this poverty line over time. Turning to the first issue, there is an infinite number of ways a person can purchase an adequate number of calories (e.g. 2100 Kcals a day) and some of these ways will be very cheap (if most calories consumed are in the form of the cheapest nationally available grain) or very expensive (if most calories consumed are, for example, in the form of red meat, fish, milk products, or alcohol).[15] The suggestion in Ravallion (1994) is to choose populations that are presumed to be close to the poverty line, but there are other alternatives, including expert judgments on adequate baskets, the average basket in a country, or the basket of the poorest group. There are arguments for each of those procedures and one would require a consistent choice across countries.

This relates to the more serious second problem, how to update the poverty line. The standard procedure is to maintain the basket and simply update the costs of that basket over time. While this necessary for consistent comparisons over time, it is clear that a periodic adjustment of the basket is also necessary as the food habits will change and need to be reflected. This will, however, change poverty levels and make poverty trends more difficult to interpret. In addition, international coordination would be required to ensure that these adjustments are done in a consistent fashion. Adjusting the basket regularly would have a sizable impact on poverty. For example, Reddy (2007) shows that the failure to adjust the

14 See Ravallion (1994) for a full exposition of this method and Reddy, Visaria and Asali (2008) for an application.

15 See Deaton (1997) for a discussion of these issues.

basket inherent in India's poverty line has arguably led to a strong overestimation of poverty decline since the 1970s. The reason is that the poor in India have been purchasing increasingly expensive calories (esp. the consumption of milk products and fats has increased substantially) so that the same expenditure now buys fewer calories than previously, leaving more people with insufficient calories and thus poor. This is a rather difficult conceptual issue and a satisfactory and consistent treatment of this problem would be required if one were to use national poverty lines to measure poverty at the global level.

There are also a host of empirical issues to consider. They include problems of comparability of questionnaires of household surveys, a different extent of measurement, and errors in food expenditures that would affect the construction of national poverty lines, just to name a few. Also here, the devil is in the detail as has been shown in Deaton and Kozel (2005) who survey the great debates on poverty in India where these issues are the centre of the debate.

Clearly, this alternative approach of using consistent national poverty lines to measure poverty at the international level would either require extensive international coordination and standardisation or would require an international agency, such as the World Bank, to take all these household surveys and build up comparable national poverty lines for as many countries as possible. Both paths are not entirely infeasible. The first route has been chosen in the creation of the System of National Accounts where all countries of the world agreed to specific rules for the calculation of national income, GDP, and other aggregate statistics. And the second route the World Bank has already gone down quite far in its work on global poverty as well as its work on national poverty. Thus it would not appear to be entirely infeasible to try out such an alternative approach. If implemented successfully, such an approach would obviate the need for the periodic drastic revisions of poverty levels and would also present a more accurate picture of poverty trends over time. To be sure, the conclusion on poverty trends would, as discussed above, not be substantially different from those based on the current method favoured by the World Bank, but they would be based on a better foundation.

Conclusion

The rather drastic revisions of global poverty have revealed significant problems in the measurement of levels and trends in global poverty. This chapter has discussed the nature of these problems and highlighted some potential solutions. It appears that the current method of calculating poverty using a regularly revised international poverty line is beset with considerable conceptual and empirical problems. Instead, it is well worth considering an alternative where global poverty is monitored using internationally consistent national poverty lines. It is time that such an approach was actually tried to investigate whether the conceptual and empirical problems inherent in this alternative approach could be handled.

At the same time, it is important to highlight that there are other, in many ways, more substantive problems than the measurement issues that were the focus of this chapter. First, for most countries we do not have any data on poverty so are unable to say much about levels and trends. Second, the vast majority of countries, particularly in Sub-Saharan Africa, but also countries in other regions of the world, are currently far from reaching the first MDG by 2015. The currently worsening global economic environment will make further extreme poverty reduction even more difficult (see Bourguignon et al. 2008). Thus the focus in terms of policy has to be on those countries to ensure that they are able to make progress towards the reduction of extreme poverty. As discussed in great detail in Bourguignon et al. (2008) this will require changes both in national policies as well as in international environment and aid policies.

References

Anand, S. et al. (eds) (2009), *Debates on the Measurement of Poverty* (Oxford: Oxford University Press).

Bhalla, S. (2004), 'A Comparative Analysis of Estimates of Global Inequality and Poverty', *CESifo Economic Studies* 50:1, 85–132.

Bourguignon, F. (2003), 'The Growth Elasticity of Poverty Reduction', in Eicher, T. et al. (eds).

Bourguignon, F. et al. (2008), *Millennium Development Goals at Midpoint: Where do We Stand and Where do We Need to Go?* (Brussels: EU Commission).

Chen, S. and Ravaillion, M. (2007), 'Absolute Poverty Measures for the Developing World, 1981–2004', *Proceedings of the National Academy of Sciences* 104, 16757–16762.

Chen, S. and Ravallion, M. (2008), 'The Developing World is Poorer Than We Thought, But No Less Successful in the Fight Against Poverty', *World Bank Policy Research Working Paper* No. 4703.

Deaton, A. (1997), *The Analysis of Household Surveys* (Baltimore: Johns Hopkins University Press).

Deaton, A. and Dupriez, O. (2008), 'Poverty PPPs Around the World: An Update and Progress Report', Mimeographed, Development Data Group, The World Bank.

Eicher, T. et al. (eds) (2003), *Inequality and Growth* (Cambridge, MA: MIT Press).

Haddad, L. and Kanbur, R. (1990), 'How Serious is the Neglect of Intrahousehold Inequality?' *The Economic Journal* 100, 866–881.

Heston, A. (2008), 'The 2005 Global Report on Purchasing Power Parity Estimates: A Preliminary Review', *Economic and Political Weekly* 43:11, 65–69.

Heston, A., Summers, R. and Aten, B. (2006), 'Penn World Table Version 6.2' (Center for International Comparisons of Production, Income and Prices at the University of Pennsylvania).

Klasen, S. (2000), 'Measuring Poverty and Deprivation in South Africa', *Review of Income and Wealth* 46:1, 33–58.
Klasen, S. (2007), 'Gender-Related Indicators of Well-Being', in McGillivray, M. (ed.).
Klasen, S. (2008). 'Poverty, Undernutrition, and Child Mortality: Some Inter-Regional Puzzles and their Implications for Research and Policy', *Journal of Economic Inequality* 6:1, 89–115.
Klasen, S. and Misselhorn, M. (2007), 'Determinants of the Growth Semi-Elasticity of Poverty Reduction', *Ibero-America Institute for Economic Research Working Paper* No. 176 (Göttingen: Ibero-America Institute).
McGillivray, M. (ed.) (2007), *Human Well-Being: Concepts and Measurement* (Basingstoke: Palgrave Macmillan).
Ravallion, M. (1994), *Poverty Comparisons* (Chur: Harwood Academic Press).
Ravallion, M., Chen, S. and Sangraula, P. (2008), 'Dollar a Day Revisited', *World Bank Policy Research Working Paper* No. 4620.
Reddy, S. (2007), 'Poverty Estimates: How Great is the Debate?', *Economic and Political Weekly* 10 February 2007.
Reddy, S. (2008), The World Bank's New Poverty Estimates: Digging Deeper into a Hole'. Available at <http://www.socialanalysis.org> [last accessed 22 January 2009].
Reddy, S. and Pogge, T. (2009), 'How Not to Count the Poor', in Anand, S. et al. (eds).
Reddy, S., Visaria, S. and Asali, M. (2008), 'Inter-Country Comparisons of Income Poverty Based on a Capability Approach', Mimeographed, Barnard College.
Sen, A. (1984), 'Poor Relatively Speaking', in Sen, A. (ed.).
Sen, A. (ed.) (1984), *Resources, Values and Development* (Cambridge: Harvard University Press).
Sen, A. (1985), *Commodities and Capabilities* (Amsterdam: North-Holland).
Summers, R., Heston, A. and Aten, B. (2006), *The Penn World Tables Version 6.2* (Center for International Comparisons of Production, Income and Prices at the University of Pennsylvania).
World Bank (1990, 2000/01), *World Development Report* (New York: Oxford University Press).
World Bank (2007, 2008), *Global Monitoring Report* (New York: Oxford University Press).

Chapter 2

Identifying Absolute Global Poverty in 2005: The Measurement Question[1]

Michael Ward

Introduction

Poverty is precisely how we define it and how any concept is defined determines how it is quantified. Identifying the extent and magnitude of poverty is thus essentially a methodological question embodied within a measurement choice. The notion of poverty, as opposed to the features that it reflects, is quantitatively elusive – not least because it is widely recognised as possessing many dimensions. This chapter first reviews the way absolute poverty is conventionally measured at the national level and goes on to describe how international poverty, as perceived by the World Bank and as incorporated in the Millennium Development Goals (MDGs), is defined. The problem of using official purchasing power parity (PPP) estimates for robust poverty assessment is explored and questions are raised about the validity of using the latest 2005 PPP numbers to identify the present number of poor in the world.

Leaving aside some significant issues of whether poverty is best measured in terms of income or wealth, including access to productive assets like land and property, or is primarily a concept based on societal foundations related to adequate social functioning and status in the community, the fact of poverty ultimately represents a relative rather than an absolute concept. Seen from the perspective of inter-temporal and inter-spatial analysis, 'absolute' poverty, even as a minimum level of survival, is not independent of an evident time dimension. Someone may be able to survive on the most basic minimum of a 'bread and water' or rice diet, but only for a limited period. What may be officially considered as 'absolute' poverty in contemporary US or Europe in the first decade of the twenty-first century is very different from what it was in the early nineteenth century. The actual state of poverty at present in the US is also clearly widely different from that seen in India or Africa.

1 The contribution of Michael Ward is an incomplete draft, as he sadly passed away in autumn of 2008. Nevertheless, the editors decided to include his insightful contribution in its current state, with minor editing. The contribution does not include any references which we hope readers will understand.

National Poverty Criteria

Each country defines poverty in its own way, taking account of local circumstances, demographic features, prevailing social conditions, the relevant time dimension and the economic policy context as well as political and ideological imperatives. Universally, however, governments of rich and poor countries alike have adopted a philosophy that provides a minimal level of support for those living in poverty. Various national criteria have been adopted to define the level of living below which individuals and households cannot be allowed to sink because their personal health and nutrition would be endangered or put at an unacceptable risk. The notion that it is a state responsibility to ensure at least the basic survival of its citizens is a step in the direction of an implicit recognition of fundamental human rights.

Governments, faced with competing demands for the limited resources at their disposal and being conscious, at the same time, of the need not to provide a permanent social safety net that might discourage poor people from seeking the means for their own longer term sustainability, have generally acquiesced in a minimum basic needs approach throughout the course of history.

The initial template of officially 'acceptable' poverty policy (if not of public approval) which set the seal on providing only the most basic support to the poor, was laid down in England and Wales in the early nineteenth century. The adoption of a radical utilitarian rather than humanitarian approach to poverty alleviation led to the accompanying establishment of the principle of 'least eligibility'. The New Poor Law Act introduced by Edwin Chadwick in 1834 simultaneously provided universal public support while introducing a strong disincentive deliberately intended to encourage most people – and especially those considered indolent, vagrant, morally weak and generally idle – not to avail themselves of what was on offer. Poor people who applied for relief were entitled to receive food and shelter but only inside the 'workhouse' and at a level below that enjoyed by the lowest paid member of the working class. This criterion was seen as providing a sufficient deterrent to people seeking parish handouts financed from local rates and was designed to serve as a strong deterrent to the able-bodied poor who were to be persuaded to find work rather than remain voluntarily 'idle' (as was generally presumed). This recognised physical 'rights' to life but not the need for human dignity.

In practice, this adoption of a minimum standard of physical provision has survived to the present day. In the absence of a readily available independent standard, the cost of meeting a criterion determined as a basic nutritional intake defined in terms of minimum calorie requirements has been widely established. This sets the level of living perceived as adequate for economic effort and social functioning. Different age, sex and occupational status have to be taken into account to determine this nutrition based core component of a poverty datum line (PDL). This standard, when converted into current values, has to be further adjusted upwards – based on the observed budgetary outlays of the poorest households and the share of food expenditures in their regular budgets – to account for other important elements of everyday survival like shelter, fuel and clothing. All such items are necessary to preserve longer term household sustainability, security and well-being.

A minimum PDL, as a measure of absolute poverty, is often unrealistic as it represents a situation that few people actually experience. It is a level to which few would want to be exposed but also, nevertheless, one below which certain seriously disadvantaged and vulnerable people, for reasons of circumstance and lack of adequate social support, may exist from time to time although under poor health and with diminished life expectancy.

Living on a PDL defined in this way results in a level of existence where the quality of life can be significantly affected by very limited access to regular paid employment, life-enhancing opportunities and communally available services like education, public and personal health facilities and other non-market goods and services. Access to all these amenities is often dependent on citizenship, residency status, religious, ethnic and tribal affiliation and the place where a person lives. The presence of critical non-parametric attributes in the complex poverty equation makes quantification and the identification of who is poor more difficult and imprecise. This opens the door to the local subjective evaluations, qualitative appraisals and arbitrary selection criteria.

From National to International Criteria

To support global analysis and help clarify the priority issues for the fairer implementation of international policies of support to low income countries, the incidence of poverty – at least in the sense of income deprivation and resource scarcity – has to be determined in terms of the acquisition of an equivalent common basket of goods and services. The composition of this 'basket' should fulfil the normal requirements and basic needs of residents. In other words, a notion of poverty must be viewed in terms of a comparable international purchasing power that allows people to acquire a varying basket of goods and services in their respective countries to satisfy an array of basic needs related to their normal patterns of expenditure behaviour. The basket identified would permit a uniform minimum level of sustainability.

Viewed in this light, absolute poverty is determinable and comparable across countries in real terms. But it may not be representative because of discrepancies in relative price structures between countries, recognising the fact that consumption structures differ to reflect indigenous tastes and preferences and institutional factors. The use of estimated purchasing power parities allows for the different observed spending patterns in various countries because the price weights are implicitly adjusted to account for their relative significance in their respective national expenditure contexts.

Finding a Common Numeraire Value

The principle of making international comparisons is methodologically straightforward although far from simple to implement empirically. In each country national values are expressed in local currency terms. To convert all reported domestic transaction values [PnQn] incorporated within GDP into international price terms, the various components of GDP expenditure, including capital outlays and government spending, are divided by their relevant prices [Pn] to derive a real quantity [Qn]. When multiplied by a statistically derived international price [Pi], a set of comparable values [PiQn] is generated across countries for every particular category of GDP expenditure. Under the successive phases of the International Comparisons Programme (ICP) that was first launched in 1975 and since then conducted roughly every five years, the latest and most extensive exercise to have been completed relates to 2005. In this 2005 benchmark, national expenditures in all but the poorest countries have been broken down into more than 150 distinct sub-categories.

In the past, international comparisons of real economic status were always conducted using official exchange rates. Exchange rates possess the uncommon virtues of being convenient, up to date, readily available and easy to use. For a long time, therefore, governments, international agencies and analysts would invariably turn to GDP or GNP (now more correctly defined as Gross National Income) and to GDP per head, all expressed in terms of US dollars using official exchange rates, in order to compare income levels and to determine a country's assumed development status. National poverty measures were converted in the same way compounding one problem of comparability on another. This is because principal exchange rates, even if modified to incorporate unofficial exchange and black market rates or adjusted using moving averages to dampen fluctuations, while still useful in analysing financial transactions, debt and fund transfers, do not provide appropriate conversion factors for getting at real economic values. This is not only because, in many countries, exchange rates tend to fluctuate, often irrationally, from one time period to the next but also because they do not reflect relative price levels as was once assumed they would in long term equilibrium under international trade theory.

The criterion adopted by the World Bank to define poverty is the widely recognised 'one dollar per head per day' (in 1985 PPP dollar terms) level. This well-known standard has become universally accepted in its application to international and global assessments. While a low income threshold measure, it is seen as an unambiguous 'social' indicator. It nevertheless possesses a logical empirical link to selected contemporary official national poverty lines of a number of low income countries. These national PDLs, expressed originally in national currencies, were converted into their PPP dollar equivalents and then a simple average of them was taken. Such a standard, however, cannot remain fixed because price levels and relative prices change over time. Thus, by 1995, the equivalent international dollar criterion had shifted upwards to $1.08 and in 2005 it was estimated to be $1.25 per head per day, again based on calculations of adjusted national poverty lines. This procedure is methodologically appealing, but it is heavily dependent on how well and effectively the poverty lines of the poor countries concerned can be updated to the latest required benchmark. There is no guarantee the new international dollar standard will adequately track the pace of global inflation.

PPPs and Price Levels

A PPP is simply the amount of local currency needed to acquire, for example, what one US dollar could purchase in terms of goods and services in the US. Thus, countries with low exchange rates in relation to the dollar would need far more local currency to buy the equivalent quantity of such items and, mutatis mutandis, one dollar spent in a low income country would buy much more than it would in the US. In exchange rate terms, if the US is taken as the point of reference, some countries are 'cheap' to live in – that is, their general price levels are lower – while others are more 'expensive' because their prices are mostly much higher than in the US.

Intuitively, it follows there has to be, in principle, a mean price level for the world as a whole representing the average of all individual country price levels. The application of the respective prices for the various components of GDP comprising this price level (as indicated in the simple procedure above) results in the equalisation of price levels throughout the world, thus allowing the comparison of economic aggregates and variables in real terms. How this international price level comprising all prices for every good and service globally transacted in a year is derived, nevertheless, remains a matter of some debate and is subject to both theoretical and empirical limitations.

The conceptual issues

Conceptually, the issue is one of choosing the most appropriate aggregation procedure. The main question here is whether the prices belonging to the same basic expenditure categories in all countries should be treated equally or whether the volume (and value) of transactions conducted in each country should be weighted according to their respective importance. Whatever method is adopted, by construction, the resulting 'international price level' will inevitably fall somewhere between the level of prices that obtains in the most expensive country in the world and that in the country with the lowest set of prices.

In every successive phase of the ICP, the most consistent finding has been that low income countries tend to have the lowest price levels. It is thus inevitable that if their domestic prices are replaced across the board by the higher international prices, this will raise their apparent GDP and make them appear richer than what they have come to think they are. By the same token, higher income level countries, as measured conventionally by GDP or GDP per capita, would appear to be somewhat poorer in PPP terms.

The main source of contention has been that if an aggregation procedure that takes account of the value and volume of total transactions is adopted, then this will, in some sense, 'bias' the international price level closer to the level of prices in the OECD countries. This is exactly the result a weighted price index reflecting international GDP outlays will automatically generate. But other analysts have argued strongly that what really matters in a comparative global context is the level of prices that is more likely to be faced by the majority of people in the world. If the latter aggregation formula is adopted, the largest low income countries, such as China, India, Indonesia and Brazil, exhibiting significant income inequalities and containing very rich enclaves that, consequently, give rise to diverse consumption patterns that cover a wide range of products and outlet types will exert a much stronger relative influence over the average international price structure.

The diagram (Figure 2.1) depicting for the year 2005 the global distribution of total income (shown below the x-axis) and individual incomes per head (shown above the x-axis) by their relative frequency, clearly underlines what lies behind the crux of this dilemma. By far the vast majority of the world's population live on low incomes and only a small proportion of very rich people in the world, mostly in the OECD countries, command the bulk of world income. The overall pattern and shape of these distribution curves has remained very much the same for 1970, 1980, 1990 and 2000.

Thus, the choice of index formula to aggregate the observed bilateral ratios of country prices really matters in a cardinal sense, and especially when it comes to measuring poverty levels, although in an ordinal context there appears to be little difference. The poorest country, under whatever scheme of measurement weighting is applied, will always appear the poorest.

The empirical problem

An average can only be compiled from the data available. From a purely practical viewpoint, it has not proved possible to compile price and GDP expenditure data from all countries. Countries have had to agree voluntarily to participate in the ICP and this exercise is both highly resource intensive and managerially demanding. It has not proved feasible for many smaller and poorer countries to take on such a time and resource-consuming task when most are already hard pressed to meet all the regular official statistical demands on their budgets and work plans.

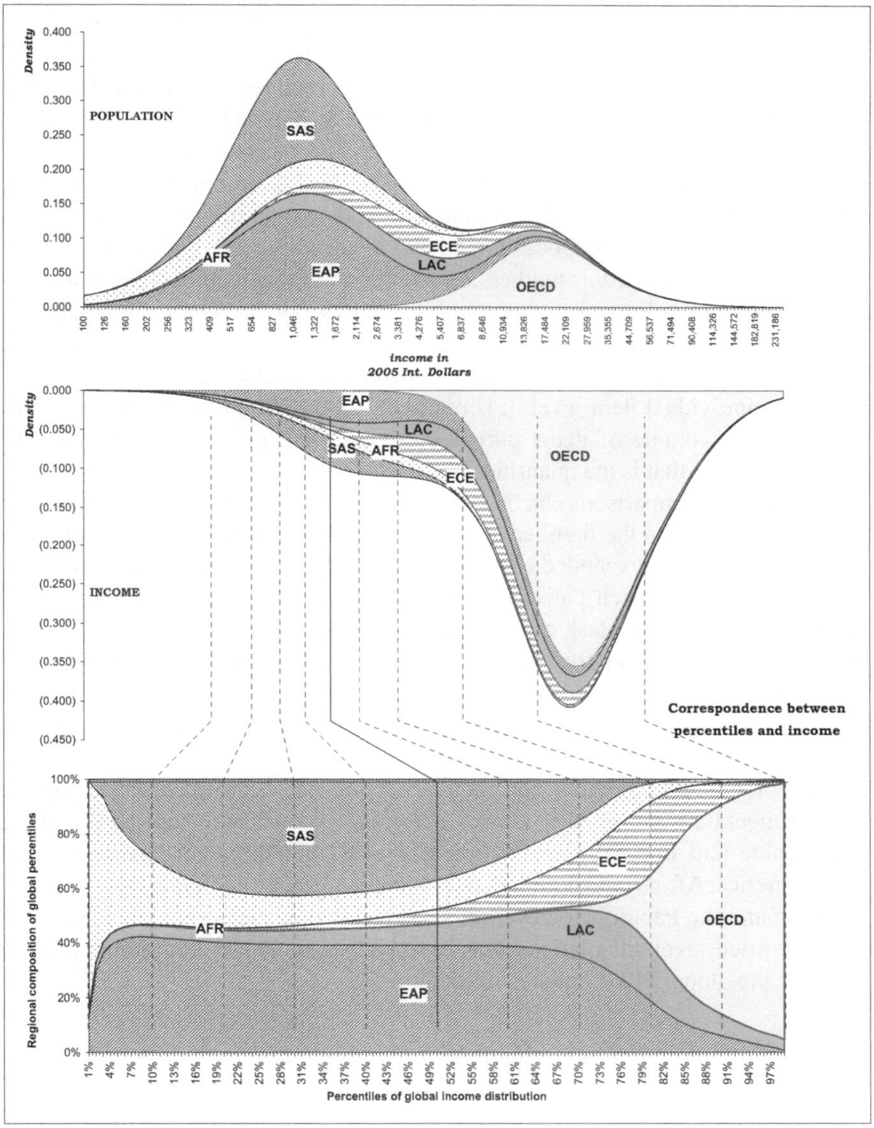

Figure 2.1 World income distribution 2005
Source: Based on an extension of Dikhanov 2005, 11–12.

Even when countries have agreed to participate, there is a huge problem of coordination over matters of timing and product selection and some have found they are unable to cover the whole panoply of data requirements to calculate PPPs for the benchmark year chosen. Thus, over time, a changing number of countries as well as different ones have participated in the various phases of the ICP. Since the computed average international price level is dependent only on those countries that take part in a given round and on the range of data they are able to collect, the implicit international price level in each successive phase of the ICP, while coherently defined, is neither consistent nor, in fact, comparable. If a major country, like India, drops out of the programme in some years or a new one comes in, like China, then the comparative PPP GDP levels – and sometimes the relative positions of countries in the international income hierarchy – can change.

At the individual item level, it is relatively simple to find a unit price, p, that relates to the volume of items purchased, pq, so that pq/p=q will describe the number of units, that is the quantities, sold. So, for a specific type of loaf of bread, real (quantum) comparisons can be made between places as well as over time. The problem arises when the number of types of items are multiplied to include, say, different breads and expanded to cover pastries and cakes. (The choice available from an ordinary French patisserie or Italian bakery shop gives just some idea of the magnitude of the task of collecting prices for all the items in this category offered for sale). To quantify the real amount represented in the bakery basket, it would then be necessary to weight the various prices according to their relative importance in the basket in order to estimate a relevant average price for all the goods it contains.

The task of coordination and data collection has been made easier by the compartmentalisation of the global ICP into distinct but logistically more manageable and internally more homogeneous administrative regions such as Latin America, Africa (and within that, Francophone and Anglophone sub-regions) and Asia and the Pacific. However, this has resulted in the derivation of separate regional price level calculations that have had to be linked and harmonised to generate the global PPP estimates for countries.

PPPs and GDP

It follows that expanding this data activity to embrace not just all bread and cereals, or even everyday foodstuffs including meat fish, vegetables, etc as well as beverages – let alone other goods and services comprising personal household expenditure – poses a mammoth, if not impossible, statistical task. But it does not stop there because, to obtain equivalent comparable measures of GDP in PPP terms, it is also essential to identify those expenditures, and prices relevant to them, that are appropriate for annual government outlays and capital formation in investment goods. Somewhat different approaches are necessary to deal with these major categories that are comprised of, respectively, either mostly labour service or distinct and indivisible 'lumpy' outlays.

Economic transactions are occurring continuously through time and GDP represents the value of all goods and services produced by a country and made available for consumption by its residents during a given time period, usually a year. GDP expenditures can be broken down and classified into their major consumption and use categories and respective sub-headings but any finer detail at a product group level is rarely available. The various sub-headings, referred to as 'basic headings', represent the lowest level of expenditure detail for which data can be found in most countries. Within these headings, that have to be standard across all countries, the ICP has laid down a common methodology for selecting comparable and, as far as possible, representative products that need to be identified for pricing.

The way these products should be priced in order to obtain consistent estimates of the relevant deflated values for each expenditure heading is also specified. This is because the derivation of another significant statistical artifact, the 'annual national average price' of the products belonging to each heading, must be uniformly determined. The average price must relate to all months of the year and cover all locations and types of sales outlet as well as service providers. From these data, an appropriate overall implicit unit value for the combined product group defined in each respective basic heading can be determined.

PPPs are designed to provide a common, uniformly defined method for deflating observed GDP expenditure aggregates (and their sub-components) in terms of national currencies and then converting them into economic magnitudes that are expressed in comparable international price terms. This is the conventional way of solving the problem of measuring price level differences through PPPs. However, there is another way and that is to view the whole question not as a spatial GDP 'deflation' exercise but as a problem to estimate the difference in price levels for marketed goods and services. Examining price level differences between countries directly at the product level represents, in effect, a method of estimating the different cost of living faced by people in different countries and communities. Extracting the issue from the highly contentious problems of treating capital formation outlays for both machinery and construction purposes in a comparable manner when having to calculate PPPs for GDP, would seem to be a more appropriate way to measure real differences in final household consumption. Using this approach would provide an alternative means of tackling the specific concern to estimate income (consumption) poverty levels.

PPPs for Poverty Analysis

There are serious drawbacks to using GDP PPPs, or even sub-aggregate consumption expenditure PPPs, to estimate the incidence of income poverty. At the same time, the possibility of partitioning GDP into those elements relevant to different socioeconomic groups is, inevitably, constrained. Nevertheless, with household income and expenditure survey (HIES) information becoming increasingly available over an extensive range of countries, if not for comparable time periods (or that actually cover the whole country), the ability to identify the pattern of lower quintile household outlays is much easier. But problems still remain because such surveys may not refer to the same time period or cover the whole country, particularly the rural population. In addition, to generate specific poverty numbers, most household survey data will need to be modified to take account of different household size as well as its age and sex composition.

Other relevant factors that have to be taken into account are:

- The poor have limited access to transport and have no adequate storage facilities; thus, they do not have much opportunity to purchase their requirements from those cheaper larger out of town stores and factory outlets frequented by most other people.
- Because the poor have little savings and restricted recourse to lines of credit and are paid only at haphazard intervals, they tend to pay for things as and when they need them. They usually cannot take advantage of 'sales' and other limited period price concessions available to the rest of society.

Rural and urban prices are often significantly different, especially in large countries like China, India, Brazil and Indonesia that have widely dispersed populations. Some population concentrations may also be superimposed by ethnically or tribally distinct groups that enjoy different lifestyles and spending patterns.

- Half of the world's population lives in rural areas. Before 2008, the proportion was higher the further back in time taken. An even larger percentage of the world's poor are rural inhabitants. In this case, many poor households are able to acquire their basic food needs a lot cheaper from local farm markets. Furthermore, some of their household consumption of food will be home produced on the farm or on an adjoining garden plot.
- On the other hand, the rural poor also have to pay proportionately higher prices for manufactured household goods, including clothing, hardware items and other basic needs.
- Basic services like education, personal medications, public health facilities, clinics, and local public utility supplies to help lift people out of poverty may not be available to some rural communities.
- Poor households often buy in smaller quantities and that tends to raise the unit price paid for these products compared with goods sold in, say, supermarkets. If credit is extended to a poor household by a particular local outlet, the poor may have reduced recourse to buying cheaper products on cash sale elsewhere.
- The poor sometimes resort to buying items of lower quality in order to be able to afford them, particularly in the case of certain perishable goods.

> Packages of, say, tea or cigarettes or bottles of oil may also be halved and sold at proportionally higher prices.

All this means that if PPPs are to be separately calculated for the poor, they should take account of the effects of location and the residency status of poor households as well as the nature of the outlets from where they make most of their purchases on total expenditures. It is not sufficient simply to re-weight the existing average annual national prices obtained from the general ICP survey according to the observed consumption patterns of the poor with respect to the basic heading level weights. The derived outlay shares will conceal many significant differences in purchasing behaviour.

Difficulties with the 2005 ICP Results

The summary GDP PPP results from the latest 2005 ICP survey round were disseminated on the World Bank's website at close of business on 17 December 2007. The preliminary poverty numbers were subsequently issued at an online conference meeting that was broadcast from the Research Department of the World Bank in Washington DC on Monday 26 August. Despite being the most expansive survey in terms of country participation, the most extensive in respect of the number of product items covered and by far the most expensive in the matter of the total budget spent and resources of time and staff allocated to the programme, the results published and the actual methodologies applied immediately ran into considerable criticism. The poverty numbers have been constructed on the basis of the published PPP data.

Some big question marks hang over the data. The first relates to the information compiled for China. The ICP survey in China was confined to twelve main cities. There is irrefutable evidence, drawn from academic research and official figures, of wide differentials in prices between urban and rural areas. If rural prices are left out, it means that half of the country that has access to much lower prices, especially for basic food outlays (that represent a large share of low income family budgets), was not covered. At the same time, not least because of the considerable efforts made by the Chinese authorities to find comparable items to price on the comprehensive regional/global product list, it seems many of the urban prices obtained were more reflective of 'western' purchases rather than representative of ordinary urban Chinese household spending.

The inevitable outcome of this has been a higher derived average price level for China that most independent observers did not anticipate. This means the reported incomes and expenditures for China are far lower than would be assumed – and seem incompatible with the officially reported growth rates for the past 20 years. Since China figures prominently in the regional and, hence, global PPP calculations and because of the extensive spill-over effects associated with the multilateralisation of all binary country price ratios methodology embedded in the

ICP methodology, there are also cumulative repercussions for the derived price levels for other countries. This inexorably compounds the overall PPP problem indeterminately.

There is some prima facie evidence that a similar concern might also apply to the price data compiled for India. If this is the case, then the price level for the whole Asia and Pacific region will be biased. This will then distort the poverty figures, pushing them significantly upwards, especially because of the large number of poor people in both China and India in 2005.

What lies behind both these issues is the fact that physically comparable products, if they are not equally representative, tend to be relatively higher priced in at least one of the countries in a binary comparison. This is simply because, by definition, they are sold in smaller quantities. A second big issue relates to the shifting international dollar equivalent.

This shifting standard has to be implemented, otherwise the numbers in absolute poverty would progressively decline every year as, inexorably, the rate of inflation pushes income levels above the cut-off threshold. In reality, actual poverty is likely to increase anyway if inflation is high. The problem is that the standard does not effectively track inflation. Successive World Development Indicators, also disseminated by the World Bank, shows no country experiencing inflation between 1985 and 1995 or between 1995 and 2005 as low as that implied in the equivalent international dollar values. This means that the reported poverty numbers based on the latest $1.25 per head per day criterion are likely to be significantly lower than what they are in reality.

Another problem relates to the way the various ICP regions were linked, for the first time, through the 'Ring' methodology rather than via the use of specific 'bridge' countries that spanned two regions as used in previous ICP exercises. In practice, the ring countries that exerted the strongest influence in the Asia region appear to have accentuated the higher price effects.

Finally, the implementation of productivity adjustments to certain costs to estimate a truer value of government spending, but only in selected countries and regions, has led to evident bias. A further form of bias may well have been introduced by the actual productivity adjustment method applied.

Some Concluding Observations

It has been admitted that the 2005 results are not comparable with any of the previous phases of the ICP. There were sound reasons for deliberately introducing new procedures and for fully incorporating India into the global comparison. The first real inclusion of China is also to be warmly welcomed but greater direction, closer supervision and more care in precisely how data are compiled will need to be taken by the ICP Global Management team in the future. The methods employed in Latin America as well as in much of Africa at the very detailed data collection level remain shrouded in mystery but are known to have been different from those used in Asia and the participating EU/OECD managed countries. There is no overriding unique local circumstance that should allow regions not to follow standard methods and uniform operational procedures.

Given the confounding problems of the price level differences and the shifting international dollar criterion, the main upshot of this exercise is that it is now impossible to compare 2005 PPP results and estimated poverty levels with any previous benchmark years. It is thus difficult to say for sure whether the politically sensitive MDGs with respect to poverty reduction are being met or are on track for 2015. Nor is it now clear whether absolute poverty has become more of a problem in China than it is in India or Africa. Not having the most suitable and transparent data to make key policy choices constitutes a serious drawback to strategic planning.

References

Dikhanov, Y. (2005), 'Trends in Global Income Distribution, 1970–2000, and Scenarios for 2015' (UNDP). Available at <http://hdr.undp.org/en/media/globalincometrends.pdf>.

Chapter 3

How World Poverty is Measured and Tracked

Thomas Pogge

Our current understanding of world poverty and its evolution over time is heavily focused on counting the number of poor people. This counting is based on a narrow conception of 'absolute' or 'extreme' poverty, closely tied to hunger: people are counted as poor only if they fall short of 'the income or expenditure level below which a minimum, nutritionally adequate diet plus essential non-food requirements are not affordable' (UNDP 1995, 223).

For the last 20 years or so, the World Bank has taken charge of this counting exercise. The Bank employs for this purpose an international poverty line (IPL) widely known as 'a dollar a day'. The Bank had initially defined this line in terms of the purchasing power that $1.02 had in the US in 1985, but has since redefined it three times. Its latest definition is in terms of the purchasing power that $1.25 had in the US in 2005. Once the IPL is fixed, poverty is quantified simply by the number of those living below the IPL, and a reduction of poverty as a reduction in this number.

Invoking the Bank's tracking method and figures, the world's governments have repeatedly promised to halve world poverty by 2015. One such promise was grandly made at the 1996 World Food Summit in Rome, where 186 governments pledged themselves 'to achieving food security for all and to an ongoing effort to eradicate hunger in all countries, with an immediate view to reducing the number of undernourished people to half their present level no later than 2015' (World Food Summit 1996). An 'immediate' view that takes 19 years to solve just half of the world poverty problem is not exactly ambitious, to be sure – just imagine Franklin Roosevelt pledging in 1942 to cut the ongoing harm caused by the Nazis down to half by 1961! But at least the pledge seemed manageable, implying an annual reduction of 3.58 per cent in the number of poor people.

Yet the world's governments soon decided that they had promised more than they were willing to deliver. In the year 2000, they declared the first Millennium Development Goal (MDG-1) was 'to halve, by the year 2015, the proportion of the world's people whose income is less than one dollar a day and the proportion of people who suffer from hunger' (UN General Assembly 2000, article 19). This formulation retains the idea of halving the problem by 2015, and yet smartly diminishes the ambition by focusing not on the *number* but on the *proportion* of poor and hungry people. This proportion is a fraction consisting of the number of poor people in the numerator and world population ('the world's people') in the denominator. With world population expected to increase by 2015 to about 120 per cent of what it was in 2000 (UN Population Division 2007), a reduction in the number of poor people to 60 per cent of what it was in 2000 suffices to cut the proportion in half. By redefining what is to be halved, the world's governments raised the acceptable number of poor people in 2015 from 836 million (1996 benchmark minus 50 per cent) to 1,004 million (2000 benchmark minus 40 per cent), according to the current World Bank statistics (Chen and Ravallion 2008, 34). They also lowered the promised annual reduction in the number of poor people from 3.58 per cent to 3.35 per cent.

It is not important whether governments focus on the number or the proportion of poor people. What's more important is the dilution of the 2015 goal and the effort to obscure this dilution. The dilution can be expressed in either idiom: The number of poor is to be reduced by 50 per cent according to the Rome Declaration and by only 40 per cent according to the Millennium Declaration. Or: The proportion of poor is to be reduced by 58.33 per cent according to the Rome Declaration and by only 50 per cent according to the Millennium Declaration. Either formulation makes apparent that the goal-posts were moved to add 168 million to the number of those whose extreme poverty in 2015 will be deemed morally acceptable – an extra 168 million human beings for whom 'a minimum, nutritionally adequate diet plus essential non-food requirements' will be out of reach. This dilution was successfully obscured from the public, and kept out of the media, by opaquely switching from 'number' to 'proportion' while retaining the language of 'halving poverty by 2015'.

Since its celebrated adoption by the UN General Assembly, the poverty promise has undergone further dramatic dilution through two important revisions. The current UN interpretation and tracking of MDG-1 expresses the poor no longer as 'a proportion of the world's people', but as a 'proportion of people in the developing world' (e.g. United Nations 2008, 6), thus taking advantage of a faster-growing denominator. It also back-dates the baseline envisioning that the halving should take place 'between 1990 and 2015' (ibid.) rather than between 2000 and 2015. Because the population of the developing world in 2015 is expected to be 146 per cent of what it was in 1990 (UN Population Division 2007), a reduction in the number of poor to 73 per cent of what it was in 1990 is now deemed sufficient to halve poverty by 2015. Shrinking the reduction to be achieved and also lengthening to 25 years the period in which to achieve it, this revision of MDG-1 lowers the promised annual reduction in the number of poor people down to 1.25 per cent. This revision also raises the acceptable number of poor people in 2015 to 1,327 million (1990 benchmark minus 27 per cent), according to the current World Bank statistics (Chen and Ravallion 2008, 34).

One remarkable consequence of the UN's back-dating of the baseline is that China's reported massive poverty reduction in the 1990s – the number of Chinese living in extreme poverty supposedly declined by 265 million during that decade (ibid.) – can be counted as progress toward MDG-1. The revision of MDG-1 thus led UN Secretary-General Kofi Annan tragicomically to report to the General Assembly (United Nations 2002, 8 and 22) that for the world's most populous region – East Asia and the Pacific – the 2015 poverty target had been fully met already in 1999, a full year before this goal had even been adopted!

There is little doubt that the UN will announce, in 2015, that the goal of halving world poverty has been achieved. But this success will depend decisively on having replaced the initial understanding of this goal as requiring a 50 per cent reduction in the number of poor people from the 1996 level (promised at the 1996 World Food Summit in Rome) with a new understanding of this goal as requiring merely a 27 per cent reduction from the substantially higher 1990 level.

The nearby table summarises what this dilution means in human terms: The number of extremely poor people that the world's governments deem acceptable in the year 2015 has been revised upward by 491 million. The reduction in the number of extremely poor people that the world's governments had promised in Rome has correspondingly been cut back by 491 million: Once 836 million, the reduction promised for 1996–2015 is now 345 million.

Table 3.1 A promise diluted

	Baseline year	**Baseline number of poor (millions)**	**Promised reduction by 2015**	**Target for 2015 (millions)**	**Required annual rate of reduction**	**Target for 2005 (millions)**
World Food Summit	**1996**	1672	50%	836	3.58%	1204
MDG-1 as adopted	**2000**	1673	40%	1004	3.35%	1411
MDG-1 as revised	**1990**	1817.5	27%	1327	1.25%	1505

The story of the sly revision of the grandiose commitment of Rome and, more generally, of how the world's governments are managing the 'halving of world poverty by 2015' illustrates one main reason for the persistence of massive poverty: The poor have no allies among the global elite. Hundreds of officials in many governments and international agencies were involved in shifting the goal-posts to the detriment of the poor. Thousands of economists and other academics understood what was happening. So did thousands of people in the media, who had been reporting on the Rome Summit and the MDGs – with some of them expressly denying that the revisions were worth reporting (Pogge 2008, note 18). Most of these privileged harbour no ill will toward poor people. They merely have other priorities. And they don't care how their pursuit of these priorities may affect the global poor.

Problems with Tracking Poverty as the Number or Proportion of People Living Below Some IPL

The first and most obvious problem with tracking poverty by means of a headcount figure is that it indefensibly prioritises people living just below the IPL: Moving such people above the IPL is the cheapest and easiest way of reducing the poverty headcount. But there is no good reason for ignoring changes in people's economic situation when these occur below or slightly above the IPL while counting as progress any move from a penny below to a penny above this line.

A second, related problem is that, when poverty is tracked as a headcount, our picture of the evolution of poverty may be excessively sensitive to the level at which the IPL is set. The problem is easily illustrated because the World Bank researchers leading the poverty count, Martin Ravallion and Shaohua Chen, provide headcounts not only for their own chosen IPL of $1.25 PPP 2005 (daily consumption),[1] but also for three other poverty lines denominated in 2005 international dollars. The following table displays, for each of these four poverty lines (listed in the leftmost column) the headcount change between various base years (listed in the top row) and the year 2005. (A minus sign in a cell indicates that the poverty headcount has fallen in the column period relative to the row's poverty line.) Column 6 shows how the actual change in the number of poor people during 1990–2005 compares to the 17.2 per cent reduction in this number that would put the world on track for achieving the 27 per cent reduction that the diluted MDG-1 envisions for 1990–2015.

1 See Chen and Ravallion (2008, 34–35). 'PPP' stands for 'purchasing power parity', and '$1.25 PPP 2005' stands for the purchasing power that $1.25 had in the US in 2005.

Table 3.2 How success against poverty depends on the level of the IPL

Period/ Poverty Line	1981–2005	1984–2005	1987–2005	1990–2005	Relative to path of diluted MDG-1	1993–2005	1996–2005	1999–2005
$1.00 PPP 2005	-43%	-35%	-28%	-33%	**89% ahead**	-29%	-22%	-23%
$1.25 PPP 2005	-27%	-23%	-19%	-23%	**34% ahead**	-22%	-16%	-17%
$2.00 PPP 2005	2%	-1%	-2%	-6%	**67% behind**	-8%	-7%	-10%
$2.50 PPP 2005	15%	9%	6%	2%	**112% behind**	-1%	-3%	-5%

The table shows that the reportable headcount progress depends very strongly on the level chosen for the IPL. No matter what time period one may examine, the change in the poverty count during this period looks better the lower the IPL is set. Relative to the UN's newly favoured 1990 benchmark, for instance, poverty has in the 1990–2005 period fallen by nearly 33 per cent relative to the $1 PPP 2005 poverty line – way ahead of the 17.2 per cent reduction needed to put us 'on track' for meeting MDG-1. And in the very same period poverty has *increased* by 2 per cent relative to the $2.50 PPP 2005 poverty line – moving us *away* from the MDG-1 target number. If one of the two lower lines is chosen, the world is well on schedule for realising the 27 per cent headcount reduction required to achieve the diluted MDG-1. If one of the two higher lines were chosen, we would probably get nowhere near this 27 per cent reduction by 2015.

How then does the World Bank decide upon the level of its IPL? It is widely accepted that the IPL should express a narrow conception of absolute poverty that is closely tied to hunger (see opening sentence). How does the World Bank convert this shared minimalist understanding of poverty into a specific level for its IPL? We have a rich historical record for answering this question because the Bank has in fact successively employed and defended four distinct IPLs denominated in international dollars of three different base years: 1985, 1993, and 2005. The Bank has done so while contending that it is desirable to change the poverty line from time to time to keep it up to date. It is indeed true that an IPL denominated in dollars of a recent base year leads to a more accurate picture of poverty around that year – but it is also true that such an updated poverty line gives us a less accurate picture of poverty in earlier years. So periodic switching of IPLs is not needed for the sake of attaining a more accurate picture of the long term poverty trend.[2]

The Bank has defended all four of its successive IPLs as 'anchored to what "poverty" means in the poorest countries' (Chen and Ravallion 2008, 9). How

2 It is possible, though, that the PPPs available for one base year are more reliable than those of another – perhaps on account of participation by more countries or more comprehensive price data. If the 2005 PPPs are better in this sense than the 1993 PPPs, say, then they may indeed support a more accurate picture of the 1981–2005 poverty trend.

do they know what 'poverty' means in the poorest countries? The Bank infers its answer from one single set of information: The official domestic poverty lines used in poor countries. The details of this 'anchoring' have varied, however. In its first exercise, the Bank chose $1.02 PPP 1985 per day as the IPL on the ground that the domestic poverty lines of eight poor countries – converted at 1985 PPPs – were close to this amount (Ravallion, Datt and Van De Walle 1991, 348–49). This IPL was quickly rounded off to a more memorable $1.00 PPP 1985 per day (Chen and Ravallion 2001, 285, note 7). Later, the Bank chose $1.08 PPP 1993 per day as the IPL because this was then the median of the ten lowest domestic poverty lines as converted at 1993 PPPs (ibid., 285). And for its most recent exercise unveiled in the summer of 2008, the Bank has chosen $1.25 PPP 2005 per day as the IPL because it is the mean of the domestic poverty lines – converted at 2005 PPPs into 2005 US dollars – of the 15 poorest countries (Chen and Ravallion 2008, 10).

It is unclear why political decisions made by rulers or bureaucrats in a few poor countries[3] should be thought a reliable indicator of what 'poverty' means to poor people all over the world. And the fact that the Bank has been involved in setting domestic poverty lines for many poor countries cannot increase confidence in the exercise: The Bank's setting of the IPL at a certain level cannot be justified by its proximity to the levels at which the Bank itself has set national poverty lines.

The Bank's successive substitutions have resulted in a tightening of the poverty criterion in most countries and a broadening in a few (Reddy and Pogge 2009, Table 1). The case of the US is not atypical. If we use the US consumer price index (<www.bls.gov/cpi>) to convert the Bank's four successive IPLs into 2005 dollars, we get:

$1.02 PPP 1985 = $1.85 (2005)
$1.00 PPP 1985 = $1.81 (2005)
$1.08 PPP 1993 = $1.45 (2005)
$1.25 PPP 2005 = $1.25 (2005)

The last and now exclusively used IPL comes to roughly $9.50 per person per week in 2009 – or $41 per month or $500 per year (ibid.). A US resident would count as poor by the World Bank's new standard only if she could purchase, in the US, *all* of her 2009 consumption of goods and services – including food, water, clothing, shelter, utilities, and medical care – for under $500.

Perhaps it is obvious that the Bank's latest IPL is absurdly low. But we should confirm this judgment. To do so, we should look for guidance not to official African poverty lines converted at PPPs, but to straightforward domestic evidence. The US Department of Agriculture has for many decades published data about what it costs to adhere to an elaborately designed low-cost food plan that has variously

3 The 15 poorest countries are given as Malawi, Mali, Ethiopia, Sierra Leone, Niger, Uganda, Gambia, Rwanda, Guinea-Bissau, Tanzania, Tajikistan, Mozambique, Chad, Nepal, and Ghana (Chen and Ravallion 2008, 10). Nine of these have very small populations and 13 are located in sub-Saharan Africa.

been called ‘the Restricted Food Plan for Emergency Use’, the ‘Economy Food Plan, developed as a nutritionally adequate diet for short-term or emergency use’, and the ‘Thrifty Food Plan’ (USDA 1999, 2). In 2005, the cost of purchasing this minimal diet for a family of four was (depending on family size and children’s ages) between $3.59 and $4.97 per person per day.[4] If this was the cost of a minimal diet in the US, then we can safely conclude that the Bank’s IPL of $1.25 PPP 2005 is absurdly low in its base country and base year in the US in 2005[5] – especially if we remember that the $1.25 per day would need to cover not merely nutrition, but also minimal requirements of water, clothing, shelter, utilities, and medical care.

What can be said to justify the Bank’s chosen IPL level? It is obvious that the Bank cannot justify its decision by saying that the IPL must be set so low in order to show the world to be on track toward achieving MDG-1. As we have seen, a low IPL entails much prettier trend figures than would be derived from higher IPLs. But this cannot be a *justification* for choosing a low IPL.

Another defence of the Bank’s chosen IPL level would point out that the blatant insufficiency of $1.25 per day in the US of 2005 proves nothing because, in the locations where in 2005 very poor people actually lived, dollars bought much more than in the United States. This defence involves a common misunderstanding of the Bank’s procedure. Dollars converted at market exchange rates did indeed buy more in poor countries than in the US. But the Bank is using for its conversions not market exchange rates, but PPPs which supposedly preserve purchasing power. Thus the Bank counts someone who lived in India or Vietnam on the exchange-rate equivalent of $0.40 or $0.45 per day in 2005 as non-poor because this amount, converted at 2005 PPPs, equals or exceeds $1.25.[6]

This raises the question whether the general-consumption PPPs employed by the Bank are an adequate guide to what poor people must actually pay for necessities. Can we conclude from the fact that $1.25 per day was not enough to meet the basic needs of a human being in the US in 2005 that the PPP equivalent of $1.25 per day in any other currency was similarly insufficient? In the author’s view, PPP conversions indeed fail to preserve command over basic necessities (cf. page 60 and more fully Reddy and Pogge 2009). But the Bank cannot invoke the inadequacy of its PPPs in defence of the level of its IPL because, by doing so, it would fatally undermine the very methodology it is using, which assumes that PPPs provide suitable conversion rates for comparing incomes and consumption expenditures of poor people worldwide and for fixing the level of the IPL.

Let’s restate this point a little more elaborately. It has been shown that consumption expenditure of $1.25 per person per day is much too low to access even the most basic subsistence minimum in the US in 2005. It follows that the

4 See <www.cnpp.usda.gov/USDAFoodCost-Home.htm>, prices for June of 2005.

5 See also Zimmerman (2008) for some anecdotal evidence.

6 The PPPs the Bank uses are available on the web at <http://siteresources.worldbank.org/ICPINT/Resources/icp-final.pdf>, drawn from Table 1, column ‘individual consumption expenditure by households’.

use of 2005 PPPs to convert this amount into another currency cannot be relied upon to yield an amount sufficient to purchase in 2005 the most basic subsistence minimum in the territory of that other currency. This follows from considering two jointly exhaustive possibilities. Suppose PPPs reliably preserve purchasing power with respect to basic necessities. Then any 2005 foreign currency equivalent of $1.25 per person per day was as inadequate abroad as $1.25 per person per day was in the US. Alternatively, suppose PPPs do not reliably preserve purchasing power with respect to basic necessities. Then a person's position relative to the dollar-denominated IPL – calculated by means of PPPs – does not tell us whether this person has access to a minimally adequate set of basic necessities.

There is one more possible justification of the very low IPL chosen by the Bank and employed by the UN for tracking MDG-1. This justification invokes the normative significance of the IPL. We are monitoring the evolution of extreme poverty not merely out of curiosity but also with the aim of its eventual eradication.[7] Given this commitment to eradicate extreme poverty, one might say, we ought to define the IPL in such a way that the magnitude of the world poverty problem implied by this definition is reasonably related to the world's resources: We should not define poverty so broadly that its eradication becomes wholly impractical. Doing so might even be counterproductive by discouraging efforts to reduce poverty to the extent that we can.

Table 3.3 How the size of the global poverty gap varies with the level of the IPL

Poverty line expressed in US-dollars PPP 2005 per person per day	Poor people in 2005		Aggregate shortfall from the poverty line in percent of the global product	
	Number in billions	Average shortfall from the poverty line	at PPPs	at market exchange rates
$1.25	1.40	28%	0.33%	0.15%
$2.00	2.58	40%	1.3%	0.6%
$2.50	3.14	45%	2.2%	1.1%

This table (figures based on Chen and Ravallion 2008, 23; 32–36), provides the data we need to assess this worry. Using the IPL favoured by the Bank and the UN, we find that the aggregate shortfall of the 1.4 billion people living below this IPL amounts to merely 0.15 per cent of the global product – or about $70 billion per annum or one-ninth of US military spending (<http://www.cdi.org/PDFs/What%20is%20the%20Defense%20Budget.pdf>). It is this poverty problem that the world's privileged see themselves as reducing at the stately pace of 1.25 per

7 Talk of the eventual eradication of extreme poverty survived from the World Food Summit (1996) all the way to current MDG-1 monitoring (United Nations 2008, 6).

cent per annum, with the affluent states contributing about $12 billion annually in official development assistance for basic social services.[8]

Were we to double the Bank's IPL, both the number of poor and their average shortfall from the poverty line would greatly increase. A seven times larger 1.1 per cent change in the distribution of the global product would then be required to eradicate poverty so defined. Yet, even this shift would hardly be discouragingly large – not when one considers that poverty causes some 18 million premature deaths annually (WHO 2004, 120–25), thus killing at over twice the rate of World War II during its worst years. Winning that war cost the lives of 23 million allied soldiers as well as half or more of the gross domestic products of the US, UK, and USSR during the war years (Harrison 1988, 184; cf. Harrison 2000). Ending world poverty would require no young people to be sent into battle. And it would – even on as broad a definition as $2.50 PPP 2005 – not noticeably affect the economies of the affluent countries. It would lower the growth path of these countries a bit so that they would reach any future standard of living a little later than would otherwise be the case – perhaps half a year or a year later on as broad a definition of poverty as $2.50 PPP 2005. It is for the sake of relatively trivial gains, then, that we let poverty destroy billions of human lives.

A third problem with the World Bank's counting of the poor arises from the fact that the exclusive focus on monitoring income and consumption expenditure leaves out factors that are relevant to poverty as intuitively understood. Someone who survives by working in a cold climate, which requires additional expenses for staying warm, is poorer than another who can earn the same income without having to bear such extra costs. Similarly, someone who reaches the IPL by working 70 hours a week is poorer than another who can maintain the same consumption expenditure by working only 20 hours per week. Any plausible measure of poverty must take account of necessary labour time – including here not merely paid work, but also the work on family food production, housekeeping, and child rearing, which is typically unpaid and very predominantly performed by women and girls.

A fourth problem arises from the Bank's reliance on household surveys that seek to value, in local currency, the totality of a household's consumption or income. This amount is then simply divided by the number of household members to determine their economic position. This simple division ignores variations in course-of-life needs: As persons' needs vary with age, so do the requirements of poverty avoidance.[9] The Bank should not then ignore a household's age composition when assessing the adequacy of its consumption expenditure. The simple division also ignores how consumption and labour are distributed within each household, and

---

8 See <http://milleniumindicators.un.org/unsd/mdg/SeriesDetail.aspx?srid=592&crid=;> the latest figures currently available are for 2006.

9 Recall how the Thrifty Food Plan maintained by the USDA is taking age into account.

thereby systematically overlooks, in particular, gender biases in the distribution of work, food, education, and health care. A closer look would often reveal what the Bank's method renders a priori impossible: That some – typically female – household members are poorer than others.

A fifth problem arises from how the results of household consumption surveys, expressed in the currencies of many countries and years, are compared against the IPL. How does the Bank determine whether the consumption of an Indian household in 1987, say, valued at some amount of 1987 Rupees per person per day, is above or below $1.25 PPP 2005?

The Bank makes such determinations through two transformations. It uses PPPs of the base year to convert its chosen IPL into base-year amounts of all other currencies (e.g., into 2005 Rupees). It then uses national consumer price indices (CPIs) to convert the results further into national currency amounts of other years (e.g., into 1987 Rupees).

This conversion method is unreliable on account of the CPI and PPP conversions it involves. Price comparisons across years (within the same country) and across countries (within the same year) yield different results for diverse commodities: The price of computers may be falling even while the price of rice is rising, and dollars may buy more bread but less maid services in the US than yuans do in China. CPIs and PPPs aggregate such diverse price data, weighting the prices of the various commodities according to their role in national (CPI) and international (PPP) consumption expenditure. This fact renders CPIs and PPPs unreliable within a poverty measurement exercise, because national and international consumption patterns do not come close to reflecting the consumption needs of the very poor. The prices of basic foodstuffs, for instance, have a significance in the lives of poor people that is vastly greater than their influence on CPI and PPP calculations reflects. The doubling of these prices during 2006–08 made much less of a difference to national CPIs, and hence to the official poverty statistics, than to the poor who typically must spend well over half their income on basic foodstuffs. Conversely, prices of cars or services play a much larger role in CPI and PPP calculations than in the lives of poor people. There is no assurance, then, that plausible poverty comparisons across space and time can be generated by using national CPIs and PPPs in order to map any amount, denominated in any currency of any year, onto the common currency of the IPL.

To illustrate, imagine a simple world with three commodities: *necessities*, *discretionaries*, and *services* (always in this order). If their prices do not move in lockstep, the CPI will reflect a weighted average of their price movements, based on the national spending pattern. By relying on the CPI, the World Bank thus loses track of the price of necessities. Falling prices of discretionaries (e.g., consumer electronics) may lead to a falling CPI even while rising bio-fuel demand is driving up food prices. Poor people on constant incomes become poorer relative to what they need to buy (necessities), yet by the Bank's calculations richer (relative to what their country's population is consuming).

Similar errors are introduced through the use of PPPs, as can be shown with a numerical example. Suppose the prices of our three commodities, in pesos, are 5, 6 and 1 in some poor country and $3, $4 and $9 in the US. What is the PPP? The answer depends on the spending patterns in *both* countries. Suppose this pattern is 30 per cent/50 per cent/20 per cent in the poor country and 10 per cent/50 per cent/40 per cent in the US. This yields a bilateral PPP of 1.55 – each peso is deemed to be equivalent to $1.55. (Here the hypothetical peso is valued so highly in dollars because it buys nine times more services and because services constitute so large a portion – 40 per cent – of US consumption expenditure.) But this bilateral PPP is inadequate for assessing the incomes of the very poor: They do and must concentrate their consumption expenditure on necessities – relative to which each peso is worth only $0.60 (five pesos buy as much necessities in the foreign country as $3 buy in the US). Again, many who are extremely poor, relative to what they really need to buy, may not show up in the Bank's poverty statistics.

This distortion is compounded once third countries enter the picture. Bilateral PPPs calculated without regard to other countries would not satisfy transitivity, that is, the condition:

for all countries A, B, C: PPP(A, B) x PPP(B, C) = PPP(A, C)

Transitivity fails to hold because the left side of the equation is substantially influenced by the spending pattern in country B, while the right side is not so influenced at all. It is highly desirable, however, that PPPs be transitive because the Bank's poverty measurement exercise would otherwise not be robust with respect to the choice of base country (the relation between the domestic poverty lines of any two countries would change depending on which currency they are converted into and compared in). To ensure transitivity, the calculation of PPPs conventionally involves a final step that adjusts all preliminary bilateral PPPs to one another in a way that guarantees transitivity. As a result, the PPP assigned to any local currency is affected by the prices and spending patterns not only of its home country and the United States (base country), but also by the spending patterns of every other country. In the Bank's method, then, the classification of any person as poor or non-poor is influenced not merely by the money she has and the prices she faces, but also by the prices and spending patterns of all countries included in the PPP exercise.

The dependence of PPP calculations on the spending patterns of all other countries and on the prices of commodities that are irrelevant to poverty avoidance distorts the World Bank's poverty assessment exercise. This distortion could be reduced by leaving affluent countries out of account entirely. When counting the poor the Bank is looking only at the less developed countries – on the plausible assumption that virtually no one in the affluent countries lives below $1.25 PPP 2005. But then the Bank includes the affluent countries in its calculation of PPPs, thereby allowing the prices of necessities to be drowned out by the prices of discretionaries and services (which play a much larger role in the consumption of affluent countries than in that of poor countries). The Bank would do better if it excluded affluent countries also from its PPP calculations, using the currency of some developing country rather than the US dollar as the common measure – though this revision would only reduce, not eliminate the error.

The fifth problem with the Bank's method is then that it is hugely over-inclusive in its informational base. Intuitively, to determine whether a person is poor, we need to examine her necessary workload and consumption possibilities in regard to what she needs by way of nutrition, shelter, water, clothing, utilities, and basic medical care. The local prices of other commodities, the prices of commodities in other countries, and national spending patterns are all irrelevant. By making all this information relevant through its CPI and PPP conversions, the Bank distorts our picture of world poverty in unknown ways.

Perhaps the best evidence one can have against any method is that its applications can deliver massively divergent results. The two notions of equivalence invoked in CPI and PPP calculations invoke very different (national and global) spending patterns. As a consequence, the comparison of two amounts in different years and countries varies with the base year chosen for PPP conversion. For example, one can use the CPIs of the two countries to convert into 1993 amounts and then compare via 1993 PPPs – or one can use these national CPIs to convert into any other year and then do the comparison in PPPs of that year. One can get as many different results as there are available PPP base years.

An intuitive way of displaying the problem involves taking a national currency amount – denominated in 1993 Chinese yuan, say – on a 'round trip': Using 1993 PPPs to convert it into Bangladeshi taka, then the Bangladeshi CPI to convert into 1985 taka, then 1985 PPPs to convert into 1985 yuan, and then finally the Chinese CPI to convert it back into 1993 yuan. The final amount resulting from such a round trip is typically quite different from the initial amount, in this case 31 per cent higher (Reddy and Pogge 2009, Table 1). This is so because the CPI and PPP conversions performed involve very different notions of purchasing power equivalence, based on different consumption patterns. And the comparison of a 1993 yuan amount and a 1985 taka amount will then vary depending on whether this comparison is made via 1993 PPPs and the Bangladeshi CPI or via 1985 PPPs and the Chinese CPI (or in some other way). Using 1993 rather than 1985 as the base year raises all Chinese amounts – prices, incomes, consumption expenditures – in all years by 31 per cent relative to all Bangladeshi amounts in all years. And conversely, using 1985 rather than 1993 as the base year raises all Bangladeshi amounts in all years by 31 per cent relative to all Chinese amounts in all years.

The choice of base year thus has a large impact on the relative position of national poverty lines – often much greater than 31 per cent (ibid.). The Bank's arbitrary choice of PPP base year affects the classification – as poor or non-poor – of hundreds of millions of people, though some of these effects do cancel out, of course, as poverty is shifted from one country or continent to another.

Conclusion

Intuitively, whether people are poor and how poor they are depends on whether and to what extent they can, at reasonable cost in necessary labour, gain access to the goods and services they need to meet their basic human needs within their actual natural and social environment. To make this assessment, we need to know their age-specific human needs, the relevant environmental factors (such as climate and disease vectors) that co-determine what nutrients and other necessities persons require to satisfy their needs, the cost of the locally cheapest way of meeting these requirements in a culturally acceptable way, and the amount of labour necessary to gain access to these required goods and services.

The World Bank's poverty monitoring method bases its binary output (poor/non-poor) on the per capita cost of household consumption. It completely ignores household composition (age and gender), intra-household distribution, necessary labour, culture and other environmental factors. And it marginalises the local prices of necessities by swamping them with an enormous wealth of irrelevant data: About prices of commodities that are irrelevant to poverty avoidance, about the cost of all commodities in all other countries and other years, and about the proportions in which all national populations all over the world allocate their spending over commodities.

There are strong reasons to doubt that this method can reliably identify the poor, assess how poor they are, or reveal whether world poverty is in decline and, if so, at what rate. If you are still tempted to join the United Nations and the World Bank in celebrating 'success in the fight against poverty', you may want to take a look at the FAO-reported number of chronically undernourished people. This number – stated as 'more than 800 million' in the *Rome Declaration* (World Food Summit 1996) – reportedly exceeds 1 billion for the first time in human history (FAO 2009). The number of those who experience hunger intermittently is substantially higher.

Given the great political importance that tracking the evolution of poverty, and the possible feminisation of poverty, have assumed in the wake of MDG-1 and in the heated debates about WTO globalisation, it is high time to specify and try out an alternative approach that would draw on the right information base and would combine this information in a plausible way. The rich data produced by such an approach would not merely give us a more comprehensive picture of world poverty and its evolution, but would also enrich our empirical understanding of poverty, thus enabling more effective poverty avoidance.

References

Anand, S. et al. (eds) (2009), *Debates in the Measurement of Global Poverty* (Oxford: Oxford University Press).

Chen, S. and Ravallion, M. (2001), 'How Did the World's Poorest Fare in the 1990s?', *Review of Income and Wealth* 47, 283–300.

Chen, S. and Ravallion, M. (2008), 'The Developing World is Poorer than We Thought, but No Less Successful in the Fight Against Poverty', *World Bank Policy Research Working Paper WPS* 4703. Available at <http://econ.worldbank.org/docsearch>.

FAO (Food and Agriculture Organization of the United Nations) (2009), '1.02 Billion People Hungry', news release, 19 June 2009, available at <www.fao.org/news/story/en/item/20568/icode/>.

Harrison, M. (1988), 'Resource Mobilization for World War II: The U.S.A., U.K., U.S.S.R., and Germany, 1938–1945', *Economic History Review* 41, 171–192.

Harrison, M. (ed.) (2000), *The Economics of World War II: Six Great Powers in International Comparison* (Cambridge: Cambridge University Press).

Pogge, T. (2004), 'The First UN Millennium Development Goal: A Cause for Celebration?', *Journal of Human Development* 5/3, 377–397.

Pogge, T. (2008), *World Poverty and Human Rights*, 2nd Edition. (Cambridge: Polity Press).

Ravallion, M., Datt, G. and Van De Walle, D. (1991), 'Quantifying Absolute Poverty in the Developing World', *Review of Income and Wealth* 37, 345–61.

Reddy, S. and Pogge, T. (2009), 'How Not to Count the Poor', in Anand, S. et al. (eds), also available at <http://www.socialanalysis.org>.

UN General Assembly (2000), *United Nations Millennium Declaration* (A/res/55/2, 8 September 2000), also available at <www.un.org/millennium/declaration/ares552e.htm>.

UN Population Division (2007), *World Population Prospects: The 2006 Revision.* Available at <http://esa.un.org/unpp>.

UNDP (United Nations Development Programme) (1995), *Human Development Report 1995* (New York: Oxford University Press).

United Nations (2002), *Implementation of the United Nations Millennium Declaration: Report of the Secretary-General* (A/57/270, 31 July 2002), also available at <http://www.undemocracy.com/A-57-270.pdf>.

United Nations (2008), *The Millennium Development Goals Report 2008* (New York: UNO), also available at <http://www.un.org/millenniumgoals>.

USDA (United States Department of Agriculture) (1999), *Thrifty Food Plan, 1999: Administrative Report* (Washington: USDA Center for Nutrition Policy and Promotion), also available at <http://www.cnpp.usda.gov/Publications/FoodPlans/MiscPubs/FoodPlans1999ThriftyFoodPlanAdminReport.pdf>.

WHO (World Health Organisation) (2004), *The World Health Report 2004* (Geneva: WHO Publications), also available at <http://www.who.int/whr/2004>.

World Bank (2009), *The World Development Report 2009* (Washington: The World Bank).

World Food Summit (1996), *Rome Declaration on World Food Security*, adopted in Rome in November 1996, also available at <http://www.fao.org/docrep/003/w3613e/w3613e00.htm> and <www.fao.org/wfs>.

Zimmerman, E. (2008), 'Dining on a Dollar a Day', *Christian Science Monitor*, 29 December 2008, also available at <http://features.csmonitor.com/backstory/2008/12/29/dining-on-a-dollar-a-day/>.

PART 2
Christian Ethics on Justice and the Poor

Chapter 4
Christian Ethics and the Challenge of Absolute Poverty

Clemens Sedmak

When asked what Christian Ethics could specifically contribute to the challenge of absolute poverty, two main ideas come to mind: Firstly, Christian Ethics can help to reflect how to use inner resources in coping with absolute poverty; the concept of 'inner resources' would furthermore help to rethink the concept of 'absolute poverty'; secondly, Christian Ethics can help to clarify and justify a preferential option for the poor.

Absolute Poverty and Inner Resources

Christian Ethics works with a concept of human beings that describes human beings as 'entities with interiority'. The idea that human beings are beings with inner complexity and depth is an idea from Christian origin that has become part of the modern concept of human beings.[1] The Christian tradition provides insights into the nature of human 'interiority' by developing a concept of 'soul' (Selman 2000). This concept can be used to describe the growth, unity, and identity of the human person. It points to the inner resources of a person. Whether you prefer to talk about 'Self' rather than 'soul' – the idea is the same: Human development takes place externally and internally. Palladius of Hellenopolis describes in the prologue to his *Historia Lausica* the formation of a soul: The soul needs discipline and exercise in order to grow; it does not mature automatically merely on the basis of life experience; the characteristics of a mature person with a well developed soul are: equanimity, fearlessness, kindness and openness. Aquinas develops the concept

---

1 Charles Taylor's fine book *Sources of the Self* (Taylor 1989) reconstructs the history and philosophy of the modern concept of human beings, using categories like 'common life' and 'interiority' to characterise the changes in the main ideas of anthropology after the introduction of Christianity and then, later, the modern era. Augustine's *Confessions* can be seen as a milestone in this development (cf. O'Connell 1969), Augustine himself saw this as a turning point with his emphasis on introspection, memory, and the soul as the place of encounter between God and human nature. Augustine prepared the ground for many a modern debate (cf. Matthews 1992). Against this background the idea of 'inwardness' was born (Davis 1989).

of 'magnanimity' to describe the person who has extended the boundaries of the Self. Aquinas distinguishes magnanimity from pusillanimity ('small-souledness', 'faint-heartedness', 'petty-mindedness') and characterises it as 'greatness of the mind'. The magnanimous man tends to great things, magnanimity is above all about the hope of something difficult (*Summa Theologica*, IIa–IIae, 123, 3; 129, 2; 129, 6). It is the mature and developed person that offers a big soul. Interestingly enough, the phenomenon of 'the self-dwarfing man' has been observed in the nineteenth and twentieth centuries (Keating 2007),[2] thus nourishing the interest in inner resources.

The concept of interiority invites one to rethink the concept of poverty, especially the concept of absolute poverty. If we take human beings to be 'animals with interiority', we would accept the idea that poverty is about a restricted possibility of accessing external resources and at the same time about a restricted possibility of cultivating inner resources. Christian Ethics points to the idea of these inner resources as an important factor in understanding poverty. It is widely accepted that poverty alleviation has to focus on the relationship between persons and goods rather than on the availability of goods as such. Amartya Sen's famous move in his capability approach placed the emphasis on this relationship, thus attacking 'commodity fetishism'. However, in the light of 'interiority', one simple question may be permitted: Sen bases his understanding of human beings on aspects of Aristotelian philosophy that did not conceive of interiority in modern terms. What would change regarding the capability approach, we could ask, if one were to accept the idea of interiority as a central aspect of human beings? Wouldn't it mean, if we could continue, that inner resources such as 'commitments' gained weight and importance and that the description 'relationship between goods and persons' would be deepened by considering the relationship of the person to himself/herself?

The claim to the importance of reflecting upon a person's self, inner resources and interiority can be justified by two fields that are somewhat related to poverty studies, resilience studies and gerontology. Resilience studies have shown that there are important internal factors that are decisive in the strengthening of a person's resilience, namely a 'sense of control of the situation' (refusing to see oneself primarily as a victim) and a 'sense of direction' (having clear goals in mind).[3] Similar results can be found in gerontological studies – Tornstam's widely discussed theory of 'gerotranscendence' nourishes the idea that old age is a spiritually fruitful stage in life and that 'successful ageing' can be enhanced

2 Keating (2007) contrasts pessimistic diagnoses of Mill, Nietzsche, C.S. Lewis, and Bernanos about the loss of greatness of the soul (which is, at the same time, reconstructed as a loss of inner strength) with Aquinas' approach to magnanimity.

3 The vast and expanding field of resilience studies has been introduced by Emmy Werner (Werner 1992; 1996; Werner and Smith 1989). Conceptual issues have been clarified by Luthar (2000; 2006), and the importance of inner resources have been elaborated by Higgins (1994), Wolin and Wolin (1993), and Lifton (1994).

by tapping spiritual resources (Tornstam 2005). The gerotranscendent individual has redefined the Self in terms of reduced self-occupation, experiences higher life satisfaction and has thereby developed new relationships to others and a new understanding of fundamental existential questions. There is an increased feeling of closeness to past generations and a decrease in interest in superfluous social interaction and in material objects. In this sense, the gerotranscendent individual taps spiritual resources that allow for new means of autonomy and independence from external circumstances. It is not surprising, then, that spirituality has been identified as an important factor in 'successful ageing' (Crowther 2002; Sadler and Biggs 2006). Again, inner resources have been recognised as major factors in coping strategies when facing difficult situations.

In the light of the consideration of inner resources the concept of absolute poverty could be rethought: Absolute poverty is to be linked with a complete loss of resources, both external and internal ones. Absolute poverty implies that an affected person has no access to inner resources that would strengthen her resilience and give her a sense of orientation, motivation, and vision. Poverty, then, can be described as 'identity deprivation', as the deprivation of cultivating and using resources of identity; poverty can be characterised as 'the lack of freedoms to cultivate attitudes and capabilities in order to cultivate and maintain identity in public space'. Such a characterisation would help to bridge the gap between 'Inner' and 'Outer', between interiority and external resources.

Christian Ethics invites us to emphasise the importance of this inner dimension. It would do that in at least three ways – firstly, it would appeal to the cultivation of inner resources of people affected by poverty, secondly, it would redefine absolute poverty in terms of lack of resources including inner ones; thirdly, it would underline the importance of interiority for our own efforts in dealing with poverty.

At this point, the author would like to introduce a concept that has a long tradition in Christian thought and seems pertinent to the discussion of absolute poverty: The concept of 'acedia'. The concept of 'acedia' stands for 'indolence of heart', 'spiritual sloth', 'tedium of the spirit', 'despondency', 'boredom', and 'burnout'. Colapietro writes that acedia 'is not simply insensitivity or feelinglessness, but the feeling of feelinglessness – the acute sense that the most one feels is a dull ache' (Colapietro 1997, 368). Adam Phillips claims that boredom is always accompanied by 'that most absurd and paradoxical wish, the wish for a desire' (Phillips 1993, 71). The concept has played an important role in patristic and medieval Christian thought (Arbesmann 1958; Colapietro 1997; Kuhn 1976; Wenzel 1967) and has been understood as the most subtle and most dangerous of the seven deadly sins. The term has been developed within the framework of early monks who were sitting in their cells for decades and all of a sudden, one day, in the early afternoon when the monk was expected to study the Holy Scriptures a sense of frustration carried the monk away into a cloud of darkness. 'Acedia' reflects the symptoms of burn out and lack of energy and motivation. Egyptian desert monk Evagrius Ponticus reflected in his widely read *Practicos* on the diseases of the soul. He identified several inner diseases such as sadness, pride, avarice, anger, lust and paid special attention to the disease of *acedia*. The danger of acedia is pertinent for people in hopeless situations who may fall into apathy. Acedia has been mentioned in relationship to modern melancholia (Jackson 1986) and has been rediscovered for contemporary depression studies (Hell 2006). There is also a political dimension to acedia, namely a collective 'compassion fatigue' (Moeller 1999), or a cultural climate based on a total loss of idealism (cf. Eng and Kazanjian 2003).

Why is the concept of acedia relevant for the discourse on absolute poverty? This chapter would like to suggest two reasons: (1) Acedia is a scourge of people who have given up on life and thus a danger for people suffering from severe hardships; (2) acedia known as 'compassion fatigue' is a challenge for all involved in the discourse on poverty and poverty alleviation strategies. What are possible remedies against acedia? Here, Christian Ethics can make a difference. It can teach us that acedia can be nourished by cynicism, by impatience, by over ambitiousness – important lessons to be learnt for compassion fatigue. Remedies against acedia are: suitable conversations and readings, sharing and fasting, cultivation of hopes ('docta spes'), and the perspective on life as such. This is, of course, a philosophical question – why should we be interested in alleviating poverty at all? Here again, Christian Ethics can make a contribution to the discussion of absolute poverty. It is the reflection on a preferential option for the poor.

Christian Ethics and a Preferential Option for the Poor

One of the contributions of Christianity to the history of humanity has been the development of a concept of human dignity and a sense of universal egalitarianism and solidarity, and an idea of charity (Habermas 1999; Chadwick 1971, 55ff). The idea of altruism can be attributed to Christian backgrounds: 'It seems clear that in western culture, Christianity is the ultimate source of the modern concept of altruism ... If the modern concept of altruism derives from the Christian concept of *agape*, the ultimate source of the concept is in the Christian understanding of God' (Grant 2001, 167 resp. 190). It is against this background that Christian Ethics can contribute the concept of a 'preferential option for the poor' to the question of facing absolute poverty. It is part of the established terminology of Christian Ethics. The term has been developed in theological documents: The pastoral constitution of the Second Vatican Council of the Catholic Church, 'Gaudium et Spes', introduced the idea of a special attention for the poor by underlining the solidarity of the Church with people living in affliction (no 1). This idea was taken up by two famous gatherings of the Episcopal Conferences of Latin America, in Medellín (1968, Conclusions 1, 3) and Puebla (1979, nos 1134, 1141f, 1153f). When dealing with the challenge of absolute poverty we are confronted with the challenge of entering a commitment vis-à-vis the weakest members of the human family, namely those who are afflicted by absolute poverty. No doubt: A first step of such an option involves the recognition that poor people are members of the human family, that they are first and foremost human and only in a secondary, less important sense 'poor'.[4] Furthermore, the notion of an 'option for the poor' is to be understood against the backdrop of a prior decision, namely the decision that poverty is an expression of an unjust situation. Poverty is perceived as a social *problem,* and not as an unavoidable aspect of society. Identifying a phenomenon as a social problem presupposes values and entails decisions.[5] The above mentioned Christian concepts of egalitarian universalism and solidarity provide the instruments to reconstruct poverty as a social problem.

In connection with a discussion of the concept of a 'preferential option for the poor' the author would like to raise three aspects that will help to get a better grip on the hermeneutical value of this concept: First, a 'preferential option for the poor' is a *preferential* and not an exclusive option; an option that sets priorities.[6] Here one can also ask whether this option should be universalised, since it is couched in terms of priority and does not make any claims concerning exclusivity. This question stands or falls with the question as to the possible existence of positive obligations. Can an option for the poor be turned into a general positive obligation? In an attempt to provide a reply from the perspective of Christian Ethics it is suggested that the question of the option for the poor is a *relevant question*: A question Q is relevant for a context C when at least one adequate answer to Q would lead to a significant change in C. A relevant question is such that one cannot ignore it when one is aiming at well-balanced judgments in a given

---

4 It was Martha Nussbaum who pointed out this need for recognising human beings as members of the human family first, prior to the recognition of specific differences (Nussbaum 2003); however, given Nussbaum's well known list of basic capabilities one could get the impression that poor people are not considered fully human in Nussbaum's philosophy.

5 As early as in 1941 Richard Fuller and Richard Myers have pointed out that social problems cannot be treated as 'natural disasters'. Robert Merton has underlined the fact that talking about 'social problems' involves value judgments and power issues: 'Social problems have been identified as the substantial, unwanted discrepancies between what is in a society and what a functionally significant collectivity within society seriously (rather than in fantasy) desires to do on it' (Merton 1961, 718). Joseph Gusfield has specifically addressed the questions of power in connection with the 'ownership of social problems'; social problems are defined; definitions are linked with the authority to define and the power to put a definition into practice (Gusfield 1981). There is a sociologically relevant dimension in the definition of social problems (Jamrozik and Nocella 1998). Concerning the difference between 'social problems' and 'natural disasters' the author would like to draw the reader's attention to Jon Sobrino's interpretation of the earthquakes in El Salvador. Sobrino has made it convincingly clear that the consequences of these earthquakes reflect the vulnerability and the social security of a person or class and that in this light we can read the earthquakes as 'social problems' (Sobrino 2003).

6 Cf. Puebla 1145, 1165. Concerning interpretations of this document see Scannone (1980).

context. The question of a preferential option for the poor can indeed claim the status of a relevant question.

Secondly, an 'option for the poor' is an *option*, in the sense that it is a voluntary as well as a lasting decision. An option distinguishes itself from a one-time decision in its binding character as well as in its adopted obligations, the accepted commitments; in a word, it differs in the lastingness of the position.[7] As opposed to a decision, which is made at a certain point in time and in many cases possesses a clearly limited range, an 'option for the poor' is a decision which requires permanent 'recommitment' and thus also self-reflection; it serves as a permanent 'thorn the flesh', a lasting challenge, never seeming to reach a state at which one might say that 'now the option has been achieved'. In connection with this is the fact that an option must be free from coercion and must be understood as a type of voluntary decision. It is a voluntary action, an action beyond the call of duty, a supererogatory action. But if Christian Ethics develops a strong justification for a preferential option for the poor – what happens to the supererogatory character of this option? One could argue that the preferential option for the poor can be justified as a mandatory option from a Christian perspective. In his partly canonical article on the option for the poor contained in that authority of liberation theology, the *Mysterium Liberationis*, Gustavo Gutiérrez (1993) clearly points out that the ultimate motivation for an option for the poor is a religious one. It is a theocentric and prophetic option that takes root in, and is demanded by, the giving nature of God's love. Within a Christian perspective, drawing from biblical sources such as the book of Amos or the topos of the final judgment in the gospel of Matthew (Mt 25, 31–46) it is indeed possible to justify a preferential option for the poor as non-negotiable for Christian Ethics. Outside of a Christian context it is possible to justify the option, but it seems to be more difficult to overcome the supererogatory nature of this option – even when using Peter Singer's pertinent argumentation within the context of a utilitarian position[8] or variants of John Rawls' difference principle, which posits that social and economic disparities be corrected in such a way that they benefit those who are least well-off (Rawls 1971, 104)? One could also appeal to the advantages of a negative utilitarianism as expressed by Popper: It is simpler to strive for the minimisation of pain than to strive for the maximisation of happiness. One could make use of epistemological arguments arguing that an option for the poor raises the epistemic quality of judgments insofar as it does not only take into account established ways of thought, best examples and the mainstream. A focus on absolute poverty teaches a lot about the structure of the world. Let us take the example of world hunger: World hunger teaches us a lot about the world, and about ourselves. 'Famine acts as a revealing commentary

7 Cf. Sedmak (2001, 233–240). A preferential option for the poor has implications and consequences; cf. Collet (1992).

8 Peter Singer argues for an obligation to fight against poverty; his line of thinking could be read as an 'option for the poor' (Singer 1972); cf. similar arguments in Unger (1996).

upon a society's deeper and more enduring difficulties'.[9] World hunger confronts us with hard facts; facts that are hard to accept and facts that are hard to deny. 'One of the hardest facts of life is that living itself is so painful to large numbers of people' (Hastrup 1993, 727). Hard facts provide the friction we need in order to have concepts that work (Wittgenstein 1967, 109). If ethical concepts want to remain 'fresh', they have to be open to disruption, the kind of disruption made possible through contact with the resistance of the real world. World hunger teaches us about the structure of the global food system.[10] It forces us to look at our planet as a whole to realise that we are throwing away food on the one hand and that we allow people to starve on the other hand. World hunger teaches us about our human conditions, about our bodies. The body is the prime place of resistance to the real world and of resistance by the world. We have to face the ethical challenge of not retreating from this real world of space and time as the proper focus of our attention, of not fleeing into abstract domains of conceptual constructions. A preferential option for the poor is a commitment to not losing touch with causal realities – and not losing sight of suffering human beings. In order to justify a preferential option for the poor one could also make use of the topos of an option for the poor when discussing the question whether the way in which society deals with its weakest members can be regarded as a criterion for the ethical quality of this society.[11] Even human rights can be linked to the idea of a preferential option for the poor (cf. Brieskorn 1994).

Thirdly, we must be interested in the normative implications of a preferential option for the poor. Christian Ethics can be characterised by the fact that it does not allow for a strict separation between individual ethics and social ethics. The structural implications of a preferential option for the poor are as important as the demands it puts on the individual. Gustavo Gutiérrez and Pedro Arrupe, for example, emphasised the importance of cultivating friendships with people affected by poverty. This is probably the best remedy against 'acedia' in dealing with poverty – living friendships with people afflicted by poverty. Friendships are according to the Church Fathers – next to 'otium' and 'beauty' – necessary nourishments for the inner resources of a person; and it is through these inner resources that the motivation to provide and use external resources can be found.

9 Arnold (1988, 7).

10 Cf. McMichael (2000, 125–143) and Friedmann (1982, 248–286).

11 See Neuberger's approach (Neuberger 2005) and Bernardin's vision (Bernardin 1998). Israeli philosopher Avishai Margalit has pointed out that the way we treat deviant and weak members of our society is the ultimate test for the decency of this society (Margalit 1996).

References

Arbesmann, R. (1958), 'The "Daemonium Meridianum" and Greek and Latin Patristic Exegesis', *Traditio* 14, 17–31.

Arnold, D. (1988), *Famine: Social Crisis and Historical Change* (Oxford: Oxford University Press).

Bernardin, J. (1998), *A Moral Vision for America* (Washington, DC: Georgetown University Press).

Brieskorn, N. (1994), 'Möglichkeiten und Grenzen der "Option für die Armen" im Rahmen einer Begründung aus der Tradition der Menschenrechte', in Bucher, A. et al. (eds), 140–157.

Bucher, A. et al. (eds) (1994), *'Die vorrangige Option für die Armen' der Katholischen Kirche in Lateinamerika* (Eichstätt: Diritto).

Chadwick, H. (1971), *The Early Church* (London: Penguin).

Colapietro, V. (1997), 'Acedia: A Case Study of a Deadly Sin and Lively Sign', *Semiotica* 117:2/4, 357–380.

Collet, G. (1992), 'Den Bedürftigsten solidarisch verpflichtet. Implikationen einer authentischen Rede von der Option für die Armen', *Jahrbuch für Christliche Sozialwissenschaft* 33, 67–84.

Crowther, M. et al. (2002), 'Rowe and Kahn's Model of Successful Aging Revisited: Positive Spirituality – the Forgotten Factor', *Gerontologist* 42:5, 613–620.

Davis, W. (1989), *Inwardness and Existence* (Madison: University of Wisconsin Press).

Eng, D. and Kazanjian, D. (eds) (2003), *Loss: The Politics of Mourning* (Berkeley: University of California Press).

Friedmann, H. (1982), 'The Political Economy of Food: The Rise and Fall of the Postwar International Food Order', *The American Journal of Sociology* 88.

Fuller, R. and Myers, R. (1941), 'Some Aspects of a Theory of Social Problems', *American Sociological Review* 6, 24–32.

Grant, C. (2001), *Altruism and Christian Ethics* (Cambridge: Cambridge University Press).

Gusfield, J. (1981), *The Culture of Public Problems* (Chicago: Chicago University Press).

Gutiérrez, G. (1993), 'Art. "Option for the Poor"', in Sobrino, J. et al. (eds).

Habermas, J. (1999), 'Über Gott und die Welt. Eduardo Mendieta im Gespräch mit Jürgen Habermas', in Maneman, J. (ed.), 190–209.

Hastrup, K. (1993), 'Hunger and the Hardness of Facts', *Man* 28:4, 727–739.

Hell, D. (2006), *Die Sprache der Seele verstehen. Die Wüstenväter als Therapeuten* (Freiburg/Br: Herder).

Higgins, G. (1994), *Resilient Adults: Overcoming a Cruel Past* (San Francisco: Jossey-Bass).

Jackson, S. (1986), *Melancholia and Depression: From Hippocratic Times to Modern Times* (New Haven, CT: Yale University Press).

Jamrozik, A. and Nocella, L. (1998), *The Sociology of Social Problems* (Cambridge: Cambridge University Press).

Keating, M. (2007), 'The Strange Case of the Self-Dwarfing Man. Modernity, Magnanimity, and Thomas Aquinas', *Logos* 10:4, 55–76.

Kuhn, R. (1976), *The Demon of Noontide: Ennui in Western Literature* (Princeton, NJ: Princeton University Press).

Lifton, R. (1994), *The Protean Self: Human Resilience in an Age of Fragmentation* (New York: Basic Books).

Luthar, S. et al. (2000), 'The Construct of Resilience: A Critical Evaluation and Guidelines for Future Work', *Child Development*, 71, 543–562.

Luthar, S. (2006), 'Conceptual Issues in Studies of Resilience', *Annals of the New York Academy of Sciences* 1094, 105–115.

Magdoff, F. (eds) (2000), *Hungry for Profit. The Agribusiness Threat to Farmers, Food, and the Environment* (NY: Monthly Review Press).

Manemann, J. (ed.) (1999), 'Befristete Zeit', *Jahrbuch Politische Theologie* 3 (Münster: LIT).

Margalit, A. (1996), *The Decent Society* (Cambridge, MA: Harvard University Press).

Matthews, G. (1992), *Thought's Ego in Augustine and Descartes* (New York: Cornell University Press).

McMichael, P. (2000), 'Global Food Politics', in Magdoff, F. et al. (eds).

Merton, R. (1961), 'Social Problems and Sociological Theory', in Merton, R. et al. (eds), 697–737.

Merton, R. et al. (eds) (1961), *Contemporary Social Problems* (New York: Harcourt, Brace & World).

Moeller, S. (1999), *Compassion Fatigue* (New York: Routledge).

Neuberger, J. (2005), *The Moral State We're In* (London: HarperCollins).

Nussbaum, M. (2003), *Cultivating Humanity* (Cambridge, MA: Harvard University Press).

O'Connell, R. (1969), *St. Augustine's Confessions: The Odyssey of Soul* (Cambridge, MA: Harvard University Press).

Phillips, A. (1993), *On Kissing, Tickling and Being Bored: Psychoanalytic Essays on the Unexamined Life* (London: Faber).

Rawls, J. (1971), *A Theory of Justice* (Cambridge, MA: Belknap Press).

Sadler, E. and Biggs, S. (2006), 'Exploring the Links Between Spirituality and "Successful Ageing"', *Journal of Social Work Practice* 20:3, 267–280.

Scannone, J. (1980), 'Various Interpretations of the Puebla Document', *Lumen Vitae* 35, 353–369.

Sedmak, C. (2001), *Sozialtheologie* (Frankfurt/Main: Peter Lang).

Selman, F. (2000), *The Soul. An Inquiry* (London: St Paul).

Singer, P. (1972), 'Famine, Affluence and Morality', *Philosophy and Public Affairs* 1, 229–243.

Sobrino, J. et al. (eds) (1993), *Mysterium Liberationis* (Maryknoll, NY: Orbis).

Sobrino, J. (2003), *Terremoto, terrorismo, barbarie y utopía. El Salvador, Nueva York, Afganistán* (San Salvador: UCA Editores).
Taylor, C. (1989), *Sources of the Self* (Cambridge, MA: Harvard University Press).
Tornstam, L. (2005), *Gerotranscendence: A Developmental Theory of Positive Aging* (New York: Springer).
Unger, P. (1996), *Living High and Letting Die* (New York: Oxford University Press).
Wenzel, S. (1967), *The Sin of Sloth: Acedia in Medieval Thought and Literature* (Chapel Hill, NC: University of North Carolina Press).
Werner, E. (1992), 'The Children of Kauai: Resiliency and Recovery in Adolescence and Adulthood', *Journal of Adolescent Health* 13, 262–268.
Werner, E. (1996), 'How Kids become Resilient. Observations and Cautions', *Resiliency in Action* 1:1, 18–28.
Werner E. and Smith, R. (1989), *Vulnerable but Invincible. A Longitudinal Study of Resilient Children and Youth* (New York: McGraw Hill).
Wittgenstein, L. (1967), *Philosophical Investigations* (Oxford: Blackwell).
Wolin, S. J. and Wolin, S. (1993), *The Resilient Self: How Survivors of Troubled Families Rise Above Adversity* (New York: Villard).

Chapter 5
'De Iustitia in Mundo' – Global Justice in the Tradition of the Social Teaching of the Catholic Church[1]

Gerhard Kruip

Catholic Social Teaching

Modern Catholic social teaching is expressed in papal, conciliar, and other official documents of different levels of Church hierarchy and lay movements dealing with the economic, political, and social order of society. It has its origins in the late nineteenth century, when industrialisation and social change in Europe led to the 'social question': The presence of a poor and excluded working class that began to organise social movements questioning the existing social and economic order. At the beginning this teaching of the Church, challenged by the misery of the poor, formed a rather closed system of general social principles such as personality, solidarity and subsidiarity. Its central arguments were related to natural law and neo-scholastic theology, proposing a kind of 'third way' between liberal and socialist ideologies. With the changes introduced by the Second Ecumenical Council of the Vatican (1962–1965) – that is the new insistence in a dialogue of Church and society and a very sensible awareness of modernity – the social teaching of the Church became more open to biblical roots, ecumenical and inter-religious exchange, social sciences and modern philosophical thought. Furthermore, while the Catholic Church began to be a global religious institution present in all countries of the world (cf. Kruip 2006), the particular perspectives of local Churches in poor countries became increasingly important and found their response even in papal documents. Without neglecting the social teaching of local Churches or of lay groups within them, this chapter will refer to some important documents published by the Popes and to the final document of the Roman

---

1 The author is very grateful to Katharina Backert who corrected the first English draft of this chapter and gave this text its present readable form. Nevertheless, the author is entirely responsible for any error or misunderstanding, which might have remained in the text. Parts of the following considerations are already published in different articles in German. See Kruip (2005; 2008b). For a more general view on Christian thinking about justice see Kruip (2008c).

Bishops' Synod of 1971,[2] because this text titled 'Justice in the World' is the most important one when trying to learn something about the global perspective in the social teachings of the Catholic Church.[3]

Spheres and Extensions of Justice

The still existing poverty and misery in many parts of the world, the climate change and other ecological problems, the danger of military conflicts, failing states and terrorism, and the actual crisis of international finance markets are urgent global problems, which cannot be solved by national states alone. Global problems need global solutions. If we don't want to find only solutions in the short run or solutions merely based on the relations of power of the participating states, but seek ethically justified solutions for a more human future, then these global solutions require global ethics, at least a minimum of globally consented principles of justice. In most ethical reflections however, justice, or at least social justice concerning the distribution of goods, was originally a concept restricted to national societies, and it was the state institutions and national organisations who were the primary actors obliged to build up a more just society within national borders. Today, in processes of accelerated globalisation, the urgent need arises, that the concept of justice must be a global concept to build up just structures for the global world including distributive justice in favour of the poor, fair democratic structures, a just economic world order and so on.

The most important contribution of Catholic social teaching consists in strengthening the idea that today the extension of justice necessarily must be a global one. To clarify this idea, this chapter will draw a distinction between *spheres* and *extensions* of justice. By spheres of justice the author understands – as Michael Walzer does (cf. Walzer 1983) – different fields or areas, which are ruled by determinate and different principles of justice. To give some examples: Some kinds of relations between persons are exchange-relations ruled by the principle of reciprocity. Others are relations of cooperation ruled by the principle of proportionality in the distribution of the results of these cooperations. Some kinds of relations in the area of fundamental rights have to be organised according to strict equality of rights. On the other hand, by extension it is meant the group of persons which are affected by these kinds of relations and which must be included into the application of the corresponding justice rule. In exchange-relations this

2 Third World Bishops, mainly from Latin America, had contributed a lot to this document which has been published as it had been passed on to the synod itself – a procedure which never again was applied after any other Roman synod of bishops.

3 You will find the English translations of these documents most easily on <http://www.osjspm.org/social_teaching_documents.aspx>. The official versions in Latin are published in *Acta Apostolicae Sedis*. For an English introduction to Catholic social teaching see Krier Mich (2000) and Pontifical Council for Justice and Peace (2004).

group only consists of persons who participate in the concrete exchange, at least if others are not concerned. In cooperative relations the groups normally are more extensive, they are often not limited to the persons that really participate in concrete cooperative activities, but to a community, often even a nation, that understands itself as a community of cooperation. Concerning fundamental rights our moral intuitions tend to tell us that all persons have to be included into the extension of this kind of justice. What seems most important to the author is the understanding that to determine what could be the right spheres and the correct extensions of justice, we have no other means than a fair discourse. But this raises the same problem: What should be the extension of this discourse, who has to have the right to participate in it? Or in other words: Whom do we have to attribute the 'right to justification', the right that every action affecting him has to be justified to him? What should be the extension of the right to justification?[4] For Catholic social teaching the answer is quite clear: The whole human family.

The Concept of the Whole Human Family

The concept of the unity of the whole human family (or humankind or human race), directly related to the concept of the universal use of goods of the earth, appears in many texts of the Catholic social teaching. The author found it interesting to see whether this concept could help to ground or at least to motivate a global justice theory. Anyway, it is interesting and astonishing that the idea of global justice was present in these texts long before it started its career in philosophical discussions. This chapter can only very briefly mention the most important texts.

In *Rerum Novarum*, the first 'social encyclical' of 1891, Pope Leo XIII invites others to 'feel and understand that all men indeed have been created by God, their common Father; [...] and [...] that the goods of nature and the gifts of divine grace belong in common and without distinction to all humankind [...]' (RN 38).[5] As he underlines the right to private ownership against Marxist ideas, he refuses the use of the argument of universal ownership against private ownership, but he does not deny the argument itself: 'The fact that God gave the whole human race the earth to use and enjoy cannot indeed in any manner serve as an objection against private possessions' (RN 14). It is important to note that the context of these texts as later with similar texts in *Quadragesimo Anno* and in the radio messages of Pius XII (who did not publish any social encyclical) still is clearly national. The idea of the unity of the human family was already used, when the

4 In the conception of the right to justification by Rainer Forst, this extension necessarily is a universal one, which does not mean that all questions of justice must have this same global extension. Cf. Forst (1999; 2002).

5 Most of the other official documents of the Church social encyclicals are cited by the abbreviation of their two or three first Latin words and by numbers of paragraphs (which unfortunately in the first encyclicals don't have an official status and therefore can vary).

problems related to this use still were problems of distributive justice at the level of national societies. But in *Mater et Magistra* (1961), the first social encyclical of John XXIII, the pope complains about the unequal international relationship between political communities that are economically advanced and those in the process of development:

> The solidarity which binds all men together as members of a common family makes it impossible for wealthy nations to look with indifference upon the hunger, misery and poverty of other nations whose citizens are unable to enjoy even elementary human rights. The nations of the world are becoming more and more dependent on one another and it will not be possible to preserve a lasting peace so long as glaring economic and social imbalances persist (MM 157).

The second encyclical of John XXIII *Pacem in Terris* (1963) puts the same idea in relation to a right to immigration: 'The fact that he [the migrant] is a citizen of a particular State does not deprive him of membership in the human family, […]' (PT 25).

In the documents of the Second Vatican Council the most important text is *Gaudium et Spes*: it witnesses an extension of the concept of the common good to a global level.

> The resulting rights and obligations are consequently the concern of the entire human race. Every group must take into account the needs and legitimate aspirations of every other group, and even those of the human family as a whole (GS 26).

This also concerns the distribution of goods.

> God destined the earth and all it contains for all people and nations so that all created things would be shared fairly by all humankind […] Therefore everyone has the right to possess a sufficient amount of the earth's goods for themselves and their family. […] Persons in extreme necessity are entitled to take what they need from the riches of others (GS 69).

In *Populorum Progressio* (1967), the first social encyclical of Pope Paul VI and the first social encyclical after Vatican II, the idea of the unity of the human family is related to the 'right to development'[6] of all peoples (PP 22) and is even enlarged to past and future generations: '[…] we have obligations towards all, and we cannot refuse to interest ourselves in those who will come after us to enlarge the human family' (PP 17).

6 Note that the UN resolution about the right to development dates from 1986 (resolution A/41/128).

Both in *Sollicitudo Rei Socialis* (1987) and *Centesimus Annus* (1991), the second and third social encyclicals of Pope John Paul II, the perspective is a really global one. John Paul II protests against 'the persistence and often the widening of the gap between the areas of the so-called developed North and the developing South' (SRS 14), he talks about the 'elements and aspects which render the social question much more complex, precisely because this question has assumed a universal dimension' (14). By using the term *social question*, a traditional concept referring to the problems of social justice during the industrialisation process in Europe in the nineteenth century, he also seems to include problems of distributive justice into his concept of global justice. He refuses the concepts of 'the First World, the Second World, the Third World and at times the Fourth World. Such expressions', – says the Pope – '[…] are significant: They are a sign of a widespread sense that the unity of the world, that is, the unity of the human race, is seriously compromised' (SRS 14). In his call for solidarity the Pope claims 'a new model of the unity of the human race, which must ultimately inspire our solidarity' (SRS 40).

The present Pope, Benedict XVI, follows the same lines: In his speech, for instance, in front of the General Assembly of the United Nations on the 18th of April of 2008,[7] he spoke about the 'common good of the human family' and, concerning the 'responsibility to protect' from human rights violations he referred to the 'unity of the human family'. He insisted in his support for the idea that global rules do not limit human freedom and therefore cannot be rejected with recourse to freedom:

> In the context of international relations, it is necessary to recognise the higher role played by rules and structures that are intrinsically ordered to promote the common good, and therefore to safeguard human freedom. These regulations do not limit freedom. On the contrary, they promote it when they prohibit behaviour and actions which work against the common good, curb its effective exercise and hence compromise the dignity of every human person. (Ibid.)

He wanted his visit to the United Nations to be understood as 'a sign of esteem for the United Nations, and it is intended to express the hope that the Organisation will increasingly serve as a sign of unity between States and an instrument of service to the entire human family'. It is expected that his coming social encyclical will deal with the problem of globalisation and global justice, reinforcing the idea of the unity of the human family.

7 Available at <http://www.vatican.va/holy_father/benedict_xvi/speeches/2008/april/documents/hf_ben-xvi_spe_20080418_un-visit_en.html>.

De Iustitia in Mundo

The Roman Synod of Bishops in 1971 about 'Justice in the World' was marked by a lot of contributions of Third World Bishops, mainly from Latin America, who were influenced by the just emerging Liberation Theology. One might understand the term 'world' in opposition to the sphere of spiritual or religious activities, but this is not the opinion of the synod's members. Their natural starting point of thinking is the unity of mankind and the idea of global justice in the whole world, which is expressed in a very direct, not primarily theological language.

As an assembly of bishops 'gathered from the whole world, in communion with all who believe in Christ and with the entire human family', from the beginning of their consultations, they aimed to fight for 'justice in the world' (IM 1) and to 'build a more human world' (IM 2). 'Since the Synod is of a universal character, it is dealing with those questions of justice which directly concern the entire human family' (IM 63). They started by analysing 'the serious injustices which are building around the human world: A network of domination, oppression and abuses which stifle freedom and which keep the greater part of humanity from sharing in the building up and enjoyment of a more just and more loving world' (IM 3). They observe a great paradox:

> Never before have the forces working for bringing about a unified world society appeared so powerful and dynamic; they are rooted in the awareness of the full basic equality as well as of the human dignity of all. Since people are members of the same human family, they are indissolubly linked with one another in the one destiny of the whole world, in the responsibility for which they all share. (IM 7)

On the other hand, despite these hopeful tendencies, global inequalities are growing, so that poorer countries don't have the same possibilities for development as the richer countries had in former times. One of the main problems of global justice – seen already one year before the famous Stockholm world conference on environmental problems – is 'the danger of destroying the very physical foundations of life on earth' (IM 64):

> Moreover, people are beginning to grasp a new and more radical dimension of unity; for they perceive that their resources, as well as the precious treasures of air and water – without which there cannot be life – and the small delicate biosphere of the whole complex of all life on earth, are not infinite, but on the contrary must be saved and preserved as a unique patrimony belonging to all human beings. Furthermore, such is the demand for resources and energy by the richer nations, whether capitalist or socialist, and such are the effects of dumping by them in the atmosphere and the sea that irreparable damage would be done to the essential elements of life on earth, such as air and water, if their

> high rates of consumption and pollution, which are constantly on the increase, were extended to the whole of humanity. (IM 10–11)

The ethical conclusion of the bishops is very demanding, because they claim global distributive justice:

> Those who are already rich are bound to accept a less material way of life, with less waste, in order to avoid the destruction of the heritage which they are obliged by absolute justice to share with all other members of the human race. (IM 64)

Finally they make an earnest call for action:

> We see in the world a set of injustices which constitute the nucleus of today's problems and whose solution requires the undertaking of tasks and functions in every sector of society, and even on the level of the global society towards which we are speeding in this last quarter of the twentieth century. Therefore we must be prepared to take on new functions and new duties in every sector of human activity and especially in the sector of world society, if justice is really to be put into practice. Our action is to be directed above all at those people and nations which because of various forms of oppression and because of the present character of our society are silent, indeed voiceless, victims of injustice. (IM 20)

Their suggested concrete measures appear quite innovative for 1971:

> These [measures] include the transfer of a precise percentage of the annual income of the richer countries to the developing nations, fairer prices for raw materials, the opening of the markets of the richer nations and, in some fields, preferential treatment for exports of manufactured goods from the developing nations. These aims represent first guidelines for a graduated taxation of income as well as for an economic and social plan for the entire world. We grieve whenever richer nations turn their backs on this ideal goal of worldwide sharing and responsibility. [...] Let governments continue with their individual contributions to a development fund, but let them also look for a way whereby most of their endeavors may follow multilateral channels, fully preserving the responsibility of the developing nations, which must be associated in decision-making concerning priorities and investments. (IM 66)

In the bishops' understanding, the engagement for a 'better world' (IM 4) is part 'of the Church's mission for the redemption of the human race and its liberation from every oppressive situation' (IM 6). For the bishops – and it is here that you can note the influence of the new arising Liberation Theology – God reveals himself as the 'liberator of the oppressed and the defender of the poor'. And the following statement strikes the key understanding of the relation between Christian faith and justice: 'It is only in the observance of the duties of justice that God is truly recognised as the liberator of the oppressed' (IM 30).

The Option for the Poor

The term 'option for the poor' was created in Latin America after Vatican II, when the local Catholic Church began to scrutinise its own 'signs of the time' and to adapt the results of Vatican II to its own situation.[8] The Latin American Theology of Liberation is nothing else than the contextualising of Vatican II. In a very conflictive context with growing inequalities between the rich and the poor and often marked by repression and violence by military regimes, the Christian love thy neighbour and God's promise of universal salvation demands taking priorities and deciding to help the poor first. Furthermore, Liberation Theology always insisted that Christian love had to be effective. Therefore, not only individual action and attitudes, but mainly social structures and institutions have to be changed in favour of the poor. Already in the document of the second Bishops' Conference of Latin America in Medellín in 1968, the issue of poverty was very present. The poverty of the poor was criticised and the poverty of the Church as an effective sign of its solidarity was demanded. Pastoral actions were supposed to be directed primarily to the poor and help them to get out of their misery. But the term 'option for the poor' itself only appeared in 1970 in the final document of an assembly of priests in Peru. They emphasised the situation of social conflict and called it 'class struggle'. In such a situation, which does not allow any neutrality, the universal claim for justice and charity leads to the option for the poor. It is very important to understand that the option for the poor is not an alternative or a supplement to justice, but that it is its consequence in certain situations marked by extreme inequality. The right understanding of the option for the poor therefore presupposes a concept of justice. This also means that the option for the poor is not just a biblical claim only relevant for the Christian faithful. It is as relevant and plausible for those who, without being Christians, want to realise central principles of justice and have to decide about priorities and siding for the underprivileged.

Because Liberation Theology, from its beginning, was heavily influenced by dependency theory with its importance given to asymmetrical international relations, the corresponding concept of justice was a global one. Therefore also the option for the poor can only be a decision to give priority to the poor on the world level without limiting one's actions to any national state. On the contrary, it is necessary to take into account relations of inequality and injustice all over the world and between all parts of the world. It is because of this that the poor living

8 For the following chapter cf. Kruip (2008a); Twomey (2005); Boff and Pixley (1987).

in foreign countries do not cease to be 'our own poor' who can claim our solidarity and help (cf. Boff et al. 1986).

But Liberation Theology always insisted in another important aspect of the option for the poor, too. The poor may not be treated as mere objects of help or assistance. As human beings with the same dignity as all the others they have to be recognised as subjects for their own sake, as actors of their own development. Therefore, the option for the poor demands empowerment of the poor, their full participation in decisions concerning them and the respect for their own speed of social change. In the author's impression, the present philosophical discussions about how to ground global justice often tend to neglect the subjectivity of the poor. But in the end, the poor themselves have to be the owners of their development.

The Problem of Universalisability of Christian Ideas of Global Justice

In the discussed teachings of the Catholic Church, the theological background is very clear and was already mentioned. *Gaudium et Spes* is very explicit: 'God, who has a parent's care for all of us, desired that all men and women should form one family and deal with each other as brothers and sisters' (GS 24). This attitude goes back to a universal claim at the very beginning of Christianity. In Mt 28, 19 to 20, Jesus says to his disciples: 'Therefore go and make disciples of all nations, baptising them in the name of the Father and of the Son and of the Holy Spirit, and teaching them to obey everything I have commanded you'. It is quite clear that this pretension is related to a very strong claim of absolute authority, which finds its historical effects in the medieval *orbis christianus* and the claims of global power of the Popes, for instance during the colonisation of the Americas, when the Pope divided the World into two areas of influence, one for Spain, another for Portugal. But at the same time, by the thinking of Bartolomé de Las Casas and Francisco de Vitoria, another effect of this claim of universality was the idea of human rights, which were also attributed to Native Americans.

Does this mean that these concepts of the unity of the human family were purely Christian concepts restricted to faithful understanding, or can they also be grounded philosophically in the context of global justice theories as they are now discussed in political ethics? Grounding these concepts in Christian faith may be consoling for Christians, but it doesn't help very much in arguing with others, no matter whether they are adherents of other religions or atheists. One indicator that shows that this idea of the unity of mankind is not only a Christian thought seems to be the Universal Declaration of Human Rights, which in its preamble refers to the 'recognition of the inherent dignity and of the equal and inalienable rights of all members of the human family [, which] is the foundation of freedom, justice and peace in the world'.[9]

9 English text at <http://www.ohchr.org/EN/Pages/WelcomePage.aspx>.

In the Hanover Institute of Philosophical Research we organised a research group in cooperation with the Center for Interdisciplinary Research of the Bielefeld University. Recently we published the results (Kaplow et al. 2005). We argued that it could be successful to start from a universal 'sense of injustice', which in its core seems to be common to all men and women among all religions and cultures. It's clear that we don't mean a sense as in the sense of smell, but rather in the sense of the sense for good music or the sense for emotional energy in human relations, for instance. It's also clear that this sense of injustice is not pre-cognitive but includes cognitive concepts of justice and at least implicit moral rules. Nevertheless, many philosophers, from David Hume to Paul Ricœur and Judith Shklar, have argued that it could be easier to know what injustice is than to define what justice means. If every person, at least when being a victim of injustices, is able to feel moral indignation, and if more and more people feel affected by injustices committed all over the world, this universal sense of injustice today also includes a global perspective and cries for global action. The sense of injustice, at first, is individual and local, but a growing number of people get affected by injustices in other places far away from one's own country. Indeed, in the last years we could observe that through the mass media and the work of global civil organisations a consciousness of interdependency among all in the world has been growing.

The concept of the unity of humankind nevertheless cannot be grounded on such a global sense of injustice, because this sense of injustice will only work if the extension of justice, that permits us to speak of injustice, is a global one that integrates all human beings. Therefore, it must be grounded in the idea of the dignity of every person and the moral community which is formed by the consequence of that dignity, namely that every person has the right that moral and legal norms concerning him or her must be justified to him or her. In a globalised world all are concerned, and therefore this moral community of persons in the sphere of the right of justification must be a global one and include all human beings. This does not mean that the extension of justice should be a global one in all spheres of justice, but at least when determining different extensions of different spheres of justice, the extension of the right to justification must be a global one. It is hoped that the idea of the dignity of all persons does not depend on Christian traditions alone, but that it can be grounded by philosophical reflections that are independent from any kind of religious faith.

It is quite clear that the concept of the unity of the human family has important consequences in many fields of ethical reflection about global justice. This chapter must be limited to some very short remarks about how these consequences should be: It seems quite clear that we have to guarantee a minimum for dignity to surive for every child, every woman, and every man, which implies a kind of social security system on a world level. We must find solutions for a more just distribution of goods, so that the poor will participate in the welfare of the rich instead of becoming increasingly poorer while the rich get richer. We must elaborate rules for international migration, not by starting with national sovereignty but with the understanding that national borders and migration policies must conform to a global social responsibility for the poor in other countries. Borders, as private ownership, are under a social mortgage. If in principle the goods of the earth belong to all, then there must be strict criteria to refuse permission for others to cross any borders. We need a better and more just distribution of the use of ecological resources so that there can remain opportunities for the sustainable development of the poor. We need fair play in world trade, which forces the rich countries to reduce their protection policies in agriculture and to allow the poor countries – corresponding to their needs – a gradual and partial integration into the world market. We need just procedures in global decision-making, so that the great number of the poor can be really represented proportionally in world institutions which have to be democratic institutions for global governance in benefit of all, and that means primarily for the poor. We need global policies to find the right regulation regimes for international financial markets to avoid any further financial crisis and its terrible consequences in the future.

Finally, we will emphasise one last idea: The Catholic Church could raise its credibility in this field by realising the unity of the human family in its own structures, procedures of decision-making, internal distributions of goods and its fight for more global justice. The Synod of the Bishops of 1971 expressed it well: '[…] unless the Christian message of love and justice shows its effectiveness through action in the cause of justice in the world, it will only with difficulty gain credibility with the people of our times' (IM 36).

References

Bhargava, R. et al. (eds) (2008), *Justice. Political, Social, Juridical* (New Delhi: Sage).

Boff, C. and Pixley, J. (1987), *Die Option für die Armen* (Düsseldorf: Patmos).

Boff, L., Elizondo, V. and Lefébure, M. (1986), *Option for the Poor. Challenge to the Rich Countries* (Edinburgh: T. & T. Clark (Concilium, 187)).

Brunkhorst, H. et al. (eds) (1999), *Recht auf Menschenrechte. Menschenrechte, Demokratie und Internationale Politik* (Frankfurt/Main: Suhrkamp).

Forst, R. (1999), 'Das grundlegende Recht auf Rechtfertigung. Zu einer Konstruktivistischen Konzeption von Menschenrechten', in Brunkhorst, H. et al. (eds), 66–105.

Forst, R. (2002), 'Zu einer kritischen Theorie transnationaler Gerechtigkeit', in Schmücker, R. et al. (eds), 215–232.

Göllner, R. et al. (eds) (2006), *Kirche der Zukunft – Zukunft der Kirche* (Münster: Lit).

Kaplow, I. and Lienkamp, C. (eds) (2005), *Sinn für Ungerechtigkeit. Ethische Argumentationen im Globalen Kontext* (Baden-Baden: Nomos).

Krier Mich, M. (2000), *Catholic Social Teaching and Movements*, 2nd Edition. (Mystic/USA: Twenty-Third Publications).

Kruip, G. (2005), 'Vom Sinn für Ungerechtigkeit zur Globalisierung der Gerechtigkeit', in Kaplow, I. and Lienkamp, C. (eds), 100–116.

Kruip, G. (2006), 'Katholische Kirche in einer globalisierten Welt', in Göllner, R. et al. (eds), 117–136.

Kruip, G. (2008a), 'Die Option für die Armen. Was bedeutet sie in Deutschland?', *Amos International* 2:2, 23–31.

Kruip, G. (2008b), 'Eine andere Welt ist möglich'. Globalisierung der Gerechtigkeit', *Trierer Theologische Zeitschrift* 117:3, 235–252.

Kruip, G. (2008c), 'Traditional Conceptions of Justice in Christianity', in Bhargava, R. et al. (eds), 94–115.

Pontifical Council for Justice and Peace (ed.) (2004), *Compendium of the Social Doctrine of the Church* (Città del Vaticano: Libreria Editrice Vaticana).

Schmücker, R. et al. (eds) (2002), *Gerechtigkeit und Politik. Philosophische Perspektiven* (Berlin: Akademie-Verlag).

Twomey, G. (2005), *The 'Preferential Option for the Poor' in Catholic Social Thought from John XXIII to John Paul II* (Lewiston, NY: Edwin Mellen Press).

Walzer, M. (1983), *Spheres of Justice. A Defence of Pluralism and Equality* (New York: Basic Books).

Chapter 6
Religions and Global Justice: Reflections from an Inter-Cultural and Inter-Religious Perspective

Johannes Müller and Michael Reder

Introduction: Why Think About Religions and Global Justice?

Justice is one of the main concepts in ethics in the last three decades. Since John Rawls published his famous *Theory of Justice* (Rawls 1971), justice became the key concept in discourses of political philosophy and social sciences analysing political structures. Justice is also a favoured slogan of civil society concerning various issues, and politicians discuss social justice worldwide.

Presently, there are quite a lot of political aims on the agenda of world politics which are related to the notion and adaptation of justice concepts. Sometimes, there are competing concerns regarding justice which cannot be easily harmonised, e.g. in the current political discourse climate protection and poverty reduction both have regard to the concept of justice. Actually, both targets are mutually dependent and necessary for a sustainable development. But, since it is not possible to satisfy all claims simultaneously and completely, ethical concepts like 'global justice' are needed to enable an equitable distribution in such conflicts (Wallacher and Reder 2008).

Global justice is not only an ethical concept which has to be reasoned from a philosophical point of view. Not less important is its acceptability in different socio-cultural contexts, at least when we get down to concrete global and at the same time local problems like poverty or climate change. Therefore, communitarism emphasises the importance of cultural roots and heterogeneity of justice as an ethical concept. Authors like Michael Walzer argue against Rawls, that we can only talk about justice 'in plural' (Walzer 1994). The idea of global justice will only be accepted, if socio-cultural contexts are integrated in its notion. Thus, acceptability presupposes an open dialogue with other cultural contexts and the people who are living there. Probably the most important socio-cultural factors in nearly all developing countries are religions.

Religions are an important cultural background of societies all over the world. In post-war Europe religions seemingly lost their public role at least. The idea of secularisation was rampant (cf. Dobbelaere 2002; Martin 2005), whereas in traditional societies religions kept their integrative function. There was the impression that in democratic societies this function was taken over by a secularised reason in a broad communication process which would bring about a consensus. Religion seems to block this 'communicative action' (Habermas 1984) and therefore has to be overcome. Hence, religion is not more than just a phase in the history of modern societies.

Times have changed and today quite a number of academics who favoured this thesis have had second thoughts about religion again. Jürgen Habermas is probably the most famous one. He sees modern societies in danger of 'derailing'. As an antidote, deliberative democracy needs sources for motivation and religions could be such moral resources (Habermas 2008).

Irrespective whether this argument might be convincing, it is clear that religion will not just become extinct (Rorty and Vattimo 2005; Reder and Schmidt 2008). Keeping in mind that cultural contexts are important for the idea of global justice, we should think about the relation between religion and justice in a global context. Of course, there are various ways to look on the role of religions dealing with justice-related issues and specific justice problems. This chapter tries to present some thoughts from a social science (sociology, political sciences, and cultural anthropology) as well as a political philosophy perspective. The argument is not following a specific religious tradition (theology), except for some hints. And it will speak in the plural 'of religions' in order not to reduce the perspective to only one religion.

Religions are Ambivalent Phenomena

In its history, each religion has been a source of injustice, violence and inhumanity as well as a source of justice, peace and human rights. This concerns all great religious traditions, e.g. Christendom, Islam or Buddhism. The history of the Christendom in Europe is just one obvious example.

The main roots of this ambiguity presumably will not to be found in the religions themselves. Political, economic and social conditions are always other important roots for this ambiguity of religions. Religions quite often were exploited to improve social conditions of particular groups or to strengthen a political order in favour of such groups.

Nevertheless, religions and religious beliefs also contribute to this ambivalence. This is most obvious in internal religious conflicts, e.g. the wars between Catholics and Protestants in the sixteenth and seventeenth centuries or the fights between Sunni and Shia in Islam. Hence, the ambiguity of religions is also a characteristic from an internal point of view.

Religious Sources are Open for Different Interpretations

In the sources of all religions evidence or at least arguments can be found for a positive as well as a negative judgement on the position of religions regarding justice issues. Hence, the reference to such sources is only partly helpful because they are open for quite contradictory interpretations. The philosophical tradition of hermeneutics shows that texts are always open to different interpretations (Kennard 1999). Both the background of the writer and the circumstances of the reader can never be absolutely eliminated from an interpretation.

In addition, the issue of religious texts is a transcendent one. Transcendence means that humans can never grasp this absoluteness or God himself. Their knowledge in this respect will always be very limited compared to what they do not know. Human thinking is necessarily bounded by immanent borders. The tradition of negative theology rests on this comprehension. This tradition could be found in almost all world religions. Nicholas of Cusa (1997) in the Christian tradition or Al-Ghazzali (cf. Wittingham 2007) in the Islamic tradition are both outstanding examples for this. Keeping in mind all these restrictions, religious sources always need to be interpreted because it is impossible to reach an absolute knowledge about God under whatever name.

Differences in interpretation also have led to diversity in all religions, and even schisms which seem to be a characteristic of all religions. The process of interpretation is complex and quite dependent on the respective time and place. A striking example is the role of women (Müller 2007a). Therefore, it is of major importance what kind of and how much authority is ascribed to interpreters, how the relationship between 'holy texts' and 'less holy interpreters' is defined, and what rules of interpretation (hermeneutics) are applied. Furthermore, the recruitment and formation of religious leaders is very crucial because they are often more influential than political leaders.

Discrepancies Between Theory and Practice

In the religious field too, theory and practice are very diverging for different reasons. In his famous article on *Religion as a Cultural System*, Clifford Geertz (1966) makes the distinction between pure and applied religion because even religious people switch between different viewpoints. Phenomena like syncretism or dual religious systems demonstrate that people combine and mix beliefs and ethics which are not reconcilable according to theologians (Schreiter 1985, esp. 144–158). Religions are 'mixed phenomena'. It can never be pointed out, what 'the real' or 'the pure' religion is. This applies also to the ethical implications of religions like the notion of justice. There never exists one homogeneous or fixed catalogue of all values concerning one religion.

Religious fundamentalism as one important root of injustice (Timmerman 2007) is ignoring this discrepancy and demands and tries to enforce strict observance of teaching and morality. There is no room for different positions and human weakness. In this way, they are searching for an 'original religion', which they want to make authoritative for all believers.

If someone wants to understand the role of religion and in what way different religions reflect on their 'mixed forms', it is not enough to study their theoretical foundations. Sometimes religions ignore their real diversity in their theoretical works and impose rigid practices on their adherents. Sometimes it is just the other way around: they get lost in so many different or even disparate practices that their internal unity is at risk. Sometimes theory is better than practice, in other cases it is practice which is better than theory. The late expert on Islam, Richard Gramlich, once said with regard to violence: 'In most of its history, Islam proved to be more tolerant than has to be expected from its teaching. Christianity proved to be less tolerant than would be expected according to the fundamental commandment of love proclaimed by Jesus' (cf. Kerber 1991, 80).

The Truth Claim of the Religions Includes Potential for Conflict

The interpretations of religious sources have to be taken very seriously since they have a specific quality because of their claim to proclaim the truth. What distinguishes religions from other cultural systems is the reference to an absolute authority (God under many names), an authority which by definition cannot and has not to be questioned or even challenged. In general, they pretend or at least presuppose that there exists no contradiction between their truth and the results of human reasoning. This crucial issue in the dialogue between religions and sciences can only be discussed in a constructive way, if faith and reason are regarded as connected in a dialectical way (Reder 2008). Religion is talking about the relation between transcendence and immanence without being able to objectify it. Authors like the already mentioned Nicholas of Cusa express this idea convincingly (Bulhof 2008).

But there exists a plurality of religions. Most of them and particularly the missionary religions including Christianity and Islam regard their beliefs, at least nowadays, as universal offers. This plurality results in a strong competition and sometimes even in more or less violent conflicts which entail a lot of injustice. This 'market of religions' is regarded as a threat by the established religions and often labelled as proselytism. A specific challenge is posed by evangelical and pentecostal churches on the one side and fundamentalist Islamic groups on the other side.

In this situation it is very crucial that religious leaders and interpreters of 'holy scripts' are aware of the radical difference between the word and will of God on the one hand and their own statements, preferences and convictions on the other hand. This implies the notion that everything they say is embedded in particular socio-cultural contexts. An epistemologically critical point of view concerning absolute truth sensitises facing religious fundamentalism and is also a good starting point for inter-religious dialogue. This must not imply a strong cultural relativism, but an awareness of socio-cultural conditions of religious ideas. Again, a lecture of communitarism which points out this relation between ideas and their socio-cultural background might also be helpful for religious leaders all over the world.

Close Relationship Between Religions and Cultures

Social sciences started talking about a 'cultural turn' about ten years ago. Similar to the linguistic turn in the 1960s when philosophers focused on language, today cultural conditions of social phenomena are taken into account and analysed more and more. Hence, culture is a special category to analyse and take seriously the diversity of society in the age of globalisation. Bearing in mind these aspects, it is emphasised that the world society is not a homogenous body, but a dynamic interaction between different cultural perspectives and even cultural reasons.

As already shown, the history of religions, too, is closely connected with cultures from which the internal plurality of religions emerged. The respective cultures have left their positive as well as negative marks. This process is ongoing and has its own dynamic which cannot be controlled by religious leaders.

Even the sources and original shape of religions, generally regarded as points of reference, were always embedded in particular socio-cultural contexts because human beings can only think and converse in this way. The idea of a pure beginning of a religion is nothing else than an imagined construction. Hence, religions always reflect the strengths and weaknesses of the respective culture, even though they claim universal world views and ethical imperatives which indeed transcends any particular culture and enables them to internal reforms. Thus, religion is no substance, no 'Ur-Religion' as Friedrich Schleiermacher already pointed out in the beginning of the nineteenth century. Religion and culture are always interconnected in his perspective (Schleiermacher 2003).

For this reason, the relationship between religions and cultures, including the historical dimension, is the key issue for any argument on the contribution of religions to justice or injustice, an aspect which often is not taken into account enough. This issue is also essential in the dispute about faith and reason. On the one hand authors like Habermas argue that we have to distinguish clearly between faith and reason. On the other hand some theologians contend that faith is the fulfilment of reason (cf. the famous discussion between Habermas and Cardinal Ratzinger: Habermas and Ratzinger 2005). Both positions have to be rejected. Faith and reason are rather both sources of religion and both are in a close interaction with cultural traditions and developments (Reder 2008). This is why participants of a dialogue should start reflecting more about the interaction between faith and reason and their cultural conditions.

Religions have a Tendency to be Exploited

Religions – not different from cultures – create a strong emotional adherence among their believers. To act with a transcendent authority in the background always involves and mobilises a lot of people who follow this authority with high motivation. This can have destructive as well as constructive consequences. One could even speak of an inherent tendency or openness of religions to (fundamentalist) instrumentalisation (Meyer 1995).

That is the reason why differences between, as well as inside, religions have a strong potential for conflicts and can be misused and exploited for nearly any end. This makes it possible for the parties to a conflict to connect their ends with specific religious (or ethnic-cultural) identities, mostly not in accordance with the spirit and intention of the religions. Even though these are only social constructions, which mostly are very far away of reality, they are very influential if people believe in them. The famous *Clash of Civilisations* (Huntington 1996) is just one outstanding example.

Religions are in a Continuous Process of Change

Cultures are not unambiguous or unchangeable factors but continuously adapt to new challenges both from inside and outside. This has to be underlined against a widespread cultural essentialism. That means there are always conflicts inside of cultures and between them (cf. Senghaas 2002). This is also true for religions because they are embedded in cultures. A famous example is the position of the Catholic Church regarding freedom of religion which changed radically in the course of time. For this reason, competition and controversies in struggling for being a 'good religion' are not an evil but necessary for surviving, even though this is a difficult and sometimes painful process.

In this context it is important to emphasise that religion cannot and may not be reduced to only one function or even only their social function. Some authors tend to do so and focus too much on the moral competence and function of religions. The moral implications are of course important but they are always rooted in the worldview or metaphysics of the respective religion which in different times and contexts are reinterpreted again and again. Of course, if religions try to advocate for justice in modern societies, they can play a constructive social role. But religions are multidimensional phenomena and as such may be reduced to this function. If we take notice of the continuous process of change of religions, we can see that religions have various functions for different groups and that these functions are also changing through history. These other functions (e.g. cultural function) are also important for their understanding of, and activity for, justice.

Cooperation for Common Human Concerns

There are numerous examples of a peaceful coexistence and cooperation of religions on the basis of mutual acceptance of differences. Religions have also the potential for enriching one another and looking for common solutions of global problems. This requires an inter-religious dialogue on different levels and in different ways (Müller 2007b).

Experiences in multi-religious societies show that inter-religious dialogue is most successful where people live together in their daily life just as a matter of fact. Even in situations of conflict, a 'dialogue of action' has turned out to be the best way to start a process of reconciliation. Action for common human concerns demands above all an appropriate way of proceeding and personal dedication. Different religious beliefs do not much matter in this respect. Such cooperation can be realised in the context of a social project, e.g. for street children, but as well in the form of a political project, e.g. the resistance against the building of a dam which forces many people to be relocated, often without proper compensation. In the latter case, the shared experience of massive injustice unites people.

The 'dialogue of action' primarily has to take place locally and at the grass-roots level. Thus, it is not surprising that churches in multi-religious societies like Indonesia have more experience in this field. But the 'dialogue of action' is also a challenge for the Christian relief organisations in rich countries which have long supported their partners in developing countries. The main end of such inter-religious development cooperation in a broader sense is human development and the fight against poverty. Even though it is not explicitly directed towards exchanges among people of different religions, it is in fact facilitating such contacts. Inter-religious development cooperation in a narrow sense presupposes the intention to include members of other religions into the decision-making and management of projects. Furthermore, these projects should have as their main motive the aim to ensure further constructive and peaceful inter-religious living and working together. Particularly in religiously pluralistic societies, the initiative for such projects can also be taken by members of other religions (cf. Banawiratma/Müller 1999).

Such a 'dialogue of action' is not necessarily intended or experienced as an inter-religious dialogue, because this might even become an obstacle for cooperation. But anyway, practical inter-religious cooperation will always take place which creates mutual trust and esteem. This is a solid basis or perhaps even a precondition for the theological dialogue on these different religious beliefs. Furthermore, dialogues of action are not just discussions that are very far away from reality or trivial talking without any commitment, but they represent dialogues in a proper sense. They get their credibility from their dedication in the service of men and women.

Conclusion

Liberals like Rawls (Rawls 1971) or Rorty (Rorty and Vattimo 2005) tend to reduce religions to the private sphere. In their perspective, religions could be a foundation for the individual schemes of live and private world interpretations. But they should not play a role in the public sphere.

This notion of and approach to religion and its role in society is far from sufficient and misleading. Religions are part of society, not only on the individual level (e.g. as civil society, moral background or cultural actor). Therefore, religions should be integrated in public reasoning about justice. Of course, religions are ambivalent phenomena and sometimes they tend to support injustice rather than justice. But this is no argument to reduce them to the private sphere.

The biggest challenge for religions is to consider the inter-connection between religion and culture. If they do so, they could avoid a fundamentalist point of view and support justice in a heterogeneous world, where the dynamic interaction between different cultures is one main characteristic.

References

Banawiratma, J. and Müller, J. (1999), 'Contextual Social Theology. An Indonesian Model', *East Asian Pastoral Review* 36:1–2.

Bulhof, I. (ed.) (2000), *Flight of the Gods. Philosophical Perspectives on Negative Theology* (New York: Fordham University Press).

Dobbelaere, K. (2002), *Secularization. An Analysis at Three Levels* (Bruxelles: Peter Lang).

Geertz, C. (1966), *Religion as a Cultural System. Anthropological Approaches to the Study of Religion*, Banton, M. (ed.) (New York: Praeger), 1–46.

Habermas, J. (1984–87), *The Theory of Communicative Action*, transcribed by McCarthy, T. (Cambridge: Polity Press).

Habermas, J. (2008), *Between Naturalism and Religion* (Cambridge: Polity Press).

Habermas, J. and Ratzinger, J. (2005), *The Dialectics of Secularization: On Reason and Religion* (Ignatius Press: San Francisco).

Huntington, S. (1996), *The Clash of Civilizations and the Remaking of World Order* (New York: Simon & Schuster).

Kennard, D. (ed.) (1999), *The Relationship Between Epistemology, Hermeneutics, Biblical Theology and Contextualization. Understanding Truth* (Lewiston/New York: Mellen).

Kerber, W. (ed.) (1991), *Wie tolerant ist der Islam?* (München: Kindt).

Kerber, W. (ed.) (1995), *Religion: Grundlage oder Hindernis des Friedens?* (München: Kindt Verlag).

Martin, D. (2005), *On Secularization. Towards a Revised General Theory* (Aldershot: Ashgate).

Meyer, T. (1995), 'Fundamentalismus und Universalismus in Moral und Politik', in Kerber, W. (ed.), 165–183.

Müller, J. et al. (eds) (2007), *Frauen – Gewinnerinnen oder Verliererinnen der Globalisierung?* (Stuttgart: Kohlhammer).

Müller, J. (2007a), 'Frauen – Stiefkinder der Weltreligionen?', in Müller, J. et al. (eds), 79–95.

Müller, J. (2007b), *Interreligious Cooperation for Human Development. Africa and Europe*, by Müller, J. and Reder, M. (eds) (Münster: Lit-Verlag), 198–203.

Nicholas of Cusa (1990), *On Inter-religious Harmony: Text, Concordance and Translation of De pace fidei*, Biechler, J. and Bond, H. (eds) (New York: Lewiston).

Nicholas of Cusa (1997), *De docta ignorantia. Selected Spiritual Works*, translated by Bond, H. (New York: Lewiston), 85–206.

Pratt, V. (1970), *Religion and Secularisation* (London/Basingstoke: St. Martins Press).

Rawls, J. (1971), *A Theory of Justice* (Cambridge, MA: Belknap Press).

Reder, M. (2008), 'Religion in der Öffentlichkeit und die Vielfalt ihrer Kulturellen Explikationen. Lebenswelt und Wissenschaft', *XXI. Deutscher Kongress für Philosophie (Sektionsvorträge)*. Available at <http://www.dgphil2008.de/dokumentation/sektionsvortraege.html>.

Reder, M. et al. (eds) (2008), *Bewusstsein von dem, was fehlt. Eine Diskussion mit Jürgen Habermas* (Frankfurt/Main: Suhrkamp Verlag).

Rorty, R. and Vattimo, G. (2005), *The Future of Religion*, Zabala, S. (ed.) (Columbia: Columbia University Press).

Schleiermacher, F. (2003), *Der christliche Glaube nach den Grundsätzen der evangelischen Kirche im Zusammenhange dargestellt*, 2nd Edition. (KGA I/13; ed. Schäfer, R.) (Berlin: Walter de Gruyter).

Schreiter, R. (1985), *Constructing Local Theologies* (Maryknoll, NY: Orbis).

Senghaas, D. (2002), *The Clash Within Civilisations: Coming to Terms with Cultural Conflicts* (London: Routledge).

Timmerman, C. et al. (eds) (2007), *Faith-based Radicalism. Christianity, Islam and Judaism between Constructive Activism and Destructive Fanaticism* (Bruxelles: Peter Lang).

Wallacher, J. and Reder, M. (2008), 'Principles of Justice. Climate Negotiations Need a Precise Ethical Concept', *Climate Change and Global Poverty* 5:8, see also <http://www.climate-and-justice.de>.

Walzer, M. (1994), *Thick and Thin. Moral Argument at Home and Abroad* (Notre Dame: University Press).

Wittingham, M. (2007), *Al-Ghazali and the Qur'an. One Book, Many Meanings* (London: Routledge).

PART 3
Global Theories of Justice and Responsibility

Chapter 7
On the Concept of Global Justice

Peter Koller

Global Ethics and Justice

Demands of global ethics

Every comprehensive system of ethics includes two sorts of binding moral demands: First, the perfectly universal demands of *general morality* that apply to all people vis-à-vis others independently from their specific social relationships, such as the commandment not to hurt or kill others without justification or the duty to help people in need, if such help is easily possible; and, secondly, the more limited demands of *justice* which are context-dependent in the sense that they refer to particular social relationships among the parties involved, such as the precept that contractual transactions are to be fair and the requirement that a punishment ought be proportionate to the committed wrong. Accordingly, it is assumed that a comprehensive system of *global ethics* will also include two sorts of demands concerning the relationships among nations and their individual members: Some perfectly universal demands of global morality, on the one hand, and certain context-dependent demands of global justice, on the other (Barry 1989).

As to the first sort, the *perfectly universal demands of global morality*, there are good reasons to assume that we all do have a number of moral duties towards strangers, be they individuals, collectives or whole nations, regardless of whether or not we are related to them in a particular way that may result in further moral obligations. These duties of global morality may be classified along two dimensions: Their determinacy, on the one hand, and their object, on the other. In regard to their determinacy, we may distinguish between *strict* and *loose* duties, depending on whether they submit us to some clearly determined ways of conduct or leave us a significant degree of discretion; and as to their object, our duties can be divided into *interpersonal* and *institutional* ones, depending on whether they concern our conduct vis-à-vis other people or the institutional arrangements of our social world. On the basis of these classifications, this chapter assumes there are four kinds of perfectly universal duties of global morality: (1) the *strict interpersonal duty* of not harming other peoples or their individual members without reasonable justification; (2) the *loose interpersonal duty* to render help to foreign people in need, if such help does not involve significant sacrifices; (3) the *strict institutional duty* to comply with the existing rules of international law, provided that they facilitate a world order which appears preferable to an international state of nature;

and (4) the *loose institutional duty* to contribute to a generally acceptable global order to a degree which can be reasonably expected.

In the author's opinion, there are no further perfectly universal, context-independent duties of global morality which accord to widely shared moral intuitions and appear to be generally defensible too. Even though the four duties just mentioned are highly vague and open to various interpretations, it is obvious that they alone cannot provide a sufficient moral basis for a generally defensible international or global order. Thus, it is plausible to assume that an appropriate moral conception of international or global affairs must also include certain demands of justice, that may be summarised by the notion of *international* or *global justice* depending on whether they refer to the relations among individual nations or to the structure of the global order as a whole. In order to be able to identify these demands, it will be helpful to take a glance at the basic vocabulary of justice.

Fundamental demands of justice

The demands of justice differ from perfectly universal standards of morality by the fact that they always apply to specific social relationships where the actors have conflicting interests as to the advantages or burdens of their interaction, such as exchanging assets, awarding achievements, dividing goods, exercising power, compensating torts, etc. There is, however, a great variety of such relationships that hardly can be reduced to a common denominator. Therefore, it is necessary to differentiate between various typical forms of interaction and to check whether there are plausible standards of justice that fit with them, in order to find out whether such standards exist at all. This strategy was already pursued by Aristotle when he distinguished between two sorts of justice that are usually named 'distributive' and 'commutative' justice (Aristotle 1954, Koller 2001, 27f). This distinction leads to the right direction, but is still too simple. In the author's view, it is requisite to distinguish between four kinds of justice each of which refers to a specific elementary type of social relationship:

- distributive justice → communal relationships
- transactional justice → exchange relationships
- political justice → power relationships
- corrective justice → wrongness relationships

This classification enables us to identify a number of widely shared and reasonable, though rather weak demands of justice that apply to the rules and institutions of social life. Each type of social interaction includes specific conflicts whose fair resolution requires appropriate principles of justice. We will now sketch the kinds of justice and their respective demands briefly (Koller 2001, 19ff).

Distributive justice applies to *communal relationships*. These are interpersonal constellations whose participants have a common claim to certain goods or are commonly bound to bear certain burdens. So people maintain a communal relationship, when and insofar they share some common goods or common burdens or both. Justice demands that common goods and burdens are to be distributed in a way that is reasonably acceptable to all parties involved. There is a general principle of distributive justice that works for all distributive problems, although the specific criteria that apply to them vary with their special features. This is the *principle of equal treatment* which runs as follows: The goods and burdens of a communal relationship are to be distributed *equally* among all parties unless an unequal distribution is justified by reasons acceptable to all parties concerned from an impartial viewpoint. Taken alone, the principle of equal treatment is rather weak and abstract, but it is not completely empty, for it acquires significant strength when it is combined with further information (Rawls 1971, 62; Feinberg 1973, 99ff; Miller 1976, 24ff).

Transactional justice focuses on *exchange relationships*, i.e. contractual transactions through which independent persons, each of whom is endowed with particular rights and entitlements, voluntarily agree on a mutual transfer of some of their assets among each other. Justice demands that such transactions occur in a way which makes sure that they are to the benefit of all parties involved, so that none of them has reason to complain about the outcome. In advanced societies with competitive markets, transactions are deemed to be just, if the parties involved voluntarily agree on them under conditions which enable them to pursue their best interest. These conditions require that all parties involved have equal legal competence, sufficient knowledge of the relevant facts, and basic rational capacities in order to make well-considered choices. Furthermore, contractual agreements must not be distorted by inequalities of power due to which a party would be able to dictate the terms of trade. Since these conditions, if met, make sure that exchange relationships operate to the benefit of all parties involved, they define the basic requirements of a *fair market* (Roover 1958; Gijsel 1984; Koller 2008).

Political justice deals with *power relationships* that occur when an agent effectively claims the authorised power to determine the ways or circumstances of conduct of other people through binding decisions backed by force. There are good reasons to assume that, at least in large social unions, some forms of power are necessary in order to secure a just and efficient social order. Since, however, any such power involves significant dangers, it is subject to certain requirements of justice in order to keep it within acceptable limits. It is generally agreed that power is not an end in itself, but a means to achieve a rightful and efficient social order. Accordingly, power is deemed to be just only if it serves *legitimate purposes* and is exercised in an *impartial way*. Its purposes are twofold: First, enforcing the well-founded duties and rights of individuals, particularly human rights, and, secondly, facilitating projects of cooperation to the benefit of all people involved, such as the provision of public goods (Höffe 1987, 62ff).

Eventually, *corrective justice* applies to *wrongness relationships*. These occur when people commit wrongdoings by flouting binding social norms, violating the rights of other persons, or breaching their duties toward others. This constellation demands for a correction of committed wrongs in order to restore the social order by compensating the victims or punishing the wrongdoers for severe crimes. The ways of such correction are the object of *corrective justice*, which itself includes two parts: *Restitutive* justice which deals with the just compensation of damages, and *retributive* justice that concerns the question as to whether and how wrongdoings ought to be sanctioned through punishment. Both sorts of corrective justice are based on certain requirements of *proportionality*, which cannot, and need not, be discussed in the present context (Sterba 1980; Coleman 1992).

Complex notions of justice

Notwithstanding their analytical differences, the various elementary kinds of justice are actually interlinked, since, in social reality, human interaction usually takes place within complex social networks that combine some or even all forms of relationships under consideration. So the different kinds of justice and their demands are bound together through manifold interrelations some of which are conceptual, while others are contingent.

The author would like to point out one *conceptually necessary* interrelation between distributive justice and the other kinds that is of particular importance: The *fundamental role of distributive justice*. Let us first take a glance at transactional justice. According to any plausible conception of transactional justice, an exchange relationship can be deemed to be just only if it starts from a previous distribution of the respective rights and possessions of the parties involved that itself is acceptable, i.e. by and large just or at least not extremely unjust, so that the parties involved are entitled to dispose of the goods and services which they want to exchange. This condition, however, eventually presupposes some standards of distributive justice and general morality, for the question of whether or not it is met cannot sufficiently decided on the basis of transactional justice alone because of its reliance on an acceptable initial distribution of the rights and possessions of the parties under consideration. And the same is true of political and corrective justice, since they are also concerned with social affairs whose participants are already endowed with certain rights and assets. Consequently, distributive justice is in fact fundamental to all other demands. And this fact explains why it lies in the centre of most disputes on justice in political discourse.

If the various basic demands of justice, taken together, are applied to complex social orders, they facilitate the formation of more complex ideas of justice in regard to the orders under consideration. If applied to the order of modern societies, they amount to the idea of *social justice* (Koller 2003), and they suggest the idea of *international* or *global justice*, if applied to international relations or the entire global order (Koller 2009).

A Comprehensive Concept of Global Justice

Demands of global justice

For a first approximation, it is suggested that we interpret the notion of global justice as a comprehensive concept that includes a plurality of demands on international and global affairs rather than looking for a single master principle of global justice. So it is proposed to understand global justice as the *totality of demands of justice that can be reasonably applied to international relations and the global order*. The author would like to argue that all kinds of justice mentioned previously come into play, namely distributive, transactional, political, and corrective justice. Since this claim is more difficult to defend in regard to distributive justice than in the other cases, this chapter will take a glance at the latter first and then deal with the issue of global distributive justice.

The global order is subject to *transactional justice* when different nations or their members maintain trade and exchange relationships. Transactional justice requires that international trade relations and global market processes take place under *fair rules and framing conditions* which make sure that all participating peoples and nations can derive appropriate benefit from them. To this end, those rules and framing conditions must ensure that no nation is mighty enough to dictate unilaterally the terms of trade to its own advantage, and that international exchange transactions are balanced to the effect that they are not distorted by asymmetrical market restrictions. This demand does not necessarily require a system of free trade. Yet, a well-known theory of international trade, the theory of comparative advantage, maintains that free international trade relationships are to the benefit of all countries involved, even if they start from very different stages of economic development. Even though this theory seems to be subject to some reservations, it may support a preference for free international trade, provided that the countries involved keep their national markets equally open, unless exceptions are justified by other requirements of justice (Franck 1995, 413ff; Kapstein 2006, 45ff; Stiglitz and Charlton 2006).

The demand of *political justice* applies to international and global affairs to the extent in which these affairs actually include or require authorised power. In order to circumvent the difficult question as to the form of such power, we will emphasise two rather obvious requirements of political justice on the global level: First of all, an appropriate global order ought to be capable of *counteracting two main evils* of our present world as far as possible: (1) gross and massive violations of basic human rights, such as genocides, ethnic cleansing, and avoidable famines (Buchanan 2004, 118ff; Chwaszcza 2007); and (2) the irreversible destruction of global natural resources, such as the oceans, earthly climate conditions, and rain forests (Kaul, Grunberg and Stern 1999). Furthermore, power in international affairs ought to lie in the hands of transnational authorities that have *sufficient strength and independence* in order to enforce the rules of international law in an *impartial* way (Franck 1995, 173ff; Buchanan 2004, 233ff).

The demand for *corrective justice* arises in the context of international relations when nations or some of their members commit severe wrongdoings against other peoples or their individual members – wrongdoings that require compensation or retribution. Though one may quarrel about the implications and the weight of corrective justice in international affairs, it is plausible and widely acknowledged that, in principle, nations as organised collective bodies are to be liable to take appropriate corrective measures for wrongs committed by their agents or members in accordance with their procedures of collective decision making. Yet, in many cases, particularly in those concerning past wrongs a long time ago, corrective justice among nations is a highly disputed and sensitive issue, that even may tend to endanger international peace rather than promote it. At least in such cases, corrective justice should not be regarded as a matter of primary importance. When it occurs, however, that the demand for correcting past wrongs coincides with the requirements of transactional, political and distributive justice, as frequently happens, this demand can supplement, support and strengthen these other requirements (Barkan 2000; O'Neill 2000, 129ff; Meyer 2005, 135ff).

Global distributive justice

The most contested issue of global justice is the question as to whether and to what extent international relations and the global order are subject to *distributive justice* (Buchanan 2004, 191ff). A number of thinkers, including Rawls (1999, 113ff), advocate the view that distributive justice doesn't have any significance in the context of international or global justice. This chapter contradicts this view and argues for a concept of global justice that integrates distributive justice to the extent to which the international or global order has distributive effects on the communal affairs of different nations or humankind as a whole. In the author's view, the role of distributive justice in international relations depends on *contingent facts*, namely the actual structure of the world, especially the degree of international and global interdependencies. The more individual nations and peoples become interconnected and interdependent, the greater is the domain of their communal affairs that are subject to distributive justice. When we consider the present situation of the world, we find at least three issues that evoke the demand for distributive justice: The extent of the nations' political autonomy within the global order, the negative effects of societal activities across borders, and international economic cooperation based on division of labour.

The first issue, *the extent of the nations' political autonomy* within the global order, is already present in a world where the national economies are relatively separated, but it increases with the process of globalisation. It is assumed that a just international order ought to grant to each nation the right to political self-determination to the extent that is compatible with a peaceful and generally beneficial global order (Koller 2000, 102ff). The second issue, *the negative effects of societal activities across borders*, results from the fact that the social and economic activities of individual societies increasingly have negative effects on other countries and even the whole world. This fact raises the demand for a just distribution of the benefits and costs of border-crossing social and economic activities: The costs must be distributed in proportion to the benefits which the individual nations derive from those activities. When such a distribution cannot be achieved through market regulations, corrective justice requires that the nations who fare better have to pay appropriate compensation to those who are worse off (Barry 1989; Singer 2002, 14ff). Thirdly, there is the issue of *international economic cooperation based on division of labour*. The nations increasingly melt together to comprehensive units of economic cooperation based on division of labour, in which all, more or less, contribute to the production of earthly wealth and become more and more dependent on each other. Even though this cooperation mainly operates on the basis of market transactions, it creates a problem of distributive justice, since market processes alone cannot secure a just distribution of their outcomes. So distributive justice also applies to the benefits and burdens of international cooperation based on division of labour. So the global order has to be designed in a way that international cooperation works to the benefit of all peoples, in particular the less developed and poor.

Global justice and the present world

As a result, the idea of global justice combines a variety of demands that flow from all elementary kinds of justice. Even though these demands are rather vague, they are clearly not met by the present international system. In fact, this system suffers from extreme injustices in the light of each demand. The demands of *transactional* justice are grossly violated by the prevailing systems of global trade and international finance, at least as far as the relationships between rich and poor countries are concerned. The trade system highly favours the interests of the rich countries to the disadvantage of the poor, and the international credit system operates in a way that results in a permanent flow of wealth from the poor to the rich countries (Woods 1999; Oxfam 2002; Hertz 2004; Stiglitz 2006). Nor does the present international order meet the demands of *political* justice. When we just look at the global level, we encounter a peculiar situation: On the one hand, there is a global legal power, the UNO, that suffers both from ineffectiveness and distorted decision-making mechanisms; on the other hand, there is a pretty small group of real super powers, particularly the USA, whose governments are mainly led by their national self-interest rather than the common good of the international community (Höffe 1999, 267ff; Czempiel 2002).

Last but not least, the present world system is also in contradiction to *distributive* justice. As to the first issue, it greatly fails to meet the requirement that every nation's political autonomy is compatible with a peaceful global order, since it concedes to each state government two rights or privileges: The right of exercising control of its country's natural resources at will, including selling them, and the right of raising credits in behalf of its country that bind future governments. These two rights – the 'resource privilege' and the 'borrowing privilege', as Thomas Pogge (2002, 112ff, 146ff) has called them – entice corrupt regimes to enrich themselves at the cost of the people by disposing of their land's resources and raising credits. Furthermore, the present order violates the demand for a proportional distribution of the costs and benefits of societal activities across borders, because the rich nations derive the lion's share of benefits from the use of natural resources belonging to the common heritage of humankind at the cost of the poor countries and future generations (Singer 2002, 14ff). And finally, the existing form of international economic cooperation is also not defensible, for it works in a way so that some nations take the benefits, while others are left with empty hands (Oxfam 2002).

In the light of these results, it becomes pretty obvious that the present international system suffers from a great variety of gross injustices. And these injustices appear even more scandalous, when one considers that they mutually reinforce each other, as they all work to the benefit of the rich and mighty nations at the cost of the poor. Consequently, it is still our task not only to interpret the world, but also to change it.

References

Aristotle (1954), *Nicomachian Ethics*, Ross, D. (ed.) (Oxford: Oxford University Press).

Barkan, E. (2000), *The Guilt of Nations. Restitution and Negotiating Historical Injustices* (Baltimore/London: Johns Hopkins University Press).

Barry, B. (1989), 'Humanity and Justice in Global Perspective' (1982), in Barry, B. (ed.), 434–462.

Barry, B. (ed.) (1989), *Democracy, Power and Justice. Essays in Political Theory* (Oxford: Oxford University Press).

Buchanan, A. (2004), *Justice, Legitimacy, and Self-Determination. Moral Foundations for International Law* (Oxford: Oxford University Press).

Chwaszcza, C. (2007), *Moral Responsibility and Global Justice. A Human Rights Approach* (Baden-Baden: Nomos).

Coleman, J. (1992), *Risks and Wrongs* (Oxford: Oxford University Press).

Czempiel, E.-O. (2002), *Weltpolitik im Umbruch. Die Pax Americana, der Terrorismus und die Zukunft der Internationalen Beziehungen* (München: C.H. Beck).

Feinberg, J. (1973), *Social Philosophy* (Englewood Cliffs, NJ: Prentice-Hall).

Franck, T. (1995), *Fairness in International Law and Institutions* (Oxford: Oxford University Press).

Gijsel, P. (1984), 'Individuum und Gerechtigkeit in ökonomischen Verteilungstheorien', in *Ökonomie und Gesellschaft, Jahrbuch 2: Wohlfahrt und Gerechtigkeit* (Frankfurt/Main/New York: Campus), 14–66.

Hertz, N. (2004), *I.O.U. The Debt Threat and Why We Must Defuse It* (London: Fourth Estate).

Höffe, O. (1987), *Politische Gerechtigkeit* (Frankfurt/Main: Suhrkamp).

Höffe, O. (1999), *Demokratie im Zeitalter der Globalisierung* (München: C.H. Beck).

Hurrell, A. et al. (eds) (1999), *Inequality, Globalization, and World Politics* (Oxford: Oxford University Press).

Kapstein, E. (2006), *Economic Justice in an Unfair World. Toward a Level Playing Field* (Princeton/Oxford: Princeton University Press).

Kaul, I., Grunberg, I. and Stern, M. (eds) (1999), *Global Public Goods. International Cooperation in the 21st Century* (New York/Oxford: Oxford University Press).

Koller, P. (2000), 'Westfälisches System oder globale Friedensordnung?', in *Politisches Denken. Jahrbuch 2000* (Stuttgart/Weimar: Metzler), 96–118.

Koller, P. (2001), 'Zur Semantik der Gerechtigkeit', in Koller, P. (ed.), 19–46.

Koller, P. (ed.) (2001), *Gerechtigkeit im politischen Diskurs der Gegenwart* (Wien: Passagen).

Koller, P. (2003), 'Soziale Gerechtigkeit – Begriff und Begründung', *Erwägen-WissenEthik* 14:2, 237–250.

Koller, P. (ed.) (2006), *Die globale Frage. Empirische Befunde und Ethische Herausforderungen* (Wien: Passagen).

Koller, P. (2008), 'Markt, Tauschgerechtigkeit und Macht', in *Normative und institutionelle Grundfragen der Ökonomik. Jahrbuch 7: Macht in der Ökonomie* (Marburg: Metropolis), 215–240.

Koller, P. (2009), 'International Law and Global Justice', in Meyer, L. (ed.).

Meyer, L. (2005), *Historische Gerechtigkeit* (Berlin/New York: de Gruyter).

Meyer, L. (ed.) (2009), *Legitimacy, Justice and Public International Law* (Cambridge: Cambridge University Press).

Miller, D. (1976), *Social Justice* (Oxford: Oxford University Press).

O'Neill, O. (2000), *Bounds of Justice* (Cambridge: Cambridge University Press).

Oxfam International (2002), *Rigged Rules and Double Standards. Trade, Globalisation, and the Fight against Poverty* (Oxford: Oxfam).

Pogge, T. (2002), *World Poverty and Human Rights* (Cambridge/Oxford: Polity Press).

Rawls, J. (1971), *A Theory of Justice* (Cambridge, MA: Harvard University Press).

Rawls, J. (1999), *The Law of Peoples* (Cambridge, MA: Harvard University Press).

Roover, R. de (1958), 'The Concept of the Just Price: Theory and Economic Policy', *The Journal of Economic History* 18, 418–434.

Singer, P. (2002), *One World. The Ethics of Globalization* (New Haven/London: Yale University Press).

Sterba, J. (1980), *The Demands of Justice* (Notre Dame/London: Notre Dame University Press).

Stiglitz, J. (2006), *Making Globalization Work* (New York: Norton).

Stiglitz, J. and Charlton, A. (2006), *Fair Trade For All. How Trade Can Promote Development* (Oxford: Oxford University Press).

Woods, N. (1999), 'Order, Globalization, and Inequality in World Politics', in Hurrell, A. et al. (eds), 8–35.

Chapter 8
Poverty and Responsibility

Stefan Gosepath

In this world, it is all too often the case that people exist in absolute and not just relative misery. Large parts of the earth's population live in poverty; they suffer from diseases; they are subjected to natural disasters or cruel wars accompanied by displacements and depredation; they die in famines, or at the least suffer greatly from a lack of food, access to basic health commodities, water, housing, and basic sanitary facilities; or they find themselves subject to other forms of plight. These are all states of need that threaten the very existence of those people. It is both generally and reciprocally accepted that such states constitute disadvantages that entitle these people to compensation, if the following conditions are met: As a rule, these persons must have entered into these circumstances through no fault of their own, and they must be unable to remove themselves from them without extraordinary sacrifices and external help. The persons in question must be unable to deliberately influence their circumstances, or at least only be able to influence them to an insignificant degree. The restrictions the circumstances place upon these people must objectively stop them from achieving things that are universally regarded as essential, including first and foremost the satisfaction of basic human needs.[1] Under such conditions, people are threatened with the violation of basic needs, including bodily integrity, security and subsistence. People who cannot afford a combination of the various goods and abilities sufficient to satisfy these basic needs and to achieve those things we regard as essential are called destitute; they exist in a state of need.

According to a widely shared understanding, circumstances that are generally and reciprocally accepted to be states of emergency entitle those in need of help through no fault of their own to social support. When confronted with poverty, destitution and misery – possible qualifications for self-inflicted poverty aside – we have a very clear intuition as to what we should do. Destitute persons are entitled to the help of those who live in better circumstances. Almost everybody would agree that such conditions are truly terrible for those affected. Their plight is a moral wrong, that is, an immoral situation, and therefore, for moral reasons, it should be eradicated without fail. Most people would regard helping other persons in urgent, life threatening need and deferring one's own interests while doing so as an obvious moral obligation. Very few would be so cold-hearted as to deny any feeling of obligation at all to help in an emergency.

1 Cf. Hinsch (2002, chap. V); Gosepath (2004, chap. V.1.5).

Even if one agrees that all 'decent' people share the idea that states of need justify a claim for support, it is still difficult to give a plausible concept of help in case of need, not just for a random 'man on the street', but also for philosophical conceptions of morality. The answers to the following questions are especially unclear and contentious: (1) Who should help in case of need? Who is responsible for correcting the state of need? (2) Who exactly should receive help in case of need – just the people nearby or all members of a society, or even those living far away? (3) To what extent should we provide help in case of need? What should we deny ourselves in order to help others in case of need? (4) Are we at all *obligated* to help in case of need and if so, in what sense?

Out of this complex of problems, we will for now single out the first question for a brief discussion: (1) Who should help in case of need? Who is responsible for correcting the state of need?

Firstly, moral agents are generally responsible in a weak sense and to varying degrees for all things they can influence (or could have influenced) with their acts. If one accepts this position, one must turn to the question of attributing this general responsibility for removing wrongs to certain persons (or groups). If persons as members of groups are also responsible for the correction of wrongs they did not cause, which member of these groups exactly should be the one to correct the wrong or the state of need? The principles of morality must always refer to identifiable subjects who must be specified in the moral principle in question.[2] The difficulty lies in the identification of the persons who should actually correct the morally wrong circumstances. In some cases there are a number of persons who would be able to act accordingly, and some of them must be attributed a special responsibility; in other cases, the task of correcting the wrong or the states of need places excessive demands on individual persons. In both cases, the obligation is in danger of eroding, because in these cases of emergency nobody actually acts although everybody agrees that there is a need for action. It is morally unacceptable to be confronted with a real, massive plight and with misery that could be eradicated and then to simply allow it to continue and implausibly claim that no one is responsible for helping. Instead, one must ensure that at least in extreme cases of emergency the responsibility to help can always be attributed to someone. It is not a question of rights: They are always empty if no actual addressees for the obligation to implement them are named. Rather, the question is how to identify the right responsible agents out of the large contingent of persons able to fulfil the obligation and, according to secondary moral reasons, obligated to afford the help that is needed.

Now, who should be the one to help? Who has the specific obligation to do it? The addressees of moral obligations are first of all we as members of the comprehensive community of all human beings, and this means us as individuals and all of us together; and as such members we are primarily required to respect the subjective moral rights of others and to act accordingly. According to the classic

2 Cf. O'Neill (2001).

model of personal responsibility, the individual human being is the subject of responsibility.[3] Individuals have the responsibility and the obligation to establish just conditions. Individuals are primarily the subjects of responsibility, first and foremost for their own actions and inactions. As individual persons, we must accept responsibility for our individual actions and their results insofar as we can change them to the best of our knowledge through our actions or inactions. This is required by the moral principle of subsidiarity, according to which individuals are primarily responsible for achieving what is in their power instead of leaving the tasks to the community.[4] The individual has an obligation as well as a right to personal responsibility and self-help.

Clearly individual attributions of responsibility are not sufficient for all cases of responsibility for changeable, morally wrong states of affairs. To demand that individuals by themselves establish just conditions (everywhere and at once) is often excessive. The individual moral responsibility for the correction of unjust grievances and wrongs must be restricted.[5] For practical reasons alone a general individual obligation to better the circumstances could not be fulfilled – after all, no one can remove all grievances by themselves. An individual obligation to help in case of need would also be an excessive moral demand for individuals who should be able to arrange their life autonomously according to their 'basic projects' and in accordance with equal chances and liberties for everyone. After all, the autonomous arrangement of the agents' lives is a moral value that is important enough that we have a legitimate interest in affording them the (necessary) space. This is another reason why the individual moral responsibility for removing unjust grievances must be less extensive.

Therefore, individuals cannot be wholly responsible for correcting a generally deficient state of affairs; they may however contribute something towards its improvement. This duty to help those in need addresses all members of the moral community of human beings and demands of them in their capacity as 'citizens of the world' to create institutions which may effectively put a stop to such rights violations, for (all) individuals collectively share a common moral responsibility. Because such states of need can only be remedied through the (coordinated) actions of many, this is a communal task. Thus in such a case individuals assign responsibility to collectives as a means of fulfilling their individual responsibility.

But the responsible collective in question is not necessarily one of perpetrators or of culprits. It is not only those causing injustice who have the duty to alleviate or correct it. Because in many cases injustice is not brought about through culpable causation and because individuals are often not up to the task of rectifying an injustice, those who are capable of doing so at an acceptable cost have the duty

3 Cf. Gosepath (2006, 388).

4 Cf. Gosepath (2004, chap. III.6.1); see also Gosepath (2005).

5 Cf. Schlothfeldt (2006).

to help. This position ascribes the responsibility to help in a crisis to individuals collectively, even though these individuals do not have a 'causal responsibility'.[6]

One could, it is maintained, structure this collective responsibility for the correction of injustice along the lines of the concept of liability. We all have a considerable interest in mechanisms designed to prevent damages (pre-emptive effect of liability regulations) and to correct them or compensate for them in case damages do arise. This is why we together as a society should agree on such mechanisms (i.e. we should do so for moral reasons). In this scenario, a group may be held collectively responsible even though not all of its members bear the blame.[7] This is a case of vicarious liability without partial responsibility. Collective liability for risk or absolute liability (instead of tortuous liability) means to be held responsible for the actions of others. In the case of responsibility or liability for injustices it is often not possible to assign distributive blame to the group, i.e. the blame cannot be allocated among the individual members. Thus the group should be held responsible for correcting such wrongs, precisely because they cannot be imputed to the individual members. There is only one possible way of fulfilling this duty, and that is through effective cooperation. This is why collective liability in the last resort creates a duty to cooperate: Prospectively to provide for possible risks and retrospectively to cope with the shared responsibility for manmade ills and injustices. The duty is to come together to engage in collective action and to create institutions to collectively manage common responsibility.

In order to account for the individual distributive (joint) responsibility in an initially randomly composed group, a responsibility which at the same time opens up the possibility of effectively putting an end to injustices without overly burdening the individuals, it is necessary to institute a coordinated collective based on principles of fairness. If a randomly composed group can transform itself into a collective which is capable of acting and of developing procedures of decision-making in a situation in which rational human beings should have a clear understanding of the moral nature of the action required, then such a group can be said to be responsible.[8]

The collective does not necessarily need to be an established and institutional entity to be able to engage in responsible action. Loose aggregates of people may be considered for the assumption of collective responsibility if they meet the above conditions. This is particularly relevant where deficiencies requiring collective action exist but where responsible institutional collectives have not yet been firmly established, such as in the case of world poverty. In order to account for the particular individual (joint) responsibility a collective must be established according to principles of fairness which can, in a continuous and steady manner, effectively put an end to the existing serious grievances. Based

6 For this slightly unfortunate expression for a particular kind of responsibility cf. Hart (1986).

7 Cf. Feinberg (1968).

8 Cf. Teubner (1994, 118).

on previous experience we can say that a state-like structure would best meet the requirements for a solution of the problem of coordinating shared responsibility. Various alternatives are however presently emerging and are being discussed as part of the concept of 'Global Governance'.

Once an effective collective is established, possibly taking the shape of a state-like organisation, one would expect it to guarantee as a rule the individual adherence to primary moral reasons by means of legal sanctions as well as to regulate the individuals' commonly shared responsibility with the purpose of creating a just state of affairs. Thus one advantage of collective liability is that the compensation for deficiencies is made easier. The second advantage is that responsibility and liability become internalised. For legal rules of liability aside, we wish to achieve and should achieve a situation where certain individuals feel responsible and accept and, if possible, internalise the distribution. Only then can we achieve a viable social practice effectively regulating responsibility. A third advantage is that, ideally, agents begin adjusting their risk calculation and thus improve the level of foresight.

A more precise definition of the individuals' duties is, however, required, if we are to know exactly who is responsible for what. Furthermore, because the group members together defined the desired goal, the group is responsible for the actions undertaken in achieving that goal. The collective responsibility is thus distributed among members in the form of sub-tasks. Therefore, collective responsibility is not a substitute for individual responsibility; instead, the former complements the latter with an additional element, i.e. that amount of partial responsibility assigned by the community of responsibility. The group members meet their shared responsibility by reasonably allocating their duties in the form of a social and moral division of labour, whereby individuals are either evenly taxed or whereby only a few people are assigned tasks for which they are adequately compensated. Thus, when specifying individual responsibilities, a certain degree of re-individualisation of collective liability is involved by which the group determines the internal measure for the distribution of burdens.

Finally, the creation of collective responsibility presents itself as follows: In a first step, actions, rights and obligations are ascribed to the collective agent as such. In a second step, profits and losses are individually distributed among the members according to their causal, moral and functional responsibility as well as to criteria of effectiveness and personal bonds. It is here that different criteria can be combined and weighed against each other. It thus makes sense from a moral point of view to maintain that the causing of an injustice is the most important measure for the attribution of responsibility.[9] Only where this cannot be applied exclusively because the moral demands on the culpable individual become excessive should different criteria be applied, such as how much individuals contribute to the risk of exacerbating injustices or in how far they tolerate or profit from injustice. The

9 For this principle cf. Barry (2005), 'Understanding and Evaluating the Contribution Principle', and 'Applying the Contribution Principle'.

criterion of ability may also be applied. Where even this is impossible, all members should assume an equal share of responsibility. A two-step procedure such as ours is attractive because it combines the advantages of collective liability with the appeals of an individualised approach. Collective liability ensures that the victims of moral ills receive compensation even where no individual causation can be determined; the individual distribution of this approach generates an individually assignable share of the duty to alleviate injustices. Thirdly, in recognition of the joint responsibility, a system of insurances should be introduced along with a statutory duty to insure. This generates a reasonable and fair allocation of individuals' rights to protection from moral wrongs. Where people are generally willing to participate in such a scheme, the burden for the individual member can be kept to a relative minimum, and no excessive moral demands are made. Where people are not prepared to enter into this scheme voluntarily, the coordinated collective must resort to sanctions in order to ensure that all members satisfy their fair share of the collectively shared responsibility for fair conditions.

In conclusion we may say that this political construction of collective responsibility enables us to specify the addressee of the duty to help as well as to solve the problem of coordination and excessive moral demands. We may thus hope that the global social ills, insofar as this is empirically possible, can be corrected or at least significantly alleviated.

References

Barry, C. (2005), 'Understanding and Evaluating the Contribution Principle', in Føllesdal, A. et al. (eds), 100–135.

Feinberg, J. (1968), 'Collective Responsibility', *Journal of Philosophy* 65, 674–688. Reprinted in May, L. and Hoffman, S. (eds) (1991), *Collective Responsibility (Lanham)*, 53–67.

Føllesdal, A. et al. (eds) (2005), *Real World Justice: Grounds, Principles, Human Rights, and Social Institutions* (Kluwer/Springer).

Gosepath, S. (2005), 'The Principle of Subsidiarity', in Føllesdal, A. et al. (eds), 153–166.

Gosepath, S. (2006), 'Verantwortung für die Beseitigung von Übeln', in Heidbrink, L. et al. (eds), 387–408.

Gosepath, S. (2004), *Gleiche Gerechtigkeit. Grundlagen eines Liberalen Egalitarismus* (Frankfurt/Main: Suhrkamp).

Hart, H. (1968), 'Postscript: Responsibility and Retribution', in Hart, H. (ed.), 211–230.

Hart, H. (ed.) (1968), *Punishment and Responsibility* (Oxford: Oxford University Press).

Heidbrink, L. et al. (eds) (2006), *Verantwortung in der Zivilgesellschaft. Zur Konjunktur eines Widersprüchlichen Prinzips* (Frankfurt/Main: Campus).

Hinsch, W. (2002), *Gerechtfertigte Ungleichheiten* (Berlin/New York: de Gruyter).

Lübbe, W. (ed.) (1994), *Kausalität und Zurechnung. Über Verantwortung in Komplexen Kulturellen Prozessen* (Berlin: Walter de Gruyter).

O'Neill, O. (2001), 'Agents of Justice', in *Metaphilosophy* 31 (2001), 180–195. Reprinted in Pogge, T. (ed.) (2001), *Global Justice* (Oxford: Blackwell) and in Kuper, A. (ed.) (2005), *Global Responsibilities* (New York/London: Routledge), 37–52.

Schlothfeldt, S. (2006), *Pflichten von Individuen und Gruppen bei der Behebung gravierender Übel. Ein Plädoyer für eine gemeinsame Verpflichtung, Habilitationsschrift* (Paderborn: mentis).

Teubner, G. (1994), 'Die unsichtbare "Cupola". Kausalitätskrise und kollektive Zurechnung', in Lübbe, W. (ed.), 91–143.

Chapter 9
Absolute Poverty and Global Inequality[1]

Darrel Moellendorf

> There is no question of relieving others at the cost of hardship to yourselves; it is a question of equality. At the moment your surplus meets their need, but one day your need may be met from their surplus. The aim is equality. (Paul of Tarsus, 2 Corinthians, 8:13–14)

Our world contains staggering poverty. A recent World Bank study estimates that 1.4 billion people are living on less than $1.25 PPP a day, and 2.4 billion on less $2 PPP a day (Chen and Ravallion 2008).[2] There is controversy surrounding the accuracy of these figures.[3] But no one denies that billions of people are living in absolute poverty. This is a moral catastrophe that replays itself every day, all the more horrible because the costs of eliminating it are so paltry. Thomas Pogge argues very powerfully that a program of transfers to the desperately poor, the starving and dying children of the world for example, could be instituted without causing any significant hardship to the very wealthy (Pogge 2008, 9–10 and 211). Moreover, according The United Nations Development Programme in 1998 the total assets of the 200 richest people in the world were $1,042 billion; at a cost of less 1 per cent of the net wealth of these super rich ($7–8 billion) access to primary education could be provided to every child around the world (UNDP 1999, 38).

---

1 I would like to thank Christoph Broszies, Henning Hahn, the graduate students in their course on global justice at Universtität Bremen, and the participants in the workshop on Absolute Poverty and Human Rights at Universität Erfurt for discussions that helped me to improve this chapter. I would also thank the organisers of that conference for the opportunity to make a presentation. I began work on this chapter while receiving support from the Deutscher Akademischer Austausch Dienst, and enjoying the hospitality of the Institut für Interkulturelle und Internationale Studien at Universtität Bremen. I completed it at the beginning of a membership at the Institute for Advanced Study with the support of the Friends of the Institute for Advanced Study. I am deeply grateful to all of these organisations for their generous support.

2 'PPP' stands for 'purchasing power parity', which is meant to be a measure of the equivalent in the local currency of what $1.25 or $2 would buy in the US, in this case at 2005 prices. The enterprise of establishing such equivalencies is, of course, very complex and controversial. The report by Chen and Ravallion is in fact based upon a newly revised PPP.

3 For criticisms of the World Bank's approach see Reddy (2008). For a reply see Ravallion (2008).

Our world also contains deep and persistent inequality. The *World Development Report 2006* offers several examples. One is the under five mortality rate. 'A baby born in Mali in 2001 had an approximately 13 per cent chance of dying before reaching the age one, with this chance declining only slightly (to 9 percent) even if the baby were born into the top quintile of the asset distribution. By contrast, a baby born in the United States the same year had a less than 1 percent chance of dying in its first year' (World Bank 2006, 56). More generally, in 2001 the mortality rate for children under five was nearly 26 times higher in the countries of Sub-Saharan Africa than in the OCED countries (UNDP 2003, 38–39). According to the World Health Organisation, 'Over 60% of deaths in developed countries occur beyond age 70, compared to about 30% in developing countries' (WHO 2002, 44). Returning to the Mali–US comparison, consider education inequality: 'The average American born between 1975 and 1979 has completed more than 14 years of schooling (roughly the same for men and women, and in urban and rural areas), while the average school attainment for the same cohort in Mali is less than two years, with women's attainment less than half that for men, and virtually zero in rural areas' (World Bank 2006, 56). With the onset of adulthood the cumulative effects of these childhood inequalities is huge income disparity. In 1994 the average income in Mali at $54 per month was less than $2 PPP per day; in the US it was more than 20 times greater, $1,185 per month (World Bank 2006, 56). Considering the broader picture, the richest 5 per cent of the world's population earns 114 times that of the poorest 5 per cent. The total income of the richest 1 per cent is equal to that of the poorest 57 per cent. And the income of 25 million richest Americans is nearly as much as that of the 2 billion poorest people in the world (Milanovic 2002). Income inequality is, however, even less extreme than wealth inequality. The assets of the richest three people in the world are more than the combined GNP of all of the least developed countries (UNDP 1999, 38).

One important reason for reducing global inequalities is that it could serve as a means for eliminating absolute poverty under which so many people suffer. The fact that poverty could be eliminated by only very slightly reducing global inequality supplies an important premise to an argument that inequality is unjust.[4] The author believes that there is another less instrumental reason for maintaining that justice requires reducing global inequality. This reason is less instrumental in the sense that it does not derive from the service that reducing inequality plays in realising other morally important social arrangements. This chapter will sketch an argument for this view by discussing five premises that support the conclusion.

4 Charles Beitz is correct to point out that although such reasoning argues against inequalities of this sort (where poverty is great and the costs of eradicating are low) it cannot be employed to justify equality generally. See Beitz (2001).

Human Dignity and the Respect that it Requires are Appropriate Bases of the Justification of Principles of Global Justice

The inherent dignity of persons and the respect that is appropriate to such dignity is a useful place to start because of the wide appeal that these ideas have. Several important human rights documents, agreed upon during the twentieth century, begin by affirming the inherent dignity of persons. These are documents that a great many political elites have committed their regimes to observe and that provide hope for millions who are seeking more just political, economic, and social structures. And they typically acknowledge their basis in human dignity. The Preamble to the Universal Declaration of Human Rights begins, 'Whereas recognition of the inherent dignity and of the equal and inalienable rights of all members of the human family is the foundation of freedom, justice, and peace in the world …' (UDHR 1948). The Preambles of both the International Covenant on Civil and Political Rights and the International Covenant on Economic, Social and Cultural Rights postulate a basis in human dignity: 'Considering that, in accordance with the principles proclaimed in the Charter of the United Nations, recognition of the inherent dignity and of the equal and inalienable rights of all members of the human family is the foundation of freedom, justice and peace in the world …' (ICCPR 1976 and ICESCR 1976). Moreover, Article 5 of the African Charter on Human and Peoples Rights affirms that, 'Every individual shall have the right to the respect of the dignity inherent in a human being …' (ACHPR 1986).

To be sure, invoking the wide appeal of the claim that persons possess inherent dignity is to rest on a pragmatic point, a contingently accepted normative understanding of persons, not to appeal to a necessary moral truth or to the conclusion of an argument about deep moral foundations. But this seems appropriate to the task of justifying principles of justice. In the final section of *A Theory of Justice*, John Rawls distinguishes between justification and proof.

> [J]ustification proceeds from what all parties to the discussion hold in common. Ideally to justify a conception of justice to someone is to give him a proof of its principles from premises that we both accept, these principles having in turn consequences that match our considered judgments. Thus mere proof is not justification. A proof simply displays logical relations between propositions. Proofs become justification once the starting points are mutually recognized … (Rawls 1999, 508)

To begin as Rawls does is to commit oneself to a view of what an account of justice is about, namely that it seeks a resolution to practical problems, where there are sufficient values held in common for such a resolution to be possible. Accounts of justice are practical normative conceptions about how to order human affairs, suitable to the circumstances in which there is disagreement about such matters, but deeper agreement on some values. A person seeking a justification then has one eye on the social context, seeking to provide arguments that might provide the basis for a reasoned resolution to on-going disputes.

To invoke the inherent dignity of persons is to claim that all persons have a special moral status or standing. The attribution of human rights to persons is an example affirming that standing of persons. Human rights documents, which invoke the inherent dignity of persons, take that moral status of persons to be the warrant of a demand on institutions that their power be constrained and directed in ways expressed in the documents.

The inherent dignity of persons makes the attitude of respect appropriate. More specifically, respect of the kind that Stephen Darwall distinguishes as recognition respect. '[W]e respect something in the recognition sense when we give it standing (authority) in our relations to it' (Darwall 2006, 123). Recognition respect is the acknowledgment of this authority, which all humans have, to demand that the use of institutional power that affects them be appropriately constrained and directed. These constraints and directions are summed up in the human rights documents. Because the inherent dignity is a status possessed equally by all persons, human rights are equal for all persons. Equal treatment under common institutions is the baseline expectation.

Respect for Human Dignity Requires that the Institutions of Associations of a Certain Type Fulfil the Standards of Social Justice

In this section we briefly defend the claim that duties of justice exist between persons who have a pre-institutional moral duty of equal respect if those persons are co-members in an association that is (1) relatively strong; (2) largely non-voluntary; (3) constitutive of a significant part of the background rules for the various relationships of their public lives; and (4) governed by norms that can be subject to human control.[5] With respect to (1), an association is strong to the extent that it is (a) enduring; (b) comprehensively governed by institutional norms; and (c) regularly affecting the highest order moral interests of the persons associated with it. With respect to (2), an association is non-voluntary to the extent that there is no reasonable alternative to participating in the association.[6]

The defence of this claim involves the comparison of two different circumstances: In the first the four conditions unambiguously do not obtain; in the second they unambiguously do. Now, suppose that duties of justice do not exist between persons in the first circumstance. Persons have general moral duties to one another but no duties to obey, reform, or construct social institutions; there are no significant mediating institutions. In the second circumstance there are such institutions which, *ex hypothesis*, affect the highest order interests of persons in a

5 This idea is discussed further in Moellendorf (2006).

6 This account of non-voluntariness reads like a stipulation but the author believes that there are good reasons to accept it. See Cohen (1988, 239–254).

manner that conditions their public lives, but which although are changeable by collective effort are escapable for individuals only at unreasonably high moral expense. Imagine further that from the beginning of their lives, through no choice of their own, the life prospects of persons are dramatically different under these institutions, some having profoundly inferior prospects than others.

Now suppose the sceptic claims that in the second circumstance standards of justice do not apply, and there is therefore no sensible claim of injustice, despite the different life prospects of persons. The reasoning might go as follows: If duties of justice did not exist between persons when they were isolated, then they do not exist when they are not. But this would be to claim that the rules upon which the institutional order, which could be changed and which resulted in profoundly inferior life prospects for some members of the order, are not subject to the standards of justice. Although this might be the case if we assume that people have no pre-institutional moral duties to one another, it cannot be the case if persons owe one another a morally basic duty of respect. If respect requires anything of persons it surely at least demands justice of the institutions that inescapably govern social interactions and issue in significant effects upon persons.

The Global Economy Satisfies the Conditions of the Type of Institution that Must be Justice-Conforming

The previous section claimed that four conditions taken together constitute sufficient conditions for the application of standards of social justice. In this section it is argued that the institutions of the global economy satisfy these four conditions.

First consider strength. The strength of an association is a function of its (a) duration; (b) the extent of its governance by norms; and (c) the degree to which it affects the highest order interests of persons. The association created by the processes of economic globalisation is not a fleeting phenomenon. Rather it is a structural feature of capitalist economic development that has gathered pace recently with technological changes, but that has been observable since at least the early colonial era. It is governed primarily by the norm of competition for market share that requires firms to innovate ceaselessly and to reduce production costs. But norms of governance are also in place through, for example, the regulatory framework established by the World Trade Organisation (WTO) and the reciprocal recognition of the property law regimes of states. The WTO requires member states to abide by negotiated trade rules that are guided by four basic principles: Non-discrimination, Reciprocity, Market Access and Fair Competition (GATT 1994).

The globalisation of trade, investment, and finance has had profound effects on the highest order interests of persons. The author notes six such effects: (1) In some cases, state supported export-led development strategies have produced significant gains for the social development of countries (Chang 2002); (2) Foreign direct investment (FDI) is very often a requirement of domestic financing as well as financing from third party countries (Sit 2001); (3) Generally, globalisation has been associated with an increase in job insecurity (Standing 1999); (4) It has also been associated with a general trend towards increasing inequality within countries (Corina 2003); (5) Some of the poorest and most vulnerable people in the world have become worse-off in comparison to the rich. In the 1990s children in Sub-Saharan Africa were 19 times more likely to die than children in the world's richest countries. By 2003 this figure had grown to 26 times (UNDP 2003, 39); and (6) with the increased globalisation of speculative investing has come the increased danger of a generalised economic crisis. Consider the effects –sometimes referred to as network effects – far beyond Asia of the Asian economic crisis in the late 1990s (Keohane and Nye 2002, 199–200). The crisis did extensive damage to emerging markets. Eventually Russia defaulted on its debt and Brazil narrowly avoided complete financial collapse. States with economies heavily dependent upon exporting basic resources such as petroleum and precious metals faced dramatic declines in their GDP as a result of the crisis, 14–18 per cent in Angola and Kuwait and 9 per cent in Zambia (UNDP 1999, 41). As the author writes this an object lesson in global network effects is unfolding. The US Federal Reserve has offered AIG an $85 billion loan, needed because of losses it incurred from international credit default swaps, on grounds that if AIG were to fail to meet its obligation to insure the bonds purchased by banks around the world, the global financial effects could be catastrophic (Andrews et al. 2008). Regardless of whether persons are directly engaged with the global economy, their local economy is profoundly affected by international trade, FDI, lending, and speculative investing.

Second, consider non-voluntariness. Although state leaders are formally free either to deepen engagement with the global market or not, the fact that nearly every country in the world is a member of the WTO is evidence that there is no reasonable alternative development path. Moreover, in many cases, citizens of countries that choose this development path have no choice in the matter.

Third consider the significance of the background rules of the global economic association for the public rules that affect persons' lives. We have already canvassed several considerations relevant to this matter two paragraphs above, in discussing how the rules of trade and investment affect persons' lives. So, here we merely note two serious limitations that WTO rules have on the domestic policies that countries may pursue. First, the policies that states may employ in the pursuit of infant industry protection are limited by WTO rules. But there is extensive historical evidence that such protection is necessary for the economic development of countries (List 1966; Chang 2002). Second, the WTO's TRIPs provisions dramatically curtail the ability of states to encourage the production of life-saving pharmacological therapies. According to TRIPs Article 28, patent protection prohibits the 'making, using, offering for sale, selling, or importing' without consent of the patent-holder (TRIPs 1994). In effect, holding a patent gives the holder monopoly power in the market for the period of the patent. According to Article 33 this is 20 years (TRIPs 1994). Consider the effect on India, whose laws previously provided patent protection for pharmaceutical processes for only seven years and provided no patent protection at all for pharmaceutical products (Hoekman and Kostecki 1994, 154). Without product patent protection firms may reverse-engineer pharmaceutical products and produce them according to their own processes. Since typically this is done without investing nearly as much in research and development as is required for invention, prices for pharmaceutical products are driven down, thereby allowing greater access for the poor. With the advent of TRIPs, this avenue of production is closed, with disastrous consequences for the poor.

Finally, the requirement that norms be subject to human control is obviously satisfied. There is no doubt that market competition can be limited, directed, or counterbalanced by deliberate public policy. And obviously WTO rules and property law regimes can be amended. So, there is no reasonable doubt that the global economic association satisfies this condition.

Respect for Human Dignity Requires that the Principles which Justify Institutions Governed by Standards of Justice, are Such that Participants in Those Institutions Can Reasonably Accept Them

As noted in the first section, recognition respect of the inherent dignity of persons is the acknowledgment of the authority, which all persons have, to demand that use of institutional power that affects them be appropriately constrained and directed. These constraints and directions are enumerated as rights in the human rights documents. The determination of whether the constraint and direction of institutional power is appropriate is a matter of justification. To what might justification appeal in order to be consistent with human dignity? The answer must be based on an interpretation of the premise of human dignity that is consistent with it being the basis of human rights.

To begin, institutions that observe human rights offer persons the ability to pursue goals and values without interference, so long as they observe the same institutional rules for other persons. Consider, for example, the manner in which Article 3 of the Universal Declaration of Human Rights constrains the use of power and force: 'Everyone has the rights to life, liberty and the security of person' (UDHR). Observance of the article requires that institutions do not infringe on the life, liberty and security of others. Pogge is correct to argue that when a right is violated, the moral demand that we halt the violation is a consequence of the negative duty against infringing on it (Pogge 2008, 70–73 and 177–178). But observance of human rights not only constrains the use of power, it also directs it. For observing Article 3 requires not only a negative duty of non-interference, but also a duty to ensure (at least) the requisite institutional functioning for policing and prosecuting wrongdoing (Shue 1996). Constructing institutions in order to observe human rights, then, involves seeing persons as sources of practical reasons; reasons, for example, to limit institutional reach and to ensure that institutions make adequate provisions.

Respecting human dignity then can be seen as taking humans as sources of practical reasons in this sense outlined above. Rawls states this as taking persons to be 'self-authenticating sources of valid claims' (Rawls 2001, 23). This is a conception of inherent dignity as the status to make claims on institutions which they ought to observe. But if the source of the reason that guides the use of institutional power is the claim that persons may make to have it so guided, then the principle which underlies the institutional construction must be one that persons can reasonably endorse. An institution directed by a principle that persons cannot reasonably endorse, is an institution that is not respecting persons as sources of practical reasons. There is, then, another sort of respect for human dignity, in addition to the recognition respect that institutions can express in their functioning. This we shall call *justificatory respect*. Justificatory respect requires that the principle that guides institutional functioning be such that it can be reasonably endorsed by the persons participating within the institutions.[7] Respect for human dignity then requires a justification of institutional principles that can be reasonably accepted by those who live under them.[8]

Reasonable acceptance is not equivalent to actual acceptance. The justification cannot be held hostage to the unreasonable demands of persons. In order not to be question begging such a justification must involve an account of the reasonable conditions under which principles could be accepted that is not itself dependent on the principles justified. There are various attempts at this offered in, for example, the constructivist accounts of Habermas, Rawls, and Scanlon.[9] This is clearly a major philosophical project. But, it is hoped that the next section will be convincing that enough can be said for present purposes without having to develop anything like a full account of the justification of principles.

Constructivist accounts take the justification of principles to be a function of whether we could endorse them as generally binding from a perspective that is suitably qualified so as to prevent the endorsement from being affected by unreasonable threats. In establishing a common perspective from which each person can endorse principles that are binding on everyone, constructivist accounts also offer a justification especially suited to the premise of the equal dignity of persons. Each person is equally respected by the demands of the justification that

7 On the idea that respect for human dignity has implications for both institutional operation and the justification of principles according to which they operate see also Darwall (2006, 244).

8 Compare this to Rainer Forst's account of a right to justification in Forst (2007, 291–327); and in Forst (2005). Compare this also to Darwall (2006, 272): '[O]ne demand that anyone has the authority to make is that he not be subject to demanding (coercive) conduct that cannot be justified by second-personal reasons'. See also Gosepath (2004, 200–211). Finally, see Rawls (1999, 513), '[R]espect for persons is shown by treating them in ways that they can see to justified'.

9 See for example Habermas (1983, 53–125; 2004, 324–356), Rawls (1999, 15–19 and 118–123; 1980) and Scanlon (1982; 1998).

prevent one from promoting a principle as binding on persons unless one accepts it as also binding upon oneself.

The Criterion of Reasonable Acceptance Establishes a Presumption of Equal Treatment Under the Rules of the Institutional Order

The principle 'institutions should be arranged so as to realise maximally the interests of persons in group G' cannot be reasonably accepted *pro tanto* by persons who are not members of group G. Without some further justification persons not in G could not reasonably be expected to support this principle since it seems to favour members of G arbitrarily. Since G could be any group whatsoever there is a *pro tanto* case for a principle of equal treatment, such as 'institutions should be arranged so as to realise equally the interests of all those living under the institutions'.[10]

On the face of it there are four plausible exceptions that could support a difference between the *pro tanto* endorsement of a principle of equal treatment and the principle when finally justified: (1) Some persons could deserve to have their interests treated less well because of something they have done to harm the interests of others; (2) some persons could voluntarily consent to lesser realisation of their interests or to taking certain risks of this outcome; (3) there might be differences in morally important needs requiring more resources to satisfy; or (4) offering incentives that produce differential outcomes could benefit everyone in comparison to their condition under equality. The *prima facie* principle of equality might not, then, upon further consideration, be appropriate because of one of these exceptions.

Conclusion

The premises that we have been discussing comprise the following argument:

- Human dignity and the respect that it requires are appropriate bases of the justification of principles of global justice.
- Respect for human dignity requires that the institutions of associations of a certain type fulfil the standards of social justice.
- The institutions of the global economic order satisfy the conditions of the type of institution that must be justice conforming.
- Respect for human dignity requires that the principles, which justify institutions governed by standards of justice, are such that participants in those institutions can reasonably accept them.

10 See also Gosepath (2004, 200–211).

- The criterion of reasonable acceptance establishes a presumption of equal treatment under the rules of the institutional order.
- Therefore, respect for human dignity requires the institutions of the global economic order satisfy a presumption of equal treatment.

Taking persons as possessors of inherent dignity establishes a *prima facie* principle of equality under institutions, including distributive institutions. This suggests a method for considering whether distributive inequalities between people who share common and unavoidable institutions are, all things considered, just despite their violation of the *prima facie* equality principle: One must consider whether the exceptions to equality adumbrated section 5 apply.

It is highly implausible to believe that these exceptions apply when considering the bulk current global inequality. The child growing up in Mali, for example, has done nothing to deserve her inferior health and education prospects. Nor has she voluntarily chosen them or put herself at risk having them by her choices. It is outrageous to suppose that her needs are so much less than the child growing up in an OCED country. Finally, the arguments of Pogge and the UNDP concerning the relative costs of eliminating absolute poverty also lend credence to the claim that alternative institutions can be devised that would better realise the child's interest in health. It's certainly not the case that everyone is benefiting from these massive global inequalities. If we assume the inherent dignity of this child and children like her in the underdeveloped world, we have good reasons to believe that the inequalities between their life prospects and children growing up in OCED countries are seriously unjust.

References

ACHPR, African Charter of Human and Peoples Rights (1986), *The African Charter of Human and People's Rights*. Available at <http://www1.umn.edu/humanrts/instree/z1afchar.htm> [last accessed 22 September 2008].

Andrews, E. et al. (2008), 'Feds $85 Billion Loan Rescues Insurer', *The New York Times*, 17 September 2008. Available at <http://www.nytimes.com/2008/09/17/business/17insure.html?sq=credit%20debt%20swas&st=cse&adxnnl=1&scp=1&adxnnlx=1221746792-ZMs7pvGOBxr5yoQSFRxAiw> [last accessed 18 September 2008].

Beitz, C. (2001), 'Does Inequality Matter?', in Pogge, T. (ed.).

Chang, H. (2002), *Kicking Away the Ladder: Development Strategy in Historical Perspective* (London: Anthem Press).

Chang, H. (ed.) (2003), *Rethinking Development Economics* (London: Anthem Press).

Chen, S. and Ravallion, M. (2008), 'The Developing World is Poorer than We Thought, but no Less Successful in the Fight Against Poverty', *Policy Research Working Paper, World Bank*. Available at <http://econ.worldbank.org/docsearch> [last accessed 22 September 2008].

Cohen, G. (1988), *History, Labour, and Freedom: Themes from Marx* (Oxford: Oxford University Press).

Corina, G. (2003), 'Globalization and the Distribution of Income Between and Within Countries', in Chang, H. (ed.).

Darwall, S. (2006), *The Second Person Standpoint* (Cambridge, MA: Harvard University Press).

Forst, R. (2005), 'Die Würde des Menschen und das Recht auf Rechtfertigung', *Deutsche Zeitschrift für Philosophie* 53:4, 589–596.

Forst, R. (2007), *Recht auf Rechtfertigung* (Frankfurt/Main: Suhrkamp Verlag).

GATT (1994), Article I:1. Available at <http://www.wto.org/english/docs_e/legal_e/legal_e.htm#finalact> [last accessed 22 September 2008].

Gosepath, S. (2004), *Gleiche Gerechtigkeit: Grundlagen eines Liberalen Egalitarianismus* (Frankfurt/Main: Suhrkamp Verlag).

Habermas, J. (1983), *Moralbewusstsein und Kommunikatives Handeln* (Frankfurt/Main: Suhrkamp Verlag).

Habermas, J. (2004), *Wahrheit und Rechfertigung* (Frankfurt/Main: Suhrkamp Verlag).

Hoekman B. and Kostecki, M. (1994), *The Political Economy of The World Trading System* (Oxford: Oxford University Press).

ICCPR, International Covenant on Civil and Political Rights (1976), Available at <http://www.unhchr.ch/html/menu3/b/a_ccpr.htm> [last accessed 17 September 2008].

ICESCR, International Covenant on Economic, Social and Cultural Rights (1976), Available at <http://www.unhchr.ch/html/menu3/b/a_cescr.htm> [last accessed 17 September 2008].

Keohane, R. (ed.) (2002), *Power and Governance in a Partially Globalized World* (New York/London: Routledge).

Keohane, R. and Nye, J. (2002), 'Governance in a Globalizing World', in Keohane, R. (ed.).

List, F. (1966), *The National System of Political Economy*, translated by Sampson S. and Lloyd, M. (New York: Augustus M. Kelley Publishers).

Milanovic, B. (2002), 'True World Income Distribution, 1998 and 1993: First Calculations Based on Household Surveys Alone', *Economics Journal* 112:476, 51–92.

Moellendorf, D. (2006), 'Equal Respect and Egalitarian Justice', *Social Theory and Practice* 32:4, 601–616.

Pogge, T. (ed.) (2001), *Global Justice* (Oxford: Blackwell Publishers).

Pogge, T. (2008), *World Poverty and Human Rights*, 2nd Edition. (London: Polity Press).

Ravallion, M. (2008), 'Global Poverty Reassessed: A Reply to Reddy', *International Poverty Centre: One Pager* 66. Available at <http://www.undp-povertycentre.org/pub/IPCOnePager65.pdf> [last accessed 22 September 2008].

Rawls, J. (1980), 'Kantian Constructivism in Moral Theory', *Journal of Philosophy* 77:9, 515–572.

Rawls, J. (1999), *A Theory of Justice*, Revised Edition. (Cambridge, MA: Harvard University Press).

Rawls, J. (2001), *Justice as Fairness: A Restatement*, Kelly, E. (ed.) (Cambridge, MA: Harvard University Press).

Reddy, S. (2008), 'The New Global Poverty Estimates: Digging Deeper into a Hole', *International Poverty Centre: One Pager* 65. Available at <http://www.undp-povertycentre.org/pub/IPCOnePager65.pdf> [last accessed 22 September 2008].

Scanlon, T. (1982), 'Contractualism and Utilitarianism', in Sen, A. and Williams, B. (eds).

Scanlon, T. (1998), *What We Owe Each Other* (Cambridge, MA: Harvard University Press).

Sen, A. and Williams, B. (eds) (1982) *Utilitarianism and Beyond* (Cambridge: Cambridge University Press).

Shue, H. (1996), *Basic Rights*, 2nd Edition. (Princeton: Princeton University Press).

Sit, V. (2001), 'Globalization, Foreign Direct Investment, and Urbanization in Developing Countries', in Yusuf, S. et al. (eds).

Standing, G. (1999), *Labour Flexibility: Seeking Distributive Justice* (New York: St. Martin's Press).

TRIPs (1994), *Annex 1C of the Marrakech Agreement Establishing the World Trade Organization*. Available at <http://www.wto.org/english/docs_e/legal_e/27-trips_03_e.htm> [last accessed 22 September 2008].

UDHR, Universal Declaration of Human Rights (1948), *Universal Declaration of Human Rights*. Available at <http://www.un.org/Overview/rights.html> [last accessed 17 September 2008].

UNDP, United Nations Development Programme (1998), *Human Development Report 1998*. Available at <http://hdr.undp.org/en/media/HDR_1999_EN.pdf> [last accessed 23 September 2008].

UNDP, United Nations Development Programme (2003), *Human Development Report 2003*. Available at <http://hdr.undp.org/en/media/hdr03_complete.pdf> [last accessed 23 September 2008].

WHO, World Health Organization (2002), *Global Burden of Disease in 2002: Data Sources, Methods and Results*.

World Bank (2006), *World Development Report 2006*. Available at <http://www-wds.worldbank.org/external/default/main?pagePK=64193027&piPK=64187937&theSitePK=523679&menuPK=64187510&searchMenuPK=64187283&theSitePK=523679&entityID=000012009_20050928150847&searchMenuPK=64187283&theSitePK=523679> [last accessed 17 September 2008].

Yusuf, S. et al. (eds) (2001), 'Facets of Globalization: International and local Dimensions of Development', *World Bank Discussion Paper* No. 415 (Washington, DC: World Bank).

Chapter 10
Sufficientarianism both International and Intergenerational?[1]

Lukas Meyer

Introduction

An egalitarian understanding of justice may well be appropriate for well-ordered liberal societies (Rawls 2001, 8; Rawls 1999, Part I); it is, however, a sufficientarian understanding or a humanitarian duty of aid that is appropriate for global and intergenerational relations – or, so, John Rawls (Rawls 1999, 106, 118; Rawls 2001, 159) and others have argued (Kersting 2001; Blake 2002; Brock 2005; Miller 2005; Nagel 2005; Satz 2003; Beckermann and Pasek 2001, Part I; Meyer 2003b and 2005, chap. 2; Wall 2003). Far stronger reasons, however, speak on behalf of a sufficientarian conception of intergenerational justice than on behalf of a conception of international justice. First, there are special reasons in favour of a sufficientarian understanding of intergenerational justice. These reasons reflect an interpretation of the significance of the non-identity problem and of our uncertainty as to the consequences of our actions for the well-being of future people. Here, we will only discuss the normative implications of the non-identity problem. Second, the reasons often cited in favour of a sufficientarian understanding of global justice – namely, the undesirability of a world state, the global pluralism of conceptions of the good as well as problems of measuring relative differences globally – speak, in fact, far more strongly on behalf of a sufficientarian understanding of intergenerational justice, owing to non-contingent features of intergenerational relations. Here, we will only discuss the normative significance of problems in measuring relative differences globally and over time. Third, some of the most common instrumental reasons in favour of an egalitarian understanding do not hold for the relations among non-contemporaries.

1 I should like to thank David Heyd, Peter Koller, Andrew Williams, Dieter Birnbacher, Keith Bustos, Julian Culp, Sarah Kenehan, and Dominic Roser. Special thanks to Stanley Paulson and, as always, to Barbara Reiter.

Egalitarian and Sufficientarian Conceptions of Justice

Egalitarian conceptions comprise first those that include truly egalitarian reasons for action as Thomas Scanlon understands them – reflecting the notion of equality as having intrinsic value (Scanlon 2000) – and, secondly, those conceptions that have a continuous tendency to lead to equality, and in particular the priority view (Parfit 1997, 213). Conceptions of weak and strong sufficientarianism differ from both egalitaristic understandings (Frankfurt 1987; Crisp 2003; Casal 2007). Sufficientarian conceptions have a tendency to lead to equality only below the threshold. Above the threshold neither improving the position of the worse off nor even promoting equality, as such, are of concern. To simplify matters, we will identify sufficientarian justice with strong sufficientarianism that gives absolute priority to those below the threshold. The conception of strong sufficientarianism differs most clearly from both egalitarian understandings. Furthermore, strong sufficientarianism differs from both weak sufficientarianism and the priority view in precluding trade offs between persons above and below the threshold.

Before inquiring into a sufficientarian understanding of intergenerational and global justice, we might clarify further the subject matter of our discussion. The author understands sufficientarian claims to be claims backed by considerations of justice. In other words, the author does not share the view either that justice can be equated with egalitarian justice or that considerations of sufficiency justify humanitarian reasons only (Nagel 2005, 118). Those who defend such an understanding also tend to assume that the sufficiency threshold lies very low; that is, the threshold specifies a minimal value – and, as mentioned above, they hold that claims to a well-being at that threshold are not to be understood as justice claims. How the threshold value is to be understood substantially should, however, be left as an open question. A sufficiency threshold can be understood in such a way that people have justice claims to a threshold level of well-being that lies far above the minimum level required by humanitarian reasons.

Some disputants, most prominently Harry Frankfurt (Frankfurt 1999; Kersting 2002; Krebs 2003), hold the view: (1) that a sufficientarian understanding of justice holds generally, that is, for well-ordered societies as well as for international and also intergenerational relations. Accordingly, they deny that even cooperative structures sponsored and protected by a liberal state go hand-in-hand with egalitaristic claims to equality or to weighted improvement of well-being. A different and more popular view is: (2) With respect to these special cooperative schemes there is far-reaching reasonable dissent about justified inequalities even among those who hold that an egalitaristic conception is valid for these schemes (Rawls 2001, 47–50; Gutmann and Thompson 1996).

Brian Barry and others were correct in stressing that liberal cosmopolitanism does not entail an egalitaristic understanding of justice (Barry 1999a, 35; Pogge 2002, 169; Miller 2005, 65). Barry says that cosmopolitanism combines three elements: That individual beings have (ultimate) value and not collective entities, that each human being has equal moral value, and that the first two clauses apply to all human beings. Thus, we may not weigh the value of people differently according to features such as race, sex, or nationality and exclude some people from equal moral consideration either. While cosmpolitanism, so understood, excludes racist and extreme nationalist doctrines, it is equally compatible with many different substantive moral doctrines and corresponding understandings of justice. Importantly, it is compatible with both egalitarian and non-egalitarian conceptions of justice, for the three elements mentioned do not specify the criterion according to which we ought to consider equally all human beings. Liberal-cosmopolitan equal consideration may require either the elimination of relative differences of benefits among all people or the prioritarian improvement of the position of the less well-off or that all people have enough. Also, equal consideration allows one to hold differing conceptions of justice for different subjects; for example, holding an egalitarian conception for well-ordered liberal societies and a sufficientarian conception for international and intergenerational relations is allowed. In any case, a sufficientarian understanding of justice can be understood to reflect a notion of equal respect that is owed to all people. Egalitarian and non-egalitarian conceptions of justice interpret differently what it means morally to treat people as equals.

Both (1) those who hold a sufficientarian conception of justice; and (2) those who defend the view that there is reasonable dissent about justified inequalities within well-ordered societies can also hold the view that a plurality of legitimate basic political units characterised by differing shared conceptions of, in particular, domestic justice is a valuable feature of the world in which we live (Meyer 2000; Miller 2005). An egalitarian understanding of global justice is likely to be in conflict with such a view. Such an understanding attributes egalitarian justice claims to all people wherever they live and thus stands in conflict with, first, non-egalitarian interpretations of domestic justice. The egalitarian conception is likely to require both more (namely for persons who are not members of one's own society) and less (for members of one's own society) than the domestic sufficientarian conceptions do. Claiming, secondly, that an egalitaristic understanding is exclusively valid for well-ordered societies of the liberal type is clearly incompatible with an egalitarian understanding of global justice. The latter requires more, namely equal consideration of the relative differences among all people or the prioritarian improvement of the situation of the less well-off wherever they live. However, the lower the threshold of a sufficientarian understanding of global justice the more likely it is that it is compatible with both egalitarian and non-egalitarian conceptions of domestic justice. This, it is assumed, is the political or ideological reason for the popularity of the view – namely, among members of the affluent societies – that the relevant threshold of global sufficientarianism is to be specified in terms of a minimal humanitarian standard of well-being (Nagel 2005, 126).

We will begin our discussion by inquiring into, what is taken to be the most important particular reason for holding that a sufficientarian understanding of justice is appropriate for the relations between currently living people and their future non-contemporaries. We will then discuss one reason often cited in favour of international sufficientarianism. This reason, as this chapter hopes to show, speaks more strongly in favour of intergenerational than international sufficientarianism. In this chapter's concluding remarks attention will be drawn to the fact that some of the more common instrumental reasons in favour of an egalitarian conception of justice are irrelevant in the intergenerational realm.

The Non-Identity Problem and Sufficientarianism

A particular reason for holding a sufficientarian understanding of intergenerational justice relies upon a certain response to the so-called non-identity problem (Schwartz 1978; Kavka 1982; Parfit 1984, Part IV). The non-identity problem concerns the very possibility of intergenerational justice. Consider a policy of making intensive and extensive use of exhaustible resources for the aim of increasing the welfare of currently living people. If the policy is criticised for harming future people on the ground that this policy will predictably worsen their conditions of life and, thus, is likely to violate their welfare rights, a defender of the policy could reply by saying: Many, if not all of our actions have (indirect) effects not only on the conditions of life, but also on the composition of future persons, that is, on the number, existence, and identity of future persons. This is also true for actions that allegedly harm future persons. If the omission of the allegedly harmful action meant that the allegedly harmed person did not come into existence, then that person cannot be said to have been harmed by this action – or, at any rate, according to the normal understanding of harm.[2] With respect to persons whose existence is dependent upon the allegedly harming action, they cannot be worse off owing to this action than they would have been had this action not been carried out. For in that case, they would not have existed.

Some philosophers hold the view that future people whose existence depends upon currently living people's actions cannot have rights vis-à-vis the latter people's actions. Others argue that currently living people can violate the rights of future people even if the former cannot harm the latter (Kumar 2003). If so, future people cannot have welfare rights vis-à-vis currently living people. Or we can attempt to limit the practical significance of the non-identity problem. Some have suggested limiting the relevant actions to those that are not only likely but indeed necessary conditions of the existence of the concerned person (Roberts 1998). In addition, or alternatively, they attempt to delineate an alternative understanding of harm, the so-called threshold conception of

2 The common understanding is the subjunctive-historical interpretation of harm: an action (or inaction) at time t_1 harms someone only if the agent causes (allows) this person to be worse off at some later time t_2 than the person would have been at t_2 had the agent not interacted with (or acted with respect to) this person at all. For a detailed discussion see Meyer (2003b, 147–149 and 155–158).

harm,[3] according to which future people can be said to be harmed by currently living people's actions even if these actions are among the necessary conditions of the existence, identity or number of future people. According to a threshold understanding of harm an action harms a person if as a consequence of that action the person falls under a normatively defined threshold – this is to be understood as a sufficient condition of harming a person (Meyer 2003b, 152–158). The threshold understanding is unaffected by the non-identity problem, for here the finding of harm does not require a hypothetical comparison with the situation that would have occurred in the absence of the harming action. Such a notion of harm limits the practical significance of the non-identity problem to different degrees depending upon how the threshold is substantially defined (Meyer 2003a, section 3.2).

Such reasoning seems to suggest a specification of the relevant threshold as a *sufficientarian* standard defined in terms of absolute, noncomparative conditions. One could hold a unitary view of the threshold according to which one, and the same threshold would be applicable to all decisions. Even if we held that the same list of rights were attributable to all people (wherever and whenever they live), for example, those which are meant to protect basic capabilities of human beings, what these rights amount to will reflect contemporary social, economic, and cultural conditions (Sen 1984; Nussbaum 2000, 132).

Specifying the standard by attributing equal minimal rights to people is only one possible interpretation of the threshold. We might, instead, want to define the threshold in accordance with the two egalitarian conceptions, distinguished as follows: First, egalitarian considerations that address relative differences between people can help to specify the standard – and in at least two ways. We might hold that the standing of people relative to their contemporaries is important and that the threshold notion of harm ought to reflect, say, the average level of well-being that people realise, or that future people will realise: The higher the average level of well-being the higher the threshold level of harm should be set. According to one interpretation of such an egalitarian reading, presently existing people harm future people by causing them to realise a (much) lower level of well-being than their own contemporaries (Sher 1979, 389). In addition or alternatively, we might hold that the threshold level ought to reflect, say, the average level of well-being of the present generations upon whose decisions the existence, identity, and well-being of future people depend. According to such an interpretation, presently existing people harm future people by causing them to realise a (much) lower level of well-being than they enjoy themselves (Barry 1999b, 109). Still, even if egalitarian considerations that reflect a concern with the relative differences between people can contribute to the specification of the threshold, a plausible threshold is not going to be based on that concern, but will reflect primarily a concern with the absolute level of well-being of persons. Otherwise – this is an implication of the

3 This understanding can be expressed in the formula: an action (or inaction) at time t_1 harms someone only if the agent thereby causes (allows) this person's life to fall below some specified threshold.

first interpretation – any level of well-being would be considered justified as long as all future people fare equally badly. This presupposes attributing intrinsic value exclusively to equality – an implausible view. Moreover, to define the threshold standard of well-being of future people as the level of well-being achieved by currently living people (whatever it may be) is less than plausible, unless we were to attribute intrinsic value exclusively to intergenerational equality, so understood. This view would deny that currently living people may stand under a duty of justice positively to save for future people so that they will achieve a sufficientarian level of well-being (Rawls 2001, 159).

The second way in which egalitarian considerations can help to identify the standard is to rely on the priority view for specifying the threshold. On this interpretation, future people fall under the threshold unless they are as well-off as the priority view requires. However, this understanding gives rise to unreasonable demands on the currently living. For, given the large number of future people whose level of well-being can be affected by the decisions and actions of currently living people, the priority view will make unreasonable demands on the currently living. In assessing alternative options we would have to weigh the claims to improvements as well as to take into account both the size of the benefit and the number of beneficiaries; if the number of future people is sufficiently large, we would then have to choose the option that improves their well-being even if both their claims to improvements in well-being are weak and the benefits they receive are small. If the number of future people is sufficiently large, currently living people will stand under an obligation to improve their well-being even if in fulfilling the obligation they will lose (very) much in well-being and the improvements in well-being of future people are small or even trivial.

The objections to specifying the threshold in terms of the egalitarian conceptions as distinguished here present a particular reason for holding that the specification of the threshold ought to be informed by a sufficientarian understanding of justice, at least for intergenerational relations. In defining the relevant threshold we may also rely on considerations that reflect the significance of relative differences among future people or people who belong to different generations including the currently living. Considerations characteristic of the priority view may, also, be considered relevant for the specification of the threshold. It is implausible, however, to hold the view that we might define the relevant standard as reflecting egalitarian reasons solely of the two types distinguished: Reasons for diminishing relative differences among people and those for the prioritarian weighting of claims to improvements in well-being. By defining a threshold of well-being according to which both currently and future living people are able to reach a sufficientarian conception allows us to avoid the misleading implications of both egalitaristic conceptions: First, avoiding or reducing differences must not lead to a state of affairs in which people are worse off than they ought to be. Secondly, claims against currently living people are unreasonable if in fulfilling them the currently living people will bring about minimal or even trivial improvements of the well-being of future people but suffer losses themselves, causing them to fall under a plausible threshold level of well-being.

If these objections are valid, we have strong particular reasons for interpreting intergenerational justice in terms of a conception for which a sufficientarian threshold is of central significance. At the same time, the reasons for a sufficientarian understanding of intergenerational justice are not equally relevant for the relations among contemporaries – never mind whether we think of these contemporaries simply as people wherever they may live, or as members of a well-ordered liberal society, or as found in different basic political units. For the reasons reflect particular features of intergenerational relations: The non-identity problem simply does not arise in relations among contemporaries. The problem does not arise among institutionalised transgenerational legal entities such as Rawls's peoples or states understood as subjects of public international law, either. Also, the objections to egalitarian conceptions of intergenerational justice – to both the prioritarian conception and the conception relying on the notion that equality is of intrinsic value – reflect, in part, particular features of intergenerational relations: The large number of future people leads to unreasonable demands on currently living people; further, we can demand of currently living people that they positively save for future people only in the context of intergenerational relations. Thus, the reasons for a sufficientarian understanding of intergenerational justice are at least in part specific reasons and are not relevant for understanding either global justice or the notion of justice that holds among contemporary members of well-ordered societies.

Reasons for a Sufficientarian Conception of International Relations

A good number of reasons have been put forward on behalf of a sufficientarian understanding of international relations. Here, we can discuss only one of them. Some authors (Miller 2005, 4–10; Brock 2005, 348–350) claim that we cannot measure globally what we would need to measure in order to be able to determine what in accordance with egalitarian conceptions of justice is owed to people who belong to different societies. We cannot say what an egalitarian justice, to quote David Miller, 'means in a culturally plural world' (Miller 2005, 9), for we can neither assess the relative differences among people who live in very different, historically formed cultural and social contexts nor can we determine how well-off they are in a way that bears on the prioritarian attribution of weighted claims to improvements in well-being. In response, we ought to consider whether the alleged difficulties of measurement are simply greater than the difficulties of measurement in single societies or whether the difficulties of measurement are principally different and of a kind that they should be regarded as insuperable given the global pluralism of conceptions of the good and socially shared forms of life. Proponents of both egalitarian and non-egalitarian conceptions of justice agree that no problems that are principally different arise with respect to the measurement of some goods and especially the basic goods of survival when compared with the well-being of people wherever they might live. This is not to deny, of course, that the means necessary for supplying these goods vary and thus also the costs involved in providing and securing them; reaching, for example, the tolerable minimum of well-being in an OECD country requires secure access to a different set of goods than in a country of the so-called Third World. Applying a minimal sufficientarian threshold globally rather than within a single society does not, however, seem to entail principally different problems of measurement.

Principally different problems might arise, however, where we compare goods that are relevant for people's well-being above such a minimal threshold. People's well-being depends upon access to valuable options whose existence depends in turn upon collective and, often, also participatory goods whose supply is secured within bounded societies whose members share a particular historically and culturally formed understanding as to why these options are valuable to them (Meyer 2000). Access to such options – professions, social roles, being a mother or a father, and societal activities in sports and culture – is of vital importance to the well-being and social status of members of a society. For realising the value of self-respect, backed by social recognition, depends upon having access to such options and having success in pursuing them.

It seems plausible both that problems of comparatively measuring the well-being of individuals both within single societies and globally will vary depending upon which goods we compare and that we will face problems of measurements more often in international relations given the far more far-reaching global pluralism of both conceptions of the good and available life options when compared with a reasonable pluralism within a single (Rawlsian well-ordered liberal) society. Thus, a conception of global egalitarian justice will be able to take into account only a selection of goods – which raises questions about the meaningful applicability of the conception – or will have to make generalised assumptions about the significance of various goods for the realisation, say, of the value of self-respect. The assumption, given that the value of self-respect is equally transculturally significant, is that we can rely upon the value of self-respect for comparative measurements of the well-being of people (or for the prioritarian assessment of weighted claims to improvements in well-being).

Comparatively to measure the well-being of people is even more difficult in intergenerational relations, however. For our knowledge of the relevant conditions of life of future people is limited and this epistemic situation of ours seems insuperable. At least two considerations support the view that in our efforts to carry out such measurements with respect to future people we face principled different reasons. First, the particular way of life of future people is likely to depend in part upon those new and today unknown technologies to which they will have access. However, we cannot or can only with great difficulty predict technological developments (Birnbacher 1988, 168). Second, the collective way of life of future people will depend, in part, upon their own individual and collective decisions. We are not in a position to predict how they will decide to organise their lives socially or how they will want to live individually and we cannot hope to determine these decisions either, that is, where we believe that the individual and collective autonomy of future people ought to be secured (Meyer 1997, 145–150). We also know that the decisions of their predecessors will have an impact on what options more remote future people will have as individuals and collectively; we cannot hope to determine the decisions of intervening generations either and for the same reason.

Thus, it might well be true that we are in no position to know what we owe to more remote future non-contemporaries in accordance with egalitarian conceptions of justice. We are in no position to determine their pertinent relative differences, for the particular historically formed cultural and social contexts that the lives of remote future people will have are uncertain to us. We do know, however, that these particular contexts will be of decisive importance for the particular level of well-being that future people will enjoy. Accordingly, we cannot hope to determine today how well-off future people will be. We are in no position to know what impact our actions will have on the relative well-being of future people or their particular level of well-being, for their individual well-being will depend to a large part on socially shared understandings of what options are valuable as well as on who has access to them and how successful they are in pursuing them. At the very least, our discussion suggests that the epistemic problems of determining what is owed to future people in terms of sufficientarian threshold are less weighty.

Concluding Remarks

In conclusion it is worth pointing out that instrumental advantages of equality among contemporaries are of very little, if any, relevance where relations among non-contemporaries are concerned: There is no correlation between economic and political equality among non-contemporaries. This is one of the more common justifications for greater equality among citizens of one society: Large differences in wealth or income will make it possible for the rich to exercise impermissible power over the poor, which might, or is indeed likely to, lead to unacceptable inequalities in people's liberty rights. There is, however, an unchangeable power asymmetry between non-contemporaries (Barry 1989, 189, 246). Furthermore, it makes no sense to claim that greater income equality among non-contemporaries will further intergenerational harmony, reduce intergenerational envy, or strengthen a sense of intergenerational solidarity or communal belonging (Beckermann and Pasek 2001, 49).

References

Barry, B. (1989), *Theories of Justice. A Treatise on Social Justice* (Berkeley: University of California Press).

Barry, B. (1999a), 'Statism and Nationalism. A Cosmopolitan Critique', in Shapiro, I. (eds).

Barry, B. (1999b), 'Sustainability and Intergenerational Justice', in Dobson, A. (ed.).

Beckermann, W. and Pasek, J. (2001), *Justice, Posterity, and the Environment* (Oxford: Oxford University Press).

Birnbacher, D. (1988), *Verantwortung für zukünftige Generationen* (Stuttgart: Reclam).

Blake, M. (2002), 'Distributive Justice, State Coercion, and Autonomy', *Philosophy & Public Affairs* 30.

Brock, G. (2005), 'The Difference Principle, Equality of Opportunity, and Cosmopolitan Justice', *Journal of Moral Philosophy* 2.

Casal, P. (2007), 'Why Sufficiency Is Not Enough', *Ethics* 117.

Clayton, M. et al. (eds) (2000), *The Ideal of Equality* (Houndsmill: Macmillan).

Coates, A. (ed.) (2000), *International Justice* (Aldershot: Ashgate).

Crisp, R. (2003), 'Equality, Priority, and Compassion', *Ethics* 113.

Dobson, A. (ed.) (1999), *Fairness and Futurity. Essays on Environmental Sustainability* (Oxford: Oxford University Press).

Fotion, N. et al. (eds) (1997), *Contingent Future Persons. On the Ethics of Deciding Who Will Live, or Not, in the Future* (Dordrecht: Kluwer Academic Publishers).

Frankfurt, H. (1999), 'Equality and Respect', *Social Research* 64.

Gutmann, A. and Thompson, D. (1996), *Democracy and Disagreement* (Cambridge, MA: Harvard University Press).

Kavka, G. (1982), 'The Paradox of Future Individuals', *Philosophy and Public Affairs* 11.

Kersting, W. (2002), *Kritik der Gleichheit. Über die Grenzen der Gerechtigkeit und der Moral* (Weilerswist: Velbrück).

Krebs, A. (2003), 'Warum Gerechtigkeit nicht als Gleichheit zu begreifen ist', *Deutsche Zeitschrift für Philosophie* 51.

LaFollette, H. (ed.) (2003), *Oxford Handbook of Practical Ethics* (Oxford: Oxford University Press).

Meyer, L. (1997), 'More than They Have a Right to. Future People and Our Future Oriented Projects', in Fotion, N. et al. (eds).

Meyer, L. (2000), 'Cosmopolitan Communities', in Coates, A. (ed.).

Meyer, L. (2003a), 'Intergenerational Justice', in Zalta, E. (ed.). Available at <http://plato.stanford.edu/archives/sum2003/entries/justice-intergenerational>.

Meyer, L. (2003b), 'Past and Future. The Case for a Threshold Notion of Harm', in Meyer, S. et al. (eds).

Meyer, L. (2005), *Historische Gerechtigkeit* (Berlin and New York: de Gruyter).

Meyer, L. et al. (eds) (2003), *Rights, Culture, and the Law. Themes from the Legal and Political Philosophy of Joseph Raz* (Oxford: Oxford University Press).

Miller, D. (2005), 'Against Global Egalitarianism', *The Journal of Ethics* 9.

Nagel, T. (2005), 'The Problem of Global Justice', *Philosophy & Public Affairs* 33.

Nussbaum, M. (2000), 'Aristotle, Politics, and Human Capabilities. A Response to Antony, Arneson, Charlesworthy, and Mulgan', *Ethics* 111.

Parfit, D. (1984), *Reasons and Persons* (Oxford: Clarendon Press).

Parfit, D. (1997), 'Equality and Priority', *Ratio* 10.

Pogge, T. (2002), *World Poverty and Human Rights. Cosmopolitan Responsibilities and Reforms* (Cambridge: Blackwell).

Rawls, J. (1999), *The Law of Peoples* (Cambridge, MA: Harvard University Press).

Rawls, J. (2001), *Justice as Fairness. A Restatement* (Cambridge, MA: Harvard University Press).

Satz, D. (2003), 'International Economic Justice', in LaFollette, H. (ed.).

Scanlon, T. (2000), 'The Diversity of Objections to Inequality', in Clayton, M. et al. (ed.).

Schwartz, T. (1978), 'Obligations to Posterity', in Sikora, R. (eds).

Sen, A. (1984), *Resources, Values and Development* (Cambridge, MA: Harvard University Press).

Shapiro, I. et al. (eds) (1999), *Global Justice* (New York: New York University Press).

Sher, G. (1979), 'Compensation and Transworld Personal Identity', *Monist* 62.

Sikora, R. et al. (eds) (1978), *Obligations to Future Generations* (Philadelphia: Temple University Press).

Wall, S. (2003), 'Just Savings and the Difference Principle', *Philosophical Studies* 116.

Wenar, L. (2001), 'Contractualism and Global Economic Justice', *Metaphilosophy* 32.

Zalta, E. (ed.), *The Stanford Encyclopedia of Philosophy.* Available at <http://plato.stanford.edu>.

Chapter 11
The Alleged Dichotomy between Positive and Negative Rights and Duties[1]

Elizabeth Ashford

Liberty rights are uncontroversially held to be universal human rights. 'Special' welfare rights, which are grounded in special acts or special relationships are equally uncontroversial. But there has been considerable dispute over whether welfare rights can be general human rights, held by every human being simply by virtue of their humanity.

The aim in this chapter is to reinforce, from a different angle, two of Shue's principal arguments against there being a fundamental distinction between liberty rights and welfare rights such that only the former are genuine human rights. The first argument is that the enjoyment of the right to subsistence is essential to the enjoyment of any other rights, and so has to be acknowledged as a basic human right.[2]

The second argument addresses the duties imposed by welfare rights. Shue points out that the view that welfare rights can only be special rights is underpinned by our inherited picture of the duties imposed by rights as 'full of dichotomies', between positive and negative duties, perfect and imperfect duties, and general and special duties. On this inherited picture, liberty rights are held to impose primarily negative duties, whereas welfare rights are taken to impose primarily positive duties.[3] Negative duties are taken to be perfect and general, and to be stringent duties of justice that correspond to human rights. Positive duties, by contrast, are

---

1 A longer version of this contribution will be appearing in *Global Basic Rights*, ed. Charles Beitz and Robert Goodin (Oxford: Oxford University Press, forthcoming). I am grateful to Charles Beitz, Simon Caney, Rowan Cruft, Katrin Flikschuh, Pablo Gilabert, Robert Goodin, David Miller, Adina Preda, Henry Shue, Hillel Steiner, Leif Wenar and the members of a workshop on human rights at the University of Oslo for their extremely helpful comments on previous drafts.

2 See Shue (1996).

3 Shue also offers a sustained argument against dividing welfare rights and liberty rights into positive and negative rights, respectively, by showing that both kinds of rights impose both positive and negative duties. The focus of the argument in this chapter is to reinforce Shue's argument against the dichotomies between duties themselves, and show that even if we do accept a division of rights into positive and negative rights by distinguishing the primary duties they impose from secondary duties to enforce those primary duties, this does not indicate that welfare rights can only be special rights.

held to be either imperfect duties that do not correspond to rights, or special duties that can only correspond to special rights rather than human rights. Shue suggests that these dichotomies present an overly schematic picture of such duties.[4]

Shue's first argument, that the right to subsistence is a basic right, is that enjoyment of subsistence is a necessary precondition for the enjoyment of other rights, such that it is impossible to secure other rights without securing the right to subsistence. Our focus, in contrast, is on the substantive relationship between the right to subsistence and other rights. It is argued that while it might be conceptually possible to fully secure other rights in the absence of securing the right to subsistence, it is not possible to achieve the full securing of those rights in a way that can plausibly be held to be in the interests of the right-holder unless the right-holder's access to subsistence has been secured.

Turning to the second argument, it is then argued that because of this substantive interdependence, some liberty rights cannot be adequately respected until the right to subsistence has been fulfilled. Until the right to subsistence has been secured, even the primary duties imposed by such liberty rights may be imperfect in nature (in the sense that they are not exceptionless duties that strictly bind agents' conduct at all times, and they are not fully delineated). Thus negative duties of justice corresponding to liberty rights may in fact be imperfect. We conclude that imperfect duties may be general duties of justice owed to every human being, and that the imperfect nature of the positive duties imposed by welfare rights prior to their institutionalisation is no reason to deny that they constitute duties of justice. This supports Shue's claim that we should not be strait-jacketed by the standard dichotomies between duties that underpin the view that welfare rights cannot be human rights. The author therefore aims to reinforce Shue's argument about the interdependence between the right to subsistence and other rights, and in the light of this to reinforce at the same time his argument against our inherited picture of the rigid dichotomies between duties.

We begin the first section by discussing Shue's account of the interdependence between the right to subsistence and other rights, and in section two we argue for a substantive interdependence between them. Section three then turns to the implications of this substantive interdependence for the nature of the duties imposed by human rights, focusing on the right against child labour. It is argued that unless the right to subsistence has been secured, even the primary duties imposed by this right are most plausibly seen as imperfect in nature, and we conclude that the standard dichotomies between positive and negative duties are overly rigid.

Shue's Necessary Precondition Argument

Shue argues that enjoyment of the right to subsistence is essential to the enjoyment of any other right. He takes rights to be claims that the object of the right be

4 See Shue (1988, 687–704).

guaranteed a reasonable level of security, and argues that until the right to subsistence has been securely established, persons cannot enjoy reasonably secure access to the objects of other rights, including traditional liberty rights. Establishing a right to a reasonable level of security involves protecting the object of the right against standard threats. Lack of subsistence, or a threatened lack, is one of the most common and severe threats to the enjoyment of other rights. First, adequate nutrition is a precondition for the enjoyment of any rights involving rational autonomous activity. Second, unless continued enjoyment of subsistence has been guaranteed, people are liable to coercion and intimidation through threats of deprivation 'which can paralyse a person and prevent the exercise of any other rights as surely as actual protein or calorie deficiencies can'. He concludes that the enjoyment of the right to subsistence is 'necessary for enjoying' other rights.[5]

A response that has been given to Shue's argument is that it is possible to guarantee reasonably secure access to the objects of liberty rights in the absence of guaranteeing the right to subsistence, so that the secure enjoyment of the right to subsistence cannot be said to be literally essential to the secure enjoyment of liberty rights. Shue discusses one such objection offered by Mark Wicclair.[6] Wicclair's objection is that the right not to be tortured could be secured without securing the right to subsistence through implementing measures to ensure that the duty not to torture was strictly enforced. As the objection runs, while starvation is undoubtedly terrible, the fact remains that starvation without torture is better than starvation with torture. Shue's reply is that unless persons have been guaranteed reasonably secure access to subsistence they could not be said to actually enjoy security against torture, because they would be vulnerable to being drawn into a bargain (with, say, a sadistic millionaire) of undergoing torture in exchange for subsistence.

A riposte to this argument that has recently been given by Cohen (2004) is that people could be protected against such contracts too, through enforcing a prohibition on them. This could ensure that each person enjoyed freedom from torture to a reasonable level of certainty.[7]

The possibility of prohibiting torture contracts does show that it is conceptually possible to guarantee the right not to be tortured in the absence of guaranteeing the right to subsistence. As we will now argue, however, Shue's example of the torture contract brings out a crucial substantive interdependence between the two rights.

---

5 See Shue (1996, 31).

6 In an endnote in Shue (1996,184–7).

7 Andrew Cohen argues for this, in Cohen (2004, 264–276).

The Substantive Relationship Between the Right to Subsistence and Other Rights

At the root of the relationship between the right to subsistence and other rights, it is suggested, is that the interest in subsistence is so important that it is liable to outweigh the interests protected by other rights, where the two interests come into conflict. As Shue's torture contract case illustrates, given the urgency of the interests protected by the right to subsistence, even extremely harmful and degrading treatment relative to an uncontroversial baseline, such as torture, is likely to constitute a better option than the alternative option of continuing to lack subsistence. The reason a prohibition on the torture contract would be needed in order to guarantee the right against torture in the absence of securing the right to subsistence is because in such circumstances, entering into such a contract is likely to be in the overall interests of the destitute individual. This is because the interest in subsistence is likely to outweigh even the interest in freedom from torture. But this means that securing a person's right against torture by preventing such contracts, without at the same time securing their right to subsistence, would not be of benefit to them, but on the contrary would make them worse off, and further reduce their capacity to exercise their autonomy. Since the prohibition of such contracts is the only way in which the right against torture could be guaranteed in the absence of securing the right to subsistence, we conclude that the full securing of the right against torture cannot be achieved in a way that can be plausibly held to be in the interests of the individual right-holder until that right-holder's access to subsistence has been secured.

Suppose, for example, a mother entered into such a contract with a sadistic millionaire as the only way of saving her children from dying of malnutrition, because she judged the mental agony of watching her children preventably die and the permanent marring of her life this would cause to be worse than the physical agony and lasting psychological damage caused by torture, and to be a greater undermining of her autonomy given that her most central goal was to nurture her children. If she were legally prevented from making such a bargain without being given an alternative opportunity to earn a subsistence income, and her children died as a result, she might reasonably complain that the legislators had worsened her suffering and degradation. She might also reasonably complain that they had shown moral hypocrisy, on the ground that they could not claim to have protected her right not to be tortured out of concern for her interests or respect for her dignity as a rational autonomous agent, given that their actions had led to her greater suffering, and had deprived her of her only available opportunity to realise her most important end, of saving her children.

So, while it is conceptually possible fully to secure the right against torture without securing the right to subsistence, this can only be achieved by banning the torture contract, which cannot be plausibly held to be in the interests of the right-holder. This indicates that the right against torture cannot be fully enjoyed in the substantive sense in which the right is worth having unless the right-holder's access to subsistence is secure.

It should be stressed that the author is not appealing to a utilitarian argument about maximising overall welfare, but to what is in the best interests of the individual right-holder. Following the standard interest-based account of rights, rights are taken to be grounded (at least in part) on the importance of certain interests of the individual right-holder. On any interest-based account of rights we need some kind of objective ranking of interests, to work out what interests are important enough to ground rights. It is argued that on a plausible objective ranking of interests, the interest in subsistence is so important that it is liable to outweigh the interests protected by other rights – even torture – where those interests come into conflict. That means that if we ban exchanges in which people agree to give up the object of a right in exchange for subsistence, without ensuring the right-holder has other opportunities to earn a subsistence income, this will standardly and predictably worsen the plight of that individual right-holder and restrict even further their opportunity to exercise their autonomy, which, it is suggested, is in tension with claiming that our motivation for securing the right by banning such exchanges is grounded in concern for that right-holder's individual interests and autonomy.

It might be argued that it does not follow from the fact that an individual might be benefited by agreeing to forgo the object of a right in exchange for something else that that individual cannot be said to enjoy the right. However, what is distinctive about the right to subsistence is, first, that the interest in subsistence is so important that on an objective ranking of interests it is standardly and predictably likely to outweigh the interest in other rights should the right holder be offered an exchange, so that attempts fully to secure those other rights by banning the exchange are standardly and predictably detrimental to the interests of right-holder. Second, lacking subsistence is unsustainable, which means that the 'choice' of forgoing a right in exchange for subsistence is not a voluntary one. The torturer's contract case, for example, ought to be classified as coercion.

Shue's appeal to the torture contract case can be plausibly read as an illustration of his general claim that if people lack subsistence, they are standardly coerced into forgoing the objects of their other rights, and so cannot be said to have secure enjoyment of the objects of those rights. Cohen's riposte is, in effect, that people can be protected against this coercion, so that they can be said to have secure enjoyment of their other rights even if they lack subsistence. But if we focus on what is involved in securely enjoying those other rights in the substantive sense in which such security is worth having, this riposte lacks plausibility. At the root of the coercion is the fact that until people have subsistence, their plight is unsustainable. Responding to such coercion by banning contracts in which the right-holders forgo the objects of those other rights in exchange for subsistence forces them into a situation that they reasonably judge to be even more unsustainable and restricts even further their opportunity to exercise their autonomy. In the torture contract case, for example, it forecloses the only opportunity available to the mother to realise her most important end of saving her children, which she reasonably judges to be the most unbearable outcome of all.

It should also be stressed that the author is not denying that important and genuine steps can be taken towards protecting other rights such as the right not to be tortured independently of securing the right to subsistence. Instead it is claimed that *full* enjoyment of such rights – enjoyment to a reasonable degree of security – cannot be said to have been achieved, in the substantive sense of enjoyment in which such security is worth having, until subsistence has been secured. Wicclair's claim that torture heaped *on top of* destitution makes the right-holder worse off is not denied. The author's claim, rather, is that any destitute person is potentially benefited by a torture contract, in which the torture is *in exchange for* subsistence. In short, while lack of subsistence without torture is better than lack of subsistence with torture, it is also the case that torture with subsistence may be better than freedom from torture without subsistence. This argument allows, then, that protections against many standard threats to the right against torture will benefit right-holders who are destitute (such as protections against police brutality, and so on). Our argument is that the full securing of the right against torture cannot be said to have been adequately achieved until the right-holder's access to subsistence has been secured, because one very important standard threat will remain: The destitute will always be vulnerable to being drawn into bargains in which they exchange freedom from torture for subsistence because they are likely to benefit from such exchanges; and responding to this threat by attempting to ban such exchanges is inadequate, for the reasons that have been given.

It should also be noted that while the torture contract case is, as Shue notes, rather a bizarre example,[8] in the case of other rights, such as the right against child labour, to which we will now turn, the right-holders' interest in the object of the right and their interest in subsistence frequently come into conflict. In such circumstances, attempts to impose a ban on child labour in the absence of other institutional reforms to address the extreme poverty associated with it can standardly have a devastating impact on the interests of the children. It can lead to their starvation or to their taking an even worse form of work such as prostitution.[9]

As we will now suggest, the case of child labour casts doubt on a common conceptual argument against welfare rights such as the right to subsistence that is directed at the nature of the duties they impose. The argument is that unless

8 Though variations of it are not uncommon, if we consider, for example, that many of the women who are abused in the making of films for the most violent end of the pornography industry are extremely poor prostitutes, often from Latin America.

9 Kaushik Basu discusses this in Basu (1999, 1083–1119). Of course the relation between child labour and severe poverty, and the best approach to eradicating child labour, are extremely complex issues. See for example Grootaerd and Kanbur (1995, 187–203). For an excellent discussion of the normative issues raised by child labour, see Satz (2003, 297–309).

welfare rights are institutionalised the duties they impose are imperfect in nature, in the sense that they do not bind agents' conduct strictly at all times, and they are not fully delineated. Imperfect duties, it is argued, cannot be duties of justice. Institutionalised positive duties, on the other hand, are perfect duties of justice, but are special duties that correspond to special rights rather than being general duties that correspond to human rights. This line of argument is especially prominent within the Kantian tradition, but is also part of our inherited picture of the nature of the duties imposed by human rights.

Child labour constitutes a harm relative to a fairly uncontroversial baseline, and a harm that a Kantian account will take particularly seriously, given its impact on the developmental interests of the children. As we will now argue, however, in circumstances in which the child labour is the only feasible alternative to destitution, to take the duties it imposes to be perfect in nature is implausibly divorced from the interests of the children.

The Nature of the Duties Imposed by the Right Against Child Labour

According to the standard dichotomies between duties, what is key to the distinction between negative duties of justice such as the duty not to coerce, and imperfect duties of aid, is that the former are strict and fully delineated perfect duties even in the absence of institutional structures. Regardless of what institutional structures are in place, we know who owes exactly what primary duties to whom: Every agent is under a clear-cut, exceptionless duty not to coerce or harm anyone else. The role of social institutions is simply to enforce these antecendently specified duties (O'Neill 2000, 105; 1996, 131–2).[10]

The right against child labour is often understood as imposing perfect duties, that is, fully specified duties not to send one's children out to work and not to employ child labourers that can and should be completely fulfilled in all circumstances, independently of the institutional structures that are in place. Accordingly, the role of social institutions has often been taken to be simply to enforce such duties: The right against child labour has been widely acknowledged, and a common response to this acknowledgement has been to attempt to enforce the duty not to send one's children out to work or to employ child labourers through monitoring and punishing violations of this duty, in isolation from implementing other institutional reforms to tackle the chronic severe poverty that is closely associated with child labour.

However, in circumstances in which child labour is the only feasible alternative to destitution, the duties imposed by the right against child labour may have neither of the two principal features of perfect duties. Like the torture contract, child labour constitutes a harm relative to an uncontroversial baseline. It may

10 Onora O'Neill is a particularly influential and forceful advocate of this argument. See, for example, her *Bounds of Justice* (O'Neill 2000, 105); and *Towards Justice and Virtue* (O'Neill 1996, 131–132).

also plausibly constitute coercion, as does the torture contract.[11] However, there is a crucial contrast between them. In the case of the torture contract, the conflict between the right-holder's interest in subsistence and their interest in freedom from torture is entirely avoidable and gratuitous, and results solely from the cruelty of the millionaire. It is therefore perfectly plausible to take the millionaire to be under a strict duty not to torture. In the case of child labour, however, when certain economic conditions are in place, child labour may be the only feasible alternative to destitution. In such circumstances, the conflict between the children's interest in subsistence and their interest in freedom from child labour may be unavoidable. If parents really do face the choice between sending their children out to work as child labourers or allowing them to starve, it is not plausible to take them to be under a strict, exceptionless duty not to send them out to work. This would give insufficient weight to the interests of the children, given that lack of subsistence is likely to have an even more devastating impact on their developmental interests than child labour. Rather, where the conflict between the children's interest in freedom from child labour and their interest in subsistence is unavoidable the parents may have to engage in a tragic trade-off, and their duty not to send their children out to work as child labourers may be outweighed by their duty to provide them with or avoid depriving them of their only available opportunity to attain subsistence. Moreover, it is not only in very rare circumstances that this tragic trade-off between the two duties is liable to occur, but whenever the children's access to subsistence is insecure.

A possible Kantian response to this argument might be to argue that the scope of the right against child labour is limited so that it does not apply in these circumstances.[12] Kantians have stressed that while perfect duties themselves are exceptionless duties that strictly bind agents' conduct at all times, the scope of such duties has built-in qualifications.[13] It might be argued, then, that one such qualification that is built into the scope of the duty not to employ child labourers is that this duty does not apply in circumstances in which the alternative is destitution. If so then it is not the case that the duty not to employ child labourers is outweighed, because it does not apply in these circumstances. On this account, then, there is a clear-cut, perfect duty not to employ child labourers, and a corresponding clear-cut negative right, but these do not exist in situations where employing child labourers is the only way for their family to get by.

It might be argued that the rationale for limiting the scope of the right against child labour so that it does not exist in situations of destitution is that in this context such a right would not be in the overall interests of the children, precisely because it conflicts with their greater interest in subsistence. However, if the right against child labour is grounded on the detrimental impact that child labour has on the

11 This is discussed in the full version of this contribution.

12 This response was suggested to the author by Leif Wenar.

13 Thomas E. Hill, Jr., emphasises this point, in 'Meeting Needs and Doing Favours' (Hill 2002).

children's developmental interests, then it is not plausible that the right would no longer *exist* in situations of destitution. The detrimental impact on the children brought about specifically by child labour is the same in a context in which child labour is the only feasible alternative to destitution as in a context in which the children subjected to it are more affluent, even though in the former context this harm is outweighed by the even greater harm posed by lack of subsistence. Therefore to deny that the destitute have the same right against child labour is in tension with acknowledging their equal moral status. Moreover, the logic of the argument would imply that the destitute lack many of the rights possessed by others, given that they would often be likely to benefit from contracts in which they forgo the interests normally protected by rights in exchange for subsistence. This would be a kind of unappealing converse to Shue's argument in defence of the claim that the right to subsistence is a basic right.

On the other hand, however, although it is not plausible to limit the scope of the duty not to coerce so that it does not apply in these circumstances, it may be plausibly argued that it is not reasonable to hold the parents responsible for the harm to their children caused by child labour, if they are acting in their overall best interests in the circumstances. In that case, given that it is not plausible to deny the children have the right against child labour, then child labour has to be taken to be a systemic harm in these circumstances.

If, on the other hand, we do take the parents to be under a duty not to send their children out to work as child labourers,[14] given that this duty is systemically outweighed by the children's interest in subsistence, then child labour again has to be taken to be at least principally a systemic harm in these circumstances; since the parents are trapped and are not in a position to fulfil the duty not to send their children out to work if they have no alternative opportunity to secure their subsistence, then institutional structures under which these alternative opportunities are unavailable have to be seen as playing a constitutive role in deprivations of the right against child labour, and securing such opportunities has to be seen as part and parcel of fulfilling the right against child labour.

On either view, it is not plausible to take parents to be under a strict, exceptionless duty not to send their children out to work that can be fulfilled regardless of the institutional structures in place, and to take the role of institutional structures as being simply that of enforcing such a duty. Unless institutional structures are in place under which the right to subsistence has been secured, then either parents are not under such a duty, or they are under this duty but are not in a position to fulfil it because it is systemically outweighed. In either case, securing institutional structures under which the right to subsistence has been guaranteed should be

14 This interpretation might be considered to be supported by the thought that if parents do face a tragic choice in which they opt to send their children out to work to prevent their starvation, this decision will leave a moral residue, and calls for deep regret and, where possible, compensation.

seen as essential to fulfilling the right against child labour, and until this has been achieved, child labour has to be principally seen as a systemic harm.

In certain circumstances, it may also be implausible to take individual employers to be under strict duties not to employ child labourers. Of course, the relation between child labour and subsistence is extremely complex. Nevertheless, if the employers are really not in a position to pay wages that are sufficient to enable the parents to support the whole family, and by ending the children's employment would be depriving them of their only available chance of attaining a subsistence income, then it may not be plausible to take them to be under a strict duty not to employ child labourers. Again, it may be much more plausible to take child labour to be principally a structural harm that calls for a coordinated institutional response than to identify specific employers as specifically responsible for particular violations of the right.

Insofar as child labour is a systemic harm, the duties it imposes also lack the second feature of perfect duties: It is not possible to identify specific perpetrators of specific violations of the right, and the content of the duty is not clear-cut. If we were to look for perpetrators of violations of the right against child labour, the parents and employers of child labourers would be the obvious candidates. However, as has been argued, it is not plausible to take parents or employers to be under a strict duty not to send their children out to work, or not to employ child labourers, respectively, if fulfilling such a duty unavoidably conflicts with providing the children with or avoiding depriving them of a subsistence income. Rather, in such cases the duty that the right against child labour principally imposes is a duty to seek institutional reform, an integral part of which is to ensure that adequate economic opportunities are in place so that child labour is not the only available alternative to destitution. The duty to seek institutional reform is likely to lie with a huge number of agents, and has not itself been specified and allocated among them. Therefore the content of this duty is not fully defined, and it may not be possible to identify specific agents as the perpetrators of specific rights violations.

It is only if the right to basic necessities has been secured that it is plausible to take parents and employers to be under strict and clearly defined duties not to send their children out to work and not to employ child labourers, and to identify these agents as the perpetrators of specific violations of the right against child labour if they violate such duties.

These duties may function in much the same way as perfect duties, given that they are fully delineated and that they can and should always be completely fulfilled. It is important to stress, though, that in a central respect they are not perfect duties in the standard sense: They are not duties that are fully defined and that strictly bind agents' conduct whatever the circumstances, and, in particular, regardless of the institutional structures that are in place, since the strictness and fully delineated nature of these duties is contingent on the fact that social institutions are in place that have secured the right to subsistence.

To conclude, it is not an essential feature of rights that they impose perfect duties. In order to determine the duties imposed by a right we need to consider the nature of the interests the right is meant to protect and the relationship between these interests and other interests that may be threatened, and the nature of the protection all these interests require.

In the case of the right against child labour, for example, if we are to give adequate weight to the developmental interests of the children, it follows that securing the right to subsistence is part and parcel of fulfilling the right against child labour, and it is only after the right to subsistence has been secured that the right against child labour imposes perfect duties that can and should be completely fulfilled. Thus, whether the right against child labour imposes perfect duties is contingent on whether the right to subsistence has been secured.

The author therefore hopes to have reinforced Shue's argument about the interdependence between the right to subsistence and other rights, and in the light of this to have reinforced his argument that in our thinking about welfare rights we should not be strait-jacketed by our inherited picture of the standard dichotomies between duties that underpins the view that welfare rights can only be special rights.[15] As been argued, there is a crucial substantive interdependence between the right to subsistence and other rights, in that the value to right-holders of enjoying fully secure access to the objects of other rights depends on their enjoying secure access to subsistence. Given the urgency of the interest in subsistence, it may be reasonable to sacrifice the objects of other rights in order to obtain subsistence. It follows that the full securing of other rights cannot be said to have been achieved in a way that can be plausibly held to be in the interests of the individual right-holder unless the right to subsistence has been secured. Furthermore, in the case of certain liberty rights against harm and coercion, when institutional structures are in place under which the right to subsistence is insecure there may be circumstances in which the conflict between enjoyment of the rights and enjoyment of subsistence is unavoidable. In such circumstances, these liberty rights cannot be adequately respected until the right to subsistence has been secured. It is only after the right to subsistence has been secured that these liberty rights impose duties that are fully defined and that can and should be completely fulfilled at all times. This indicates, first, that liberty rights cannot be adequately secured, and in some cases even adequately respected, until institutional structures are in place under which the right to subsistence has been secured, and, second, that in just the same way as with welfare rights, in the absence of just institutional structures, the negative duties imposed by certain liberty rights may be imperfect in nature.

In the light of this we can now finally return, albeit briefly, to the question of whether the right to subsistence ought to be seen as a special right or a basic human right held by every human being simply in virtue of being human. If the duties imposed by genuine liberty rights can be imperfect, then the imperfect nature of duties of aid that correspond to welfare rights, prior to the institutionalisation of

15 Shue (1988, 687–704).

such rights, is no reason to deny that these are duties of justice that correspond to human rights. Rather than being constrained by the standard dichotomies between duties we should focus on the interests the right protects, and the relation between these and other interests. The interest in subsistence is as important as the interests protected by any other right and is essential to a minimally decent and autonomous life. Furthermore, the right to subsistence is a basic right in the substantive sense that the value to the right-holder of full enjoyment of other rights is dependent on their secure enjoyment of subsistence. In the case of certain liberty rights, moreover, the right to subsistence is basic in the further sense that these rights cannot be adequately respected until the right to subsistence has been secured.

References

Basu, K. (1999), 'Child Labour: Cause, Consequence and Cure, with Remarks on International Labour Standards', *Journal of Economic Literature* 37, 1083–1119.

Beitz, C. and Goodin, R. (eds) (forthcoming), *Global Basic Rights* (Oxford: Oxford University Press).

Cohen, A. (2004), 'Must Rights Impose Enforceable Positive Duties?', *Journal of Social Philosophy* 35, 264–276.

Grootaerd, C. and Kanbur, R. (1995), 'Child Labour: An Economic Perspective', *International Labour Review* 134, 187–203.

Hill, T., Jr. (2002), *Human Welfare and Moral Worth* (Oxford: Oxford University Press).

O'Neill, O. (1996), *Towards Justice and Virtue* (Cambridge: Cambridge University Press).

O'Neill, O. (2000), *Bounds of Justice* (Cambridge: Cambridge University Press).

Satz, D. (2003), 'Child Labour: A Normative Perspective', *The World Bank Economic Review* 17, 297–309.

Shue, H. (1988), 'Mediating Duties', *Ethics* 98, 687–704.

Shie, H. (1996), *Basic Rights: Subsistence, Affluence, and U.S. Foreign Policy*, 2nd Edition. (Princeton: Princeton University Press).

Chapter 12
Complicity in Harmful Action: Contributing to World Poverty and Duties of Care[1]

Barbara Bleisch

It has been argued recently that, from a moral point of view, we are not merely obliged to help the victims of absolute poverty, but that we must above all stop harming them. This claim is based on the empirical assumption that world poverty is to a significant extent caused by an unjust and harmful world order imposed on poor countries by the inhabitants of the wealthier ones. Thomas Pogge argues therefore that we all have 'a *negative* duty not to uphold injustice, not to contribute to or profit from the unjust impoverishment of others' (Pogge 2002, 197; see also Pogge 2002, 21, 66sqq., 172; Pogge 2004, 273). In this chapter, we will not discuss the empirical question whether the institutional global order is indeed decisive for the persistence of world poverty. We will rather assume that world poverty is amongst local factors caused by global rules and by our contributing to and profiting from them. Yet, from this assumption it does not follow that the normative question about the moral responsibility for the destitution of the poor is already answered. After all, there is the widespread view that even if we all as consumers, investors, managers and citizens of democratically ruled countries are somehow causally involved in exploiting mechanisms, our contribution is so marginal and loose that the responsibility for the distress lies entirely or at least primarily in the governments of the affected countries.[2]

In this chapter, we will firstly argue that the immediacy and the dimension of one's causal contribution is – contrary to widespread belief – not necessarily decisive for the extent of the moral fault and the compensation owed respectively. As will be claimed, we cannot attribute retrospective responsibility for a certain

1 I thank Norbert Anwander and Susanne Boshammer for helpful comments on earlier drafts of this chapter.

2 What Pogge has in mind is admittedly an institutional rather than an interactional thesis: According to this view, the absolute poor are harmed by a global order forced on them by the rich countries. The poor are thus not wronged by individual or collective actions. That is why Pogge does not have to show that *individual* actions contribute – no matter how indirectly – to world poverty, but only that the global order does so. He has to show, however, that individual actions and omissions contribute to the alleged harmful world order. The allocation problem of responsibility thus shifts onto the level of contributing to harmful institutions.

wrong without a normative background theory about what does and what does not belong to our sphere of moral attention. Such a background theory could profit, as will be argued secondly, from the concepts of 'due diligence' and 'duties of care' used in criminal law: Duties of care ask us not to put others at risk knowingly. Thereby they determine the sphere of moral attention – the factors one has to take into account when acting. Several human rights documents and global corporate citizenship initiatives (amongst them most prominently the UN Global Compact[3]) incorporate a similar idea with regard to transnational corporations: They require that businesses are not complicit in human rights abuses and that they act (among other things) according to a duty of care.

Causal and Moral Responsibility

If we want to know who is responsible for a bad situation, we usually start by asking who has brought it about. In many cases it seems possible to ascribe the main part of responsibility for a certain incident to a single and readily identifiable actor: The speeding driver is responsible for the car crash; the cook who used spoiled eggs for the tiramisu is responsible for the food poisoning of the guests; and the building workers are responsible for the death of a child who fell into an unsecured building pit.[4] However, there are other cases where the background story of a certain incident is less clear because there are hundreds of causal factors and players involved. This is especially true on a global scale: instead of some clear-cut offenders and victims, we find billions of actors and victims, most of them with changing roles depending on the situation. No doubt that Robert Mugabe is responsible for most of the incredible misery of Zimbabwe's people. Yet, Mugabe's possibilities to oppress and deprive his people are only as strong as his supporters and beneficiaries are. Without thousands of people contributing to the establishing and upholding of brutal regimes, the dictators could not remain in power and not oppress the already very poor. Thomas Pogge therefore claims:

> How harmful corrupt leaders in poor countries are […] is strongly influenced by whether the global order recognizes such leaders […] as entitled to sell us their country's resources, to borrow in its name, and to use the proceeds to buy the means of internal repression. (Pogge 2005a, 47)

3 The second principle of the UN Global Compact requires: 'Businesses should make sure they are not complicit in human rights abuses', see <http://www.unglobalcompact.org> (last accessed 17 October 2008).

4 Note that in these examples, there is no deliberate harm. To deliberately harm others is obviously wrong, but we sometimes also ascribe moral responsibility to negligent actors.

The same is supposedly true for corporations: Shell was certainly responsible for the environmental damage and the civil commotions in Nigeria in 1995, but without Shell's shareholders sustaining the proceedings and customers buying from Shell including those fuelling by using Shell, the corporation would not have been able to pursue its harmful strategy as it did. Sani Abacha in turn could not have oppressed his people without corporations like Shell engaged in the local oil production – he simply would have lacked the funds to sustain his personal army. Although there are certainly more or less powerful actors who are more or less responsible for at least some of the injustice, it seems reasonable to assume that from a *causal* point of view, a lot of people (if not all) are involved in the harmful practices that contribute to extreme poverty. But supposing that we are (more or less) *causally* involved, are we *morally*?

The concept of 'complicity' connects causal and moral responsibility:[5] An accomplice plays not only a decisive causal role in the commitment of a crime; she does so in a morally blameworthy way. But when does a contributor become an accomplice at the same time? To put it differently: How can we get from the ascription of causal responsibility to a proper ascription of moral responsibility and blame respectively?

With regard to the destitution of the extreme poor, some authors ascribe moral responsibility to all of us arguing that we are all involved in the unjust world order as consumers, as investors and as mere citizens of democratically ruled countries.[6] But this seems precipitate for two reasons: Firstly, not every involvement in the formation of a harmful action is a proper part of its causal explanation. Secondly, not every causal involvement in a certain harmful action is also morally relevant.

Let us first have a look at the first differentiation. The idea is the following: The individual contribution of northern consumers, investors and of businesses seems to be so marginal compared to local factors such as corrupt rulers, wars, geographic factors or historic facts like colonialism that it seems somehow odd to claim that you and I are responsible for the misery of those suffering from absolute poverty. Since the idea that we contribute to the distress in Southern countries seems somehow far fetched, some philosophers have suggested that we are not genuinely contributing to harmful practices, but at the most *enabling* them. Peter Schaber, for example, argues that although we may, by Pogge's resource privilege, *enable* the rulers in resource-rich countries to pocket gains for their personal army and luxury without considering the poor, we do not *contribute* to this thievery. Enabling conditions, as Jonathan Dancy defines them, are considerations that

5 This connection is also mentioned in several background documents to the UN Global Compact. See, for example, the Reports of the Special Representative of the Secretary-General on the Issue of Human Rights and Transnational Corporations and other Business Enterprises (Ruggie 2008).

6 Thomas Pogge argues, for example: 'As ordinary citizens of the rich countries, we are deeply implicated in these harms' (Pogge 2002, 142). See also Pogge (2002, 23) and Pogge (2005a, 36).

are required for an explanation to go through, but which are not themselves part of the explanation at stake (Dancy 2000, 127; see also Schaber 2007). Enabling conditions are thus to be distinguished from considerations that are 'a proper part of an explanation' (Dancy 2000, 127).[7] That is why it would sound odd if the cook who prepared the spoilt tiramisu said that, after all, the (uninformed) waiter contributed to the upset stomach of the guests, too. Hence not every causal factor counts as involvement in the sense of a proper contribution to an incident.

This differentiation is important for us because it seems to be quite reasonable to make use of the differentiation between contributing and enabling factors not only for the *causal explanation*, but also for the *moral evaluation* of a certain situation (see Miller 2007). If someone contributes knowingly to the wronging of third parties, he obviously makes a moral mistake and he owes the victim compensation. By contrast, some philosophers have suggested that the mere enabling of injustice is morally neutral: If someone provides an opportunity for others to harm a third party, he does nothing wrong himself and should not be blamed for the resulting injury. Peter Schaber gives the following example (Schaber 2007, 147sqq.): A philosopher who frequently borrows books from a library removes them sometimes without booking them correctly. This makes it impossible for others to find those books if required. But if the librarian ordered less interesting books, the philosopher would not remove them. While the librarian enables the philosopher to act wrongly, he is of course not to be blamed for the damage. Schaber concludes that enabling misbehaviour is not blameworthy in itself.

However, there is doubt over this conclusion. Although in the given example the enabler is indeed not at fault, enabling wrongdoing is not always unproblematic.[8] Firstly, it is difficult to keep apart contributing and enabling factors properly.[9] Secondly, it is doubtful that the example of the librarian is analogous to our contribution to world poverty. It goes without saying that the books have to be ordered before they can be removed. Likewise children have to be born before they can die from malnutrition. But the fact that western businesses engage, for example, with the arms trade and contribute that way to civil wars, displacement of the poor and hunger, is a far more direct involvement in the wrong than the librarian's ordering of books. Of course, our involvement varies in immediacy and

7 Hart and Honoré make a similar distinction, differentiating between *causes* and *mere conditions*. See Hart and Honoré (1959, 8–23, 30–41, 58–70).

8 Of course, there are situations in which enabling injustice is indeed morally irrelevant. Let us think, for example, of an art collector who – by hanging expensive pictures in his flat – provides an opportunity to steal those pictures for the thief. The art collector is of course not *morally* involved in the theft. See Anwander and Bleisch (2007, 179).

9 Hart and Honoré point to the fact that the differentiation between 'causation' and 'enabling' is not strict but context-dependent (Hart and Honoré 1959, 31). See also Dancy (2000, 127).

in dimension from case to case. But in addition, the differing evaluations of our participation in the harmful action depend on the description of the situation.

Yet, independently of how the situation and the causal involvement of all stakeholders are best described, there is a third point. The decision whether a contribution to a bad situation is morally relevant cannot be traced back solely to the question of the *extent* of the involvement. The question is rather whether I am – through my role or situation – in charge of taking into account possible negative consequences of my action. Hugh LaFollette argues:

> For most of what is important in our lives, the question is not am I *solely* or even *predominantly* responsible for harm, but whether am I [sic!] *responsible enough*? We must ask: did I play a *sufficiently important* role that it is proper to attribute responsibility to me – to blame me for mistakes (and to expect me to atone for them) or to praise me for my successes? (LaFollette 2003, 248f)

The following example may illustrate this point: In South Africa, every eighteen hours a woman is shot by her husband or ex-husband.[10] The local arms dealers' involvement in this situation is – from a causal point of view – considerable. If there were no arms shops and arms producers, it would be much more difficult for the murderers to obtain suitable weapons and commit the crimes in question. Yet, it would be exaggerated to claim that the local arms dealers contribute to the outrages, even if they enable them. The South-African government also provides enabling conditions for the crimes – although very indirect ones: Since the government does not tighten the weapons law, it is in the first place possible for individuals to get a gun so easily. Although the arms dealers and the government only enable the outrages and even if the causal involvement of the arms dealers is more direct than that of the government, the government bears more responsibility in this case. But why should that be so? This is because the government has the prospective responsibility to protect the citizens whereas the owner of the arms shop is not subject to such an obligation.

It is mistaken therefore to assume that the moral evaluation of causal involvement simply tracks its immediateness or importance. Instead it relies on a normative background which links the network of causal factors to a network of moral factors. It is therefore not enough to demonstrate that we are all somehow causally involved in the injustice. Causal involvement in a mischief is certainly very often evidence of a moral fault. But firstly, it is not always. And secondly, the more intricate the causal chain is, the lesser evidence of a moral fault we have. This is so because the ascription of retrospective responsibility depends not generally on the *causal* responsibility, but also on the *prospective* responsibility to do or omit certain things in a given situation. It is therefore impossible to tackle the question about retrospective moral responsibility (and the required restitution

---

10 See <http://www.news.amnesty.org/index/ENGPOL300102005> (last accessed 17 October 2008).

respectively) unless we have clarified who is prospectively morally responsible for the prevention of certain harmful conditions. To be able to evaluate the individual contributions to injustice, we therefore need to know what our prospective obligations are or – to put it otherwise – what does and what does not belong to our individual sphere of moral attention. Without a clear picture of the division of moral labour in a prospective sense, the distinction between bigger or smaller and more or less direct contributions (and between genuine causations and mere enabling conditions) is quasi morally blind.

Admittedly, in many cases, this blindness carries no weight: *Either* the prospective responsibility is clearly attributed to someone by a social role or by a contract. The pool attendant is, for example, by contract prospectively responsible for the children in the pool and retrospectively responsible and to be blamed if a child drowns. And the parents of a child are to be blamed if she falls off the balcony because they are responsible by their role to look after her. *Or* both forms of responsibility coincide in the case of clear-cut negative duties: We all have the prospective responsibility not to wrong others and, if we do nevertheless, to rectify injustice retrospectively. But within confusing chains of acts and omissions including an unclear division of moral labour, it becomes dubious who is in 'moral charge' of what and who is accountable for damage accordingly.

To sum up, it is difficult to ascribe moral responsibility for world poverty to individual actors. It is not only difficult to perceive and to estimate the individual's causal contribution to the misery, but causal and moral responsibilities are above all not necessarily on a par. The responsibility to rectify injustice and to prevent future harm lies sometimes not in those who contributed mainly to the misery but in those who are obliged to keep an eye on the situation by virtue of their social role. The above mentioned building workers, for example, are not only causally, but also morally responsible for the death of the child falling into the unsecured building pit because it is their duty to secure the construction site. What we need, thus, is a concept of global moral labour division distributing the fields of moral attention.

To ask for such a concept is, admittedly, not inventive. Those who argue for positive duties to eradicate severe poverty usually also advocate such an idea. But what this chapter claims is on the one hand that even those who start from the assumption that we are involved in world poverty cannot avoid developing a concept of a division of moral labour in a prospective sense. On the other hand, the alleged idea of moral labour division does not rely on the justification of positive duties to help the starving (although we may of course also have such obligations). It is rather based on our involvement in a harmful order. It structures the normative background of our involvement so that we can determine whose contribution is not only causally, but also morally relevant. Only if we know what belongs to whose field of duty, are we able to attribute retrospective responsibility to certain actors.

How could such a concept of a division of responsibilities be shaped? In the case of positive obligations some authors have proposed to distribute responsibilities in accordance with (among other things) capacity, capability or fair shares. But with regard to our involvement in unjust practices this seems unfair: Why should a billionaire (disposing of a much bigger financial capacity than a building worker) be responsible to pay for the surgery of the insured boy in the example above? This might be plausible in the case of mere positive duties, but does not make sense when asking about retrospective responsibility. Neither would it be justified to pass on the costs to the person who has the lion's share of the causal responsibility – say, for example, to another boy who jostled the unlucky fellow for the fun of it. In the context of the attribution of retrospective moral responsibility it is helpful to consider concepts used in tort law, namely negligence and duties of care. Let us turn to these concepts now.

Negligence and General Duties of Care

In law, it is of course actionable to wrong another person deliberately – either by an act or by an omission. With regard to world poverty our contribution usually is not a deliberate one. Of course we want to maximise our utility and profit from cheap goods, but it is not our goal to wrong the already poor. Rather, we harm the destitute by negligence. An example for negligent harm is the following: If I play with a gun carelessly and then shoot someone by accident, I might be chargeable for a negligent killing. And if I fail to put up a warning sign when I polish the floor in front of my shop in the airport building, I might be culpable for a negligent omission if a passenger slips and breaks her leg. In these cases, the accusation is based on a violation of a general duty of care:[11] The culprits acted negligently, and this negligence and carelessness is *in itself* something they are to be blamed for. The idea of a general duty of care is based on the attempt to protect each other from the realisation of a danger which our own conduct may represent for others. This duty is not based on roles or contracts, but has to be respected whenever our own conduct puts others at risk.

Applying this concept to the situation of world poverty, we can say that even if we do not exploit the very poor actively and on purpose, and even if our causal contribution to world poverty is very small, we must not put other people at risk knowingly. Even if we do not know precisely how extreme poverty comes about and whether a certain contract, bargain or commerce will deteriorate the situation, and even if other factors are much more important for the existence of extreme poverty, we must abstain from putting the poor at risk of persisting in the situation or from even deteriorating it. Maybe Thomas Pogge has had in mind something similar in saying that we are obliged, 'not to support and not to pocket gains from an unfair institutional order *that forseeably contributes to severe deprivations*'

11 In the case of omissions, duties of care are – depending on the legislation at stake – called differently than in the case of actions. To simplify matters we will talk about 'duties of care' in both cases.

(Pogge 2004, 279; emphasis BB; see also Pogge 2005b, 60). If the management of a corporation has reason to believe that trading with a certain leader might put the people in his country at risk because by trading with him a bloody and oppressive regime might be supported, it has a duty of care to quit its trade relations.

It is important to note that the idea of a general duty of care does not involve that one contributes to a wronging *for sure*; it suffices to know that by doing something one *risks* contributing or wronging a third party. To resume the example of playing with a gun: If I knew that by playing with the gun I will surely shoot someone, I would not act negligently, but intentionally (which is of course worse).

Hence, although it might be difficult to argue that we are involved in harming the poor by contributing to the injustice they suffer from, we often endanger the poor by our conduct. A danger is nothing else than an anticipation of a presumably occurring harm. Performing our duty of care means not to put others at the risk of suffering this presumably occurring harm.

Fair enough, one might object, but this suggestion does not answer our normative question about individual responsibility, but only postpones it to a different level: What is at issue now is a reasonable concept of putting at risk and endangering others. Which potential side effects of my conduct do I have to evaluate to be sure that I do not possibly endanger someone?

As has been said, the risk must be *foreseeable* for the actor in order to blame him. With companies this is often the case: They often know exactly that by their purchase of resources, their investment or production, they put the environment and the people at risk of remaining in poverty or even deteriorating their circumstances. Interestingly enough, the United Nations Global Compact mentioned above asks the subscribers to implement a principle of due diligence in order not to be complicit in harmful action. The second principle asks the subscribing corporations to make sure that '... they are not complicit in human rights abuses'. The document mentions three different types of 'complicity': Firstly, 'direct complicity' occurring when a company knowingly assists a state in violating human rights; secondly, 'beneficial complicity', in which a company benefits directly from human rights abuses committed by someone else;[12] and thirdly, 'silent complicity', which means '... the failure by a company to raise the question of systematic or continuous human rights violations in its interactions with the appropriate authorities'.[13] Since a lot of corporations do not know precisely what the effects of their investments and trade relations will be, the Global Compacts asks them to act according to due diligence, 'a process whereby companies not only ensure compliance with national laws but also manage the risk of human rights harm with a view to avoiding it' (see Ruggie 2008, chap. I.2).

---

12 On the issue of profiting from harm, see Anwander and Bleisch (2007) and Norbert Anwander's contribution to this book.

13 See <http://www.unglobalcompact.org/AboutTheGC/TheTenPrinciples/Principle2.html> (last accessed 17 October 2008).

Admittedly, the 'normal citizens' often do not have the relevant information about possible risks. In fact, the author is deeply convinced that many people are not as cold-hearted, egoistic and morally lazy persons as Peter Singer and other philosophers suppose them to be, but are, first of all, confused by all the divergent information on an admittedly complex problem. To act according to a general duty of care, we must take into account what we can possibly know. A judge will not accept the claim that the accused mother did not think of putting her baby at risk by not clearing away strong drugs, for every sane person knows that swallowing drugs may endanger little children. Acting carefully is based on *evidence*, on the possibility to pre-estimate the risk of a possible damage. To fulfil their duty of care, ordinary citizens of affluent countries must hence above all vote for governments who fulfil their duty of care respectively, and ask for more information regarding the goods they consume and the services they accept. Ordinary people have above all a duty to inform themselves and to think and act politically.

Conclusion

If it is true that a considerable part of world poverty is caused by an unjust world order for which we are causally responsible, then the question arises who exactly is to be blamed for man-made poverty and who exactly has to remedy the distress. Although presumably all of us are somehow causally involved in the unjust order by contributing to it, moral responsibility cannot be traced back to causal responsibility solely. It is also misleading to assume that the moral blame diminishes the looser the causal involvement is. Sometimes our contribution is better explained as an enabling of injustice. Apart from the difficulty to discriminate between enabling and contributing elements, it is moreover far from clear that our moral responsibility in case of mere enabling can be disregarded. It has been argued that our involvement in world poverty might sometimes be better understood as an *endangering* and as a *violation of a general duty of care*: Even if the lion's share of the causation of extreme poverty could be traced back to local factors, we have a duty of care not to put third parties knowingly at risk. Those who know more about possible risks are typically those who bargain with and produce in poverty-ridden countries. Hence their responsibility to carefully examine possible endangerments exceeds the responsibility of the mere citizens of wealthy countries. Yet, they in turn have the duty to inform themselves about possible endangerments stemming from their consumption of goods, their lifestyle and the government they have elected.

References

Anwander, N. and Bleisch, B. (2007), 'Beitragen und Profitieren. Ungerechte Weltordnung und individuelle Verstrickung', in Bleisch, B. et al. (eds).

Bleisch, B. et al. (eds) (2007), *Weltarmut und Ethik* (Paderborn: Mentis).
Chatterjee, D. (ed.) (2004), *The Ethics of Assistance. Morality and the Distant Needy* (Cambridge: Cambridge University Press).
Dancy, J. (2000), *Practical Reality* (Oxford: Oxford University Press).
Frey, R. and Wellmann, C. (eds) (2003), *Blackwell Companion to Applied Ethics* (Oxford: Blackwell).
Hart, H. and Honoré, A. (1959), *Causation in the Law* (Oxford: Clarendon Press).
LaFollette, H. (2003), 'World Hunger', in Frey, R. et al. (eds).
Miller, D. (2007), 'Wer ist für globale Armut verantwortlich?', in Bleisch, B. et al. (eds).
Pogge, T. (2002), *World Poverty and Human Rights. Cosmopolitan Responsibilities and Reforms* (Cambridge: Polity Press).
Pogge, T. (2004), 'Assisting the Global Poor', in Chatterjee, D. (ed.).
Pogge, T. (2005a), 'Real World Justice', *Journal of Ethics* 9:1/2, 29–53.
Pogge, T. (2005b), 'Severe Poverty as a Violation of Negative Duties', *Ethics and International Affairs* 19:1, 55–48.
Ruggie, J. (2008), 'Promotion and protection of all human rights, civil, political, economics, social and cultural rights, including the right to development. Clarifying the Concepts of "Sphere of influence" and "Complicity". Report of the Special Representative of the Secretary-General on the Issue of Human Rights and Transnational Corporations and other Business Enterprises', available at <http://www.business-humanrights.org/Documents/RuggieHRC2008> [last accessed 17 October 2008].
Schaber, P. (2007), 'Globale Hilfspflichten', in Bleisch, B. et al. (eds).

Chapter 13
Transnational Political Elites and Their Duties of the Common Good

Eike Bohlken

Transnational elites have a specific potential to shape the processes of globalisation for the better or for the worse. According to a *philosophical* and *normative elite theory*, this specific potential involves a specific responsibility. Those who have the power to transform the social structure of whole polities and economies by obtaining an elite position bear a greater responsibility than the average citizen. On the national state level this responsibility can be developed in terms of the common good leading to a set of duties derived from it. In the author's project 'Transnational elites and their duties of the common good. Ethical claims on political, financial and cultural elites in the processes of globalisation' the author discusses whether a similar responsibility and corresponding duties of the common good can be stated on a transnational level as well.

This chapter will focus on transnational *political* elites. First, this chapter will give a definition of transnational political elites. Secondly, we will try to clarify the concept of a transnational common good by reference to a set of basic common or public goods necessary for the mere existence as well as for the cultural autonomy of each human being. Finally, we will outline what kinds of duties can be derived from the basic transnational common good for transnational political elites. In a non ideal world the conception of the basic common good is intrinsically related to absolute poverty since the realisation of the first implies the overcoming of the latter. Therefore, a well grounded theory of a transnational or even global common good and of the corresponding duties derived from it could play an important part in political philosophy.

Defining Transnational Elites

In search of a definition of transnational political elites, we should start with a general definition of elites and political elites. The term elite originally stems from Latin *eligere* (to elect). Between the sixteenth and eighteenth centuries French elite referred to selected commodities of high quality on the one hand and a distinct group of the aristocracy who were highly talented and had the best education, manners and leadership qualities on the other hand (*élite de la noblesse*). Between the 1890s and 1920s Gaetano Mosca, Robert Michels, and

Vilfredo Pareto, founding fathers of the new discipline of sociology, transferred the term to social and political theory. This transfer proved very successful at first. But after the devastating results of the elite-conceptions that the Nazi-Herrenrasse on the one side, and of the Soviet-Kader-elite on the other, had led to, the term became heavily biased with totalitarian and antidemocratic ideology, especially after the students' movements of 1968.

Despite the scepticism against the term as well as against the phenomenon, one cannot help but acknowledge that elites are still there, and probably – not only according to Michels' 'law of oligarchy' (Michels 1957, 366sqq.) – always will be. According to this observation, the main question is not how to get rid of elites but how to get good elites instead of bad ones – which is the starting point of a philosophical and normative elite theory.[1] But how can the elite be defined in scientific terms, avoiding such broad notions as 'the ruling class' or 'the chosen few'. In the author's opinion, the most useful definition at hand is one that German sociologist Hans-Peter Dreitzel has given in 1962. He stated:

> An elite consists of those possessing top-positions in a group, organisation or institution who advanced into these positions through an election-process based on personal meritocratic knowledge (persönliches Leistungswissen) and whose position enables them to exert power or influence either to directly sustain or transform the social structure and its primary norms beyond the goals of their own group or to serve as a role model guiding others' behaviour in a normative way because of their social status. (Dreitzel 1962, 71; translation E.B.)

According to this definition, there are three criteria constitutive for elite membership. To be a member of any elite, one should obtain (1) a leadership position in a social organisation or institution which is usually linked with (2) power or influence. He or she should have obtained that position (3) through some kind of selection process based on personal achievements. Furthermore, the two social functions of playing an important part in the sustainment or transformation of social structures and of serving as a role model for the members of elite groups and for the general public can be ascribed to elites.[2]

Members of the *political* elite, therefore, should obtain leadership positions in political organisations or institutions, should be powerful or influential, and should be elected into their positions, ideally because of certain qualifications, abilities,

---

1 Moreover, Joseph Schumpeter (1993), Otto Stammer (1951) and Eva Etzioni-Halevy (1993) have delivered convincing arguments for a democratic elite theory (see also Bohlken 2005, 96–100).

2 There are some small points one should add: The selection-process certainly can be based on achievements other than knowledge. And the influence or power one gets with the top-position in an organisation or institution should be more than mere potential and *exerted* over a certain period of time. But these additions are rather small adjustments than alterations.

and merits. National political elites encompass the governmental elite, the leaders of the opposition, and leaders of influential interest or pressure groups. They have the power or influence to shape political and social structures[3] and serve as a role model for political activity.

From National to Transnational Political Elites

Thinking beyond the limits of the nation state it is important to distinguish three partially overlapping but yet different frames of reference: The first comprises the field of *international* relations between the governments of nation states or between the citizens of several countries. A second one includes the sphere of *supranational* political entities, such as the EU or GUS, and the relations between the integrated states, governments and citizens. Finally, the third frame comprises the field of *transnational* relations between persons, organisations, and institutions operating from several countries. One main difference to the international and supranational level is that transnational relationships rely neither on citizenship nor on national identity. As Jürgen Habermas has stated, they can take place‚behind the back' of nation states and independently from the status of citizenship. Thus, the concept of transnationality marks the field for discussions about a world society (Weltgesellschaft) and the, *moral* not legal status of world citizenship or cosmopolitism. In its ultimate extension it refers to the global level. Hence, global elites are a subset of transnational elites which is the more general term to be used.

Whereas 'international' is constrained to the inter*governmental* collaboration of the government elites of nation states the term 'transnational' also matches Non Government Organisations (NGOs) and Multinational Corporations (MNCs) whose heads do not act as representatives of their countries. 'Transnationality' transcends the level of the nation state but can remain below the global level. In its, spatial extension transnationality, thus, is situated somewhere in between international relations and the processes of globalisation.

On the transnational level members of transnational political elite should possess a leadership position in a transnational political organisation or institution and should be powerful or influential enough to shape transnational political regimes. They should also serve as a role model for transnational political activity.

3 One may argue that, in general, at least inside the framework of democratic theory, sovereignty or power is with the people not with some elite groups. But in spite of this theoretical foundation, legislation and executive power for a certain period of time in fact are in the hands of a small group of political representatives. This, however, is not to say that the theoretical foundation is meaningless – for the representatives still are *representatives* under the surveillance of public control and under the threat of not being re-elected. But in the period between two elections most of political power concentrates in a few hands, though.

According to the aforesaid requirements for political elite membership, the transnational political elite consists of members belonging to three different groups: The first and most prominent group is made up by heads of supranational and global political institutions (EU, UNO etc.). The second group consists of heads of transnational NGOs (AI, Human Rights Watch, Attac etc.). A third group comprises the heads of MNCs and of supranational institutions as WTO or World Bank. One may be surprised to find the heads of MNCs and WTO declared not only members of the transnational financial but also members of the transnational political elite. In fact this declaration marks an important difference to the nation state level. The heads of MNCs or WTO are powerful political agents, influential not only for the 'policies' of their corporations or institution but also for transnational regimes. They bear an enormous potential to shape the financial as well as the political processes of globalisation.

Prima facie this argument seems to focus only on factual power pushing aside any normative questions like that of legitimacy. But if we take a closer look, we have the same or at least a similar problem with NGOs and to a certain respect even with the UN. In accordance with ideal democratic political theory, transnational political institutions and their leaders should be legitimised by democratic elections. Of course there is a difference between the EU or the UN where representatives of (mostly democratically elected) governments meet and multinational corporations or financial institutions which lack such legitimacy. Still, the democratic legitimacy of the EU and the UN is at best an indirect and procured one.

The problem of legitimacy has a normative as well as a descriptive or factual dimension. Seen from the normative perspective it is intrinsically tied to a basic problem of contract theory, respectively of a contractual theory of global justice. The striking point is that there is a systematic difference between the national and transnational political order which seems to make 'justice' and 'global justice' two different principles (cf. Gosepath and Merle 2002). This difference becomes apparent if one tries to transfer contract theory from the national to the transnational, especially to the global level. There are several objections against a global or world state. One crucial normative argument has already put forth by Immanuel Kant: Whereas there was a duty for man to leave the original position, hypothetically ascribed to her/him by contract theory, no analogue duty to establish a world state could be derived from the idea of pure practical reason and the rule of law (cf. Kant 1983, B 103 et seq., BA 32–39).

From a more pragmatic or factual point of view a world state appears to be simply ungovernable, for it would be too big, would have an extremely diverse heterogeneous demos, and would have to deal with political issues too complex and diverse to be solved by one single and central government. Furthermore, the existence of one central global government would run the risk of a totalitarian and oppressive domination.

The point that is to be made here is that the objections against a world state simultaneously seem to affect the legitimacy of transnational institutions and to some extent even the legitimacy – to be more cautious, the applicability – of the demands of global justice. The best and most legitimate transnational order will not be the legislation of a central world state but only a more or less loose net of transnational political and financial regimes, i.e. treaties, contracts. It is this absence of a global state and legislation as a model of legitimate transnational representation that makes it difficult, if not impossible, to postulate a primacy of political regulation and to draw a strict distinction between political and non political (e.g. financial) actors on the transnational level.[4]

Having already dealt with the relation between descriptive and normative aspects, we should also say something about the transition from descriptive to normative elite theory.

From Descriptive to Normative Elite Theory – The Responsibility Elite

The definition of elites cited above is a mere descriptive one. Yet, it opens the field to normative considerations. The striking features for the transition are the greater power or influence and the two functions of shaping society and serving as a role model. People of greater power or influence are able to shape financial and societal structures in a much more effective way. This means that they have greater power to promote or to affect the common good. Insofar as they can do more harm to other people by affecting the common good than the average person or citizen they bear a greater responsibility than he or she. To talk of responsibility marks a first step in the transition to normative grounds. But the transition is not complete until there is a normative principle towards which that responsibility is orientated. This vacancy can be filled either by 'justice' or 'the common good'. Whereas for many thinkers of past centuries it would have been odd to separate the two, the second half of the twentieth century saw an autonomisation of the discourse on justice based on the thesis of the primacy of the right over the good. As the author aims to demonstrate in the next section, this thesis may be misleading, since there can be a universal understanding of the common good which may help to overcome the hinted gap between justice on the nation state level and global justice. Thus, we should add the following sentence to define the normative conception of the responsibility elite:

> The greater power or influence of elite members and their specific potential for societal transformation leads to a specific responsibility of the elites for the polity and the common good.

---

4 The absence of a world government entails also that there is no institutionalised, world opposition' but only the competition of opposed political alliances of nations, the very informal institution of the world public, and the non parliamentary opposition of several transnational NGOs.

Despite this addition one problem remains. Even if the proposed argument for the transition from a descriptive to a normative elite theory is logically sound it still may seem unsatisfactory as long as there is no sufficiently precise definition of the common good. We will, therefore, try to delineate the contours of such a definition for the national and then for the transnational level in the next section.

Defining the Common Good

There are several arguments against the common good as the core concept of political philosophy. For many scholars the idea of the common good has been replaced by a theory of justice for good reasons, among them the primacy of the right over the good. First, the notion of the common good is considered to be bound to the traditional norms and values of particular communities, and thus to particular conceptions of the good life. Especially in times of transnational migration, cultural heterogeneity, and moral pluralism the notion of a clearly definable common good seems to be illusory and oppressive for those not adhering to the traditional values of the majority. As has been shown elsewhere (cf. Bohlken 2006) these objections deserve careful consideration but can be refuted.

First of all, one should distinguish between the *basic common good* and a *melior common good* as two different levels of the common good. The basic common good is made up by the set of material and immaterial goods human beings need to sustain their physical existence and cultural autonomy. These essential goods are *public* goods since they can *only* or at least can be *better* produced, provided and sustained by the social institutions of a polity. The public goods indispensable for the sustainment of *each* member of the polity are material goods (food, water, clothes, housing, a basic health care system and last but not least a healthy environment) and immaterial goods as the rule of law positivising and protecting human rights such as the right to life, liberty and security of person. Since man is not only a physical but also a cultural being (Kulturwesen) the list of goods essential for his/her existence also includes some material and immaterial goods needed to exert something the author terms cultural autonomy (cf. Bohlken 2002, 253). Cultural autonomy means access to a certain set of cultural practices (science, ethics, religion, art, and personal relations based on friendship or other kinds of love) which implies some basic education and knowledge. Again, the indispensable goods are partly material (schools, books, and the financial conditions for parents to send their children to school and not to work), partly immaterial as school attendance, knowledge (reading, writing, and calculation skills), and information as to what the named cultural practices are about and what it takes to engage in them. Methodologically, the list of these basic common goods is the result of some semi transcendental analysis[5] which asks for the *necessary conditions for man to*

5 To claim the status of a 'full' transcendental analysis seemed to be a subjection since its 'object' is not a concept and has no direct validity claims ascribed to it.

exist and to develop humanity. To call all these essential goods 'goods of the basic common good' is to say that the polity, its institutions, and particularly the political elite governing it have an obligation to produce, to provide and to sustain these goods for each present as well as for each future member of that society.

One important feature of the conception of the basic common good is that it is limited to a certain set of primary goods. Hence, a lot of (potential) public goods remain outside of it, respectively part of the *non-essential or melior common good*. The boundary between the basic and the melior common good is marked by the extension of the aforesaid semi transcendental analysis. This means on the one hand that any public good which cannot be proved to be part of the basic common good may be at best part of the melior common good and on the other hand that philosophy has nothing to say about the melior common good *in respect of content*.

Yet, three formal conclusions can be drawn: (1) the melior common good has to be considered *procedural*; (2) because of the equality of the political rights of each citizen the contents of the melior common good have to be settled by procedures of public debate and democratic acclamation – the melior common good, therefore, comprises material and immaterial goods considered valuable by the opinion of a majority of polity members; (3) there is a primacy of the basic over the melior common good – which means that even a majority of voters is not entitled to restrain the supply with basic public goods for any member of the polity.[6]

The Transition from the National to the Transnational Level

The basic transnational common good encompasses all the material and immaterial goods, proved necessary for the physical existence and cultural autonomy of human beings by semi transcendental analysis. These goods can also be called transnational public goods, for they can *only* or at least can be *better* produced, provided and sustained by transnational institutions, organisations and regimes. Prima facie the transition from the national to the transnational basic common good seems unproblematic. The transition from the nation state level to the transnational level can be made plausible by pointing to the universal character of the basic common good. Since it contains a set of primary goods essential for each human being it is not restrained to certain local or national conceptions of the good life.

Yet, one problem remains. How can we identify the anonymous 'transnational institutions, organisations, and regimes' accountable for the production, provision, and securing of the basic transnational public goods? Our attempt to answer this important question consists of three parts.

---

6 This chapter is not going to discuss the issues of the melior common good in detail since – unless the primacy of the basic common good is neglected – it is not directly connected with the problem of absolute poverty.

At first, no world state will be needed to provide the basic transnational public goods. It has been argued that 'transnationality' refers not to the central perspective of a world state but to the more open conceptions of world society and cosmopolitism. Hence, the idea of a transnational or even global common good and of duties derived from it is not necessarily linked to the existence of a global state. The notion that there cannot be a transnational common good without a world state is based on the *false premise of methodological nationalism* (cf. Albert 2007, 17). What is wrong here is the idea that the building of transnational political regimes should perform in the same way as the building of nation states. It is a mistake to identify the ultimate polity with the world state (cf. Merle and Gosepath 2002, 7f).

An alternative solution seems to be to assign something like an 'as-if' status to transnational polities. The actual difference to the concept of a world state is expressed by terms like, 'soft' or, 'global governance' as well as in the slogan 'governance without government'. They mark a paradigm shift from the ideal of the territory bound nation state towards transnational networks and regimes. Still the issues to be settled on the transnational level remain public or common since they deal with the achievement of binding decisions and the production and provision of transnational public goods.

Secondly, the transition to the transnational level can refer to a certain class of duties of the common good which appear already on the nation state level but transcend it: Even on the level of the nation state duties of the common good are not only, 'internal' duties towards members of one's own society but also *external duties* towards members of other polities whose supply with basic common goods is affected by one's actions. An example may be the export of grain from undeveloped countries for the production of meat or of bio fuel when it would be needed for nutrition in the exporting countries themselves or becomes a causal factor to increase the price of grain making it unaffordable for some people.

Thirdly, the author's main point is that we should not only look for those institutions that maybe do not exist yet but for the political elites who have the power or influence to create them or to transform existing ones for the better and thus bear a specific responsibility for the realisation of the transnational common good. Following this thread, one should like to know what kind of duties can be derived from the basic transnational common good for transnational political elites.

What Duties Can be Derived from the Basic Transnational Common Good?

This last section is going to start with a very short outline of a theory of duties of the common good that has been developed elsewhere (cf. Bohlken 2006, 99–103). Duties of the common good make up a certain type of duties that can be situated somewhere between moral and legal duties. Thus, duties of the common good form a third class of ethical duties. Like legal duties they are constrained to outward actions instead of inner attitude. Another important feature which places duties of the common good near to legal duties is that they refer only to actions or omissions which are directly linked with one's profession and/or social position.[7] Thus, the duties of the common good can be transformed into legal duties; but more often than not, this option is not exercised since duties of the common good have a stronger moment of voluntariness which would be counteracted by legal enforcement and places them nearer to moral duties. Yet, one important difference to duties of virtue is that duties of the common good can be fulfilled following one's own interest – as long as this is congruent with public interest. Finally, duties of the common good are ethically legitimate social expectations. This means they refer to claims that members of one polity can demand from one another (general duties) or from a certain group of members of that polity (special duties).[8] The ethical legitimacy of these claims depends on whether they can be derived from the common good. Social expectations which lack such a deduction can be criticised as ethically illegitimate.

According to the definition of the responsibility elite given above transnational elites have a specific responsibility to shape and transform transnational relations such as the processes of globalisation in orientation to the basic transnational common good either by their own actions or by influencing others as a role model. Following this analysis, we can formulate a first general duty, some kind of metanorm, for transnational political elites derived from the basic transnational common good. Their responsibility for the transnational common good obligates them to produce, provide and sustain all basic transnational public goods that can *only* or at least can be *better* produced, provided and sustained by transnational institutions, organisations and regimes for each human being. A closer scrutiny reveals four subordinate duties:

- to establish and secure those transnational institutions, organisations and regimes necessary to produce, provide, and secure the basic transnational public goods for each human being;[9]
- to reform existing institutions, organisations etc. to meet this task;
- to make effective and sustainable use of financial and ecological resources, thus securing the basic transnational public goods for future generations;
- to be responsive to any stakeholders, in order to find out by public debate whose stakes are ethically legitimate.

---

7 This feature may be of some interest for the discussion on duties of help since it may restrain the circle of the obligated.

8 Additionally, the aforementioned external duties of the common good towards members of different polities are to be taken into account.

9 To give an example, one may refer to the establishing of work standards negotiated by representatives of WTO and ILO.

These duties are complemented by respective duties of the non elite members of the respective transnational polities to contribute their share. Furthermore, they are corresponded by the right of the non elite members to reclaim the fulfilment or to sanction the non fulfilment of these duties by means of public debate, protest or boycott.

Conclusion

This chapter has tried to demonstrate that national as well as transnational political elites have a specific potential to shape the processes of globalisation – for the better or for the worse. From this point of view the manifold processes of globalisation are not just the result of some anonymous functional systems. The author does not want to deny that these functional systems exist and develop their own dynamics. But still they can be shaped and transformed by the efforts of some powerful actors (political and financial elites) and, to a certain extent, also by the unified social expectations and efforts of smaller or larger groups of less powerful individuals (social movements, NGOs, etc.).

For the members of transnational political elites the responsibility for the transnational common good entails a shift from national regulation to the founding of transnational organisations and institutions respectively to the negotiation and ratification of multilateral treaties, regimes and agreements necessary for the successful solution of transnational problems. Furthermore, as has been pointed out above, some financial actors enter the scene and gain not only political weight but also – seen from a normative point of view – political legitimacy. Thus the primacy of political (governmental) elites, justified by their representing the people who elected them, somehow fades on transnational grounds. Some problems including the regulation of the markets to avoid or compensate market failures have to be solved as well on the national as on the transnational level but require not only different measures but also different structures. This shift should not only be seen as a loss of power for governmental elite – which it de facto is – but also as an enrichment in the sphere of the normative. The actual increasing of power for the heads of MNC's, for example, is accompanied by an increasing responsibility for the transnational common good. This increased responsibility can and should be made subject of concrete demands by the members of present and developing transnational polities.

References

Albert, M. (2007), 'Einleitung: Weltstaat und Weltstaatlichkeit: Neubestimmung des Politischen in der Weltgesellschaft', in Albert, M. et al. (eds), 9–23.

Albert, M. et al. (eds) (2007), *Weltstaat und Weltstaatlichkeit. Beobachtungen Globaler Politischer Strukturbildung* (Wiesbaden: VS Verlag für Sozialwissenschaften).

Bohlken, E. (2002), *Grundlagen einer Interkulturellen Ethik. Perspektiven der Transzendentalen Kulturphilosophie Heinrich Rickerts* (Würzburg: Königshausen & Neumann).

Bohlken, E. (2005), 'Die Macht der Eliten. Förderung des Gemeinwohls oder Gefährdung der Demokratie?', in Veith, W. et al. (eds), 88–104.

Dreitzel, H. (1962), *Elitebegriff und Sozialstruktur. Eine soziologische Begriffsanalyse* (Stuttgart).

Etzioni-Halevy, E. (1993), *The Elite Connection. Problems and Potential of Western Democracy* (Cambridge: Polity Press).

Gosepath, S. et al. (eds) (2002), *Weltrepublik. Globalisierung und Demokratie* (München: C.H. Beck).

Michels, R. (1957), *Zur Soziologie des Parteiwesens in der modernen Demokratie. Untersuchungen über die oligarchischen Tendenzen des Gruppenlebens*, Reprint of 2nd Edition. (Stuttgart: Kröner).

Mills, C. (1956), *The Power Elite* (New York: Oxford University Press).

Mosca, G. (1950), *Elementi di Sciencia Politica* (1896), dt.: Die herrschende Klasse: Grundlagen der politischen Wissenschaft (Bern: Verlag A. Francke AG).

Pareto, V. (1916), *Trattato di Sociologia Generale* (Florenz); dt. Pareto, V. (1962), System der Allgemeinen Soziologie, Eisermann, G. (ed.) (Stuttgart: Enke).

Ruggie, J. (1998), *Constructing the World* (London: Polity).

Ruggie, J. (2004), 'Reconstituting the Global Public Domain – Issues, Actors and Practices', *European Journal of International Relations* 10, 499–531.

Schumpeter, J. (1993), *Kapitalismus, Sozialismus und Demokratie* (1950), 7th augmented Edition. (Tübingen/Basel: Francke Verlag).

Veith, W. et al. (eds) (2005), *Macht und Ohnmacht. Konzeptionelle und Kontextuelle Erkundungen* (Münster).

von Kuenheim Stiftung, E. et al. (eds) (2004), *Verantwortung unternehmen* (Stuttgart: Leipzig).

Wieland, J. (2004), 'Die Büchse der Pandora. Unternehmensverantwortung in einer Globalen Welt', in v. Kuenheim Stiftung, E. et al. (eds), 30–39.

Willis, K. et al. (2002), 'Transnational Elites', *Geoforum* 33, 505–507.

Brunkhorst, H. (2002) [illegible] *Solidarität* [illegible] (Frankfurt am Main: Suhrkamp).

Chapter 14
World Poverty and Moral Free-Riding: The Obligations of Those Who Profit from Global Injustice[1]

Norbert Anwander

Introduction

Who should bear the costs for eradicating absolute poverty? Setting aside the extreme position that it is the poor and only the poor themselves with whom all responsibility for improving their lot lies, two principal answers have been proposed. On the first view, what matters is the *capacity* to alleviate poverty. The task of fighting poverty is the duty of all those who are in a position to do so, and the extent of one's obligation is basically a function of one's capacity.[2] On the second view, what counts is one's *contribution* to the causes of poverty. At least insofar as severe poverty results from an unjust global order, alleviating this effect is the duty of those who are involved in the primary cause, and the extent of one's obligation is basically a function of one's contribution to this cause.[3]

Regardless of the dispute between these two views, a case can be made for the supplementary thesis that the burden should also be born in part by those who have *benefited* from the causes of absolute poverty. The author has previously argued against Thomas Pogge's claim that there is a negative duty not to benefit from injustice and that those who do so owe its victims compensation.[4] The author does

---

1 Many thanks to Barbara Bleisch and Thomas Pogge for critical comments and helpful suggestions.

2 For versions of this view, see Singer (1972; 2006); Unger (1996); Wenar (2007). It is important to note that the capacity criterion may be interpreted in several ways with quite different results. Beyond the blunt question of who can avert the harm, we need to distinguish between (1) those who can provide relief *most effectively*; (2) those who can provide it *most efficiently*; and (3) those who can provide it *most easily*, i.e. at least cost to themselves. And it is a further question whether the costs for relief, regardless by whom it is provided in the first place, should as a second step be shifted on to those whom it hurts least.

3 For a sustained defence of this view, see Pogge (2002; 2005).

4 See Anwander (2005), and for a reply, Pogge (2005). For a strong statement of the view that 'profiting from injustice is wrong', see also Kelly (2004).

agree, however, that such profits can be grounds for obligations. This chapter is an attempt to clarify both the grounds and the obligations.

With regard to absolute poverty, what follows is strictly hypothetical: First, we do not know what as a matter of fact the main causes of world poverty are. Second, we are agnostic as to whether we are actually profiting from whatever we can identify as the causes of world poverty. The claim is merely that *if* we are profiting from a world order which *has* these disastrous effects (or from whatever else the causes of absolute poverty are), that fact will sustain the kind of obligations that we are going to outline.

The *Profiting Principle* that is put forward is not meant to be a competitor of either of the two principal views mentioned above, referring to *capacity* and *contribution* respectively. We should acknowledge that there is not one single criterion for assigning responsibilities but a plurality of considerations that are relevant for allocating the costs of putting bad situations right. Moreover, as we will see, the suggested principle is not entirely free-standing, but in part needs to be combined with more basic views about the grounds of our responsibilities towards those who suffer from severe poverty.

Profiting and Contributing

If we want to get clear about the distinctive role that profiting plays in a correct distribution of the costs for remedying some bad situation, it is essential that we are not led astray by overly loose notions of *profiting* (or benefiting, these terms will be used interchangeably) and *contributing* respectively. For one thing that renders benefiting from injustice morally dubious and explains why those who profit typically incur rectificatory obligations is the simple fact that benefiting from injustice often goes along with contributing to it. Not only is it frequently the case that beneficiaries from injustice, if not also perpetrators themselves, are involved in 'aiding and abetting', one could even argue that it is next to impossible to identify realistic situations in which someone purely benefits from injustice without in any way contributing to it.[5]

An effective, but distracting strategy for making such a claim about the impossibility of pure benefiting true is the appeal to a rather expansive notion of contributing. For instance, one can just define concepts such as *complicity* in a way that they cover benefiting. We can see this happening when the *United Nations Global Compact* distinguishes three forms in which corporate complicity in human rights abuse can occur – direct, beneficial, and silent – and characterises 'beneficial complicity' in human rights abuses as directly benefiting from human

5 See Anwander (2005); Anwander and Bleisch (2007).

rights abuses committed by someone else.[6] Now, whereas keeping silent may plausibly be seen as an instance of complicity, we may doubt whether it is helpful to characterise such benefiting as a relevant form of complicity. One reason for being sceptical is that such benefiting need play no role at all in an explanation of those unjust conditions.

There is a further way in which profiting from injustice can be too easily linked to contributing to it. This is by giving the latter an expansive reading on which it includes *perpetuating injustice*. In this spirit we might say that some third party contributes to injustice when it enjoys some good which has been stolen by someone else. The author has made use of such examples.[7] But they are potentially misleading, because it is questionable whether wrongfully holding on to someone else's property is best characterised as an instance of profiting from injustice. Needless to say, victims of theft have a claim that they are given back what by right is theirs. It is also plausible that restitution of stolen goods plays some role in the context of world poverty. But we do not need the notion of profiting from injustice to explain the wrongness of holding on to other people's property. The very idea of property already sustains the demand for restitution. Moreover, as we will see, it is not very illuminating to conceptualise profiting from injustice on the model of enjoying stolen goods.

Profiting as Grounds of Moral Obligation

Here is how the author proposes to understand the notion of *profiting from injustice*: To begin with, *profiting* just means 'being made better off'. Profiting, as we are defining it, does not require that you actually do something, for instance actively take advantage of a situation or explicitly accept some gain. You need not even be aware of your luck. Nothing more is required than that you are in fact in a better position than you would otherwise be. But what is 'otherwise'? This raises the tricky issue of what it is in comparison to which beneficiaries are supposed to be better off. In this chapter, we must make do with the rather rough idea that the relevant baseline for comparison is the closest possible world in which there would not be the relevant act or state from which someone is thought to be profiting.[8]

6 See *United Nations Global Compact*. Principle II states: 'Businesses should make sure they are not complicit in human rights abuses'. The threefold distinction mentioned in the text occurs in the accompanying explanatory statement.

7 See Anwander (2005, 42); Anwander and Bleisch (2007, 186 et seq.).

8 One major problem with this way of identifying the relevant baseline is the following: The closest possible world in which the wrongful act does not occur or the unjust state does not obtain need not be one in which those who in the actual world are seen as putative beneficiaries would be worse off. They might even be better off in that more just world. For instance, some white businesses in South Africa which were said to have profited from the apartheid regime argued that, all in all, they would have been better off

More precisely, we are looking at that part of your gain which is to be explained by reference to the act or state in question – as opposed, among other things, to what is due to your effort, even though in that alternative world there would have been no opportunity for you to make this effort. Next, you are profiting *from injustice* when what makes you better off is an unjust act or a state of injustice. For instance, we may say that many white businesses in South Africa profited in such a way from the apartheid regime.[9]

Turning now to the *moral* position of those who have benefited from injustice, the following principle is proposed:

The *Profiting Principle (PP)*: Independent of any other obligations they may have towards the victims of injustice, those who have been benefited by an act or a state of injustice must give up their profits towards feasible measures for redressing this injustice and remedying its effects.[10]

While it may seem natural to think of situations where some tangible good has been moved from the victims of injustice to the beneficiaries, these cases are not the focus of *PP*. As pointed out before, such illegitimate transfers can and should directly be treated as issues of property. We do not need to appeal to profiting from injustice in order to find a basis for claims of restitution.

The profit that is derived from some unjust act or some state of injustice frequently occurs *at the expense* of the victim. The affluent foreigner who employs an aboriginal driver at half the wage he would have to pay other drivers, taking advantage of the discrimination prevalent in that society, profits at the expense of this particular victim of injustice.[11] What one gains, the other loses. Such a direct correlation of profit and loss is, however, not essential in *PP*. What establishes the relevant link between beneficiary and victim is just the fact that the former benefits from the *same* wrongful act/state which wrongs and harms the latter. Thus, it covers profits made by doing business with regimes that violate human rights, regardless of whether these gains immediately derive from and correspond to what the victims of injustice are being deprived of.

Moreover, in line with our definition of profiting as being made better off, *PP* is not restricted to cases in which you *voluntarily* accept some benefit or actively

if there had been no such regime (For statements to this effect, see chap. 2, 'Business and Labour', in the *Truth and Reconciliation Commission of South Africa Report*, vol. 4, 1998). In the same vein it might be held that we, citizens of affluent countries, would by no means be worse off in a fully just world.

9 See chap. 2, 'Business and Labour', in the *Truth and Reconciliation Commission of South Africa Report*, vol. 4, 1998.

10 The *Profiting Principle* should be read as appropriately hedged. The author does not want to exclude the possibility of situations where the right thing to do is to use one's resources for immediately mitigating suffering instead of giving up one's profits for the purpose of remedying the effects of the specific piece of injustice from which one has benefited. The comparative stringency of the demands postulated by *PP* are left open.

11 This example is taken from Pogge (2004, 278–279).

take advantage of some state of injustice. It suffices that one is as a matter of fact better off due to that injustice. The mere fact that one's benefit is contingent on a state which needs to be rectified or remedied is seen as grounds for having to give it up for that very purpose.[12]

Most importantly, the proposed principle looks in two directions: On the one hand, *PP* pertains to the obligations that beneficiaries of injustice have towards its *victims*. It says something about the claims that can be made by the victims of injustice against those who have profited from the causes of their plight. On the other hand, *PP* concerns the fair *distribution of burdens* for carrying out a morally necessary task, such as eradicating absolute poverty. It says something about the claims against beneficiaries that can be made by those who are willing to discharge this duty and actually do so. It is the latter, the distinctive role that profiting plays in an equitable distribution of the costs for averting very grave harm, with which this chapter is primarily concerned. But we will begin with a brief sketch of what the obligations owed to the victims are taken to be.

Obligations Owed to Victims of Injustice

Similar to and in addition to the special rectificatory claims which victims hold against the perpetrators of injustice, they can make special claims against those who have profited from what has caused their plight. Other things being equal, it seems that the obligations of such beneficiaries are more extensive than the duties of mere bystanders, i.e. of agents whose only link to the victims is their capacity to provide relief.

Exactly how far do these obligations extend? According to *PP*, there are two decisive restrictions. First, the upper level of what beneficiaries of injustice must do is strictly determined by their profits. At most they are required to give up their gains, for there is no reason why *qua* beneficiaries they should end up being worse off. This contrasts with the obligations of perpetrators, where the measure for what is owed are the harm caused and the means needed to set things right. Making up may well make them worse off, but that is perfectly acceptable. Second, what victims can claim is that beneficiaries give up their profits insofar as there is still injustice (from which the latter have profited) that has not been rectified and harm (from which the latter have profited) that has not been remedied. Once this has been achieved, however, beneficiaries may hold on to what has accrued to them. The same holds when there are no feasible measures for putting things right to which beneficiaries could contribute. Victims cannot claim that they disgorge their profits just so that no-one enjoys any net gain from injustice.

12 On whether passive, non-voluntary benefiting from injustice can make one liable to give up the profits, see Thomson (1986, 152); Fullinwider (1975, 316–318); Amdur (1979, 231); Butt (2007, 139–142).

This latter restriction on when gains must be given up may appear too lenient. Some have argued that there is a moral obligation not to profit from injustice and that it is in principle wrong to do so.[13] Others will at least feel uneasy about a world in which some benefit from the injustice done to others. But you might also go so far as to judge that a world in which there are no such profits or where they have been eliminated is morally preferable to one where some people are better off due to the injustice done to others. Whatever the merits of such views, be they expressed in deontic terms or in evaluative terms, it is important to note that they do not engage the issue that *PP* is about. This principle is meant to go some way towards answering the question with which we started off: Who should bear the costs for putting a very bad situation right? *PP* states that gains resulting from unjust acts or states of injustice are resources that must be given up and can legitimately be taken away for redressing injustice and alleviating its harmful effects. In a nutshell: The principle we are considering is not about cleaning your dirty hands, but about using some particular portion of what is in your hands towards cleaning the world.[14]

The proviso that the gains are to be used for rectifying injustice whose effects have not yet been remedied also takes care of incidents in the very distant past: Even if it could be established that someone today is a beneficiary of unjust acts committed by the Romans some 2,000 years ago, it is difficult to see how such gains could be used towards rectifying that historic injustice. The problem is not only the non-existence of victims who could make such a claim. For presumably there is also no way that such gains could be usefully employed for alleviating the effects of this injustice.

Profiting from Injustice and Moral Free-Riding

The *Profiting Principle* makes no difference when contributor and beneficiary are identical.[15] We have just seen this with regard to the additional claims that benefiting from injustice may create on the part of the latter's victims. For the claim that a person takes up (part of) the slack adds nothing when that person should have done the job in the first place. There is nothing that person *qua* beneficiary owes to the

13 See references in fn. 4.

14 There are a number of issues to do with profiting from injustice which are not covered by *PP.* The principle's silence on them should not be taken as denying their importance. One such issue is equitable profit-sharing. It is also worth considering a virtue-ethical perspective on profiting from injustice. For some suggestions, see Anwander and Bleisch (2007, 183–184).

15 Things are more complicated when several parties are involved, such as when a number of individual agents are responsible for a bad situation or there is more than one beneficiary. Needless to say, certainly in the context of global poverty, these more complicated scenarios are also more realistic ones.

victims that person is not already obliged to do *qua* perpetrator.[16] Turning now to the issue of an equitable distribution of the costs for putting some unacceptably bad situation right, it is even more obvious that *PP* has no impact when contributor and beneficiary coincide. For one single party is just not enough to distribute anything. There is not much point in saying that a person *qua* perpetrator can shift some of the costs on to her or himself *qua* beneficiary.

Whenever there is a difference between perpetrators and beneficiaries of injustice, and that includes most real world cases, the *Profiting Principle* is however highly relevant for a fair assignment of the costs for eliminating injustice and its effects. We will explain this by introducing the concept of *moral free-riding*.

A free-rider is one who obtains a benefit without paying all or part of its cost.[17] More accurately, we can say that *free-riding* occurs when one benefits from another person's action while the costs involved in it are more than proportionately covered by that person (or other people).[18] Familiar examples include 'shipowners whose vessels take navigational advantage of a lighthouse although they have neither contributed to its erection nor to its maintenance',[19] and, of course, passengers without a valid ticket.

Moral free-riding is the same, but with a twist. To be sure, all free-riding is usually considered morally wrong. Although the author certainly shares this judgement, it is not merely this negative moral evaluation that we have in mind by speaking of *moral* free-riding. The concept of moral free-riding, as we are using it here, involves a distinctively moral cost-calculation. While ordinary free-riding relates to what it takes to produce some good or to bring about some desired state, moral free-riding concerns the 'moral costs' of that good or state. Diverging from common usage – where it commonly stands for some moral value that gets sacrificed by some course of action – the term *moral costs* is used to refer to what is needed in order to make some way of conduct, some product, or some institution morally acceptable. This includes both precautionary measures and measures of reparation. Moral free-riding, we can then say, occurs when someone profits from another person's wrongful action, from situations of injustice, or generally from what is morally unacceptable, without covering some appropriate share of the moral costs. Moral free-riders benefit from a state which morally

16 Thomas Pogge has suggested that perpetrators' remedial obligations may be *more stringent* when they happen to be beneficiaries too. If this is meant to have implications for the relative strengths of victims' claims on us when we are unable to meet all our obligations, it strikes the author as rather odd (see Anwander 2005, 44). What seems more plausible, however, is the idea that profiting perpetrators must be ready to accept increased costs to themselves in discharging their remedial obligations.

17 See Gauthier (1986, 96).

18 See Gosseries (2004, 43).

19 See Gauthier (1986, 17).

ought not to be without doing their fair share in eliminating it and neutralising its negative effects.[20]

Applying these concepts to world poverty, we can say: The moral costs of an unjust global order are whatever it takes to reform it and alleviate the misery it has caused. Since morally there should be no injustice and no severe poverty, you are a moral free-rider if you benefit from such an order, while not sharing in the task of making it morally acceptable. You let others bear the costs of the morally necessary task of eradicating global poverty while profiting from its causes.

How we should assess this concept of moral free-riding and its potential application to global poverty depends on its implications. This chapter will comment on three points.

First, we should not say that beneficiaries of injustice are free-riding on its *victims*. If, as has been suggested, victims have a special claim against those who have benefited in the relevant way, the latter do indeed violate a duty if they fail to help under the specified circumstances. Yet that violation is not a matter of moral free-riding. Beneficiaries' failure to help is only unfair against those that do make an effort to fight injustice and its effects.

Second, as has just been said, the people on whom unhelpful beneficiaries are free-riding are those who make an effort to fight injustice and redress its harms. Such an analysis seems plausible enough when we are considering people who engage in these tasks just because they can: Why should people who are not otherwise connected to the severely poor make sacrifices while those who have been made better off by the injustice hold on to their gains? It seems to me that part of the reason why many ordinary citizens of the affluent countries are unwilling to give up a more substantial part of their wealth is our feeling that the various beneficiaries of the causes of world poverty (among whom we do not count ourselves and from whom we distance ourselves) should do more. But there may also be a more controversial implication. As it stands, *PP* does not exclude that *perpetrators* too can shift some of their costs on to the beneficiaries. Actually the author thinks that this is correct: Why should the perpetrators, who surely must do whatever it takes to undo the effects of their misdeeds, foot the entire bill while there are others who are enjoying the good effects their wrongful actions had for them?[21]

---

20 Admittedly, one could talk about the costs involved in upholding a state of injustice, for instance the means it takes to keep an oppressive regime in power. But surely the moral problem is not that those who merely benefit from such a regime are being unfair to the oppressors who keep the unjust system running. Insofar as fairness is an issue, the costs that matter are the *moral* costs: what is needed to undo the unjust system and its harmful effects.

21 One might worry that having beneficiaries bear some of the remedial costs is too easy on the perpetrators, who may end up not having to pay the full price for what they did. We must, however, not compound the question of who should bear the costs for remedying harm with issues of punishment.

Third, if moral free-riding is a matter of exclusively benefiting from a situation which morally ought not to be, it makes no difference whether one is profiting from injustice or from the *natural causes* of other people's misery. Insofar as there is any duty to remedy that situation, one may not hold on to profits accruing from it. Again, this is taken as speaking in favour of the proposed account rather than being a weakness of it. The *Profiting Principle* was introduced as a supplementary thesis, because far from replacing any of the principal views why we are morally required to fight global poverty, in its distributive element, it presupposes more basic views. Yet it is not wedded to any particular position, but is quite neutral among them and can supplement any such view.

Even if one is sympathetic to the general idea that we need to think about fair ways of assigning the costs for remedying morally unacceptable situations and furthermore agrees with the more specific suggestion that there is an issue of free-riding, one may wonder: Why not rely on a simpler, more straightforward moral argument of free-riding? If it is our collective duty to promote justice and to eradicate poverty, then surely each of us ought to play his part in this effort. And we could just say that someone is free-riding if he fails to share in the task of bringing about a world with more justice and less poverty. In not doing his part, he is a free-rider – quite independent of whether he has profited or not.[22]

While the author certainly does not want to deny that those who fail to do their fair share are properly called free-riders, to the author insists on the special moral significance of what the above concept of *moral free-riding* is meant to capture. The first thing we can say of those who refuse to engage in a collective moral task, such as making poverty history, or less ambitiously, averting serious harm, is just that they violate their duty. Quite apart from considerations of fairness, how they behave is wrong. Insofar as by saving costs they enjoy some advantage over others and insofar as their non-compliance puts additional burdens on others, their uncooperative behaviour can then further be characterised as unfair. From this generic issue of (un)fairness the cases addressed by *PP* are distinct in the following ways: First, the beneficiaries in question are not just better off because they have shirked their duty and not paid their share. Their gains are more immediately based on the existence of some institution, the holding of some state, and so on. For illustration, take again the lighthouse: Seeing that all too often ships, both foreign ones and ships from our own place, get lost, we come to the conclusion that it is our collective moral task to set up a lighthouse. The duty to contribute our share to this project holds even if we ourselves will never venture on the sea and have no use for a lighthouse. Surely the advantage that accrues to those who steer a ship, take advantage of the lighthouse, and thereby profit from it falls into a different category than what we would save by failing to do our duty. Second, in the cases of moral free-riding which we have been highlighting the following holds: Even if the beneficiaries in question initially lack any obligation to remedy some harm, the fact that they have been made better off by what caused it does create an obligation

22 This point has been raised independently by the people mentioned in fn. 1.

to share in this task. Unlike in the more standard cases of free-riding, we need not assume that there is already an obligation. Rather, the obligation is just based on the fact of profiting and it may be a pure obligation of fairness.

Profiting and World Poverty

It is a legitimate question to ask how relevant the *Profiting Principle* is with regard to world poverty. Specifically one would like to know whether and how much we, ordinary citizens of high-income countries, are in fact benefiting from its causes, for instance from an unjust global order. In response, we will just repeat that this thesis only concerns a normative question. As regards severe poverty in the real world, it must be taken as a conditional claim. The author is inclined to think, however, that virtually all of us are likely beneficiaries of an unjust global order. Remember that it is not part of *PP* that one profits voluntarily. Therefore, it applies even if we cannot help being better off. Neither is there a need to show that our profit is an exact counterpart of what the victims of that order have lost. It would be enough to show that some of the causes of the misery of others are also causes of increased wealth for us.

But even if it turned out that *PP* applies only to some restricted number of people, that would still be a relevant fact for the non-profiting rest of us. We can bring this out, and indeed the point of *PP* in general, by revisiting a familiar example. For the purpose of illustration let us just assume that thinking about children drowning in ponds is an illuminating way of thinking about world poverty.[23] There is a sense in which assigning tasks according to *capacity* is the obvious policy for such situations: If you are in a position to save the drowning child most effectively and most efficiently, then surely it is you who should jump into the pond and save it. But this morally contingent fact about your unique ability to prevent something very bad from happening is no reason at all why the costs in terms of time spent and clothes ruined should exclusively lie with you. In fact, there are potentially several others on to whom this burden should be shifted. For a start, those who commissioned the pond in the first place ought to bear some of the costs. Next, the toddler's family not only owes you a debt of gratitude but should also reimburse you if they can. If something like the *Profiting Principle* holds, a further plausible candidate for covering part of your expenses are the people who have enjoyed the pond's aesthetic value and whatever other pleasures it provides. For they have benefited from a piece of infrastructure that comes at a moral price. Given this benefit, their refusal to take up some of the moral costs involved in the pond would mean that they are morally free-riding on you. In the same way, those who are made better off by living in an unjust world would be mistaken to think

23 As suggested in Singer (1972). The literature on why Singer's analogy fails is vast. For a rare defence, see Cullity (2004).

that these gains come with no strings attached. Fairness may require that they give up their profits for the sake of overcoming severe poverty.

References

Amdur, R. (1979), 'Compensatory Justice: The Question of Costs', *Political Theory* 7:2, 229–244.

Anwander, N. (2005), 'Contributing and Benefiting: Two Grounds for Duties to the Victims of Injustice', *Ethics and International Affairs* 19:1, 39–45.

Anwander, N. and Bleisch, B. (2007), 'Beitragen und Profitieren. Ungerechte Weltordnung und Individuelle Verstrickung', in Bleisch, B. et al. (eds).

Bleisch, B. et al. (eds) (2007), *Weltarmut und Ethik* (Paderborn: Mentis).

Butt, D. (2007), 'On Benefiting from Injustice', *Canadian Journal of Philosophy* 37:1, 129–152.

Chatterjee, D. (ed.) (2004), *The Ethics of Assistance. Morality and the Distant Needy* (Cambridge: Cambridge University Press).

Cullity, G. (2004), *The Moral Demands of Affluence* (Oxford: Oxford University Press).

Fullinwider, R. (1975), 'Preferential Hiring and Compensation', *Social Theory and Practice* 3:3, 307–320.

Gosseries, A. (2004): 'Historical Emissions and Free-Riding', *Ethical Perspectives* 11:1, 36–60.

Kelly, E. (2004), 'Human Rights as Foreign Policy Imperatives', in Chatterjee, D. (ed.).

Miller, D. (2001), 'Distributing Responsibilities', *The Journal of Political Philosophy* 9:4, 453–471.

Pogge, T. (2002), *World Poverty and Human Rights* (Cambridge: Polity Press).

Pogge, T. (2004), '"Assisting" the Global Poor', in Chatterjee, D. (ed.).

Pogge, T. (2005), 'Severe Poverty as a Violation of Negative Duties', *Ethics and International Affairs* 19:1, 55–83.

Pogge, T. (ed.) (2007), *Freedom from Poverty as a Human Right. Who Owes What to the Very Poor?* (Oxford: Oxford University Press).

Singer, P. (1972), 'Famine, Affluence, and Morality', *Philosophy and Public Affairs* 1:2, 229–243.

Singer, P. (2006), 'What Should a Billionaire Give – and What Should You?', *The New York Times*, 17 December.

Thomson, J. (1986), 'Preferential Hiring', in *Rights, Restitution, and Risk: Essays in Moral Theory* (Cambridge, MA: Harvard University Press).

Unger, P. (1996), *Living High and Letting Die. Our Illusion of Innocence* (New York: Oxford University Press).

Wenar, L. (2007), 'Responsibility and Severe Poverty', in Pogge, T. (ed.).

PART 4
Policies and Actions

Chapter 15

Medicines for the World: Boosting Innovation without Obstructing Free Access[1]

Thomas Pogge

Summary

The TRIPS Agreement has imposed worldwide a single regime for encouraging pharmaceutical innovation through monopoly patents. Pricing advanced medicines out of the reach of poor patients and encouraging neglect of diseases concentrated among them, this regime produces avoidable disease and death on a massive scale. Appeal to natural rights of innovators cannot defend this regime: Their efforts can justify ownership of things (apples, medically effective molecules), not ownership of types of thing (a kind of fruit or molecule). Appeal to mutual advantage cannot defend the regime: Monopoly constraints on free market interaction impose great costs on the poor who often do not benefit from monopoly-driven innovation.

A just solution involves – as a complement to the patent regime – a government-financed global Health Impact Fund that encourages the development of new vital medicines by promising to reward successful innovators according to each medicine's impact on the global burden of disease. This comprehensive advance market commitment would elicit a stream of new vital medicines immediately available at or below competitive market prices. It would enhance the profit opportunities of pharmaceutical companies and decimate many of the most destructive diseases.

This chapter is part of a collective effort, funded by the Australian Research Council, the BUPA Foundation, and the European Commission, to which Christian Barry, Laura Biron, Leila Chirayath, Kieran Donaghue, Jocelyn Finlay, Aidan Hollis, Miltos Ladikas, Matt Peterson, Michael Ravvin, Doris Schroeder, Michael Selgelid, Jie Tian, Ling Tong, Kit Wellman and Judith Whitworth have contributed substantially.

1 With the kind and cost-free permission of the editors, this chapter has been reproduced with small alterations, from the English edition of *Sur: Revista Internacional de direitos humanos 8* (2008), 116–141, which is available at <http://www.surjournal.org>.

Background

Poverty has always been the fate of a majority of human beings. Massive affluence is a more recent phenomenon. Today, the affluent have vastly more income and wealth than would be necessary to free the hundreds of millions now trapped in life-threatening poverty. At current exchange rates, the poorest half of the world's population has about 3 per cent of global household income as against 6 per cent received by the most affluent 1 per cent of US households containing only three million people.[2] The bottom half of humankind owns about 1 per cent of all global wealth as against 3 per cent owned by the world's 1,125 billionaires.[3] A mere 1,125 people own three times as much as the poorest 3.4 billion.[4]

These radical inequalities are staggering. And they have been increasing rapidly – not only globally,[5] but also within most countries. In the US, for instance, the bottom half of the population saw its share of national income slashed from 26.4 per cent to 12.8 per cent since the 1970s,[6] while those in the top half per cent of the income hierarchy enlarged their share from 6.1 to 18.6 per cent.[7] In China during 1990–2004, the income share of the bottom half declined from 27 per cent to 18 per cent, while that of the top tenth increased from 25 per cent to 35 per cent.[8] In recent decades, income inequality has been clearly declining in only four countries.[9]

Such huge inequalities are especially remarkable when those at the bottom lack not merely pocket money, denying them the toys of the rich, but access to the most basic necessities of human life. And this is actually the case, both globally

2 Aggregate figure for the poor kindly supplied by Branko Milanovic of the World Bank. Figure for US households calculated from Saez and Piketty (2003, 1–39, as updated in 'Tables and Figures Updated to 2006 in Excel Format').

3 Cf. Davies, Sandstrom, Shorrocks, and Wolff (2006, Appendix 1, Table 10a); and Kroll (2008).

4 'Billion' is used in the US sense to signify 1,000 million.

5 Over the 1984–2004 globalisation period, household final consumption expenditure per capita (in constant dollars) rose 56.3 per cent in the high-income OECD countries. During the same period, real (inflation and purchasing-power adjusted) consumption expenditure reportedly rose 48.62 per cent at the median, 33.72 per cent at the 15th percentile, 31.92 per cent at the 7th percentile, 22.87 per cent at the 2nd percentile, and 9.64 per cent at the 1st percentile. See Pogge (2008a, Table 6). See also Milanovic (2005, 108–111).

6 Cf. WIDER (2007, line 4664) and Roney (2007).

7 Cf. Saez and Piketty (2003, Table A3).

8 The 1990 data are from Table 1 of Minoiu and Reddy (2008). The 2004 data are from the World Bank's World Development Indicators dataset (available to subscribers only), accessed 18 April 2008.

9 The WIDER (2007) database on the subject lists 4981 surveys for 156 countries and areas. Available data for 108 of these jurisdictions are spotty or show no clear trend. In Brazil, France, Mauritania, and Sierra Leone, income inequality appears to be clearly lower this decade than in the 1980s – in the remaining 44 jurisdictions, clearly higher.

and in most countries. The poverty endured by the bottom half of humankind poses serious dangers to their health and survival. The poor worldwide face greater environmental hazards than the rest of us: From contaminated water, filth, pollution, worms and insects. They are exposed to greater dangers from people around them: Through traffic, crime, communicable disease, and the cruelties of the more affluent. They lack means to protect themselves and their families against such hazards: Through clean water, nutritious food, good hygiene, ample rest, adequate clothing, and safe shelter. They lack the means to enforce their legal rights or to press for political reform. They are often obliged by dire need or debt to incur additional health risks: By selling a kidney, for instance, or by accepting hazardous work in prostitution, mining, construction, domestic service, textile and carpet production. They lack financial reserves and access to public sources of medical knowledge and treatments, and therefore face worse odds of recovering from disease. Mutually reinforcing, these factors ensure that the poor bear a hugely disproportional burden of disease – especially of communicable, maternal, perinatal and nutritional conditions – and a hugely disproportional share of premature deaths: 30 per cent of all deaths each year – 18 million, are from poverty-related causes. These much greater burdens of morbidity and premature mortality in turn entail large economic burdens that keep most of the poor trapped in lifelong poverty.

This cycle of mutually reinforcing poverty and disease can be broken by reducing or eradicating severe poverty. It has been argued that this can be done effectively by reforming various features of existing global institutional arrangements that – beneficial to the affluent and maintained by them – contribute greatly to the persistence of poverty.[10] But it is also possible to reduce the global burden of disease (GBD) more directly: Existing huge mortality and morbidity rates can be dramatically lowered by reforming the way the development of new medical treatments is funded. This chapter will sketch a concrete, feasible, and politically realistic reform plan that would give medical innovators stable and reliable financial incentives to address the diseases of the poor. If adopted, this plan would not add much to the overall cost of global health care spending. In fact, on any plausible accounting, which would take note of the huge economic losses caused by the present GBD, the reform would actually pay for itself. Moreover, it would distribute the cost of global health care spending more fairly across countries, across generations, and between those lucky enough to enjoy good health and the unlucky ones suffering from serious medical conditions.

The Problem

Medical progress has traditionally been fuelled from two main sources: Government funding and sales revenues. The former – given to universities, corporations, other

10 Cf. Pogge (2008b, chap. 6–8).

research organisations and governmental research facilities such as the US National Institutes of Health – has typically been *push* funding focused on basic research. Sales revenues, usually reaped by corporations, have mostly funded more applied research resulting in the development of specific medicines. Sales revenues, by their nature, constitute *pull* funding: An innovation has to be developed to the point of marketability before any sales revenues can be realised from it.

The fixed cost of developing a new medicine is extremely high for two reasons: It is very expensive to research and refine a new medicine and then to take it through elaborate clinical trials and national approval processes. Moreover, most promising research ideas fail somewhere along the way and thus never lead to a marketable product. Both factors combine to raise the research and development (R&D) cost per new marketable medicine to somewhere around half a billion to one billion dollars. Commencing manufacture of a new medicine once it has been invented and approved is cheap by comparison. Because of this fixed-cost imbalance, pharmaceutical innovation is not sustainable in a free market system: Competition among manufacturers would quickly drive down the price of a new medicine to near its long term marginal cost of production, and the innovator would get nowhere near recovering its R&D investment.

The conventional way of correcting this market failure of undersupply is to award innovators intellectual property rights that entitle them to bar competitors or to charge them licensing fees. Either way, the result of such monopolies is an artificially increased sales price that enables innovators to recoup their R&D expenses through selling products that, even at prices far above marginal cost, are in heavy demand.

Monopolies are generally denounced by economists as inefficient and by ethicists as an immoral interference in people's freedom to produce and exchange. In the case of patents, however, many believe that the curtailment of individual freedom can be justified by the benefit, provided patents are carefully designed. One important design feature is that patents confer only a temporary monopoly. Once the patent expires, competitors can freely enter the market with copies of the original innovation and consumers need no longer pay a high mark-up over the competitive market price. Temporal limits make sense because additional years of patent life barely strengthen innovation incentives: At a typical industry discount rate of 11 per cent per annum, a 10-year effective patent life generates 65 per cent, and a 15-year effective patent life 79 per cent, of the profit (discounted to present value) that a permanent patent would deliver.[11] It makes no sense to impose monopoly prices on all future generations for the sake of so slight a gain in innovation incentives.

During the life of the patent, everyone is legally barred from producing, selling and buying a patented medicine without permission from the patentee. This restraint hurts generic producers and it also hurts consumers by depriving

11 This calculation assumes constant nominal profit each year. In reality, annual profit may rise (as a medicine becomes better known) or fall (through increased competition or reduced incidence of the target disease).

them of the chance of buying such medicines at competitive market prices. Still, consumers also benefit from the arsenal of new medicines whose development is motivated by the prospect of mark-ups.

It may seem obvious that this benefit outweighs the loss of freedom. But we must consider that not everyone is either affluent enough to buy advanced medicines at monopoly prices or fortunate enough to need them only after patent expiration. Many human beings are trapped in severe poverty. Most of them derive no benefit from patented medicines because they cannot get access to them. These people can object that the patent regime gives them nothing in return for the freedom it deprives them of.[12] If the freedom to produce, sell and buy advanced medicines were not curtailed, then the affluent would need to find another (for them possibly less convenient) way of incentivising pharmaceutical research. But advanced medicines would then be available at competitive market prices, and the poor would have a much better chance to gain access to them through their own funds or with the help of national or international government agencies or non-governmental organisations. The loss of freedom monopoly patents inflict on billions of poor people is a huge loss in terms of disease and premature death. There is no associated gain that could compensate those suffering these losses; and the gains monopoly patents bring to the affluent cannot possibly justify these losses either.

This objection was less pertinent until the 1990s, when strict patent rules were mostly confined to the affluent states, which allowed the less developed countries to have weaker patent protections or none at all. This exemption of poor countries had little effect on innovation incentives because, in these countries, those able to afford advanced medicines at monopoly prices are few, relative to the one-billion population of the high-income countries. But the exemption brought relief to many poor residents of poor counties: to all those who obtained at competitive market prices advanced medicines they would not have been able to obtain at the much higher profit-maximising monopoly price.

The diversity of national regulations was destroyed in the 1990s when a powerful alliance of industries (software, entertainment, pharmaceutical, and agribusinesses) induced the Clinton Administration and other wealthy states to press strong, globally uniform intellectual property rules upon the world. Acceptance of this regime, enshrined in the TRIPS (Trade-Related Aspects of Intellectual Property Rights) Agreement of 1994, was made a condition of WTO membership which, it was then promised, would allow poor countries to reap large benefits from trade liberalisation. While the affluent states have been slow to lower their trade barriers and subsidies, they have worked hard toward implementing intellectual property rights in the less developed countries – with devastating effects, for instance, on the evolution of the AIDS epidemic.

---

12 Another objection one might make is that lucrative monopoly rewards are unfair, because the affluent enjoy crushing advantages in the innovation race.

The world responds to the catastrophic health crisis among the global poor in a variety of ways: With the usual declarations, working papers, conferences, summits, and working groups first and foremost, of course; but also with efforts to fund delivery of medicines to the poor through *intergovernmental initiatives* such as 3 by 5,[13] through *governmental programs* such as the US President's Emergency Plan for AIDS Relief (PEPFAR), through *public-private partnerships* like the Global Alliance for Vaccines and Immunization (GAVI) and the Global Fund to Fight AIDS, Tuberculosis and Malaria (GFATM), and through medicine donations from pharmaceutical companies; and with various efforts to foster the development of new medicines for the diseases of the poor, such as the Drugs for Neglected Diseases Initiative (DNDi), the Institute for One World Health, the Novartis Institute for Tropical Diseases, and various prizes as well as advance purchase commitments and advance market commitments.[14]

Such a busy diversity of initiatives looks good and creates the impression that a lot is being done to solve the problem. And most of these efforts are really doing good by improving the situation relative to what it would be otherwise. Still, these efforts are not nearly sufficient to protect the poor. It is unrealistic to hope that enough billions of dollars will be devoted to neutralising the cost imposed on the world's poor by the globalisation of 20-year patents. And it is even more unrealistic to hope that such billions will reliably and efficiently be spent year after year. It makes sense then to look for a more systemic solution that addresses the global health crisis at its root. Involving institutional reform, such a systemic solution is politically more difficult to achieve. But, once achieved, it is also politically much easier to sustain. And it pre-empts most of the huge and collectively inefficient mobilisations currently required to produce the many stop-gap measures, which can at best only mitigate the effects of the structural problems they leave untouched.

---

13 Announced in 2003, this joint WHO/UN AIDS program was meant to provide, by 2005, anti-retroviral treatment to 3 million (out of what were then estimated to be 40.3 million) AIDS patients in the less developed countries. In fact, the number of patients receiving such treatment increased by 0.9 million to reach 1.3 million by the end of 2005. See WHO (2006).

14 A prize is a specific reward offered for the development of a new medicine that meets certain specifications. It can be in the form of a cash payment or in some other form, for instance the extension of a patent on another medicine that is in high demand by affluent patients. An advance purchase commitment (APC) is a promise to buy, at a pre-set and lucrative price, a certain large number of doses of a new medicine that meets certain specifications. An advance market commitment (AMC) is a promise to subsidise the sale of a certain large number of doses of a new medicine that meets certain specifications. The only AMC issued thus far – funded by Italy, the UK, Canada, Russia, Norway, and the Gates Foundation – is for vaccines against pneumococcal disease, a major cause of pneumonia and meningitis among the poor. News reports suggest that it is designed to serve pharmaceutical industry interests first and foremost. See, for example, Miller (2007).

The quest for such a systemic solution should start from an analysis of the main drawbacks of the newly globalised monopoly patent regime. These are:

High prices

While a medicine is under patent, it will be sold near the profit-maximising monopoly price which is largely determined by the demand curve of the affluent. When wealthy people really want a drug, then its price can be raised very high above the cost of production before increased gains from enlarging the mark-up are outweighed by losses from reduced sales volume. With patented medicines, mark-ups in excess of 1,000 per cent are not exceptional.[15] When such high monopoly prices prevail, only a few of the poor can have access through the charity of others.

Neglect of diseases concentrated among the poor

Under a monopoly patent regime, such diseases – no matter how widespread and severe they may be – are not lucrative targets for pharmaceutical R&D. This is so because the demand for such a medicine drops off very steeply as the patentee enlarges the mark-up. There is no prospect, then, of achieving high sales volume *and* a large mark-up. Moreover, there is the risk that a successful research effort will be greeted with loud demands to make the medicine available at marginal cost or even for free, which would force the innovator to write off its R&D cost as a loss. In view of such prospects, biotechnology and pharmaceutical companies predictably prefer even the trivial ailments of the affluent, such as hair loss and acne, over tuberculosis and sleeping sickness. This problem of neglected diseases has become known as the 10/90 problem, alluding to only 10 per cent of all pharmaceutical research being focussed on diseases that account for 90 per cent of the GBD.[16]

Bias toward symptom relief

Medicines can be roughly sorted into three categories: Curative medicines remove the disease from the patient's body; symptom-relieving medicines improve well-being and functioning without removing the disease; preventative medicines reduce the likelihood of contracting the disease in the first place. Under the existing patent regime, symptom-relieving medicines are the most profitable, with the most desirable patients being ones who are not cured and do not die (until after patent expiration). Such patients buy the medicine week after week, year

15 In Thailand, Sanofi-Aventis sold its cardiovascular disease medicine Plavix for 70 baht ($2.20) per pill, some 6,000 per cent above the price at which the Indian generic firm Emcure agreed to deliver the same medicine (clopidogrel). See Oxfam (2007, 20).

16 See GFHR (2004).

after year, delivering vastly more profit than they would if they derived the same health benefit from a cure or vaccine. Vaccines are least lucrative because they are typically bought by governments, which enjoy a strong bargaining position. This is highly regrettable because the health benefits of vaccines tend to be exceptionally great as vaccines protect from infection or contagion not merely each vaccinated person but also their contacts.[17] Once more, then, the present regime guides pharmaceutical research in the wrong direction – and here to the detriment of poor and affluent alike.

Wastefulness

Under the present regime, innovators must bear the cost of filing for patents in dozens of countries and then also the cost of monitoring these countries for possible infringements of their patents. Huge amounts are spent in these many jurisdictions on costly litigation that pits generic companies, with strong incentives to challenge any patent on a successful medicine, against patentees, whose earnings depend on their ability to defend, extend, and prolong their monopoly rents. Even greater costs are due to the deadweight loss 'on the order of $200bn' worldwide that arises from blocked sales to buyers who are willing and able to pay the competitive market price but not the much higher monopoly price.[18]

Counterfeiting

Very large mark-ups also encourage the illegal manufacture and sale of medicines. Even when such illegal drugs are (truthfully claimed to be) pharmacologically fully equivalent, they reduce innovator profits and thereby undermine R&D incentives. When they are not fully equivalent (e.g., diluted, adulterated, inert, or even toxic), they endanger patient health and may lead to drug-specific resistance.

Excessive marketing

When pharmaceutical companies can maintain a very large mark-up, they find it rational to make extraordinary efforts to increase sales volume, often by scaring patients or by rewarding doctors. This produces pointless battles over market share among similar ('me-too') drugs as well as perks that induce doctors to prescribe medicines even when these are not indicated or when competing medicines are likely to do better. With a large mark-up it also pays to fund massive direct-to-

17 See Selgelid (2007, 218–29).

18 Personal communication from Aidan Hollis, based on his rough calculation. See also Hollis (2005, 8). Hollis there quantifies the deadweight loss in the region 'of $5 billion – $20 billion annually for the US. Globally the deadweight loss is certain to be many times this figure, because in many markets drug insurance is unavailable and so consumers are more price-sensitive'.

consumer advertising that persuades people to take medicines they don't really need for diseases they don't really have (and sometimes for invented pseudo-diseases).[19]

The last-mile problem

While the present regime provides strong incentives to expose affluent people to patented medicines they do not need, it provides no incentives to ensure that poor people benefit from medicines they do need. Even in affluent countries, pharmaceutical companies have incentives only to sell products, not to ensure that these are actually taken, properly, by patients whom they can benefit. This problem is compounded in poor countries, which often lack the infrastructure to distribute medicines as well as the medical personnel to prescribe them and to ensure their proper use. In fact, the present regime even gives pharmaceutical companies incentives to *disregard* the medical needs of the poor. To profit under this regime, a company needs not merely a patent on a medicine that is effective in protecting paying patients from a disease or its detrimental symptoms. It also needs this target disease to thrive and spread because, as a disease waxes or wanes, so does market demand for the remedy. A pharmaceutical company making a morally motivated effort to allow the poor to benefit from its patented medicine would be seriously undermining its economic position: By paying for the effort to make its drug competently available to poor patients, by curtailing a disease on which its profits depend, and by losing affluent customers who find ways of buying, on the cheap, medicines meant for the poor.

Contemplating these seven problems together, we see another reason to aim for a comprehensive solution in preference to the many stop-gap measures that have been proposed and sometimes (at least partially) implemented: The practical value of efforts to mitigate one of the seven problems may be greatly reduced by one of the other problems that remains unaddressed; and efforts to mitigate one problem may aggravate another. For example, a drug donation for the benefit of the poor, intended to mitigate the problem of high prices, may actually do more harm than good because of the weak health infrastructure (last-mile problem) in the recipient countries. Lacking competent medical instruction and package inserts in their own language, poor patients may fail to take the medicine in the right doses, at the right times, or for the appropriate length of time. Such patients may not merely remain sick; they may also develop and spread drug-resistant strains of the disease which (as in the case of MDR and XDR tuberculosis) can pose grave dangers to people everywhere.

Counterproductive effects can arise also from compulsory licenses that some governments have issued or threatened in order to gain for their populations cheaper access to patented medicines. Though specifically permitted by the

19 See the special issue on disease mongering, Moynihan and Henry (2006, 425–465).

TRIPS Agreement as reaffirmed in the Doha Declaration,[20] compulsory licenses are energetically resented by pharmaceutical companies, and governments daring to issue such licenses are routinely censured and penalised by these companies and by the rich-country governments doing their bidding. By issuing a compulsory license, a government authorises the production and marketing of a cheaper generic version of a patented medicine on condition that the authorised generic firm pays a small license fee to the patentee. Such a license, and even the mere threat of one, will typically cause the price of the relevant medicine to fall substantially in the relevant country. But this welcome relief from the problem of high prices also aggravates the neglect of diseases concentrated among the poor. Pharmaceutical companies spend less on the quest for vital medicines – especially ones with a substantial share of their potential market in less developed countries – when the uncertainties of development, testing, and regulatory approval are compounded by the additional unpredictability of whether and to what extent successful innovators will be allowed to recoup their investments through undisturbed use of their monopoly pricing powers.

Reasoning

Counterproductive effects notwithstanding, the moral appeal of compulsory licensing is compelling. Consider a life-saving medicine whose patent-holding producer sells it at $100, of which $10 constitutes the long-run marginal cost of production and distribution. The high sales price effectively excludes poor patients many of whom, if the sales price were near cost, could gain access to the medicine, with the help of some international organisation, perhaps, or on their own. What do we say to these patients who are suffering and dying even though they could obtain the medicine at the competitive market price? We tell them that, to merit access, they must pay not merely for the physical medicine but also for the intellectual property embodied in it: for the innovative idea or discovery or invention. But how can we impose such a huge mark-up for intellectual property on them, and thereby effectively exclude them from the medicine, when the cost to them of exclusion is sickness and death?

This question becomes even more pressing when we realise that including the poor adds nothing to the cost of innovation. It is a wonderful thing about the products of thought that their cost is independent of the number of beneficiaries. The intellectual labours of composing a novel are exactly the same, regardless

20 The TRIPS Agreement is Annex 1C of the Marrakesh Agreement Establishing the World Trade Organization, signed in Marrakesh, Morocco on 15 April 1994. Articles 8(1) and 27(2) are most relevant, and the full text is available at <www.wto.org/english/tratop_e/trips_e/t_agm0_e.htm>, accessed 10 January 2009. Of the Doha Declaration, Articles 4–6 are most relevant, and the full text is available at <www.who.int/medicines/areas/policy/tripshealth.pdf>, accessed 10 January 2009.

of whether it has millions of readers or none at all. Likewise for the labours of producing music, composing software, developing a new breed of plant or animal, and discovering a new medically effective molecule. Millions can benefit from such intellectual efforts without adding at all to their cost.[21] And this renders morally irresistible the conclusion that poor people, when their lives are at stake, must not be prevented from buying medicine from willing suppliers at competitive market prices. A compulsory license secures this freedom for the poor.

But what about the innovator who has put in the effort and expense to achieve the innovation? Doesn't the innovation belong to him or her or it – to give or withhold or sell at will? Many believe that there is such a natural right of first appropriation, analogous to the right of someone who takes possession of unowned objects such as apples or wood or water in a state of nature as Locke has described. Thus Robert Nozick imagines a medical researcher who synthesises a new medicine from widely available materials and refuses to share this medicine with others or to show them how to make it. Nozick argues that such a researcher is doing nothing wrong. He does not interfere with the freedom of others to acquire the same materials (of which he is leaving enough and as good) and chemically to transform these materials into the life-saving medicine if they can. He merely refuses to help them.[22]

But the analogy is deeply flawed: The person who appropriates some apples does not thereby deprive others of the opportunity to do likewise. To be sure, no one else can eat the particular apples she has eaten. But, if she leaves 'enough and as good' for others (as Locke and Nozick require) then others can collect and eat other apples.

Nozick's argument may have some plausibility (though the author would not want such a researcher among his friends). But it is of no help in the defence of intellectual property. Here the question is whether the medical researcher is entitled also to veto production of the medicine by others who learn how to make it later. Demanding such veto power, the medical researcher asserts a natural property right not over particular objects he has produced, but over an object *type*: a whole species of medically effective molecule. In doing so, he is like someone who, based on having first conceived the idea of eating apples, claims ownership of this idea and thus asserts that it is up to her to give or withhold or sell at will her permission to the apple-eating of others. This appropriation of a *type* is not supported by Locke's view. On the contrary, it clearly goes against

21 To be sure, to benefit many, the intellectual achievement must typically be physically encoded in multiple copies: in books, CDs, seeds, DNA molecule tokens, pills, or vaccines. Such physical instantiations of intellectual creations and discoveries do have a cost that rises – typically at a decreasing rate – as additional copies are made. But such physical reproduction is separable from, and adds nothing to the cost of, the creative intellectual labours. The creative intellectual ingredient into physical reproduction is entirely cost-free at the margin.

22 See Nozick (1974, 181).

Locke: Enforcing an innovator's exclusive property right over all objects of a class necessarily fails to leave enough and as good for everyone else. Moreover, it partially expropriates others. By asserting intellectual property rights, the medical researcher is denying others not merely the freedom to use what he has legitimately acquired, but also the freedom to use what *they themselves* have legitimately acquired. Through his invention, the rest of us supposedly lose our freedom to do what he did: To transform materials we legitimately own into a substance of the kind he first produced. Far from supporting monopoly rights in pharmaceuticals, the philosophical tradition friendliest to property rights thus refutes such intellectual property rights. If people have a natural right to what they produce from materials to which no one else has a prior claim, then generic producers have a natural right to do what the innovator did before them: To produce, if they can, medicine from ingredients they legitimately own and to sell such medicine to willing customers on mutually agreeable terms.[23]

But is not such freedom on the part of patients and generic producers destructive of innovation? Does it not deprive us of the powerful new medicines pharmaceutical innovators keep on producing? These questions constitute a change of venue, suggesting a defence of monopoly patents not in the courtroom of natural rights but in the courtroom of mutual advantage. Does this defence succeed? It is indisputable that powerful new medicines whose development was motivated by the hope for profits have greatly benefited some patients – namely those affluent enough to buy them at monopoly prices or fortunate enough to need them after patent expiration. If all human beings were so affluent or fortunate, then patents might be defensible as in everyone's best interest: It would then be rational for all of us to accept the cost of laying down our rights to produce, sell, and buy a new medicine invented by another in exchange for the much greater benefit of having available a broad and powerful arsenal of pharmaceuticals.

In fact, however, many human beings are trapped in severe poverty. Most of them derive little or no benefit from the marvellous arsenal of available medicines because they cannot, at prevailing prices, get access to them. For these people – and they number in the billions – it would be highly irrational to agree to lay down their freedom so that the affluent can more successfully use patents to stimulate pharmaceutical innovation.[24] In the real world, the poor do not give such highly

---

23 The most pertinent passages are Locke (1960, §27, §33); and Nozick (1974, 181–182). Nozick approves of patents but, as we show in the text, this endorsement is inconsistent with the basis Nozick offers for it. For a more extensive rejection of the Lockean claim, with specific discussion of Nozick, see Hollis and Pogge (2008, 62–68).

24 In this chapter, the author is not separately addressing utilitarian arguments for a global monopoly–patent regime. But it is obvious how they are bound to fail: Even if funding pharmaceutical innovation in a way that includes the poor is less convenient for the affluent than the existing globalised monopoly–patent regime, this inconvenience is vastly outweighed by all the sickness and premature deaths that the present regime is adding to the burdens of poverty.

irrational consent. The often devastating cost is imposed on them by others who, for their own advantage, interpose the barrier of monopoly patents between poor people and the generic companies willing to supply the medicines they urgently need. This interposition is a grievous injustice that kills millions of poor people each year.[25]

This injustice is manifest in national legislation – in India, for instance, where the poor have recently lost their legal freedom of access to medicines at competitive market prices. It is also manifest in international trading rules such as the TRIPS Agreement, which required India to implement these legislative changes as a condition of the limited access WTO membership affords Indian exporters to the markets of affluent countries. Perhaps the governments of India and other less developed countries made a reasonable choice when they imposed unjust pharmaceutical access rules upon their poor for the sake of gaining a little more fairness in international trade.[26] But the powerful affluent countries devising and imposing the present WTO regime have no such excuse. They are acting unjustly by pressing weaker countries to inflict this injustice on their poor. If rich countries and their citizens desire medical innovation, then they must find ways of funding it that either leave the freedom of the poor unreduced or else adequately compensate the poor for the loss of freedom imposed upon them.

Because it would be difficult, if not impossible, adequately to compensate poor people for disease and death, let us consider ways of funding pharmaceutical innovation that would not deprive the poor of their freedom of access to existing medicines at competitive market prices. The problem here is that leaving the poor this freedom is inconvenient for the affluent by making it difficult to collect from anyone the monopoly rents that incentivise pharmaceutical innovation. Though the affluent are often willing to buy advanced medicines at prices far above the marginal cost of production, many of them prefer to buy cheaper, even illegally. And clever brokers and smugglers, too, stand ready to exploit any substantial differential between the price charged to the rich and the competitive market price charged to the poor. Split markets with large price differentials thus generate unfairness as smugglers and the selfish affluent benefit at the expense

25 This injustice is independent of, and additional to, the great national and international injustices that keep half of humankind trapped in severe and avoidable poverty.

26 Before 2005, Indian law allowed only patents on processes, none on products. As a result, India's thriving generic pharmaceuticals industry, inventing new processes for manufacturing known medicines patented elsewhere, cheaply supplied such medicines for poor patients in India and throughout the world's poor regions. But when India signed the World Trade Organization's agreement on intellectual property in 1994, it was required to institute patents on products by 1 January 2005. These rules have little to do with free trade and more to do with the lobbying power of the American and European pharmaceutical industries. India's government has issued rules that will effectively end the copycat industry for newer drugs. For the world's poor, this will be a double hit – cutting off the supply of affordable medicines and removing the generic competition that drives down the cost of brand-name drugs (Editorial 2005).

of innovators and the honest affluent. More to the point, allowing the poor their freedom of access at competitive market prices substantially reduces the monopoly rents that can be extracted from affluent patients and thereby also the incentives of pharmaceutical companies to undertake expensive R&D efforts in the first place. To avoid all these problems with large price differentials, it is best then to level pharmaceutical prices in the opposite direction: Instead of unjustly imposing monopoly prices also on the poor (which effectively excludes most of them from advanced medicines), we should grant open access at competitive market prices also to the affluent. In this way, we avoid the problem of high prices in an efficient way. We also eliminate high mark-ups entirely and thereby avoid the problems associated therewith: wastefulness, counterfeiting, excessive marketing, and the bias toward symptom relief.

Because pharmaceutical R&D is urgently needed, loss of funding from monopoly patents must be replaced somehow – with public funds – to ensure a reliable flow long term. Such public funding can be designed to overcome the two last remaining problems of the present regime: The neglect of diseases concentrated among the poor and the last-mile problem.

Mechanisms of public financing are usually categorised under the labels of 'push' and 'pull'. A push program selects and funds some particular innovator – a pharmaceutical company, perhaps, or a university or a national health agency – to undertake a specific research effort. The intent here is that, with adequate funding, the selected innovator will develop the desired innovation, which can then be made freely available for production by competing pharmaceutical manufacturers so as to ensure wide availability at competitive market prices.

A pull program, by contrast, is addressed to many potential innovators, promising to reward whoever is first to achieve a valued innovation. Pull programs have two interrelated advantages over push programs: They avoid paying for failed research efforts and they generate strong financial incentives for innovators to work hard toward early success. The flip side of these advantages is that, in order to elicit such a serious research effort, the reward must be large enough to compensate for the risk of failure. This risk is twofold, as a research effort may fail either because the sought medicine proves elusive or because some competing innovator succeeds first. Potential innovators have incentives to try to develop a new medicine only if the reward for success, discounted by the probability of failure, is substantially greater than the expected cost of the R&D effort. In these respects, a pull program is similar to the current patent regime.

Despite this extra cost, pull programs can nevertheless be more effective than push programs, for three reasons: Push programs are more likely to fail because they get only one rather than several competing innovators to work on the problem.[27] Push programs are more likely to fail because the innovator is

---

27 A push program might assign the same task to two or three innovators. But this would double or triple the cost and thereby dramatically erode the cost advantage over its pull-program alternative.

chosen on the basis of some outsider's confidence in it whereas in pull programs each innovator's decision to try is based on *its own*, more competent and better motivated assessment of its capacities. Push programs are more likely to fail because the chosen innovator has much weaker incentives to work hard and cost-effectively toward early success. This higher probability of failure is compounded by the fact that such failures are paid for – in contrast to pull programs, which pay nothing for failed efforts. Given this contrast, pull programs are politically more easily sustainable.

Most prominent among pull programs are prize competitions that promise a reward to the innovator who is first able to produce a medicine that meets certain specifications. This reward can be specified as some monetary amount or as an APC or AMC (see fn. 14). Such rewards have been described with considerable ingenuity.[28] They clearly can be a valuable complement to existing patent rewards and have the potential of stimulating the development of medicines for currently neglected diseases.

Nonetheless, such *ad hoc* prize competitions have four drawbacks. First, politicians, bureaucrats, or experts play a crucial role by deciding which diseases should be researched, how the sought remedy should be specified, and how large a reward should be promised for a remedy meeting these specifications. Determining the direction research will take, these decisions are likely to be associated with substantial inefficiencies due to incompetence, corruption, gaming, and lobbying by companies and patient groups. But the planners' own incentives to stimulate the most cost-effective innovations are weak. And their information about the cost of specific research efforts to innovators is likely to be of poor quality, as potential innovators have reason to exaggerate both the costs and the potential utility of their efforts.[29] Given weak incentives and poor information, the planners' design of prize competitions would likely be seriously suboptimal.

The second problem arises from the fact that ad hoc rewards involve excessive specificity. Each reward must define a precise finish line, specifying at least what disease the medicine must attack, how effective it must minimally be (magnitude and duration of the improvement, percentage of patients), how bad its side effects may be (severity and frequency), and how convenient the medicine must minimally be (stability at various temperatures, frequency and mode of intake). Such specificity is problematic because it presupposes the very knowledge whose acquisition is yet to be encouraged. Since the sponsors lack this knowledge ahead of time, their specification is likely to be seriously suboptimal even if they are single-mindedly

28 See especially Kremer and Glennerster (2004).

29 This informational deficit – though not the other problems with prizes – can be overcome through a tender system: The planners would publish the specifics of the medicine they wish to have invented and then invite companies and other capable agencies to enter competing 'bids', specifying the prize each would expect for producing a qualifying medicine as well as a deadline and a penalty for delays. The planners could then select the organisation whose bid seems most attractive overall.

devoted to the goal of improving public health. Such suboptimality can take two forms. The specification may be overly demanding in at least one dimension, with the result that innovators give up the effort even though something close to the sought solution is within their reach. And the specification may be insufficiently demanding in some dimension(s), with the result that innovators, to save time and expense, deliver products that are just barely good enough to win the prize even when they could have done much better at little extra cost.[30]

The third disadvantage of ad hoc rewards is that the funding they depend on is likely to be haphazard and case-by-case. This is so because arbitrary factors and political contingencies will invariably enter into the choice of specific diseases and types of intervention around which prize competitions are organised. It is also likely that overall fund allocations will be erratic: When encountering budget problems, governments will tend to skip or to postpone planned reward competitions, and the conduct of other sponsors is also likely to be unduly influenced by extraneous factors (e.g., by their public relations needs or by how much money they must spend in the current year to retain their tax-deductible status).

A fourth serious defect of ad hoc rewards is that they fail to address the 'last-mile' problem, which is especially severe in the context of currently neglected diseases that mostly affect the poor. The fact that a new vital medicine is available in large quantities, or can be produced very cheaply by generic producers, does not yet give poor populations real access to it. The reward pulls innovators towards the invention of a new safe and effective medicine or even to its production in large quantities. But it does not pull this medicine the rest of the way to the patients who need it. It may seem that AMCs can get around this problem by making the reward conditional on the innovator finding willing buyers. But the author remains sceptical. If – as in one of Michael Kremer's numerical examples – a $14 subsidy (up to 200 million doses) is promised for each dose the innovator can sell for $1 or more, then the innovator has powerful incentives to induce or entice or bribe buyers regardless of how they intend to dispose of the medicine. If it must be used, as a condition of the subsidy, it may well be prescribed to patients irrespective of whether they need it or not.

Solution

The exclusion of the poor by the existing patent regime requires reform. Given the foregoing discussion a straightforward and moderate reform would create a supplementary mechanism that, by addressing the needs of the poor, would remedy the injustice now imposed upon them. This reform proposal comprises six elements. First, just as the patent regime[31] provides a *general* innovation incentive,

30 For an excellent discussion, see Hollis (2007, 15–16).

31 And in fact all existing intellectual property right regimes (copyrights, trademarks, etc.).

so its complement encourages pharmaceutical innovation through an incentive that is specified in general terms: As a promise to reward *any* successful new medicine, in proportion to its success. This kind of mechanism has been described as a *comprehensive* AMC.[32] Second, while the patent regime rewards medicines on the basis of the market demand each generates and then satisfies, thereby effectively excluding the poor, its complement gives equal standing to all by defining success simply in terms of human health. On this complementary track, the success of a medicine is assessed by the reduction in human morbidity and premature mortality it achieves – regardless of whether these harms are averted from rich or from poor patients. Third, in order to help overcome the last-mile problem, the rewards available under the complementary mechanism should be tied not to what a medicine *can* do, but to what it actually achieves in the world. Fourth, when such a general health impact reward mechanism is large enough, it will attract sufficient innovation and sufficient efforts to ensure real access to new medicines worldwide. This avoids any need for compulsion. Innovators can be left free to choose between the two tracks, developing on the new track high-impact medicines needed also by many poor patients and on the conventional patent track low-impact medicines desired by the more affluent. Making the health-impact track optional is also crucial for the political success of the proposal. Fifth, in order to reinforce the incentive toward facilitating real access, health impact rewards should be conditional on the medicine being priced no higher than the lowest feasible cost of production and distribution.

Sixth, health impact rewards should be funded by governments as a public good. In order to minimise burdens and deadweight losses due to taxes, the cost should be spread as widely as possible. This suggests that the complementary funding mechanism should be global (rather than national) in scope. The reasons that make the reform compelling in any one country or region make it compelling everywhere. Moreover, global scope avoids the problems associated with large price differentials. Global scope also brings huge efficiency gains by diluting the cost of the scheme without diluting its benefits: No matter how many beneficiaries we may add, the cost of achieving an innovation remains the same even while its aggregate benefit increases with the number of beneficiaries.[33] Finally, an international agreement would also reinforce the commitment of individual countries to the scheme. Pharmaceutical innovation is therefore best encouraged by promising to reward any safe and effective new medicine in proportion to its *global* health impact. Such a promise constitutes an AMC that is *fully* comprehensive: by including not merely all diseases but also all patients.

32 See Hollis (2008, 124–133).

33 In the case of medicines targeting communicable diseases, this benefit will increase super-proportionally: Each user of such a medicine benefits from others using it as well, because wide use can decimate or even eradicate the target disease and thereby reduce the probability that this disease will adapt and rebound with a drug-resistant strain (see fn. 17).

The proposal is then for the creation of a new international agency that offers to reward any new medicine based on its health impact during its first decade or so[34] – conditional on the innovator supplying it at cost wherever it is needed. This *Health Impact Fund* (HIF) would provide ample rewards for the development of new high-impact medicines without excluding the poor from its use.

To provide stable incentives, member states must guarantee funding some 15 years into the future to assure pharmaceutical innovators that, if they invest in expensive clinical trials now, they can claim a full decade of health-impact rewards upon marketing approval. This guarantee might feature fixed annual pools to be shared among registered medicines in proportion to their respective health impacts (subject to a reward rate ceiling) or it might feature a fixed monetary amount per unit of health impact.[35] These two design options differ in how they allocate the inevitable burden from uncertainty about how much health impact HIF-registered products will achieve in aggregate. The former solution makes the cost of the HIF predictable and may therefore be more attractive to governments; but it imposes one more risk upon potential innovators by leaving them in the dark about the rate of reward per unit of health impact. The latter option removes this uncertainty from innovators, but then imposes on governments considerable uncertainty about what the HIF will cost each year.[36]

There are also intermediate design options that split the burden from uncertainty between governments and pharmaceutical innovators. For example, in years in which the aggregate health impact of all HIF-registered innovations is 6 million QALYs or less, such health impact might be rewarded at a rate of $1,000 per QALY. In years in which the aggregate health impact of all HIF-registered innovations exceeds 6 million QALYs, the excess might be evenly split between governments and innovators. If the aggregate health impact of HIF-registered products is, say, 1.44 times what was expected, government funding would be multiplied by 1.2 and the reward rate divided by 1.2.[37]

---

34 This corresponds roughly to the effective patent life of 20-year pharmaceutical patents, which are filed many years before market clearance. For fuller discussion of the HIF, see Hollis and Pogge (2008).

35 Which is here assumed to be measured in QALYs. The QALY or quality-adjusted life year is a common measure of gains against the mortality and morbidity that constitute the GBD. It can be refined in various ways which we lack the space to discuss here. Basically, one QALY is an additional year of healthy life or a longer additional period of impaired life (e.g., 1.25 additional years with a 20 per cent impairment of age-specific functioning).

36 This may not be unacceptable. If more taxpayer money is spent because the HIF stimulates more successful innovation than expected, then health gains and consequent economic benefits for taxpayers will also be greater than expected.

37 More generally, one can specify in advance, for each year, the expected aggregate health impact from HIF-registered products, H, along with the expected aggregate reward payment for that year, P, and the resulting reward rate: $r = P/H$. If H turns out to be greater than expected by a factor of n (with $n>1$), one can then preserve the correctness of the

This sort of risk splitting has important advantages. It achieves reasonable predictability for both governments and pharmaceutical innovators. The flexible reward rate puts pharmaceutical innovators in a competitive position, inducing them to check one another's activities and health impact claims (if one company illicitly inflates its measured health impact, then other companies are short-changed through a reduced $/QALY rate). The flexible reward rate also establishes an observable, market-based $/QALY rate in pharmaceutical innovation.

So constructed, the HIF is scalable, allowing governments to scale up the HIF if it proves successful (down-scaling is constrained by the 15-year guarantee). Such scaling-up could take three forms: Governments can raise the reward rate ceiling (above $1,000 per QALY). Governments can increase (beyond the initial 6 million QALYs) the limit to which this maximum rate holds. And they can reduce the steepness of the drop in the $/QALY rate beyond this limit by absorbing more of the risk. Any such scaling-up can be financed through an increased commitment by the member states and/or through the accession of new members.

The establishment and scaling-up of the HIF would be facilitated by a rule that divides the cost of the HIF in proportion to the member states' respective gross national incomes (GNIs). Thus, if one member state's GNI is 3.7 times that of another, than the contribution assigned to the former will be 3.7 times that assigned to the latter. Such rigidity has three main advantages. First, the contributions of the various countries are automatically adjusted in a way that tracks their shifting fortunes – fast-growing countries automatically assume a larger share while countries in recession (declining GNI) find their burden alleviated. Second, such rigidity pre-empts protracted struggles over contribution proportions such as have marred the United Nations. Third, rigidity assures each country that any extra cost it agrees to bear by supporting an increase is matched precisely by a corresponding increase in the contributions of all other member states. Getting a state to agree to commit an extra $20 million is much easier if this agreement expands available rewards for pharmaceutical research by many times this amount than if (as in conventional governmental research allocations) it adds merely $20 million to the available funds.

If all countries were to agree to join the effort, each would contribute less than 0.01 per cent of its gross national income to reach $6 billion. As citizens, we would all pay an additional 0.01 per cent of our gross income in taxes ($1 for every $10,000 in gross income) and, by agreeing to do so, gain the equivalent of several million years of healthy life against the GBD. If countries representing only one third of the global product were willing to contribute to the $6 billion cost, their citizens would contribute 0.03 per cent of their gross incomes – still a

equation by multiplying P by n^k and dividing r by $n^{(1-k)}$ (with $0<k<1$). When $k=½$, the burden is shared equally between governments and innovators; the example in the text illustrates this case. If k is fixed above ½, governments absorb more of the burden. If k is fixed below ½, innovators absorb more.

trivial amount relative to its impact and mitigated, of course, by the much greater affordability of HIF-registered medicines.

The solution is then to create – parallel to the existing patent regime – a Health Impact Fund that gives pharmaceutical innovators a standing option to forgo exploitation of their monopoly powers on any medicine worldwide in exchange for a guaranteed payment stream proportioned to this medicine's impact on the GBD. Innovators choosing the health impact track would also have to agree to offer zero-priced licenses for the manufacture and sale of their products after the end of their respective reward periods.

Let us recapitulate how the HIF track would provide a full systemic solution to the seven problems described earlier.

(1) *Diseases concentrated among the poor* insofar as they substantially aggravate the GBD, would no longer be neglected. In fact, the more destructive ones among them would come to present some of the most lucrative R&D opportunities for biotechnology and pharmaceutical companies.

(2) *Bias toward symptom relief* would be absent from HIF-encouraged R&D. The HIF assesses each registered medicine's health impact in terms of how its use reduces mortality and morbidity worldwide – without regard to whether it achieves this reduction through cure, symptom relief, or prevention. This would guide firms to deliberate about potential HIF-track research projects in a way that is also optimal for global public health – namely in terms of the expected global health impact of the new medicine relative to the cost of developing it. The profitability of research projects would be aligned with their cost effectiveness in terms of global public health.

(3) *High prices* would not exist for HIF-registered medicines, and innovators would typically not even wish for a higher price on their HIF-registered medicines. The reason is that a higher price would greatly reduce a drug's health impact rewards by impeding access to this drug by the poorer half of the human population. On the HIF track, health benefits to the poorest of patients count equally with health benefits to the richest.

(4) *Wastefulness* would be dramatically lower for HIF-registered medicines. There would be no deadweight losses from high mark-ups. There would be little costly litigation as innovators would often welcome generic competitors who, by increasing access to the medicine, would boost the innovator's health impact reward. Given this situation, innovators might often not even bother to obtain, police, and defend patents in many national jurisdictions. To be eligible for rewards proportioned to the global health impact of a new medicine, an innovator needs to show *only once* that it has a patentable product.

(5) *Counterfeiting* of HIF-registered medicines would be much less attractive: With the genuine item available very cheaply, much less profit can be made from producing and selling fakes.

(6) *Excessive marketing* would also be much reduced for HIF-registered medicines. Because each innovator is rewarded for the health impact of its addition to the medical arsenal, innovators get no reward for switching patients over to a new drug that is no better than its predecessor and would consequently never register it with the HIF. Innovators would have incentives to urge a HIF-registered drug upon doctors and patients only insofar as such marketing results in measurable therapeutic benefits for which the innovator stands to be rewarded.

(7) *The last-mile problem* would be mitigated because each HIF-rewarded innovator would have incentives to ensure that patients are fully instructed and properly provisioned so that they make optimal use (dosage, compliance, etc.) of its medicines, which will then, through wide and effective deployment, have their optimal public-health impact. Rather than ignore poor countries as unlucrative markets, pharmaceutical companies would, moreover, have incentives to work together toward improving the health systems of these countries in order to enhance the impact of their HIF-registered medicines there.

Conclusion

This chapter describes and justifies a complement to the existing patent regime that would generate a flow of pharmaceutical innovation without depriving the poor of their freedom to buy new medicines at competitive market prices. In response one might ask why the Health Impact Fund here described should be confined to new medicines. There are other means for reducing the GBD, such as access to safe drinking water, adequate nutrition, clean sanitation, proper hygiene, protections (such as mosquito nets) against disease-carrying animals, off-patent medicines, and many more. Why reward only new pharmaceutical remedies when there are alternative, perhaps more cost-effective ways of averting the same diseases?

A partial answer is that the efforts encouraged by HIF rewards would not be neatly confined to new medicines. Once a firm has registered a new drug, its reward will depend on how this drug affects the evolution of mortality and morbidity attributable to its target disease (the disease for which it is indicated). This impact will depend on many factors some of which – for example, the quality of health-care delivery in poor countries – the firm can affect. By helping to improve such health-care delivery, an innovator can magnify its medicine's impact, which is strongly affected by the extent to which doctors and nurses are locally available, know about the medicine, have it on hand, prescribe it, ensure that patients have access to it in the best dosage and in sufficient quantity, and instruct patients in its proper use.

This answer does not fully overcome the objection. There are diseases – simple diarrhoea, for instance – against which new medicines would be of limited help if any. Why should not efforts to reduce such diseases by securing access to off-patent medicines, to clean drinking water or to sanitation be funded insofar as they are no less cost-effective than the Health Impact Fund? The author has no objection to such an extension of the reward scheme here sketched. We can think of this scheme as the central module of a larger health reform project. Once this central module is specified and implemented, it can certainly be extended to other social factors essential to human health. It makes sense, nonetheless, to begin with the central module which will provide a useful paradigm for possible extensions and an impetus for further reform.

But why start with *this* module, focused on new medicines? Would the money not do more to protect the health of poor populations if it were spent on a global program of universal access to clean water or healthy nutrition? Perhaps it would. But let us not disregard the political realities. Bitter experience over many decades has shown that the world's governments are not prepared to spend tens of billions of dollars on clean water or school lunch programs. The provision of such basic goods is thought to deserve a few millions here and there, but certainly not tens of billions. The idea of spending such sums on supporting domestic corporations, by contrast, is entirely familiar and commonplace – in fact, the affluent countries are spending *hundreds* of billions *each year* on export credits and subsidies, which aggravate severe poverty abroad, in the agricultural sector alone. A politically realistic way forward might then tie together the two objectives of protecting the poor and providing business opportunities to large corporations. The HIF this chapter has sketched is meant to fit this description. There may be more cost-effective schemes for protecting the poor. But such alternative schemes are useless nonetheless if they cannot attract the funds they plan to spend. Aligning with the powerful interests of the pharmaceutical and biotechnology industries, the HIF has better prospects for success.

The author is aware that we have not had the space to discuss fully how the proposed HIF should best be designed. This is evidently a highly complex question. Addressing it adequately would require specification of the reward mechanism: Definition of an appropriate metric for the GBD, rules for allocating the GBD among the various diseases, ways of collecting sufficient data to assess ex post the global burden each disease imposes and to make plausible baseline projections some years into the future, rules for allocating specific disease burden reductions among contributing registered innovators, specific rules for determining a monetary reward for a given set of GBD reductions, adequate mechanisms for curbing corruption and gaming, and special rules for incremental innovations and for the phase-in period. Another aspect of the design concerns the agency administering the reward mechanism and the arbitration procedures for settling conflicts about the interpretation and application of the rules. A third design aspect concerns the treaty rules for funding the scheme along with the penalties for free-riding by countries that seek to take advantage of HIF-supported innovation without sharing its cost. We have an interdisciplinary and international team – supported by the Australian Research Council, the BUPA Foundation and the European Commission – hard at work on detailing workable solutions to these challenges. Our work is documented, with some time lag, at <www.HealthImpactFund.org>. A book, describing the proposal in more detail, is available there.

Let us close with two more general lessons this chapter supports. One concerns the tragicomic disputes over globalisation. The friends of WTO globalisation spend billions to have the media reiterate the benefits of free markets and free enterprise. The opponents of WTO globalisation mobilise millions of people to demonstrate against the damage free markets threaten to do to human values and well-being. In this unequal dispute, the reality of WTO globalisation is overlooked by both sides – intentionally by the proponents, most often, and inadvertently by the opponents. The reality is that WTO globalisation is opening markets where this serves important corporate interests in powerful countries, is preserving barriers to free exchange where this serves important corporate interests in powerful countries, and is shutting down free and open markets where this serves important corporate interests in powerful countries. The third type is exemplified by the case we have discussed, as large pharmaceutical corporations have won the right to use monopoly patents to block free trade in vital medicines worldwide. The second case is exemplified by the uneven fortunes of protectionism: While poor WTO members are forced to open their markets, wealthier members maintain their tariffs and anti-dumping duties, and most importantly their huge export credits and subsidies to domestic producers. To be sure, these protectionist measures are often theoretically illegal under WTO rules. But less developed countries usually lack the resources to bring and win cases against the US or EU. Moreover, such a country has little to gain from winning as affluent members typically continue their Treaty contraventions even in the face of clear-cut WTO rulings, confident that the weaker member will prudently refrain from imposing the retaliatory measures such rulings may entitle them to and that these retaliatory measures would not, in any case, seriously hurt them.

The other more general lesson is about political change. There is much lament about how evil corporations are putting profits above people, above health, above animal welfare, above the environment. These laments are true, but usually misdirected. The *root* of the evil lies not in how corporations do business, but in how *we* regulate and incentivise them. If we structure markets so that corporations can earn billions by getting people to smoke, then corporations will work hard to get people to smoke. If we structure markets so that corporations can earn billions by getting people to stop smoking, then corporations will work hard to get people to stop smoking. Highlighting the moral responsibilities of corporations and their leaders is appropriate even if it makes little difference to what they do. But it may also detract from *our* responsibility as citizens to structure markets so as to encourage good corporate behaviour. Having failed to do so, it is now *our* responsibility to devise politically realistic reforms, that is, reforms that the more powerful corporations and governments may well support or at least accept. This responsibility motivates the reform effort this chapter has described. We must restructure the existing global patent regime so that pharmaceutical innovators lose the financial stake in the proliferation of their target diseases and gain a financial stake in the elimination of these diseases. If we can thus redirect present incentives, then the immense powers of free enterprise will be marshalled *against* the devastating diseases that are now allowed to proliferate. If we manage to reorient pharmaceutical and biotechnology companies by aligning their profits with GBD reduction, these companies will be much more effective than the current assortment of ad hoc initiatives at defeating these diseases which bring so much misery and premature death to poor people everywhere. Working for this goal is politically realistic insofar as the envisioned structural reform is in the interest not only of the poor worldwide but also of the global pharmaceutical and biotechnology industries whose profitability it would enhance and whose tarnished public image it would help restore. These benefits come at very little cost, if any, because of the huge inefficiencies the reform reduces and because the benefits of intellectual property can be extended without cost.

References

Davies, J., Sandstrom, S., Shorrocks, A. and Wolff, E. (2006), *The World Distribution of Household Wealth*, Appendix 1, Table 10a (Oslo: WIDER).

Editorial (2005), 'India's Choice', *The New York Times*, 18 January 2005. Available at <http://select.nytimes.com/gst/abstract.html?res=F10610F8395C0C7B8DDDA80894DD404482> [last accessed 10 January 2009].

GFHR (Global Forum for Health Research) (2004), *The 10/90 Report on Health Research 2003–2004* (Geneva: GFHR). Available at <http://www.globalforumhealth.org> [last accessed 10 January 2009].

Hollis, A. (2005), 'An Efficient Reward System for Pharmaceutical Innovation', Working paper, University of Calgary. Available at <http://econ.ucalgary.ca/fac-files/ah/drugprizes.pdf> [last accessed 10 January 2009].

Hollis, A. (2007), 'Incentive Mechanisms for Innovation', *IAPR Technical Paper*. Available at <http://www.iapr.ca/iapr/files/iapr/iapr-tp-07005_0.pdf> [last accessed 10 January 2009].

Hollis, A. (2008), 'Comprehensive Advance Market Commitment: A Useful Supplement to the Patent System?', *Public Health Ethics* 1:2. Available at <http://phe.oxfordjournals.org/cgi/content/short/1/2/124> [last accessed 10 January 2009].

Hollis, A. and Pogge, T. (2008), 'The Health Impact Fund: Making New Medicines Accessible for All', *Incentives for Global Health.* Available at <http://www.healthimpactfund.org>.

Kremer, M. and Glennerster, R. (2004), *Strong Medicine: Creating Incentives for Pharmaceutical Research on Neglected Diseases* (Princeton: Princeton University Press).

Kroll, L. (2008), 'The World's Billionaires', *Forbes*, 5 March 2008. Available at <http://www.forbes.com/2008/03/05/richest-billionaires-people-billionaires 08-cx_lk_0305intro.html> [last accessed 10 January 2009].

Locke, J. (1960), *Two Treatises of Government*, Laslett, P. (ed.) (Cambridge: Cambridge University Press).

Milanovic, B. (2005), *Worlds Apart: Measuring International and Global Inequality* (Princeton: Princeton University Press).

Miller, J. (2007), 'Vaccines for Africa "Face 700% Mark-up"', *The Independent*, 18 November 2007. Available at <http://news.independent.co.uk/health/article3172164.ece> [last accessed 10 January 2009].

Minoiu, C. and Reddy, S. (2008), 'Chinese Poverty: Assessing the Impact of Alternative Assumptions', *Review of Income and Wealth* 54:4. Available at <http://www.socialanalysis.org> [last accessed 10 January 2009].

Moynihan, R. and Henry, D. (eds) (2006), *PLoS Medicine* 3:4. Available at <http://collections.plos.org/plosmedicine/diseasemongering-2006.php>.

Nozick, R. (1974), *Anarchy, State and Utopia* (New York: Basic Books).

Oxfam (2007), 'Investing for Life', *Oxfam Briefing Paper*, November 2007, 20. Available at <http://www.oxfam.org/files/bp109-investing-for-life-0711.pdf> [last accessed 10 January 2009].

Pogge, T. (2008a), 'Growth and Inequality: Understanding Recent Trends and Political Choices', *Dissent* 55:1, 82–93. Available at <http://www.dissentmagazine.org/article/?article=990> [last accessed 10 January 2009].

Pogge, T. (2008b), *World Poverty and Human Rights: Cosmopolitan Responsibilities and Reforms*, 2nd Edition. (Cambridge: Polity Press).

Roney, M. (2007), 'The Global Millionaire Boom', *Business Week*, 18 October 2007. Available at <http://www.businessweek.com/bwdaily/dnflash/content/oct2007/db20071017_916634.htm> [last accessed 10 January 2009].

Saez, E. and Piketty, T. (2003), 'Income Inequality in the United States, 1913–1998', *Quarterly Journal of Economics* 118, 1–39, as updated in 'Tables and Figures Updated to 2006 in Excel Format', July 2008. Available at <http://elsa.berkeley.edu/~saez/>, Table A3 [last accessed 10 January 2009].

Selgelid, M. (2007), 'Ethics and Drug Resistance', *Bioethics* 21.

WHO (2006), *Evaluation of WHO's Contribution to '3 by 5'* (Geneva: WHO). Available at <http://www.who.int/hiv/topics/me/3by5%20Evaluation.pdf> [last accessed 10 January 2009].

WIDER (World Institute for Development Economics Research), 'World Income Inequality Database (2007)'. Available at <http://62.237.131.23/wiid/wiid.htm>, line 4664 [last accessed 10 January 2009].

Chapter 16

Not Only 'a Simple Math Equation': Business Organisations as Agents for Poverty Reduction

Michael Schramm and Judit Seid

The measurement and analysis of poverty is a widely discussed issue and various definitions and concepts exist. The fact is, and what everybody agrees on: Too many people are living in poverty. According to the World Resource Institute 4 billion people – the majority of the world's population – live in relative poverty, that means they have incomes below $3,000/year PPP[1] and constitute the so called base of the economic pyramid (Hammond et al. 2007, 3). The Copenhagen Declaration that resulted from the World Summit on Social Development in 1995, defines absolute poverty as 'a condition characterised by severe deprivation of basic human needs, including food, safe drinking water, sanitation facilities, health, shelter, education and information. It depends not only on income but also on access to services' (UN 1995, 41).

Eight hundred and fifty million people worldwide – more than one in eight – suffer from hunger. Eight hundred and twenty million of the hungry are from developing countries (FAO 2006, 8). Ten million people die every year from hunger and hunger-related diseases,[2] 1.1 billion people don't have safe water (UNDP 2006, 5), 2.6 billion lack basic sanitation (ibid., 2006, 112) and more than 115 million children are still out of school (ibid., 2006, 267).

In Theory, Everything seems Pretty Clear

The economic point of view

In 2003, former HP Chief Executive Carly Fiorina stated in Toronto, that the moral thing (reducing poverty and hunger all over the world) on one hand and the

1 Purchasing Power Parity: PPP conversion allows us to compare the basis of purchasing powers of the currencies in the respective market, free from differences in price levels across countries.

2 Source: The United Nations' World Food Programme: <http://www.wfp.org/aboutwfp/introduction/hunger_who.asp?section=1&sub_section=1>.

business thing (making profits or to be successful in business) on the other hand is only a 'simple math equation':

> Increasing our competitiveness, doing the smart business thing as well as the right moral thing is for us a real simple math equation … Let me give you the math. We live today as a technology company in a world where only ten percent of the world can afford to buy our products today. And we also live in a world where increasingly, we are finding shortages of engineers and scientists to invent the technology for the future. So, as we look ahead and think about sustainable growth for our company – not just for the next quarter, but for the next decade and the decades beyond – we know that many of the markets, the customers, the talent, the partners, and the ideas are going to come from that other 90 percent of the world that is underprivileged, underaccessed and underserved. It is in our profound, enlightened self-interest to ensure that we tap more talent in more markets – that we build more markets capable of buying and using and understanding our products and technology, and that we build customers around the world. Again, this to me is about the marriage of social and environmental objectives to business objectives, and that's an opportunity to create new value and raise the level of competitiveness of a company. (Fiorina 2003)

First, Fiorina's argument makes a diagnosis: Currently large parts of the world population are excluded from the productive transactions of the global market. Only 10 per cent of the world population can afford the Hewlett Packard products as consumers. Also as producers (and for the development of ideas to new products) the talents of 90 per cent of the people out there are lying fallow. Starting out from this diagnosis of an exclusion of large parts of the world population, she names the inclusion of this majority of the population as an ethically desired aim (as '*the right moral thing*') and justifies this aim with the positive economic effects connected with that – both with regard to the world economy (a bigger world market = a broader prosperity) and with regard to the company's business (more innovative ideas and more consumers especially for the company Hewlett Packard by an actual usage of the economic potentials of the world market). For Carly Fiorina the only consequence can be a broad extension of the global markets ('*build more markets*') – more markets, where more suppliers and more consumers create a higher prosperity, markets, where the 90 per cent of the world population, excluded at the moment, are integrated actively to take advantages out of these markets. And in this respect there is no fundamental conflict between social and business concerns, no conflict in principle between ethical and economic objectives, but a kind of matrimony between ethical and economic purposes ('*the marriage of social to business objectives*').

So, things seem to be pretty clear from the economic point of view. What about the moral point of view?

The moral point of view

In 2007, philosopher Thomas Pogge wrote about 'Freedom from Poverty as a Human Right': 'We need only the political [*and moral*] will to realise these freedoms through a concerted effort' (Pogge 2007a, 9). If we only had the Kantian 'good (moral) will', the right moral thing would be realised. The problem of poverty would be solved. Hunger would be eliminated from this planet. It would really happen.

If the economic point of view and the moral point of view support this purpose, why don't we get from A (economic or moral theoretical reasoning) to B (actual abolition of poverty)? In our view, the answer has to do with two things: First, there is a difference between theoretical justifications (economical justifications as well as ethical ones) and practical implementations. And second, we have to take a look at organisations, because only organisations can be the agents of change.

The Difference Between Justification and Implementation

Theoretical (economical, ethical etc.) justifications for a certain objective (e.g. poverty reduction) are insufficient for a feasible (practical) implementation in several aspects:

Conflict of justified moral norms in actual situations

Philosopher Juergen Habermas distinguishes between two different levels of moral argumentation: The first level is the 'discourse of justification' ['*Begründungsdiskurs*']. This level of moral argumentation is about the justification of a certain moral norm in principle (e.g. 'You shall not lie'). The second level consists in the 'discourse of application' ['*Anwendungsdiskurs*']: This is the discussion about the appropriateness of conflicting moral norms in a certain local situation, e.g. the inhibition to lie versus the protection of life: It isn't appropriate to tell a killer truthfully where he can find his victim; in this conflict the protection of life is the higher value. If you are familiar with the concept of Habermas you know that both discourses are ethical ones: Habermas only knows 'moral justification- and application-discourses' ['*moralische Begründungs- und Anwendungsdiskurse*'] (Habermas 1991, 141).

The difference between 'reality' and 'actuality'

A second difference emphasises the – let's say – 'ontological' status of moral norms in the world we live in. Philosopher Alfred N. Whitehead proposed a terminological differentiation between two forms of existence: The first is termed '*actuality*', referring to the current facts, that which *is*. The second, he calls '*reality*', and by this term a potential, but achievable existence is designated, that which *could be*. 'The future has [...] reality in the present, but no [...] actuality' (Whitehead 1929/1979, 215). Reality is something that can become actual[3] and '[t]he present is the [...] process whereby reality becomes actual' (Whitehead 1929/1979, 214).[4]

Applied to the status of moral norms that means: Moral norms may be ethically justified (e.g. freedom from hunger as a human right). However, this valid ethical justification only founds a moral reality (a mere moral existence), not yet an actual existence in the 'physical' world we live in. On the one hand, this moral reality of moral norms is (more or less) independent from the actual status quo, and actuality cannot wipe this moral reality out of existence.[5] On the other hand this moral reality of justified moral norms alone doesn't provide their application or implementation in the actual world. And the reason for this is the poly-dimensionality of the world we live in.

Polydimensionality of the actual world

The world we live in (the actuality) is a polydimensional one: Not only the moral point of view may matter, but also the economic point of view or technological aspects, political circumstances, juridical conditions and so on. All these dimensions are realities, which are (or can be) important for the development of the actual world.

If we want certain ethical claims (e.g. freedom from hunger) to become actual, it is surely not sufficient to indicate only the moral point of view, since the economic code also matters. The realisation of poverty reduction is not just an

3 'It is the reality of what is potential' (Whitehead 1929/1979, 66).

4 Whitehead is the creator of the so-called 'process philosophy', in which the actual and present world is understood as a *process*. An actual process presupposes possibilities which can be actualised: 'The process [...] is the transformation of the potential into the actual' (Whitehead 1936/1968, 151), so '[t]he process is the achievement of actuality' (Whitehead 1927/2007, 114). His main work is titled 'Process and Reality' (Whitehead 1929/1979). The term *reality* describes the potentials for the actual processes of the current world. Whitehead also carries out another distinction, namely the one between '*general*' or '*pure*' potentiality on the one side and '*real*' potentiality on the other. He calls the *general* or *pure* potentials '*eternal objects*': 'The *eternal objects* are the *pure potentials* of the universe' (Whitehead 1929/1979, 149). These *pure* (or general) potentials are the absolute realm of all conceivable potentials for current processes, which, to the far predominant part however, cannot be actualised here and now. The *real* potentials on the other hand are really achievable. They are something that could be actualised here and now. So, there is 'the "*general*" *potentiality*, which is the bundle of possibilities [...] provided by the multiplicity of eternal objects, and [...] the "*real*" *potentiality*, which is conditioned by the data provided by the actual world. *General potentiality* is absolute, and *real potentiality* is relative to some actual entity' (Whitehead 1929/1979, 65) or the given actuality.

5 In this sense Pogge (2007b, 13) is right: '[E]ven all governments together cannot legislate such rights [*e.g. freedom from poverty as human right*] out of existence'.

application of this ethically justified objective. The stepwise implementation of poverty reduction is a polydimensional process, which always has to take several aspects into account; moral aspects as well as economic or political ones.

Organisations as Agents of Change

The second point emphasises the significance of organisations as effective agents of change.[6] According to the New Economics of Organisation, institutions have a certain function and organisations follow objectives. Institutions are not actors and organisations are (collective actors). So we first suggest, that *only organisations are effective agents of* (institutional etc.) *change* and secondly we want to point out that the implementation of poverty reduction is a polydimensional process, and we therefore need a *network of different types of organisations* for a sustainable fight against poverty and hunger.[7]

Business Companies as Agents of Change

If we focus on companies as agents of change, the question arises:

Why companies?

There are several answers to this question:

- Oftentimes we need other actors than the domestic governments. If local governments of developing countries are oppressive and economically incompetent, other actors (organisations) have to close the gap.
- Companies can/could be effective agents, because they are equipped with capital and know-how.
- Global players are on-site.
- Companies are interested in tapping (emerging) markets (of consumers as well as producers).[8]

---

6 Douglas North carries out a terminological distinction between 'institutions' and 'organisations': 'Institutions are the rules of the game' (North 1990, 3); but organisations are 'groups of individuals bound by some common purpose to achieve objectives' (ibid., 5).

7 The Global Compact is, for example, a (multi-stakeholder) compact of organisations (political organisations, e.g. UNHCHR, ILO, UNDP; civil society organisations, e.g. NGOs; business organisations, e.g. companies).

8 'It is easy to understand why multinational corporations have played such a central role in globalisation: it takes organisations of enormous scope to span the globe to bring together the markets, technology, and capital of the developed countries with the production capacities of the developing ones' (Stiglitz 2006, 197f).

But there is an important restriction for business companies, as stated in the next chapter.

Constraint: Companies are polydimensional organisations, but always organisations of the global economic system

Companies are polydimensional organisations, which have to process their transactions in different 'language games'[9] (codes): e.g. economy, law, technology or morality. In this sense, a firm is an organisation, which has to play and to master different types of language games (codes). Not only the language game of the market, which codes everything in prices, but also the language games of law, technology, politics and morality. Nevertheless: it is the economic code (cost/profit or expenditure/return)[10] which functions as a framing code, as a restriction, that no company can afford to ignore. Not everything in the corporation is economic, but every operation of a company has economic consequences.[11]

---

9 Wittgenstein's concept of the 'language games' names the different (possible) uses of words and languages (Wittgenstein 1953/2001, §7). 'But how many kinds of sentence are there? Say assertion, question, and command? – There are countless kinds: countless different kinds of use of what we call "symbols", "words", "sentences". And this multiplicity is not something fixed, given once for all; but new types of language, new language-games, as we may say, come into existence, and others become obsolete and get forgotten. [...] Here the term "language-game" is meant to bring into prominence the fact that the speaking of language is part of an activity, or of a form of life' (ibid., §23). Wittgenstein names, for example: giving orders, reporting an event, making a joke, solving a problem in practical arithmetic, thanking, cursing, greeting, praying (ibid., §23). So, the 'meaning' of a word is not defined by the object any more, but by the use of the word in the language game, encoded by a local situation type. 'For a large class of cases – though not for all – in which we employ the word "meaning" it can be defined thus: the meaning of a word is its use in the language' (ibid., §43).

10 See Luhmann (1997; 1989). Luhmann's Social Systems Theory describes the evolution of society through functional differentiation. An (individual or collective) actor is forced to use certain 'binary codes' to communicate a particular concern. Every communication operates by selected codes: e.g. the economic, the political or the juridical code. So every functional differentiated system (economy, politics etc.) is defined by a distinct 'program', which appreciates only certain aspects. All the others belong to an 'environment', which cannot be perceived by the system. The market system for example exclusively uses a monetary code (costs), a company however is a polylingual organisation, which has to process a set of different codes.

11 '[F]irms are polylingual systems. Unlike the market, which has to code every event in prices in order to be able to communicate it, firms have to be able to simultaneously or selectively evaluate and process relevant events in many different "language games" – economy, technology, law, process, morality. The economic code – expenditure/return or cost/profit – has a lead function in the overall bundle of the polylingual resources of the firm when it comes to decisions; this reflects the fact that it is the market system that structures the environment of the firm. Firms are organisations of the economic system: everything

Governance: How to implement the moral objective of poverty reduction

Given this restriction, there are still different dimensions important for a corporation, which aims at the implementation of a moral objective, e.g. poverty reduction. German economist and business ethicist Josef Wieland distinguishes four arguments, relevant for the actualisation of the moral dimension (*m*) of an economic transaction (T):

$$Tm_i = f(aIS_i, bFI_{ij}, cIF_{ij}, dOCC_i)$$

$$(a .. d = -1, 0, 1)$$

i = specific transaction; j = specific location

The basic idea of Wieland's 'ethic of governance' consists in the consideration that all problems of business ethics can be reproduced micro-analytically as the moral dimension of distinct economic transactions.[12] The governance function now differentiates between four arguments, which are crucial for the actualisation of the moral dimension (*m*) of a business transaction (T).

- *IS* stands for individual self-commitments (principles of the virtue, rational advantage calculations or other mechanisms). The indicator *i* signalises that there are differences from person to person and from transaction to transaction.
- *FI* displays the formal institutions which are relevant for the local transactions of a given company in a certain country, state or region. Examples are national laws for environmental protection or against corruption.
- *IF* stands for the informal institutions that could get effective with regard to a certain economic transaction. Religious or moral convictions of a given local culture are part of these informal institutions as well as the organisational culture of a business company. For example, the moral assessment of corruption may be deeply established in the cultural basic convictions of a certain society.
- And finally, *OCC* means the coordination and cooperation mechanisms of a certain organisation, by which transactions (guidelines, proceedings of business processes, policies and procedures) are led, steered and checked. Without these mechanisms there could be no effective implementation of moral requirements in business transactions (e.g. renunciation of child labour or corruption).

---

relevant in firms has economic relevance or consequence. But not everything in the firm is economic' (Wieland 2001a, 79sqq.).

12 See Wieland (2001b, 9sqq.).

The values (*-1, 0* or *1*) of the coefficients *a .. d* display whether the arguments *IS*, *FI*, *IF* and *OCC* of the function are effective or not.

The challenge now is to merge or to balance all these dimensions in a comprehensive way. We think there is no general answer on how to do this – it always depends on the company, on the people involved, on the country where you operate and so on. To substantiate this difficulty we will outline three case studies.

How to be profitable in an integer way Nestlé was founded in 1866 and is the world's largest milk company since the early 1900s. Milk Districts were part of Nestlé's business model from the very beginning. Nestlé originally developed its milk district model in Switzerland but the company's expansion was – and still is – driven by the fresh milk supply. That is the reason why in 1920 Nestlé turned to start production in emerging countries, first in Araras, Brazil.[13]

Establishing milk district models in emerging countries doesn't only mean signing contracts with small farmers, setting up a factory and establishing an efficient milk collection system. Apart from that it also means to implement a program to improve milk quality – for example to provide farmers with training and advice on dairy farm practices and crop production.

Nestlé's milk district models are very successful for both sides, the company and the farmers. Nestlé usually enters areas where opportunity before was scarce and trains the locals, guarantees wages, provides long term jobs and develops a quality end-product. According to Martial Genthon, Nestlé's technical director of global dairy operations, 'it is always the most remote area that is the poorest and less developed. So bringing a milk collection center to an area like that is a blessing for the village, and starts the whole economic development of the place' (Goldberg and Herman 2006, 12).

Nestlé's milk districts generate higher incomes for farmers and the community at large. They are growing on average by 2–5 per cent annually, but some of them were growing as much as 10 per cent. Farmers were doubling their output and increasing their disposable income because consumption of milk products and sales increased dramatically in most of the emerging markets. And Hans Jöhr (Nestlé's corporate head of Agriculture) confirms that usually 'one dollar flowing back to the rural area gives another three or four dollars to the local economy' (Goldberg and Herman 2006, 12).

The business model Nestlé chose with its milk districts demonstrated that a win–win situation is possible. Nestlé is economically successful but their activities also improved family living conditions in the areas they were active, provided consistent education to children and cultivated stronger livelihoods. Farmer's incomes were higher and the district's rigid criteria concerning milk quality played

13 If not stated differently information is taken from the case study 'Nestlé's Milk District Model: Economic Development for a Value-Added Food Chain and Improved Nutrition' from the Harvard Business School.

an important role in an improved state of health and nutrition and therefore had a positive impact on poverty reduction.

Regarding the milk district models 'Nestlé integrated its corporate objectives into one model that was responsive to poverty alleviation and malnutrition while simultaneously attaining its corporate strategic long-term revenue and profit goals' (Christiansen 2008, 11).

How to make the moral thing profitable Flores is an island in Indonesia and offers a lush vegetation. Agriculture is the principle source of income for the two million people living on that island. Nevertheless – according to the World Bank definition – these people are poor because they live on an average of half a dollar a day.

Johannes Schwegler had been living and working in Indonesia for the Swisscontact foundation until the year 2005. He saw the agricultural wealth on Flores and was asking himself how to better use all these natural resources for the benefit of the poor.[14] He was looking for a product which could be competitive on the world market and he found the cashew nut. The cashew nut grown on Flores is of one of the best qualities worldwide, however the farmers had no choice than selling it unprocessed to chinese wholesalers with basically no return.

This is where Johannes Schwegler and Swisscontact came in. They developed a method to cold crack the nuts in such a way not to destroy any valuable ingredients, they improved access to market information for the farmers and they founded the Cashewnut Consulting Centre where trainers were educated to give qualified training to farmers and where the whole processing of the cashew nuts takes place. Swisscontact, in addition, helped the farmers to get the IMO certification of organic and eco-friendly products.

The project was started by the principles of sustainability and granting a perspective to the people in one of the poorest regions of Indonesia. But it was doomed to fail because the farmers had no buyers for their organic nuts and would have been forced to sell them for low, dictated prices on the conventional market. Johannes Schwegler convinced Jochen Wolf and Martin Steckdaub to take the risk and they decided to buy 60 tons of nuts and try to set up a distribution network in Europe – that was the birth of Flores Farm (GmbH). When they started they had no idea whether it would work or not to sell these nuts in Europe. That was three years ago and today Flores Farm is a successful and profitable little company. What keeps them going, 'is the production and trade of natural foods of the highest possible quality – combined with granting a bit of independence for emerging countries' (Wolf, in Kovacsics and Degert 2006).

How to invest in human capital Migros was founded in 1925 and is today the largest retail store in Switzerland and one of the biggest 500 companies in the

14 If not stated differently, information is taken from the TV documentation 'Wie eine harte Nuss geknackt wird [How to crack a hard nut]'.

world. There had always been a special attention on the problem of child labour at Migros and they were aware that bans alone would not be the solution. Therefore they were looking for new ways to solve the dilemma of families in the developing world who send their children to work because they need the money to survive.

In December 2000, the Migros Kids School (Tirupur, South India) opened it's gates for 43 kids (2008: 1,011 kids). The kids receive education there as well as meals and medical care services. To finance the expenses a label system (of K.I.D.S. – kids in deficient situations) had been created, which can help generate buying incentives for western consumers interested in morals. Local Migros's suppliers can voluntarily buy these labels from K.I.D.S (2 rupies apiece) and the running charges (books, school uniforms, salaries, school bus and electricity or water supply etc.) of the school are (partly) financed with the proceeds of this label selling. Also other Migros suppliers are helping the Kids School by not sending business gifts at Christmas and instead donating the money to the kids.

Surely, this Migros Kids School is little more than a drop in the ocean, but for more than 1,000 kids it is an alternative to child labour or street prostitution.[15]

Beyond the Theories

Economic or moral theories are important, but neither the good moral will only nor the simple math (of cooperation returns) shows us a way from A to B.

First, we have to face the fact, that the implementation of poverty reduction is a *stepwise process* (Karl R. Popper: 'piecemeal social engineering').

In the second place: The fight against poverty is a *polydimensional process*, which has to integrate the moral and the economic point of view.

And third, as C.K. Prahalad said, a mind shift is needed: We have to 'stop thinking of the poor *[only]* as victims or as a burden and start recognizing them as [...] creative entrepreneurs and value-conscious consumers' (Prahalad 2006, 1). Poverty is the most pressing global problem today. Even though a wide variety of poverty reduction programs and strategies have been implemented over the last few decades, not much improvement has happened. There definitely is a need of innovative solutions and one of the recent strategies is the BoP approach.[16] The BoP perspective aligns business-oriented incentives for growth, innovation and profit with the development community's efforts to create a more inclusive capitalism. When Prahalad and Hart first published their paper their core idea

15 More information: <http://www.k-i-d-s.org/projekt/projekt-1/langswitch_lang/en>; <http://www.migrosmagazin.ch/pdf/index.cfm?ausgabe=200712&seite=62>.

16 The field of research around the concept of the 'Base of the Pyramid (BoP)' is relatively young. The debate was started in 1997 when C.K. Prahalad and Stuart L. Hart wrote their first working paper 'The Strategies for the Bottom of the Pyramid', which was not published until five years later (Prahalad and Hart 2002). Since then the topic is constantly gaining momentum.

was to offer cheaper and need-oriented products to the world's economic base of the pyramid, the 4 billion people with incomes below $3,000/year PPP. In his book 'The Fortune at the Bottom of the Pyramid' (Prahalad 2004/2006) Prahalad proposes that there are tremendous benefits for multinational companies who choose to sell to the poor, since there is much untapped purchasing power at the base of the pyramid:

> Certainly the purchasing power for those earning less than US $2 per day cannot be compared with the purchasing power of individuals in the developed nations. However, by virtue of their numbers, the poor represent a significant latent purchasing power that must be unlocked. (Prahalad 2004/2006, 11)

By selling to the poor, companies can bring prosperity to the base of the pyramid and thereby help reduce poverty. Aneel Karnani however argues that there is no fortune at the base of the pyramid. The market is quite small and furthermore the cost of serving this market can be very high (Karnani 2007, 6). 'There is little [...] fortune at the bottom of the pyramid – unfortunately, it is (almost) all a mirage' (ibid., 4). He suggests that companies can help alleviate poverty by raising the income of the poor while focusing on the poor as producers.[17]

A very practical approach is now advanced by Hart. Together with Eric Simanis and others, he led the development of the Base of the Pyramid Protocol, a 'business incubation process that enables multinational corporations to generate new business opportunities at the BoP'[18] together with the income-poor communities they want to operate in. The goal is to establish sustainable and successful businesses, in a process of mutual partnership and co-creation. Ted London[19] highlights the importance of co-creation as well (London 2007, 17) and he also points out the importance of partnerships – 'mutually beneficial partnerships' (ibid., 19) – and the principle of self-financed growth (ibid., 22).

Poverty is multidimensional and therefore poverty reduction programs and strategies have to be creative and multidimensional as well. Market-based approaches, as the BoP approach is one, are not new. Aid-funded support for small and medium enterprise development and market initiatives in emerging countries has been there for many years. There are success stories to tell as well as failures. Muhammad Yunus (Yunus 2008; 2001) and the Grameen bank – who won the Nobel Peace Prize – are definitely a success story.

Anyway, one aspect is presumably decisive: For too long companies have focused on the top of the economic pyramid and the base of the pyramid – the majority of the world population living in poverty – had been the target group

17 For a critical analysis of the vision of Prahalad offers see Landrum (2007).

18 BoP Protocol: <http://www.bop-protocol.org/>.

19 Ted London is also involved in the BoP Protocol and he is the Director of the William Davidson Institute Base of the Pyramid Initiative see <http://www.wdi.umich.edu/ResearchInitiatives/BasePyramid/>.

only of NGO's and development aid of governments. More and more positive examples from the corporate world demonstrate that morality can turn out to be economical if done the right way. Doing business in the developing world is often different from doing business at the top of the pyramid. Therefore not only a mind shift is needed but also the willingness at company top-level to combine business with morality.

Sure, the moral point of view isn't only concerned with potential gains or cooperation returns (the economic point of view), but with the identity of social life. Nevertheless, in reality (in the world we live in) they are connected, and the moral point of view isn't independent from the economic dimension. So, we have to face the truth, as Shirley Chisholm (first major party African-American candidate for President of the United States; † 2005) said: 'When morality comes up against profit, it is seldom profit that loses'. But also the other way round: When profit comes up against morality, the poor are seldom those who profit.

References

Christiansen, N. (2008), 'Creating Shared Value through Basic Business Strategy', *Development Outreach* 10:2, 10–12.

Fiorina, C. (2003), *James Gillies Alumni Lecture* (Schulich School Of Business York University, Toronto, Ontario, 28 October 2003). Available at <http://www.hp.com/hpinfo/execteam/speeches/fiorina/schulich.html>.

Food and Agriculture Organization (FAO) of the United Nations (2006), *State of Food Insecurity in the World 2006*.

Goldberg, R. and Herman, K. (2006), *Nestlé's Milk District Model: Economic Development for a Value-Added Food Chain and Improved Nutrition* (Boston: Harvard Business School Publishing).

Habermas, J. (1991), *Erläuterungen zur Diskursethik* (Frankfurt/Main: Suhrkamp).

Habermas, J. (1995), *Justification and Application. Remarks on Discourse Ethics* (Cambridge-Malden: Polity Press).

Hammond, A., Kramer, W., and Katz, R., translated by Walker, J. and Walker, C. (2007), *The Next 4 Billion – Market Size and Business Strategy at the Base of the Pyramid* (Washington: World Resource Institute).

Karnani, A. (2007), *Fortune at the Bottom of the Pyramid: A Mirage*, Working Paper (Stephen M. Ross School of Business, University of Michigan, April).

Kovacsics, M. and Degert, S. (2006), *Wie eine harte Nuss geknackt wird* (TV documentation, WDR [Germany]).

Landrum, N. (2007), 'Advancing the "Base of the Pyramid" Debate', *Strategic Management Review* 1:1, 1–12.

London, T. (2007), 'A Base-of-the-Pyramid Perspective on Poverty Alleviation', *Working Paper* (William Davidson Institute/Stephen M. Ross School of Business, University of Michigan, July).

Luhmann, N. (1989), *Die Wirtschaft der Gesellschaft*, 2nd Edition. (Frankfurt/Main: Suhrkamp).

Luhmann, N. (1997), *Die Gesellschaft der Gesellschaft*, Vol. I/II (Frankfurt/Main: Suhrkamp).

North, D. (1990), *Institutions, Institutional Change and Economic Performance* (Cambridge et al.: Cambridge University Press).

Pogge, T. (2002/2008), *World Poverty and Human Rights* (Cambridge-Malden: Polity Press).

Pogge, T. (ed.) (2007), *Freedom from Poverty as a Human Right. Who Owes What to the Very Poor?* (Oxford: Oxford University Press).

Pogge, T. (2007a), 'Introduction', in Pogge, T. (ed.), 1–9.

Prahalad, C. (2004 / 2006), *The Fortune at the Bottom of the Pyramid* (Upper Saddle River: Wharton School Publishing).

Prahalad, C. and Hart, S. (2002), 'The Fortune at the Bottom of the Pyramid', *Strategy and Business* 26, 54–67.

Stiglitz, J. (2006), *Making Globalization Work* (New York: Norton).

United Nations (UN) (1995), *Report of the World Summit for Social Development.*

United Nations Development Programme (UNDP) (2006), 2006 Human Development Report: 'Beyond Scarcity: Power, Poverty and the Global Water Crisis'.

Whitehead, A. (1927/2007), 'Introduction', by Jones, J. in *Religion in the Making* (New York: Fordham University Press).

Whitehead, A. (1929/1979), *Process and Reality. An Essay in Cosmology*. Gifford Lectures Delivered in the University of Edinburgh During the Session 1927–28, ed. by Griffin, D. and Sherburne, D. (New York: Free Press).

Whitehead, A. (1936/1968), *Modes of Thought* (New York: The Free Press).

Wieland, J. (2001), 'Eine Theorie der Governanceethik', *Zeitschrift für Wirtschafts- und Unternehmensethik* 2, 8–33.

Wieland, J. (2001a), 'The Ethics of Governance', *Business Ethics Quarterly* 2:1, 73–87.

Wittgenstein, L. (1953/2001), *Philosophical Investigations* (Malden: Blackwell).

Wolf, J. (2008), *Flores Farm: Our Philosophy*. Available at <http://www.floresfarm.de/0_flores_engl/flores_2_engl.html>.

Yunus, M. (2001), *Banker to the Poor: Micro-Lending and the Battle Against World Poverty* (New York: Public Affairs).

Yunus, M. (2008), *Creating a World Without Poverty: Social Business and the Future of Capitalism* (New York: Public Affairs).

Chapter 17
The Role of Corporate Citizens in Fighting Poverty: An Ordonomic Approach to Global Justice

Ingo Pies and Stefan Hielscher

Introduction: The Problem of Global Justice

Only in recent times has global justice become a topic of political philosophy. Although certain moral aspects of international relations have long been subject to serious debates in ethics, systematic efforts to address international issues as problems of global justice started not more than 40 years ago. The most import among these issues is certainly the problem of worldwide extreme poverty.[1]

There are two fundamental reasons why the citizens of today's world society should address the problem of extreme poverty as a problem of (global) justice, and both reasons can be illustrated by scrutinising Figure 17.1. The first reason is that the development of the western world shows that there are ways to escape from extreme poverty. For millennia, the level of per capita income oscillated around the subsistence level. It was only in the early nineteenth century that the vicious circle of the Malthusian trap could be overcome. Since this breakthrough, western societies have experienced a history of exponential growth that boosted their average per capita income more than 15-fold (upper graph after 1800).

The second reason is that this unique growth path has, unfortunately, left some countries behind (lower graph after 1800). As a result, there is a huge discrepancy between the world's rich and the world's poor: While western countries have indeed managed to induce growth and therefore experience wide-spread affluence nowadays, many countries remain poor due to the absence of growth. This implies that the very experience that growth and wealth is possible for large populations in some countries transforms the historical fact of extreme poverty in poor countries into a *normative* problem of global justice. Before 1820, this would have been unthinkable.

1 First published in 1972, Peter Singer's seminal article on the moral legitimacy of famine is still today regarded as the *locus classicus* of the early work on global justice. Cf. Singer (1985).

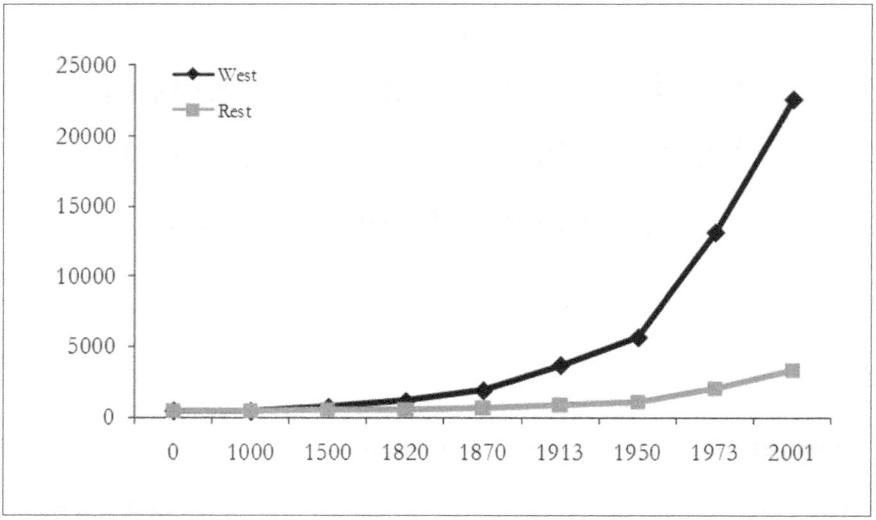

Figure 17.1 Per capita income 1000 BC–2000 AC

Given this background, to overcome extreme poverty is *the* problem of global justice. With this in mind, global justice can be interpreted as a problem of the absence of growth. Hence, there are two seminal questions to be addressed by a theory of global justice: First, how can we explain sustainable growth (that took place in some countries)? Second, how can we explain the absence of growth (in still other societies)? In order to answer these two questions, a theory of global justice needs to be based on a positive analysis that explains why there is no growth in extremely poor countries. The basic idea is: institutions matter!

This chapter compares two approaches to a theory of global justice. The first step briefly sketches an ordonomic approach, while the second step presents Thomas Pogge's cosmopolitan approach. The third step analyses and compares how both approaches generate arguments and how well these arguments are methodologically suited to address the main problem of global justice: the problem to alleviate and even to eradicate extreme poverty.

The Ordonomic Approach to Global Justice

The ordonomic approach makes use of elementary game theory and a rational-choice-based analysis of institutional arrangements in order to systematically explore the interdependencies between social structure and semantics. By 'social structure', we mean the institutional framework of society and its incentive properties; by 'semantics', we think of the terminology of public discourse and the underlying thought categories that determine how people perceive, describe, and evaluate social interactions and, in particular, social conflicts.[2]

The following discussion outlines how the ordonomic approach conceptualises the problem of global justice and, subsequently, develops contributions to a possible solution for it. The remarks are divided into diagnosis and therapy.

(1) The diagnosis of the ordonomic approach provides an answer to both seminal questions of global justice: (a) it provides an explanation for growth in modern societies; and (b) it provides an explanation for the absence of growth in poor societies.

(a) The ordonomic approach to global justice suggests viewing successful growth processes as an assurance game at the constitutional level between two actor groups: The government, including the elites that support it (Player G), and the country's citizens, taken as a group (Player C). The ordinal payoffs indicate how the players value their strategy combinations. The number before the comma applies to Player C; the number after the comma to Player G.

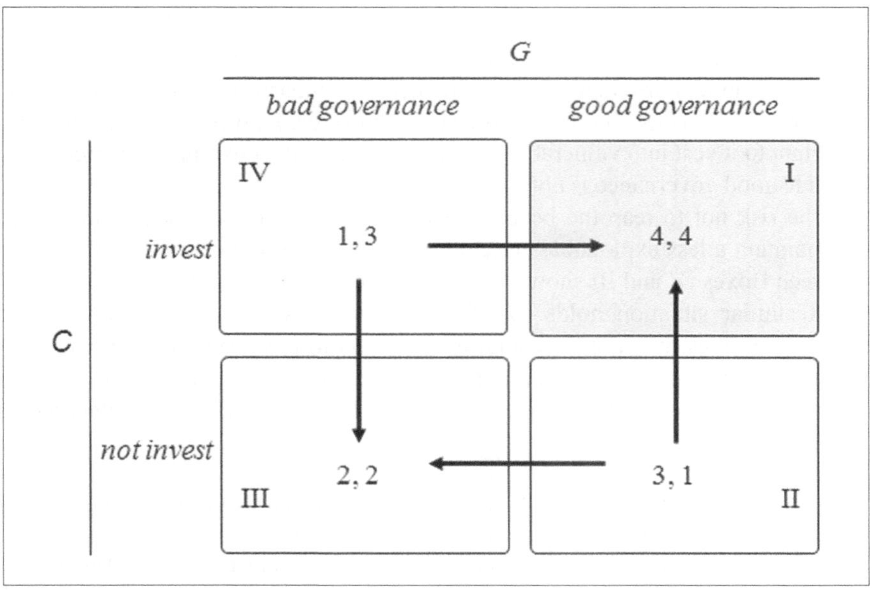

Figure 17.2 Assurance game at the constitutional level in growth societies

2 Semantics is driven by conscious or unconscious theories: our 'searchlights' – Popper (1972), 'heuristics' – Lakatos (1978), 'paradigms' – Kuhn (1962), or 'mental models' – Denzau and North (1994).

In a simple representation of this game, both actor groups have two strategies (Figure 17.2). The government, Player G, has to choose between good and bad governance. On the one hand, it has the option to create a legal system that establishes the rule of law and secures property rights. Furthermore, Player G can provide public goods – including a market-based system of private credit and insurance contracts and a well-designed system of social security. In this 'good governance' scenario, Player G facilitates access to markets for *all* country's citizens and not only for small and privileged elites. On the other hand, the government has the option to discriminate against their citizens. In this 'bad governance' scenario, only certain elites benefit from secure property rights, from the rule of law and from the provision of public goods – and citizens are excluded from access to markets, which is limited to the government's privileged supporters who profit from the resulting economic rents.[3]

The group of citizens, Player C, must choose whether to invest or not. One option is to use their (mobile) resources for small-scale agricultural production in order to provide for mere subsistence. The other option is to convert resources into capital and to invest into productive (and risky) production plans in (growing) markets.[4]

Assuming rational actors, this game can easily be solved. In both cases, Player C's individual benefit calculus leads him to respond strategically to Player G's strategic choice: Citizens like to invest into risky and productive production plans if the government provides good governance. A comparison between Boxes I and II shows $4 \succ 3$. Thus, the right arrow points upwards. However, citizens are very reluctant to invest into vulnerable market activities if the government's promise to provide good governance is not (or cannot be) made credible. In this case, citizens run the risk not to reap the benefits of their investment and instead (are forced to) maintain a less exploitable agricultural subsistence production. A comparison between Boxes IV and III shows $1 \prec 2$. Thus, the left arrow points downward.

A similar situation holds for Player G: if Player C does not invest into market activities, it is not beneficial for Player G to provide good governance. A comparison between Boxes III and II reveals $2 \succ 1$. Thus, the lower arrow points to the left. If, however, the citizens do invest, Player G finds it advantageous to

3 In recent publications, Douglass C. North, together with his co-authors John J. Wallis and Barry R. Weingast, develops a similar classification of social orders. The traditional formation of social order during history is the 'limited access order', while modern western societies are typically 'open access orders'. A limited access order is a society in which military elites form a coalition – the state. Privileges for the members of the state – i.e. monopoly rights that limit competition – stabilise this social order. In contrast, an open access order is a society in which all citizens have free access to processes of economic and political competition. In modern societies, citizens form their own organisations and exercise public pressure in order to prevent the state from granting unproductive privileges like exemptions from the rule of law. Cf. North et al. (2006) and North et al. (2007).

4 Cf. Olson (2000) and de Soto (2002).

provide good governance. A comparison between Box I and Box IV reveals $4 \succ 3$. Thus, the upper arrow points to the right.

This assurance game has two Nash-equilibria in non-dominant strategies. Furthermore, the collectively self-damaging underdevelopment Nash-equilibrium (represented in Box III) is Pareto-dominated by the Nash-equilibrium with huge prospects for mutual gains from growth (represented in Box I). Therefore, the ordonomic answer to the first question of global justice is straightforward: Rich countries are rich because they play a constitutional game in which both players – government and citizens – find it relatively easy to coordinate their strategies and to realise a mutually beneficial equilibrium. This game can be interpreted as the result of a historical learning process of mutual adaptation. Once the growth strategies of good governance and investment are combined, the strategy combination is stable and leads to the economic miracle of the western world.

(b) In order to answer the second question of global justice, the ordonomic approach suggests to interpret the absence of growth – and especially the problem of extreme poverty – as resulting from a quasi prisoners' dilemma (PD) at the constitutional level in poor countries (Figure 17.3). Just as with a genuine prisoners' dilemma, the hallmark of a quasi-PD is that it is a situation of collective self-damage: A situation in which a win-win solution cannot be realised due to an incentive structure that induces rational actors not to act in a mutually beneficial way, even though it would be in their common interest to do so. In contrast to a genuine PD, in a quasi-PD only one actor has a dominant strategy not to cooperate.

The main difference between the assurance game played in rich countries and the quasi-PD played in poor countries is simply that in the latter governments have no interest in good governance. Put graphically, both the upper and the lower arrow point to the left (Figure 17.3). There are many reasons for this. Here, we concentrate on two external factors that have played a major role in the recent history of developing countries. First, western countries have given unconditional foreign aid (and unconditional loans) to governments in poor countries, and they have – intentionally or unintentionally – supported market restricting economic policies in poor countries like state monopolies of natural resources. Second, western countries have followed the tradition to donate public emergency relief aid directly to governments in poor countries. Both western policy practices have had an influence on the constitutional game played in developing countries. These practices set a premium for bad governance in poor countries. Their effects are shown in Figure 17.3 as two transfers t_1 and t_2.

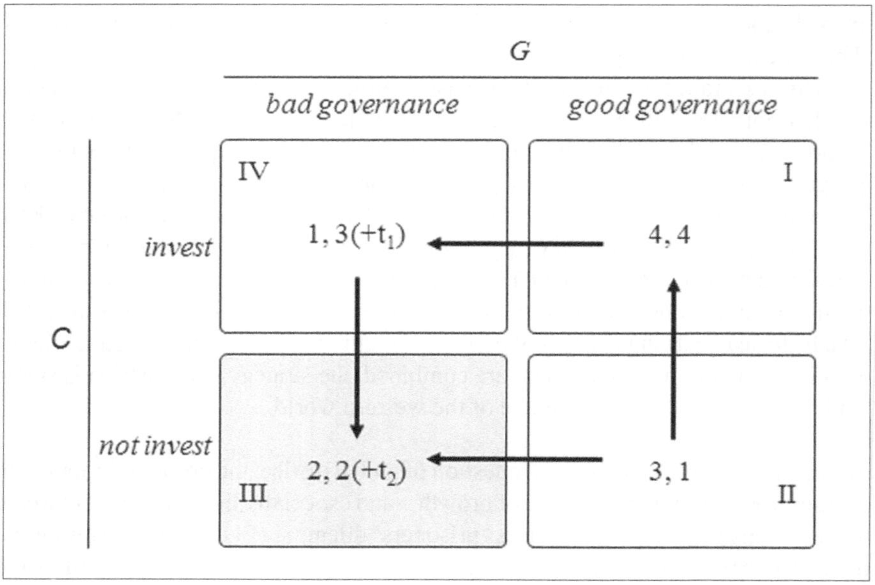

Figure 17.3 Quasi prisoners' dilemma at the constitutional level in poor societies

Transfer t_2 strengthens the tendency toward bad governance when Player G is faced with insufficient investments by the citizens – a comparison between Boxes III and II reveals $2 + t_2 \succ 1$. However, transfer t_1 may have a more fundamental impact on the cost-benefit calculus of governments. Unconditional transfers and monopoly rents are a cheap alternative to other sources of governmental income. Hence it becomes less attractive to provide good governance in order to create the institutional infrastructure for well-functioning markets and flourishing tax revenues. If t_1 is big enough, 'bad governance' becomes the dominant strategy for poor countries' governments. A comparison between Boxes IV and I shows ($3 + t_1 \succ 4$). That is why the upper arrow points to the left, which is the crucial distinction between Figure 17.3 and Figure 17.2.

This distinction has a profound consequence: Poor countries are poor because they fail to reach the growth equilibrium (Box I) and instead realise the Pareto-inferior Nash-equilibrium (Box III). They are trapped in a dilemma situation where both the government and the citizens play underdevelopment strategies. And western countries are partly responsible for this pitiful outcome because – intentionally or unintentionally – they have rewarded bad governance strategies by the poor countries' governments.

(2) This ordonomic diagnosis leads to a straightforward therapy: Rich countries and their civil society actors can (and should) help to turn the quasi-PD into

an assurance game. In order to do so, western societies should stop indirectly rewarding exploitation strategies and stop subsidising bad governance.

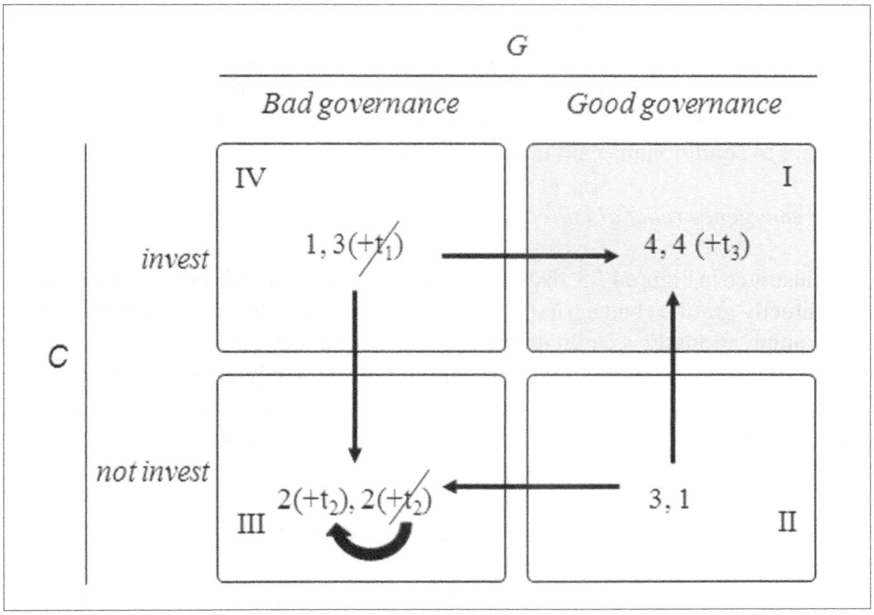

Figure 17.4 Assurance game at the constitutional level in poor societies

According to our model, one can think of three different ways how to achieve this (Figure 17.4):

Stop unconditional foreign aid to governments

As illustrated in Figure 17.3, unconditional loans or grants to governments may support bad governance in poor countries. Putting an end to this practice could therefore contribute towards restoring government credibility. This line of argument is represented in Figure 17.4 by cutting t_1. In effect, in the last 15 years much of foreign aid transfer has been reorganised and largely been made conditional on market-liberal reforms. Recently, foreign aid has been made conditional on good governance. But to put forward an effective policy of conditionality has proven to be difficult due to a problem of self-commitment among donor country governments. In the literature, the problem is often referred to as the *Samaritan's dilemma.*[5] The basic idea can be explained by a three-stage argument: In step 1, the donor countries offer a certain amount of foreign aid to the government of the recipient country in exchange for good governance reforms that would benefit its citizens. In step 2, the recipient government decides upon the allocation of resources to alternative uses. In general, the recipient government will leave the citizens with a lower level of public goods than contracted with the donors, simply because it will expect the altruistic donors to give extra foreign aid in step 3 when they observe that the citizens are worse off without extra foreign aid. Thus, many attempt to conditionalise aid lack credibility.

Give emergency relief aid directly to the poor

As illustrated in Figure 17.3, disbursing emergency relief aid directly to governments (in)directly gratifies bad agricultural and other policies that – be it intentionally or be it unintentionally – facilitate the outbreak of droughts and famines. Bypassing the government so that in cases of emergency the needy people directly benefit from relief aid could therefore contribute to restore government credibility. This line of argument is represented in Figure 17.4 by shifting t_2 from Player G to Player C.

Support self-commitments of poor country governments

Credible self-commitment of poor country governments is *the* crucial factor that turns a quasi-PD into an assurance game with a Pareto-dominant Nash-equilibrium at the constitutional level (Box I). In modern growth societies, legal institutions and civil society organisations (including companies) provide credibility for strategies of self-commitment. While the required institutional and organisational infrastructure may often be missing in poor societies, it is possible to get help for commitments from abroad and thus to import credibility. One example of credibility import from external sources is the 'Extractive Industries Transparency Initiative'. Multinational firms operating in the extractive industry in resource-affluent poor countries and poor country governments have agreed to simultaneously follow a rule of transparency: The firms committed themselves to the rule: 'publish what you pay'; the governments, by contrast, committed themselves to the rule: 'publish what you receive'.[6] Another example of credibility import from abroad is the African Peer Review Mechanism (APRM). The APRM is an instrument for monitoring and evaluating the progress of good governance in those African

5 The classic formulation of this argument stems from Buchanan (1975). Cf. Schmidtchen (2002) for a general discussion. For an application of the Samaritan's Dilemma to development policy cf. Pedersen (2001) and Gibson et al. (2005) for an application.

6 Cf. <http://eitransparency.org>.

countries who signed the New Partnership for African Development (NePAD).[7] This line of argument is represented in Figure 17.4 by a new 'transfer' t_3.

It is along these lines that the world society needs more initiatives. Supporting and sustaining credible self-commitments by governments of poor countries is the key concept here. In this sense, the global learning process to achieve a better development practice has just begun.

Thomas Pogge's Cosmopolitan Approach to Global Justice

The moral philosopher Thomas Pogge is one of the most prominent representatives of a cosmopolitan approach to global justice.[8] The problem of persisting extreme poverty is the intense focus of much of his work. Taking into account the tremendous worldwide gap between the rich and the poor, Pogge views extreme poverty as a moral scandal. His ethics aims at remedying this problem. Being a moral philosopher, Pogge has proposed both a diagnosis and a therapy for this moral grievance, and it is the incentive structure of the global institutional order that is at the centre of both.

(1) Pogge's diagnosis consists of the argument that world poverty is caused by a structural phenomenon. According to his analysis, it is the global institutional order that harms the poor in various ways: First, wide-spread protectionism of affluent countries – tariffs, agricultural subsidies and the promotion of exports – inhibit the poor from reaping the benefits of agricultural and commodity trade. Second, he thinks that WTO regulation on intellectual property rights (TRIPS) leads to a death toll that would be, in principle, avoidable. Third, he argues that the extensive use of fossil energy sources by the rich countries causes global warming that imposes a disproportionately high burden upon the poor.

According to Thomas Pogge's diagnosis, the two most important structural deficits of the international order are the 'resource privilege' and the 'borrowing privilege'. Both privileges derive from the common practice in international relations to accept as a legitimate representative and trading partner whichever group that takes control over the respective (developing) country's coercive power. In so doing, rich countries' representatives assign to the elite group the privilege (a) to borrow money in the country's name; and (b) to command over the country's resources, including the right to legally confer ownership rights of these resources. Pogge argues that both privileges involve advantages for autocratic regimes with severe negative effects to the poor in the country.

---

7 For an ordonomic analysis of the APRM/NePAD cf. Beckmann (2008).

8 The following analysis of Pogge's approach is based on Pogge (2001a; 2001b; 2002a; 2002b; 2005a; and 2005b). For a discussion of Pogge's approach to reforming the international market for pharmaceuticals cf. Pies und Hielscher (2008).

(a) The international borrowing privilege not only helps autocratic regimes and dictatorships to stay (longer) in power, even against strong popular opposition, but it also impedes and destabilises democratic transition: It hinders a successful start-up as democratic successor governments have to shoulder not only the reform efforts but also the debt burden of its, oftentimes corrupt, autocratic predecessors. Moreover, the borrowing privilege destabilises democratic transition as it provokes civil unrest by setting a premium for reactionary regime overthrows.

(b) Just as with the borrowing privilege, the international resource privilege comprises the right 'of any person or group exercising effective power within a country to confer internationally valid legal ownership rights in its natural resources'.[9] This privilege plays a similarly adverse role for the poor as it destabilises the social order and provokes civil unrest in resource-affluent poor countries. First, it is of great benefit to authoritarian rulers. Second, it provides a strong incentive to their rivals who are after such a role. Thus, in many cases, citizens do not profit from their country being affluent with natural resources.

(2) Thomas Pogge's therapy for these two major problems entails both structural reforms and compensatory measures if structural reforms are not possible. He suggests various forms of self-commitment for governments in order to solve the adverse consequences of both the borrowing and resource privileges.

In order to remedy the adverse incentive effects of the international borrowing privilege, Thomas Pogge suggests a constitutional amendment by young and poor democratic governments declaring that debts incurred by future reactionary regimes are not allowed to be repaid at public expense. According to Pogge, such an amendment should have the effect that future authoritarian regimes will be able to borrow less and at higher cost. In the long run, this would significantly reduce the reward for undemocratic government takeovers with the effect of lower incentives to attempt a coup d'état.[10]

Pogge envisages a similar constitutional amendment in order to remedy the negative consequences of the international resource privilege. In this amendment the country shall declare that 'only its constitutionally democratic governments may effect legally valid transfers of ownership rights in public property and forbids any of its governments to recognise ownership rights in property acquired from a preceding government that lacked such constitutional legitimacy'.[11] Pogge anticipates this amendment to inform potential (foreign) buyers of natural resources that they might be subject to claims of compensation once a democracy assumes power. Hence, such an amendment would reduce resource revenues for authoritarian rulers and would act as a disincentive to undemocratic coups d'état.

9 Pogge (2002b, 165).

10 Pogge (2002b, 153 et seq.).

11 Pogge (2002b, 163).

In addition to this strategy of supporting (self-)commitments of poor democratic governments, Pogge envisages compensatory and redistributive measures in order to tackle the problem of severe worldwide poverty. The Global Resource Dividend (GRD) is a case in point. Its basic idea is simple, but compelling: 'Those who make more extensive use of our planet's resources should compensate those who, involuntarily, use very little'.[12] In order to eradicate poverty, Pogge envisages a 'tax' on a limited number of primary resources and pollutants creating a revenue stream for redistribution, high enough to raise the income of the very poor above the subsistence level.[13]

Comparing Theories

At this point, the interesting question is how Thomas Pogge's theory relates to the ordonomic approach of global justice. A simple schematic model of global governance helps to compare both approaches (Figure 17.5).

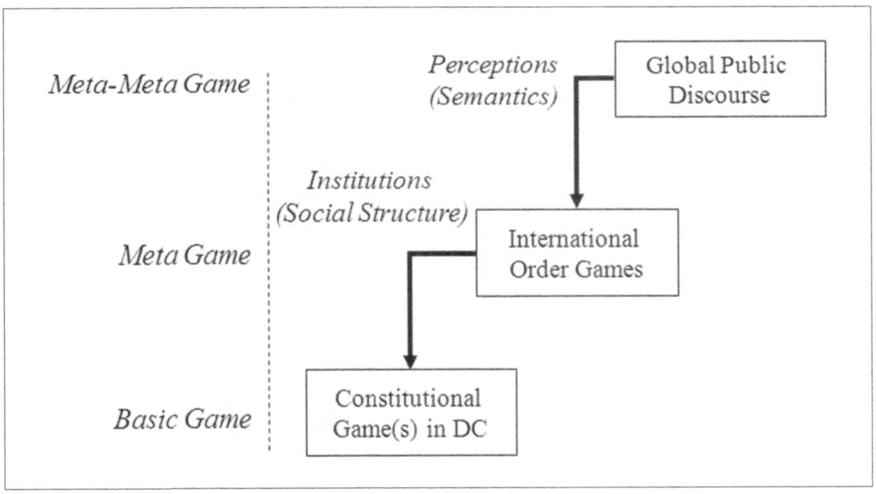

Figure 17.5 A stylised model of global governance

This model differentiates three levels of global governance: The constitutional game for growth in developing countries (DCs) is regarded as the basic game. The international (economic) order is seen as the meta game. In this meta game, the institutional rules are decided that shape the incentive properties – the social

12 Pogge (2002b, 204).

13 Cf. Pogge (2002b, 204 et seq.).

structure – of the basic game(s) in DCs. The third level is regarded as the meta-meta game. On this level, different perceptions and diverse ideas of how to solve the problem of extreme poverty are discussed in an open global public discourse. Global ethicists and theorists of global justice join this game together with civil society organisations (CSOs), transnational corporations or state actors. It is this meta-meta game that shapes the semantics of global justice and, hence, influences the institutions of global governance that form the social structure.

In comparison, both approaches agree that on the first level the problem of global justice is a problem of extreme poverty, which results from adverse incentives in the basic constitutional game in DCs. Both approaches are still in the same boat when moving to the second level. Both approaches acknowledge that the global institutional order has adverse effects on the basic games in DCs.

On the third level, the interesting question is: If ethics injects arguments in the public discourse, which kind of argument is best suited for stimulating institutional reform? In ordonomic terms: Which kind of semantics is best suited in order to successfully instruct reforms of the social structure in DCs that are required in order to help the poor? On this third level, both approaches tend to differ in the generation of arguments:

(a) Thomas Pogge's theory operates with two different categories of arguments. To a large extent, his theory operates with arguments of prudence that aim at stimulating collective action for his reform proposals. Prudential arguments are arguments of self-commitment. In a nutshell, they rely on the enlightened private interest of actors in order to further public interest. To put it graphically: They aim at an orthogonal position (dashed arrow in Figure 17.6, part a).

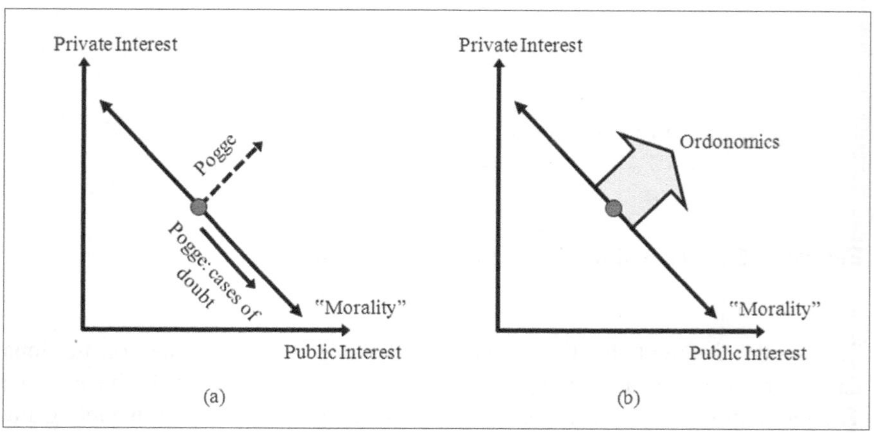

Figure 17.6 Semantics: Win-lose versus win-win

Interestingly, as a last resort Thomas Pogge's theory uses a normative fall-back option: the normative appeal to moral duties. In so doing, he changes his paradigm from arguments of prudence to arguments of obligation. Pogge (2001b, 22) writes:

> The conclusion is … that the underfulfillment of human rights in the developing countries is not a homegrown problem, but one we greatly contribute to through the policies we pursue and the international order we impose. We have not merely a [weak] positive responsibility with regard to global poverty, like Rawls's 'duty of assistance', but a [strong] negative responsibility to stop imposing the existing global order and to prevent and mitigate the harms it continually causes for the world's poorest populations. Because our responsibility is negative and because so much harm can be prevented at so little cost to ourselves, the reduction of severe poverty should be our foremost moral priority.

To put it graphically: In cases of doubt, Pogge's theory opts for the primacy of 'morality'. Such a strategy runs the utopian risk of proposing a win-lose strategy (solid arrow in Figure 17.6, part a).

(b) In contrast, the ordonomic approach consistently draws on arguments of prudence. It uses a theory design for global justice that employs a rational-choice analysis of social dilemmas in order to identify common rule-interests in the meta-meta game. A consensus of common rule-interests facilitates the rule-reform process in the meta game. The idea is to set mutually beneficial rules for better (basic) games. Ultimately, ordonomics seeks a win-win potential precisely because it wants to foster the implementation of moral objectives in the basic game. The ordonomic approach is a heuristic to find orthogonal positions (Figure 17.6, part b).

(c) Why is this win-win perspective of such vital importance? According to the ordonomic understanding of interdependencies between social structure and semantics, a theory of global justice should display two features: First, a theory of global justice should display a theory design that constructively addresses all relevant actors. In addition to political actors, an appropriate theory of global justice should envisage business firms and civil society organisations. Second, a theory of global justice should consistently operate with arguments of prudence. Such a win-win-orientation can help to stimulate profit-maximising business firms to take action as corporate citizens in processes of new governance.

For this reason, we argue that Thomas Pogge's approach has a blind spot with regard to processes of new governance. New initiatives such as the APRM or the EITI are just a few cases in point. Pogge's theory misses out the opportunity to encourage corporate citizenship as a means to make moral desiderata – i.e. the eradication of worldwide poverty – come true.

Conclusion

Modern society is best understood as a society of organisations. As an artificial coalition of natural persons, an organisation is a supra-individual entity with an essentially higher potential for individual self-commitment than ordinary citizens. In modern societies especially companies use this commitment potential to establish and to sustain mutually beneficial cooperation with their (societal and governmental) stakeholders. In this way, companies play a crucial role for technical, cultural and institutional innovation and, hence, for the creation and the dissemination of social value.

Against this backdrop, the ordonomic approach argues that a theory of justice should incorporate a theory of corporate citizenship. Such a theory should constructively address business firms as functional actors of social value creation within competitive markets. However, for a theory of global justice that addresses organisations and especially companies as relevant subjects it is advantageous to consistently operate with arguments of prudence. To put it pointedly: Worldwide prosperity and poverty reduction cannot be achieved against business firms, but only together with them. The example of EITI illustrates this argument. Companies are the major engines of growth and poverty reduction and, hence, should rank among the major subjects (and objects) of a modern theory of global justice.

References

Barry, C. et al. (eds) (2005), *Global Institutions and Responsibilities. Achieving Global Justice* (Oxford: Oxford University Press).

Beckmann, M. (2008), 'Governance durch Selbstbindung: Wider die Ausbeutungsspiele afrikanischer Eliten', *ZfP – Zeitschrift für Politik* 55:2, 199–220.

Beitz, C. (ed.) (1985), *International Ethics* (Princeton: Princeton University Press).

Brennan, G. et al. (eds) (2002), *Method and Morals in Constitutional Economics. Essays in Honor of James M. Buchanan* (Heidelberg: Springer).

Buchanan, J. (1975), 'The Samaritan's Dilemma', in Phelps, E. (ed.), 71–85.

Clark, G. (2007), *A Farewell to Alms. A Brief Economic History of the World* (Princeton: Princeton University Press).

Conill, J. et al. (eds) (2008), *Corporate Citizenship, Contractarianism and Ethical Theory. On Philosophical Foundations of Business Ethics* (Aldershot: Ashgate).

Denzau, A. and North, D. (1994), 'Shared Mental Models: Ideologies and Institutions', *Kyklos* 47:1, 3–31.

Gibson, C., Krister, A. et al. (2005), *The Samaritan's Dilemma: The Political Economy of Development Aid* (Oxford: Oxford University Press).

Kuhn, T. (1962), *The Structure of Scientific Revolutions* (Chicago: University of Chicago Press).

Lakatos, I. (1978), 'The Methodology of Scientific Research Programmes', *Philosophical Papers* 1 (Cambridge: Cambridge University Press).
North, D. et al. (2006), 'A Conceptual Framework Interpreting Recorded Human History', National Bureau of Economic Research, *NBER Working Paper Series* 12795. Available at <http://www.nber.org/papers/w12795>.
North, D. et al. (2007), 'Limited Access Orders in the Developing World: A New Approach to the Problems of Development', *Policy Research Working Paper* 4359, The World Bank Independent Evaluation Group Country Relations Division, Washington, September.
Olson, M. (2000), *Power and Prosperity. Outgrowing Communist and Capitalist Dictatorships* (New York: Basic Books).
Pedersen, K. (2001), 'The Samaritan's Dilemma and the Effectiveness of Development Aid', *International Tax and Public Finance* 8, 693–703.
Phelps, E. (ed.) (1975), *Altruism, Morality and Economic Theory* (New York: Russel Sage Foundation).
Pies, I. and Hielscher, S. (2008), 'Why the International Market for Pharmaceuticals Fails and What to Do About It: A Comparison of Two Alternative Approaches to Global Ethics', in Conill, J. et al. (eds), 169–190.
Pogge, T. (ed.) (2001), *Global Justice* (Oxford: Oxford University Press).
Pogge, T. (2001a), 'Introduction: Global Justice', in Pogge, T. (ed.), 1–5.
Pogge, T. (2001b), 'Priorities of Global Justice', in Pogge, T. (ed.), 6–23.
Pogge, T. (2002a), 'Responsibilities for Poverty-Related Ill Health', *Ethics & International Affairs* 16:2, 71–79.
Pogge, T. (2002b) *World Poverty and Human Rights: Cosmopolitan Responsibilities and Reforms* (Cambridge: Cambridge University Press).
Pogge, T. (2005a), 'Human Rights and Global Health: A Research Program', in Barry, C. et al. (eds), 190–217.
Pogge, T. (2005b), ,'Medizinischer Fortschritt auch für die Armen. Ein neues Anreizsystem für pharmazeutische Innovation', *Jahrbuch für Wissenschaft und Ethik* 10, 115–127.
Pogge, T. (2005c), 'Symposium. World Poverty and Human Rights', in *Ethics & International Affairs* 19:1, 1–7.
Popper, K. (1972), *Objective Knowledge: An Evolutionary Approach* (Oxford: Oxford University Press).
Schmidtchen, D. (2002), 'To Help or Not to Help: The Samaritan's Dilemma Revisited', in Brennan, G. et al. (eds), 470–484.
Singer, P. (1985), 'Famine, Affluence, and Morality', in Beitz, C. (ed.).
de Soto, H. (2002), *The Mystery of Capital: Why Capitalism triumphs in the West and fails everywhere else* (New York: Basic Books).

Chapter 18
Global Justice in the Context of Worldwide Poverty and Climate Change

Johannes Wallacher

Ethical Questions Raised by Climate Change

Intensified and accelerated global economic integration has quite obviously ambivalent effects on welfare accumulation and poverty reduction (Todaro and Smith 2003). Some of its mechanisms provide opportunities for overcoming poverty and underdevelopment, whereas others reinforce the risk of deepening global disparities.

On the one hand, integration into the world economy offers developing countries the opportunity to strengthen their economic development because it enables them to export more goods, to attract foreign investments and to deploy new technologies coming from abroad. As a matter of fact, a group of developing countries, notably the newly industrialised countries, have achieved enormous growth rates and as a consequence also significant progress in poverty alleviation.

On the other hand, the interconnection with international flows of goods and capital produces substantial risks which has currently become very evident by the financial and the food crises. Intensified global economic cooperation has evidently increased global welfare. However, the benefits and burdens of these interactions are distributed most unequally and worldwide disparities have particularly been amplified at the margins of global income distribution (Milanovic 2005). This raises serious questions concerning global justice (Pogge 2001 and 2002).

Meanwhile, the fight against global poverty is affected by another global crisis, namely by climate change. Industrialised countries have mainly caused climate change as most of the last 150 years' carbon emissions have occurred in the Northern hemisphere (IPCC 2007a). On the contrary, the poor in developing countries who have contributed very little to the greenhouse effect are most strongly affected by its dangerous impacts (IPCC 2007b). Due to their geographical position, they are much more exposed to extreme weather events already now and even more so in the future. Additionally, poor countries and the poor are most vulnerable to climate change as they lack suitable means to cope with extreme weather events and to adapt themselves to changing climate conditions. Already now climate change is undermining international efforts to combat poverty (United Nations Development Programme 2007). There is strong evidence that global inequalities will be further deepened if the international community does not succeed in mitigating climate change and at the same time in enabling the poor to adapt to ongoing climate change. This strong discrepancy between those who are most responsible for climate change and those who are most vulnerable poses serious ethical questions that need to be addressed and to be integrated in reasoning on global justice.

Keeping this in mind, the question of who may use the atmosphere and to what extent turns out to be a consecutive equity issue as the atmosphere's capacity to absorb greenhouse gases has now proven to be limited. Developing nations now also claim the right to use the atmosphere – or more specifically to use fossil fuels – for their economic development as the industrialised countries did over the last 150 years. This indicates that the two goals of climate protection and poverty alleviation do not consort easily.

According to the principle of sustainability, on which the international community has agreed upon since 1992, climate protection and poverty alleviation are interactive and should not be played off against each other (Ekardt 2005). The current debate on equity issues regarding climate change and poverty alleviation, however, reveals far-reaching controversies. The arguments rest on quite diverse concepts of justice from which different, partly even contrary, political strategies can be derived. The debate on how to allocate future emission rights may serve as an example (den Elzen 2002; Baer and Athanasiou 2007). One argument refers primarily to customary rights and calls for preservation of the status quo of global emission patterns to avoid distortive consequences for large emitters; others set priorities to equal per capita emission rights for all citizens of the world in the future (egalitarianism); others again favour the historic responsibility (polluters pays principle) or the capacity (ability to pay) as guiding principles for an allocation rule.

All concepts of justice comprise normative preliminary decisions. One important task of ethics consists in revealing and reflecting such – often hidden – implications. A convincing ethical reflection requires a moral point of view in order to be impartial. This also applies for ethical reasoning on global justice. Such a moral point of view is introduced below. It can serve at first as a starting point to sketch a development-centred notion of global justice (Part 2) before proceeding to address the intergenerational-extension of this concept (Part 3) in order to come to an integrated reasoning on poverty alleviation and climate change.

Development-Centred Concept of Global Justice

Human dignity as a starting point

A universal concept of global justice must depend on a moral point of view that should be justifiable in different ethical concepts and maintainable in different cultural and religious traditions. Thus, such a moral point of view and, in particular, its justification should emanate from fundamental and common human experience, such as human vulnerability or more concretely joint human experience of suffering and injustice like hunger, poverty, or discrimination (Müller and Wallacher 2005, 105–127).

These negative experiences are widely independent of cultural interpretation and are nowhere simply accepted. Prior to all reasoning, they immediately call for overcoming or at least for a plausible explanation. In human suffering as a negative experience it becomes dialectically apparent that overcoming is the goal to strive for. Even human rights can be interpreted as the response to collective human suffering in the past and therefore be conceived as imperatives in the sense of a 'Not like that!' without tracing back to specific philosophical or religious traditions (Müller 1997, 103–118).

Of course, the rejection of human suffering is just a spontaneous reaction – something like a moral sentiment – at first. Ethics, however, asks for more than this spontaneous and instinctive rejection of human suffering. It demands for critical reasoning and rational justification. Moral sentiments, however, do not simply represent subjective intuitions, but can also be a source of moral motivation and moral judgement. Moral sentiments and moral principles are linked to each other by a process of deliberative mutual adjustment (Fischer 2000).

This idea had originally been introduced by Adam Smith in his 'The Theory of Moral Sentiments' (Smith 1976/1759). John Rawls, in his 'A Theory of Justice', also resorts to this approach (von Villiez 2005, 80–87), even though he does set some different course with his method of reflective equilibrium (Rawls 1971, chap. 9) which is crucial for approaching his principles of justice. The deliberative mutual adjustment between moral sentiments and moral principles also forms the base of the 'normative logic of human reciprocity' as introduced for example by Peter Ulrich (1998, 44–49).

The point of origin of the normative logic of human reciprocity is the principle of the imagined reversal of positions which can also be traced back to Adam Smith and his moral philosophy (Smith 1976/1759). The human ability to put oneself in his fellow men's place can be seen as the '*cognitive root of morality*'. This capability allows us to sympathise with the affects of others and to reflect our own behaviour from their point of view. This imagined reversal of positions is the base for the *principle of reciprocity of legitimate claims and rights* and is also the essence of the Golden Rule which is accepted in all cultural traditions. It reads in its simplest form: 'Do unto others as you would have others do unto you!' The principle of reciprocity denotes that my moral right is inseparably connected with the fellow man's duty to keep this right, and vice versa. The imagined reversal of positions is finally broadened to a *universal concept* which transfers the idea of reciprocity of moral rights and duties from the 'face-to-face' relationship to a 'global-relationship'. In the era of globalisation this abstraction is facilitated by worldwide mass media and electronic online networks which through their pictures or reports let everyone throw a glance at hunger, poverty, or natural disasters.

Starting from this formal principle of universal reciprocity of interpersonal rights and duties, moral norms and values can be deduced. This is, first of all, the fundamental norm of *reciprocal recognition of human dignity*. The normative-ethical claims that are indiscriminately granted to all humans solely due to their human dignity are spelled out in human rights. These comprise not only civil and political but also economic, social and cultural rights. These rights are mutually interdependent and complement each other in enabling each and every human being to live a dignified life. Thus, the logic of this approach lies in an option for those who are excluded from these rights.

Comprehensive understanding of self-determinated human development

The multidimensional concept of human rights demands a comprehensive understanding of *human development*. Poverty and social vulnerability do not only mean a lack of material income, but are usually linked to inadequate opportunities for development and to wide ranging forms of social exclusion. The majority of the poor are not only excluded from social safety nets and fundamental social services, such as basic education and basic health care, but also hardly have access to formal markets. In addition, they barely enjoy essential democratic and political rights, as the poor usually have hardly any access to lawyers, judges or democratic decision-making. Regarding a comprehensive understanding of development, Amartya Sen's capability approach points out some further and helpful perspectives as it aims at expanding human freedom in its complementary and interconnected dimensions (Sen 1999).

As a consequence the perspective of individual agency has to be placed at the centre of the stage. The ones who are poor and vulnerable are not just passive recipients of poverty reduction or adaptation programmes, but have to be seen as both focus and objective, and subject and agent of all efforts to overcome social and biophysical vulnerability. It is not only an ethical commandment but also a prerequisite to reduce social vulnerability in a sustainable way.

This requires a bottom-up approach to development which corresponds to the principle of *subsidiarity*. Subsidiarity again has two interconnected dimensions – the right to participate, as well as the duty to help people to help themselves. These produce the standard by which competences are to be institutionally ordered and attributed. Individuals and intermediate groups (families, local authorities, civil society players etc.) are protected from bureaucratic centralism and abuses by higher-level social authorities. Conversely, these superior social authorities have to provide help for self-help, if necessary, and have to strengthen the capabilities of the people concerned. This applies to all levels of social life within a nation-state and also to the global order which encompasses the totality of institutions that govern international cooperation. Such an order must, on the one hand, grant adequate scope and policy-space for self-determinated development and, on the other hand, support and encourage the development efforts of the poorer countries.

Demands of global justice

Based on the previous reflections, we will now try to approach the idea of development-centred global justice in a more concrete way. When having deduced human dignity as the moral point of view, ethical reasoning on global justice is geared towards *individuals* at first and nation-states can no longer form the primary reference point. The development indicators usually applied for nation-states – for example the income per capita – only represent a mean value and fail to show the considerable inequalities within countries. Nevertheless, universal ethical principles like human dignity and an individual-centred approach do not contradict the specific role of nation-states regarding global justice. Quite the reverse! The impact of the prevailing global order on a country's development and thus on the living standard of its population does strongly depend on the national policy in question (for example Rodrik 1999). Nation-states undoubtedly carry the main responsibility for the protection of human rights in all its different dimensions. Therefore, they have an important, if only instrumental meaning.

Conversely, as already mentioned before, there are also strong externalities of the present global order. Those international interactions do in many respects restrict the developing countries' abilities and efforts to alleviate poverty. Therefore, it seems adequate for a development-centred concept of global justice to reflect on both the social interactions within one country and those among several countries on the global scale. In an ethical reasoning the principle of subsidiarity also calls for this perspective. Thus, demands of justice apply to national as well as to international relations and to the corresponding institutional frameworks.

Due to the comprehensive concept of development, there is not only one demand of justice but a plurality of them. Three main principles can be identified and all of them may be deduced from human dignity. These three dimensions of justice are mutually interdependent and complement one another.

If we focus on individual capabilites and the agency of people, then *justice of opportunities* proves to be the core demand of justice. Therefore, benefits and burdens of social interactions should be distributed in such a way that all people concerned receive the same opportunities. In the context of climate change and global poverty this means for example that poor countries need adequate opportunities and proper facilities to be able to contribute actively to climate protection without having to renounce measures of combating poverty. Taking into consideration that most poorer countries have far worse starting conditions in global competition than the industrialised ones, e.g. because of poor technological infrastructure or institutional shortcomings, they do need forms of preferential treatment in certain global rules and regulations. Justice of opportunities does undoubtedly justify such time-restricted 'positive discrimination'. Also the transfer of adjusted, emission-saving technologies into poor countries at preferential terms may easily be legitimised. Similarly, at a national level opportunities of individuals and groups who are largely excluded from participation in society are to be made stronger, for example through investments in people to increase their capabilites or their scope of capacities so that they can better cope with the risks induced by climate change.

A fundamental prerequisite for individual agency is the satisfaction of fundamental human needs, e.g. adequate nutrition, access to clean water and basic health care. Therefore, *justice meeting basic needs* is a crucial second demand of justice. Priority attention must be given to those who are even unable to meet their basic needs. As a consequence political measures, first of all, must be geared at improving the opportunities of the poor to meet these needs.

Finally, self-determined human development asks for political freedoms and fair procedures. Both are of intrinsic value for a dignified life and at the same time are an important mean to promote other dimensions of development. Political freedoms have an instrumental role as they are the prime precondition for participation in public decision-making in all its different dimensions. This for instance concerns the ability to take part in political decisions on institutional arrangements providing education, health care or social safety nets. Therefore, both justice of opportunities and justice meeting basic needs essentially rest on *procedural justice*. Justice within general framework structures depends intrinsically on how framework conditions come about and who is in charge of deciding what regulations are to be applied or to be abolished at what time. Thus, a central demand of procedural justice is the demand for justice in negotiation processes, again on the national and international level, which requires transparent procedures and participation of all concerned. In particular those who are most affected by distortive externalities must adequately be involved in consultations and decision processes. Also the aspect of transactional justice, which is usually highlighted by economists, heavily depends on fair procedures. Transactional justice demands that economic exchange should occur within framework conditions which guarantee that such transactions are to the benefit of all partners involved. The current global order however indicates considerable institutional shortcomings and structural disadvantages which tend to guarantee the status quo of individual groups in the rich countries to the disadvantage of the poor countries (Barry and Pogge 2005).

Extended Claims of Intergenerational Justice

Keeping the introductory remarks in mind, there is a need to also incorporate demands of justice between generations into the concept of global justice. In doing so, three interwoven, but different ethical issues have to be tackled (Page 2007). The first problem concerns the *scope of justice* which 'is the question of which entities possess distributive entitlements, as well as the question of which entities are bound by duties to guarantee these entitlements' (Page 2007, 4). If we put this in the context of worldwide poverty and climate change, we have to reflect the history as well as the future.

Concerning the past we have to clarify whether and to what extent the developing countries in the South who are most affected by climate change have legitimate claims to some compensation from the industrialised countries in the North as they are the ones who have caused most of the stocks of accumulated carbon emissions since the pre-industrial period. Some developing countries, in particular Brazil, now claim to get the lion's share of future emission rights in order to enhance their development (den Elzen et al. 2005). The question is, whether this demand of corrective justice appears to be plausible, as most of the emissions prior to 1990 were made in ignorance rather than by deliberate decisions. Thus, the notion of carbon debt which is sometimes referred to (Edenhofer et al. 2009, section 3.1) can be misleading, because it implies that historic emissions are interpreted as intentional wrongdoing. This aspect does at best apply for emissions from fossil fuel consumption *after* 1990, because since then the scientific evidence for global warming and for its causes has been widely approved.

Nevertheless, there are plausible reasons not to simply forget about the historic emissions and to exclude them from ethical reflection. Though the need remains to thoroughly reflect which measurements could be appropriate in order to assign the specific responsibility to rich countries for emissions produced by them in the past. Two main aspects have to be taken into account. Firstly, it has become evident that climate change having mainly been caused by rich countries has dangerous impacts on developing countries. In addition, there is a strong correlation between wealth accumulation and historic emissions (Edenhofer et al. 2009, section 3.1). Therefore industrialised countries not only have a particular historic responsibility but also a much higher capacity both to reduce emissions through low-carbon technologies and to adapt to ongoing and projected impacts of climate change.

The main focus of intergenerational justice however, concerns the *scope of duties of contemporaries to future generations*. This fundamental issue cannot be discussed in more detail here. But, however, there are very reasonable arguments to assume that future people do hold legitimate claims against us, and that in turn we have correlative duties to future generations (Meyer 2008, section 2 and 3). Looking at that in the context of climate change, intergenerational justice thus means that our generation has the duty to avoid dangerous climate change in order not to compromise the ability of future generations in general and future poor people, in particular, to live a dignified life.

A second relevant question regarding intergenerational justice is closely linked to this aspect. If we have come to the conclusion that future human beings have legitimate claims against us, we must now concretise how benefits and burdens can be distributed appropriately between present and future generations. In the current debate three different *patterns of intergenerational justice* can be identified: equality, priority, or sufficiency. Again this cannot be exhausted in this context, but – coming from human dignity as the main moral point of view – there are reasonable arguments for supporting the perspective of sufficientarianism and a threshold of sufficiency (Meyer 2008, section 4; Page 2007).

Thirdly, this threshold of sufficiency on which all future people have legitimate claims, needs to be concretised. As a prerequisite we need to define an appropriate conception of well-being which some authors denote as specification of the *currency of justice* (Page 2007, 4). The comprehensive notion of development and the development-centred concept of global justice with its three kinds of justice, as illustrated above, can be consulted in order to explicate this threshold.

Justice of opportunities for future individuals, for instance, claims that specific path dependencies have to be taken into account in present decisions in the sense that they should not compromise future options for action excessively. Considering for example infrastructure or energy supply, crucial decisions are under way right now which bear far-reaching consequences for the future and we have to be aware that these decisions establish path dependencies that can hardly be reversed.

Justice based on basic needs demands that all efforts to overcome present economic and social problems should not curtail the options of future poor people to meet fundamental needs like the security of food resources or water availability – as we can assume that these aspects will be fundamental needs even for future generations. Dangerous climate change definitely will impact on these poverty dimensions (Schellnhuber 2006, section IV).

Thirdly, present procedures and institutions on a national and international level should be shaped in a way that is conducive for procedural justice in the future. We should, for instance, encourage the participatory ability of poor people and countries through investing in 'capacity building' measures and skills in order to strengthen the poor's future negotiating power. We must also not forget that political freedoms and fair procedures are a precondition for participation not only in public decision-making, but also in public reasoning which has an important role in the formulation of norms and values (Sen 2005). Due to this, it also appears foreshortened to define a threshold of sufficiency simply as predetermined basic needs, even though these will undoubtedly be crucial in specifying the threshold of sufficiency.

Finally it is important to throw a glance at the question of how complete our judgements on justice can be. Amartya Sen does, in the author's opinion, hit a crucial point when he accentuates that 'the insistence on the completeness of justice over every possible choice is not only an enemy of practical social action, it may also reflect some misunderstanding of the nature of justice itself' (Sen 1999, 254). Thus, he highlights not only the role of public reasoning but also the meaning of partial accord with regard to judgements of justice. He recommends we should come to a 'working agreement on some basic matters of identifiably intense injustice or unfairness' (Sen 1999, 254). This is of great value if we have to come to a common understanding of ethical judgements in a plural world with different cultural and religious traditions.

Amartya Sen's reflections have an important practical value in particular in the ongoing debate on climate change and justice. For example, there cannot be a uniquely correct definition for dangerous climate change, but the suggestion to limit the rise of globally averaged surface temperature to a maximum of 2°c relative to the pre-industrial value (German Advisory Council on Global Change 2007, 4) seems to be a reasonable ethical guardrail. This guardrail has been adopted by the European Union and other countries as the official goal for their climate policy. There is some evidence that it is possible to reach this goal at acceptable economic costs (Stern 2007). At the same time, clear scientific evidence does exist that global warming above the value of 2°c would significantly raise the risk of activating tipping points in the Earth system such as the melting of the Greenland ice sheet or the changing of the monsoon dynamics in China and India (Lenton et al. 2008). This definitely would endanger future people's opportunities to live a dignified life.

References

Baer, P. and Athanasiou, T. (2007), 'Frameworks & Proposals. A Brief, Adequacy and Equity-Based Evaluation of Some Prominent Climate Policy Frameworks and Proposals', *Global Issue Papers* 30 (Berlin: Heinrich Böll Foundation).

Barry, C. and Pogge, T. (eds) (2005), *Global Institutions and Responsibilities. Achieving Global Justice* (Malden: Blackwell Publishing).

den Elzen, M. (2002), 'Exploring Climate Regimes for Differentiation of Future Commitments to Stabilise Greenhouse Gas Concentrations', *Integrated Assessment* 3:4, 343–359.

den Elzen, M., Schaeffer, L. and Lucas, P. (2005), 'Differentiating Future Commitments on the Basis of Countries Relative Historical Responsibilty for Climate Change: Uncertainties in the "Brazilian Proposal" in the Context of a Policy Implementation', *Climatic Change* 71, 277–301.

Edenhofer, O., Flachsland, C. and Luderer, G. (2009), 'Global Contract: Eckpunkte einer Globalen Klimaschutzpolitik', in Wallacher, J. et al. (eds).

Ekardt, F. (2005), *Das Prinzip Nachhaltigkeit. Generationengerechtigkeit und Globale Gerechtigkeit* (München: C.H. Beck).

Fischer, J. (2000), 'Sittliche Intuitionen und reflektives Gleichgewicht', *Zeitschrift für evangelische Ethik* 44:4, 247–268.

Fricke, C. et al. (eds) (2005), *Adam Smith als Moralphilosoph* (Berlin: de Gruyter).

German Advisory Council on Global Change (2007), New Impetus for Climate Policy, *Policy Paper* 5 (Berlin), available at <http://www.wbgu.de/wbgu_pp2007_engl.pdf> (last accessed 29 October 2008).

IPCC (2007a), *Climate Change 2007: The Physical Science Basis. Contribution of Working Group I to the Fourth Assessment Report of the Intergovernmental Panel on Climate Change*, ed. by Solomon, S. et al. (Cambridge: Cambridge University Press).

IPCC (2007b), *Climate Change 2007: Impacts, Adaptation and Vulnerability, Contribution of Working Group II to the Fourth Assessment Report of the*

Intergovernmental Panel on Climate Change, ed. by Parry, M.L. et al. (Cambridge: Cambridge University Press).

Lenton, T., Held, H., Kriegler, E. et al. (2008), 'Tipping Elements in the Earth's Climate System', *Proceeding of the National Academy of Science of the United States of America* 105:6, 1786–1793. Available at <www.pnas.org/cgi/content/full/105/6/1786> [last accessed 29 October 2008].

Meyer, L. (2008), 'Intergenerational Justice', in *Stanford Encyclopedia of Philosophy*. Available at <http://plato.stanford.edu/entries/justice-intergenerational> [last accessed 29 October 2008].

Milanovic, B. (2003), *World Apart: Measuring International and Global Inequality* (Princeton: Princeton University Press).

Müller, J. (1997), *Entwicklungspolitik als Globale Herausforderung. Methodische und Ethische Grundlegung* (Stuttgart: Kohlhammer).

Müller, J. and Wallacher, J. (2005), *Entwicklungsgerechte Weltwirtschaft. Perspektiven für eine Sozial- und Umweltgerechte Globalisierung* (Stuttgart: Kohlhammer).

Page, E. (2007), 'Justice Between Generations: Investigating a Sufficientarian Approach', *Journal of Global Ethics* 3:1, 3–20.

Pogge, T. (ed.) (2001), *Global Justice* (Malden: Blackwell Publishing).

Pogge, T. (2002), *World Poverty and Human Rights* (Malden: Blackwell Publishing).

Rawls, J. (1971), *A Theory of Justice* (Oxford: Oxford University Press).

Rodrik, D. (1999), *The New Global Economy and Developing Countries. Making Openness Work* (Washington, DC: Johns Hopkins University Press).

Schellnhuber, H.-J. (ed.) (2006), *Avoiding Dangerous Climate Change* (Cambridge: Cambridge University Press).

Sen, A. (1999), *Development as Freedom* (New York: Knopf).

Sen, A. (2005), 'Human Rights and Capabilitites', *Journal of Human Development* 6:2, 151–166.

Smith, A. (1976/1759), *The Theory of Moral Sentiments*, ed. by Raphael, D. and Macfie, A. (Oxford: Oxford University Press).

Stern, N. (2007), *The Economics of Climate Change* (Cambridge: Cambridge University Press).

Todaro, M. and Smith, S. (2003), *Economic Development*, 8th Edition. (Boston: Addison Wesley).

Ulrich, P. (1998), *Integrative Wirtschaftsethik*, 2nd Edition. (Bern: Haupt).

United Nations Development Programme (2007), *Human Development Report 2007/2008. Fighting Climate Change: Human Solidarity in a Divided World* (New York).

von Villiez, C. (2005), 'Sympathetische Unparteilichkeit: Adam Smiths moralischer Kontextualismus', in Fricke, C. et al. (eds), 64–87.

Wallacher, J. et al. (eds) (2009), *Klimawandel und Globale Armut* (Stuttgart: Kohlhammer).

Conclusion

The Paradox of Poverty Research: Why is Extreme Poverty Not in Focus?[1]

Else Øyen

In the following conclusion it is argued that extreme poverty as a research arena and a target for poverty reduction is losing out in major paradigms that have as their principal rationale the understanding of poverty phenomena in the South.[2]

Poverty research is flourishing. So are programmes for poverty reduction, political interest in poverty, global discussions on poverty, shared explanations of why poverty is so persistent, and funding of poverty-related research. Twenty years ago the situation was quite different. Poverty research was limited and the public interest was low. While the arts had a long tradition in using poverty and its causes, manifestations and consequences as central themes, the social sciences were reluctant to engage in a broader understanding of poverty than the one offered by popular myth-making and moralistic frameworks.[3]

The rationale for poverty research is not only intellectual. Many poverty researchers engage in the pursuit of poverty understanding because they see it as a worthwhile undertaking beyond ordinary research. Likewise, the rationale for the funding of such research is often an explicit or implicit expectation that the research results will contribute to more efficient poverty-reducing strategies.

Over time three major paradigms have developed in poverty research directed towards developing countries: disciplinary approaches, development theories and the human rights approach. In the following contribution it is argued that although the focus of the paradigms is on poverty, the very nature of their conceptual framework indirectly bypasses extreme forms of poverty. Thereby not only is the original focus of their research undermined, but more importantly a limited picture of poverty is drawn that ignores the needs of the most disadvantaged people.

Extreme poverty can be defined to comprise that part of a population that scores the lowest on a combination of variables expressing basic conditions for human life and survival.

---

1 First published in *Forum for Development Studies* 35:2 (December 2008).

2 The contribution is written upon an invitation from the FDS to appear under Debate and can be seen as a summing up of my earlier works where references and further arguments can be found.

3 For a more elaborate discussion, see Øyen (2004), or <http://www.crop.org>.

Disciplinary Approaches

The paradigm of a discipline is its power base. The consistent use of certain methods, concepts, hypotheses and theories defines a discipline, its arena for research and its intellectual limits. Students are taught within a disciplinary framework and their careers are based on the paradigm of the profession. Universities are organised around disciplines and huge amounts of public funding are invested to conserve the disciplinary paradigms and develop them further. Interdisciplinary teaching and research are a challenge to the disciplinary power base and have so far had meagre conditions. Trespassers are welcome only if they acknowledge the authority of the disciplinary paradigms.

Poverty research does not have a power base of its own. Many of the disciplines within the social sciences and several outside the social sciences have incorporated poverty as a research topic, some of them fairly recently and some through a well-established tradition. As could be expected, the disciplinary approaches to poverty understanding are coloured by the disciplines' theories, methodologies and previous research. The understanding of poverty is fitted into the dominant paradigms of the discipline. It follows from this that the frontiers of poverty research follow closely the state-of-the-art within the discipline in question.[4] At university level poverty is mainly taught as courses within a discipline where the emphasis is on the disciplinary paradigm's own heritage and tools. Students who do their degrees are judged by their ability to apply the paradigmatic tools rather than by applying knowledge from outside the discipline to throw light on poverty phenomena. The courses lead to careers within the discipline rather than a career in poverty research. In spite of some very important institutions on poverty research and some educational institutions, particularly in the South, focusing on poverty as a research field of its own, a profession of poverty researchers has not emerged. Poverty research is pieced together from elements of different paradigms and has not developed what could be called a specific paradigm that would provide an intellectual and organisational power base. Poverty researchers, too, often have their intellectual attention divided between their mother discipline and their chosen area of research. One of the outcomes is that the full picture of extreme poverty as a research arena does not receive sufficient attention.

The disciplines with the longest tradition in the study of poverty are economics and sociology, and to a certain degree also demography, medicine and agricultural science. As a result paradigms from these disciplines dominate the academic and political field of poverty research.

Economics is about the distribution of material resources and the effects of different distributions. Extreme poverty plays a role, as the poor by definition are found at the lower end of the distribution curves. This phenomenon has received much attention in the discipline. Within economic models it becomes important

4 Some of the arguments here are elaborated in Øyen et al. (2005); see <https://bora.uib.no/handle/1956/2260>.

to calculate the size of the problem, and effort is invested in measuring poverty in different ways and in analysing the conditions under which changes occur. The standard measure of poverty as the proportion of a population living on less than one dollar a day (now readjusted to 1.25 dollar a day) is a strong indicator of mass poverty. It is, however, a limited indicator of human life in poverty. The immense resources that have been invested in measuring poverty nationally and internationally, and researching the relationship between this kind of poverty and other social and economic variables, can hardly be justified when the issue is to throw light on the complexity of extreme poverty. Research is focused on employment opportunities for the poor, access to markets and microcredit schemes. Questions have been raised as to whether the very poorest are able to profit from these measures and generate an income. Those who live in extreme poverty are not likely to be part of the formal economy. They generate whatever means they can from the informal economy. The paradigmatic push to see entry into the formal economy as a poverty-reducing strategy may actually be counterproductive. The informal economy in low development countries is at present likely to offer better opportunities for survival than a badly organised, exploitive formal economy. Strong actors such as the World Bank have for many years pushed hard for the implementation of basic economic paradigms in countries where mass poverty prevails and have argued that mass poverty has been reduced through such measures. Whether extreme poverty has been reduced proportionally to a reduction in general poverty, however, remains an unresearched question.

Sociology is the discipline most closely associated with social problems. There are numerous qualitative and quantitative studies of deprivation, marginalisation, exclusion, the life of the underclass, inequality, distribution of skewed resources and the like, on the micro as well as the meso and macro level. The notion of citizenship and the inclusion of all citizens in a society, including the poor, has become a cornerstone of modern poverty research. Most of the research has been carried out in Western countries and within a Western cultural setting where mass poverty and the extreme poverty of former days have yielded to more moderate forms of poverty. Concepts, theories and methods have been developed within a Western culture and for a long time research on poverty in the South was carried out within paradigms alien to non-Western cultures. When the social sciences developed educational programmes for their own students in the South poverty perspectives were broadened to include both indigenous characteristics and and a more applied approach that emphasises the need to focus on poverty-reducing strategies. Whether extreme poverty is a central concept in current research is hard to say. A search for 'extreme poverty' in a new 300 page social science publication on poverty research in developing countries yielded only 13 hits, eight of which referred to official documents and only five to concrete research projects. Further searches for synonyms such as 'poorest' and 'most deprived' did not change the picture (Tekaya 2008). This might indicate that the interest in extreme poverty is more pronounced among policy-makers in the North than among than those doing poverty research in the South.

Anthropology has studied poor people throughout the life of the discipline, as for example through research on production systems, management of natural resources and land tenure. Qualitative studies embedded in anthropological knowledge provide unique insights into the lives of poor people as well as extremely poor people, and local in-depth studies supply the cultural contexts in which poverty is formed and upheld. The analysis of poverty per se is less notable. The many small studies pertaining to poverty from different regions in the South have not been brought together to form a more coherent picture of the processes of poverty formation and how the empirical variations in cultural contexts can be confronted to provide a fuller understanding of poverty in general and extreme poverty in particular.

In the past political science has been remarkably absent from poverty research. The growing emphasis on poverty nationally and internationally has led to the entry of political scientists into the field. Studies of mass movements, civil society and democracy formation are now directed towards the poor. Studies of the role of the state in the development of national and international policies for poverty-reducing interventions in the South have become part of the research agenda. Analyses of international agreements, including those concerning poverty are added to the research agenda. As policy-makers turn to extreme poverty as an important goal for interventions, political science research projects follow up. The interest in human rights as a research arena has increased. The latter is shared with the legal professions that have taken up human rights as a new and important area.

Development Research

Development studies incorporate concepts, theories and methods from the social sciences as well as from other sciences such as medicine, the natural sciences and the legal sciences. A major framework is centred around theories of the state and citizenship, and an explicit goal is to create stable and well-functioning states in developing countries, and to build a physical and social infrastructure that will increase human capital and the standard of living for the entire population – that is, including the most deprived, who are often described as the major target for the interventions.

The economists were the early interventionists with the introduction of Structural Adjustment Programmes tailored specifically to developing countries and the emphasis on economic growth as the main tool for bringing about economic progress and reduction of poverty. Thirty years of research brings home the fact that whatever else economic growth has achieved, it has not had a sizeable impact on reducing the percentage of people living in extreme poverty. The discussion has focused on the actual number of people who have moved from living on less than one dollar a day to one dollar a day (now 1.25 dollars a day). This is hardly an adequate measure. Those people are still among the extremely poor and on the margins of society. Through economic growth infrastructure has expanded and new social structures have been created. The elites have increased their economic and political power base, the old middle class has expanded, and a new middle class has grown up that has likely been recruited from the not-so-poor rather than those living in extreme poverty. The trickle-down effect has been selective in its class formation and it may take generations, if ever, to reach the poorest layers of the population.

Knowledge based on political science, sociology and the legal professions has been central in the development of institution-building. Through an improved social infrastructure such as political, financial, legal and educational institutions, the state is to be consolidated, predictable and able to offer its citizens opportunities for a better life. Concepts like democracy, human rights and political stability are central within this mode of thinking. To achieve such aims systems of voting for example are developed and monitored, and as a result percentage of voting does increase. However, the poorest are the least likely to take part. Voting and the benefits of voting do not fit into their basic needs. Even in a well-developed state with a voting system such as the United States, neither the several million homeless nor a large part of the impoverished population take part in voting. The effort and the rewards of taking part in the present voting structure do not fit with their basic needs.

The building of a legal base with courts and police is another goal in development research. While this is no doubt important in creating a more stable and reliable state, these institutions seem to be of little value to the poorest part of the population. Several studies point to the fact that the extreme poor lack not only the necessary resources and knowledge to bring a case to court, they are also and with good reason afraid of public authorities, including the police and bureaucrats. At a recent conference on 'Building Institutions for the Poor' papers were written mainly within the framework of development research. Expectations of a trickle-down effect in favour of the poor/poorest once the infrastructure was in place, were more or less taken for granted. Discussions of institutions specifically tailored to the needs of the poorest part of the population were not prevalent. It was as if the framework of development research put brackets around the participants. It was interesting to note that the economists' much scorned trickle-down effect has now taken a prominent place in development research, with the belief that over time the new infrastructure will benefit the poorest, too. The time frame for this kind of development is never offered.

If a major goal of development research is to build institutions that will help abolish extreme poverty, researchers need to consider in detail how the infrastructure promoted actually works with regard to extreme poverty. One answer is to gain an understanding of the mechanisms that exclude the extreme poor from taking part and try to address their faults. Another more radical answer lies in constructing new institutions directly tailored to the needs of the extreme poor. The latter is the most efficient if reduction of extreme poverty is the issue, although it may not be the most welcome in society at large. Measures to increase the specific infrastructure for the poorest were presented in a recent report on the need for legal protection of the basic rights to food, clean water, shelter and personal security. The report was accompanied by recommendations for financial and structural follow-ups and sent out for consultation to a set of relevant decision-makers.[5] Reactions were mainly negative: the preference was for a broader infrastructure such as visualised in the development paradigm to be prioritised. This is not surprising, but a fact which has to be taken into consideration when concern for the extreme poor is a major rationale in the development paradigm. For the development researchers it implies further explorations on how the needs of the poorest part of a population can gain political backing in the home countries, too.

The medical sciences have met a different scenario. They have not been directly involved in development research, except as planners in medical facilities. The profession's main interest has been in diseases rather than poverty. Analytically, the extreme poor are defined mainly as people with increased health risks and vulnerable carriers and victims of diseases. The medical profession has met the extreme poor with attacks on mass diseases and preventive medicine. This in turn has brought it into closer contact with the poorest populations, and it has contributed with more direct help to the extreme poor than most other professions. There have been few negative reactions from society at large. The poorest are considered by society to constitute a health risk, spreading contagious diseases that should be contained. While the extreme poor would benefit more from basic medical units located nearby, the new emphasis is on large, centrally located, high-tech hospitals. A growing middle class is taking advantage of expanding public goods, while the new hospitals provide at best only limited access for the extreme poor.

The architects of the Millennium Development Goals (MDGs) chose a different strategy where the development paradigm hardly played a role. The goals of reducing poverty in low development countries were clearly defined, the net cast wide in the sense that everybody falling below certain fairly low economic, educational and health standards was targeted, and powerful international and national organisations pledged to back the initiative. New infrastructure is expected to develop in the effort to meet the MDG goals. The present infrastructure is seen as performing a – so to speak – 'reverse trickle-down effect' when exposed to the needs of the poorest, and is expected to change accordingly. It is a daring experiment and it remains to be seen how it will develop. It is stated that the goals set for halving world poverty will be met by 2015. If the goals are reached, and several doubts have been voiced, the prediction is – in accordance with what has been said above – that those poor who reach or exceed the goals set by the MDGs will be those who are already a little better off, meaning that those living in extreme poverty are likely to be left behind once more.

The challenge for future development research lies in at least two areas. On the one hand it is necessary to define more precisely what is meant by extreme

5 Øyen et al. (2008), unpublished UNESCO document, at present not available.

poverty, who the extreme poor are, who is supposed to benefit from the planned development, how they are supposed to benefit, and what they are likely to gain over a given period of time. On the other hand it is also necessary to look at the antagonists, those who do not see any advantage in reducing extreme poverty. As has already been mentioned there are many interests linked to upholding poverty and these need to be taken into account if extreme poverty is to be abolished or even reduced.

The Human Rights Approach

The ideology of the human rights paradigm is based on the principle of indivisibility and interdependence. All human rights are considered to be equally important, as confirmed by the 1986 Declaration on the Right to Development, the 1993 Vienna Declaration and Programme of Action and the Convention on the Rights of the Child. They are seen as so closely connected that they are inseparable and one cannot be given preference at the expense of another. It can be argued that when the principles of indivisibility and interdependence are applied, they work against the removal of extreme poverty.

The human rights framework has been established both theoretically and institutionally in a way that discourses on poverty and organisations working in the area of poverty reduction have not accomplished. Legally, the status of human rights has acquired an international standing that the interests of the poor have not achieved and may never achieve on their own merit. At present there are close to one hundred independent national human rights institutes in the world which work in close cooperation on a wide set of human rights issues.[6]

Most human rights organisations link their work and arguments to poverty reduction, using a broad definition of poverty. International organisations use the human rights instruments in their arguments for eradication of poverty in general and extreme poverty in particular. Their arguments are well founded in empirical studies. For those who have worked with poor people and poverty issues there is no doubt that poverty encompasses the lack of basic human rights. The experience of people who live in poverty is one in which they are deprived of the most basic human rights such as the rights to food, shelter and work, not to speak of rights to education and health care, access to knowledge, technology and improved empowerment. Equally, the rights of vulnerable people are at greater risk of being violated. If human rights were fully respected, protected and fulfilled, mass poverty would become history.

Human rights span a wide array of rights embedded in the fundamental framework of civil, political, economic, social and cultural rights. Over time these

6 Some of the arguments here are based on Øyen, May and Tekaya (2007); and Øyen et al. (2005), including chap. VIII by B.A. Andreassen and A. Eide, 'Human Rights as an International Poverty Reduction Strategy'.

rights have been further developed and exemplified to address still more aspects of human deprivation. This ideology and well-wishing for all human beings has moved towards what at present looks like utopia. As a consequence, and in order to manage the many variables created by a still expanding human rights scenario, the concepts of 'progressive realisation' and 'core rights' have emerged. Progressive realisation refers to the fact that resources available for the implementation of even a reduced set of human rights are limited and priorities have to be made. The core rights concept refers to a hierarchy of needs where the fulfilment of certain rights is seen as more pertinent than others. Realistically, it cannot be expected that all human rights can be implemented at the same time, since full implementation not only implies that sufficient resources are available, but also requires that moral public backing and political will are in place. Therefore it is considered acceptable, although seen as a reluctant break with the principle of indivisibility, for a step-by-step process of implementation of human rights to be recommended.

The concept of core human rights might have facilitated the relationship to poverty reduction if it had been more precisely defined. Poverty consists of many elements, often referred to as a complex web of deprivation. Those elements appear in different combinations and in varying strength. Likewise, the human rights toolbox exhibits an intricate web of instruments that have different effects in different settings. One of many challenges is to provide more precise definitions of the kind of poverty intended to be reduced, the kind of human rights instrument considered effective and the link between the two phenomena. There is no one strategy that fits all situations, cultures and populations.

The reality is that different organisations (and disciplines) practise their own version of core rights since they have different areas of responsibility and are able to attack poverty within the human rights framework mainly from their own specific kind of expertise. The UN system is divided into sub-organisations with different kinds of responsibilities that are all taking part in fighting poverty and implementing the MDGs. International organisations like the Food and Agriculture Organisation and the World Food Programme, for example, both have their major focus on hunger, while UNICEF focuses on child poverty. UNESCO has its major focus on education, science, culture and communication, and analysis of poverty and the promotion of poverty reduction is characterised by the features of their allocated arena.

In practice some rights are being promoted more strongly than others. The right to education, for example, has been carried forward through the entire UN system, global campaigns and broad-based mobilisations with slogans like 'Education for all'. Commitments were made at the World Education Forum to mobilise for poverty reduction through investments in basic education. Basic education is considered a human right in itself as well as a tool to achieve other human rights and reduce individual poverty. At the same time it can be argued that poverty is the greatest obstacle to education. Although there are still about a billion adults unable to read and write the right to education has been successful in the sense that more and more children are actually going to school. However, many do not complete school and the quality of much basic education is not satisfactory. Girls, women and marginal groups, in particular, are often deprived of the right to education.

Other rights have not received the same attention, with potentially negative consequences. For example, since protection of cultural rights does not have the same standing and organisational backing as the protection of educational rights marginal groups such as indigenous and tribal peoples are often actively excluded from mainstream initiatives, disregarded by policy-makers and unclear about their rights and the way in which they can benefit from poverty-reducing initiatives. In these circumstances poverty may persist in the face of poverty-reducing policies that fail to take account of these social dynamics.

There are at least two trends within the picture presented above that work against the efficient reduction of extreme poverty. Both are connected with the extent and richness of the human rights system and the underlying principles of indivisibility and interdependency of rights. The human rights system can be seen as a system 'sans frontières', in the sense that it transcends not only geographical barriers but relates to all walks of human life and offers remedies to all kinds of violence, injustices, inflicted miseries and deprivations.

It is in this setting that choices have to be made if the abolition of extreme poverty is the target. This means that first of all it is necessary to decide who the extreme poor are. Taking into consideration that millions of people die every year from being deprived of the most basic necessities for survival, it seems obvious that securing the right to the individual's survival must be the first priority. Extreme poverty within a human rights setting translates into a lack of basic rights to food, clean water, shelter and personal security. This set of minimum survival rights must be the baseline for any poverty-reducing strategy and is necessary as a first step in the progressive realisation of human rights. This set of rights stands out as absolute and universal and can in principle not be overlooked by any government that has put its signature to the human rights agreements. Unless the right to survival is fulfilled first, all other kinds of poverty reduction become meaningless. Investments in education cannot be exploited fully. Participation in the formal economy will be very limited, and there will be no surplus energy among those deprived of basic rights to take part in political activities to improve their own situation, exercise free speech, make use of public goods and develop human capital further.

However, basic rights tend to be overlooked, among all the other rights, descriptions of poverty and principles guiding human rights implementation. It seems that human rights experts are seldom content to concentrate on these few basic rights. Still more rights are added, ones that can be called second- and third-level rights in relation to extreme poverty, in that they are important for the further development of the individual life situation once survival has been secured. After a while they seem to take priority. Poor people need to be 'empowered' to escape poverty. 'Fundamental freedoms' are essential for poor people. Trade union rights are 'equally important' for poverty reduction. The poor need to organise to 'improve their position'. They need the 'right to make legal claims' and help to get out of 'social exclusion', 'increase their cultural heritage', and so on. Many human rights NGOs specialise in one of these second- or third-level rights, as we have called them here.

All violations of human rights, many of which affect large populations, are important to take into consideration in the implementation of human rights and the battle against poverty. However, paradoxical as it may sound, they deflect attention from the abolition of extreme poverty and the basic right to survival. Somehow, the less deprived populations become more rewarding to work with, certain human rights get more attention, receive more financial backing, or are more likely to result in positive outcomes. Large organisations have concentrated on certain kinds of poverty and certain human rights, such as interest groups working with gender issues, labour organisations working with labour issues, political organisations working with freedom of speech and mass mobilisation, not to forget the disciplines zooming in on certain forms of poverty.

These different actors set the agenda, influence political actors and donors, have an impact on the public discourse, which all in turn directly or indirectly influences the choices of the research agenda. The abolition of extreme poverty is a harsh agenda to tackle. It is not made easier within a human rights framework that refrains from setting operational priorities and makes its way into international agreements through imprecise language and strategies of indivisibility and interdependence that leave behind their major goal of the abolition of poverty.

Reflections

It is a paradox that three of the major paradigms of relevance to global poverty research are not in the forefront with an operational focus on extreme poverty in the South. There seem to be several reasons for this, all interlinked.

It is an underplayed fact that investments in efficient reduction of extreme poverty in a developing society are in several ways a bad investment. It is extremely costly to bring large groups of people who live at the subsistence level up to a level where they can function as other citizens and take part in society. First of all their most basic needs must be met, needs such as sufficient provision of food for the whole family, access to a scarce and expensive resource such as clean water, and a kind of housing that will offer protection from the weather as well as a minimum of personal security. That alone costs enormous sums of money in a society where a quarter or maybe as much as half of the population can be defined as living in extreme poverty. In addition comes what can be called a second-level investment in education, health and development of skills that will enable the extreme poor to take part in the labour market. The time frame is at least a decade, and more likely two, three or four, depending on the level of achievement planned for. Unskilled or low-skilled labour is in surplus in developing countries, and the infrastructure called for to absorb masses of new workers over a relatively short period increases the costs. The total cost of such investments has not been calculated. The outcome from a low developed society's point of view is meagre. The enormous expenditures required for efficient reduction of extreme poverty need to be measured against limited resources that can be invested elsewhere with a more immediate outcome and an improved infrastructure that benefits other segments of society. For the non-poor and the not-so-poor in a developing society the first choice is not eradication of extreme poverty. So far, the discipline of economics in conjunction with other disciplines has not brought a realistic costing of the removal of extreme poverty to the fore and given it a focus in research.

The relative lack of interest in research on extreme poverty may be also be partly due to the fact that strong forces in both developed and developing countries' societies have little interest in poverty reduction in general or the reduction of extreme poverty in particular. Within this picture it has to be acknowledged that certain interests are actually served by upholding poverty and a population living on the fringes of society (Øyen 2004). In the rhetoric, poverty is usually portrayed as negative not only for the individual themselves but also for other members of the society, as well as for society at large and its future development. However, the fact is that widespread interests are actually served by upholding poverty. These interests are economic (for example, access to cheap and unorganised labour), political (for example, uninformed and non-demanding voters) and social (for example, the need for underdogs and targets for moral stereotyping). These interests can be so strong that the actors promoting them not only interfere with poverty-reducing measures; some actually contribute to producing poverty in order to defend their sphere of interest. To accommodate these interests, donors, governments and international agencies present their pro-poor plans within a framework of harmony – as if everybody were in favour of poverty-reducing measures (Øyen 2004). There is no mention of counterproductive forces. Researchers stress that a framework of conflict provides a more adequate base for analysis in moving towards more efficient poverty reduction. The harmonious, benevolent official documents, with their unprovocative and imprecise language, tend to interfere with those more realistic research agendas that depend on financing and access to data.

The fragmented approach to the study of poverty research is coloured by the lack of precision of the concept of extreme poverty and the heterogeneity of the voices calling for eradication, abolition, reduction and alleviation of extreme poverty as well as all other kinds of poverty. The calls come from many sources such as churches, donors, political organisations, moral and ethical voices. All have their reasons for why it is important to do away with extreme poverty, what causes such poverty and what it takes to remedy such a social ill. As long as they use the same wording – that is, extreme poverty – it is taken for granted that they are speaking about the same phenomenon. That is not necessarily the case. The vagueness and dualism in the concepts add to the vagueness of the research agenda. They play a contradictory role in so far as they help to downplay the more determined defenders of abolition of extreme poverty and those who are likely to have the strongest interest in promoting research on extreme poverty.

Researchers may also have a personal interest in avoiding projects on extreme poverty. Involvement in extreme poverty is altogether a bad academic investment. To do research on extreme poverty is exceedingly demanding on time, manpower, background knowledge, academic skills and resources. Extreme poverty is a complicated phenomenon that is made up of an intricate set of variables, causes and manifestations. No comprehensive theoretical framework is available to sort out this complexity in a satisfactory manner. The disciplines are at the outset oriented only towards certain limited aspects of extreme poverty. Researchers working to study the fuller picture of extreme poverty quickly become aware of those shortcomings and have to find a way of living with an incomplete understanding of the problem they are studying. That in itself is frustrating for any serious scientist. At the same time researchers are often expected to produce results that can lead to poverty-reducing strategies. One compromise is to sort out either a limited number of manageable variables concerning extreme poverty, or to move sideways into less severe and complex forms of poverty. We all need to succeed in what we are doing, and for that purpose research on extreme poverty may at present not offer sufficient success (Øyen and Javan 1997).

To do away with extreme poverty and all the suffering involved is one of the most important challenges of our time. Relevant and reliable knowledge based on research is indispensable for the development of efficient policies to meet the challenge. The research community is a key player here. In spite of all the obstacles, some of which are outlined above, the research community is a vital part of the answer to a world problem.

References

Genov, N. (ed.) (2004), *Advances in Sociological Knowledge over Half a Century* (Wiesbaden: VS Verlag für Sozialwissenschaften).

Øyen, E. (2004), 'Poverty Production: A Different Approach to Poverty Understanding', in Genov, N. (ed.), 299–315. Available at <https://bora.uib.no/handle/1956/2260>.

Øyen, E. (2004), 'The Politics of Poverty Reduction', *International Social Science Journal* 162, 459-465. Available at <https://bora.uib.no/handle/1956/2260>.

Øyen, E. et al. (2005), *The Polyscopic Landscape of Poverty Research* (Oslo: Norwegian Resarch Council). Available at <https://bora.uib.no/handle/1956/2260>.

Øyen, E. and Javan, J. (1997), *Implementing the UNDP Global Programme on Poverty Eradication and Sustainable Livelihood: A Set of Recommendations* (New York, UNDP Archives).

Øyen, E., May, J. and Tekaya, C. (2007), 'Minimum Norms in a PRSP Process. Policy Proposal Within a Human On Rights Framework: A Decision-Making Tool for Negotiators', Second Draft.

Tekaya, C. (ed.) (2008), *UNESCO Small Grants Programme on Poverty Eradication: Building National Capacities for Research and Policy Analysis. Summary of the Findings and Recommendations of Selected Research Projects* (Montreuil: Stipa).

Index

Page numbers in *italics* refer to tables.

For Product Safety Concerns and Information please contact our EU representative GPSR@taylorandfrancis.com Taylor & Francis Verlag GmbH, Kaufingerstraße 24, 80331 München, Germany